Trademark Acknowledgements

friends of ED has endeavored to provide trademark information about all the companies and products mentioned in this book by the appropriate use of capitals. However, friends of ED cannot guarantee the accuracy of this information.

Credits

Authors
Sham Bhangal
Amanda Farr
Patrick Rey

Additional Material
Seth Jackson

Content Architect
Andy Corsham

Editors
Andy Corsham
Ben Renow-Clarke
Michael Urwin

Graphic Editors
William Fallon
Katy Freer
Deborah Murray

Author Agent
Gaynor Riopedre

Technical Reviewers
Burt Abreu
Eddie Correia
Lori Denning
Brian Donnelly
Laura Kaye
Gaynor Riopedre
Zbysiu Rodak
Emma Shakeshaft

Index
Alessandro Ansa
Adrian Axinte
Martin Brooks
Andrew Criddle

Cover Design
Katy Freer

Proof Readers
Anthea Elston
Matthew Knight
Fionnuala Meacher
Mel Orgee

About the Authors

Sham Bhangal originally began his career as an engineer specializing in industrial computer based display and control systems. In his spare time he took up freelance web-design, a hobby which slowly grew until it became his main career. He now writes extensively for friends of ED and is engaged in all aspects of web design. Sham lives in Manchester, England, with his partner Karen.

Thanks go to HarryHard, a dance DJ who helped enormously in the recording studio as the sound sections were created.

This is for Karen, without whom this book would have been written much faster.

Amanda Farr is the owner and webmaster of Virtual-FX.net Flash Resources, a site that's been assisting Flash developers for over one and a half years. She's been involved in Flash development for over two years and web design and development for more than four years. She delivered a session at the Flashforward 2000 conference in New York City, and is a dedicated enthusiast in the Flash community.

An extra big thanks goes out to the editors, Andy, Ben, and Mike, to the friends of ED team, and to my two other co-authors, Pat and Sham. Without you guys this book would never have come to be! I know we all worked really hard on this.

I would like to thank the most important person in my life, Seth. You allow me to be the person that I can be. And because of that, I believe in myself and our future. And of course thanks for all the endless hours you put in making screenshots for this book!

To Ellen & Dave: you guys are the best! May all of your dreams come true. And may we all have peace and live near each other for the rest of eternity.

Mom, Jackie, Granny and Grapple! I love you guys so much. Thanks for believing in me and always being people that I can turn to for advice when I need it.

And finally Marc, Sarah and Kathleen. You guys are my best friends and always believe in my abilities. Thank you for always being here for me.

I dedicate this book to all the people who live to learn regardless of whether it's for money or for pure knowledge. And to all the other Flash resource sites out there, where you work so hard to provide great learning tools to people for little financial reward. The Flash community at its best!

Patrick Rey is a Technical Support advisor for Boston College. In his spare time you'll find him learning, documenting and developing the ins and outs of Macromedia's Flash. He describes his fascination with Flash as "like a deer caught in headlights". He's also the webmaster for Flash Addict. In June of 1999 he joined forces with Amanda Farr and Virtual-FX, realizing that writing tutorials for a site that gets 1,000,000 hits a day rather than 100 is far more rewarding.

Along with thanking the innocent trees that gave their lives so that this book might be printed, I would like to make the following dedications and thanks:

Mom – for always being there and supporting me. I will never forget all the sacrifices you made for me. I love you.

Deirdre Griffin – for the love and support that kept me going (and just putting up with me in times of chaos). I love you too.

Amanda Farr and Seth Jackson – for bringing me aboard the greatest ride of my life, and just for being good friends. It has been (and will continue to be) an honor to work with you both.

Sham Bhangal – for making impossible deadlines possible. Your technical expertise was a welcome addition to the project.

Andy Corsham, Ben Renow-Clarke, Michael Urwin and the friends of ED Team – Thanks for driving us nuts with deadlines. Oops...I mean, thanks for all your help. On a serious note – thank you guys for giving us a chance to share our knowledge and passion with the world. It was great having you guide us thru the process.

Barry Fujii - For always being there at 2 am to help me debug code and/or solve problems when my computer crashed. ("What do you mean I can't have Flash, Freehand, ICQ, AIM, Netscape, Fireworks and Winamp open at the same time?") Ha ha ha.

Chan Lieu – Remember all my hare-brained schemes I cooked up over the years? Well, my friend – it looks like one of them finally came true. Thanks for your support.

Kori Dodge – For putting up with me, teaching me, and being there. Basically for showing me the ropes of life (no not those ropes – get your mind out of the gutter...)

Bryan and Julie Kerr – Too bad this isn't a book about politics – sadly, we won't see Bryan and I argue in support of it and Julie argue against it. He he.

Lee Stewart – Read this book, learn Flash, and try not to hit any more buses.

To my other friends, co-workers, and people who were not mentioned – I am running out of space to write and the editors are trying to put me back in the cage. So here is a quick thank you. Enjoy.

Table of Contents

Table of Contents

Table of Contents

The Truth about Flash

Important stuff you should know

Home

Flash 5 and this Book: the Truth

This book aims to give you a solid foundation in the most essentials skills you need to use Flash 5. By the end of the book, you'll understand how the different components of a Flash movie fit together, you'll have used all of the key tools, and you'll have integrated all of your learning in a series of detailed creative exercises. Our mission is to launch you into orbit around planet Flash, equipped with all the tools and sustenance you need to make a safe landing.

Flash is one of the hottest content-creation technologies on the web. From its origins as an animation package, Flash has grown stronger and grown deep roots. Now Flash 5 has consolidated the multimedia capabilities that made Flash 4 so popular and buttressed them with a powerful programming engine that lets you create interactive, visually stunning, sound and feature-rich web sites. Flash is poised to make another leap and become a full web application development tool, allowing you to create any kind of site, from a home page to a corporate e-commerce site.

Flash is now used to create all kinds of site content, such as games, cartoons, adverts and jukeboxes. Perhaps its most significant role, however, is for creating *interfaces* for all those different types of sites. Its ability to present a clean, friendly and functional front end to the user is coupled with its power behind the scenes. Flash is loved by designers for its speed, quality, ease of use and clearly structured functionality, while at the same time, programmers *and* designers can use its programming language - ActionScript - to produce even more phenomenal results. Whatever kind of interface you want to build for a web site, Flash has the answer. If you've never used Flash before, you're in for a real treat.

This book will take you, step by step, through every aspect of designing your own Flash interface, gradually building up your knowledge and skills with each chapter. We'll also look at the pitfalls and practicalities that every web designer faces and teach you how to make your designs 'web friendly', and ensure that you know how to get your hard work up on the net. But before we dive into these complex issues, let's make sure we know the basics of how Flash works, and why it's such a capable authoring tool.

▶

Flash - the big Picture

When you create a Flash movie for the web, you're pulling together images, sound, text and animation, and bundling them up in a file that gets posted up on a web site.

The Flash software you install on your machine is the authoring environment in which you create your masterpiece. The 'work in progress' is stored in a file with the extension .FLA. Once you're happy with your movie and you want to publish it, Flash will convert the .FLA file into a playable file with the extension .SWF - usually pronounced 'swiff' in the Flash community. The .SWF file is then embedded in an HTML file on the server that hosts your site:

When a user visits your site, the .SWF file is downloaded into their browser and your movie is played back. All the viewer needs is the Flash Player plug-in installed on their machine: this plug-in is a reasonably compact download, and the vast majority of the world's browsers are equipped to play back Flash content.

One of the reasons that Flash is such a popular tool is that it uses **vector graphics** technology. There are two main graphic standards on the Internet: **raster** (bitmaps), and **vector**. The majority of static images that you see on the web are raster images, composed of files in formats such as .BMPs, .GIFs and .JPGs. Raster images do a good job, but a big raster image usually requires a large file size, and a large file size means a long download time. And on the web, download time is *everything*. Internet users are fickle creatures: if a site's packed with raster images and is taking too long to load, they'll just skip it and go somewhere else. This is where vectors come in. They're small, fast, and funky.

> *Vector images describe the image in terms of coordinates and mathematical transformations, which sounds complicated, but really is as simple as saying, 'put a dot here, put a dot there, and draw a line between them'. This compares with the raster technique of describing the color and position of every single pixel in the image.*

Vector graphic files are much more compact and efficient compared to rasters, and Flash is the main tool for delivering vector graphics and vector-based animations on the web. The files that Flash creates are therefore comparatively small, which is one of the factors behind Flash's success. A well-constructed Flash file will also **stream** onto the user's computer: this means that it will load the first part of the animation and start playing it back while the rest of the animation loads in the background. Streaming a file correctly is an important technique for a Flash designer, as it means that a visitor to their site is presented with something visual and enticing as soon as they enter it - removing the danger that they'll get bored and go elsewhere as they wait for the site to download.

Another disadvantage of raster images is that they're *display dependent*, meaning that if you create them to look just right on one particular display, your image could come out significantly altered if someone is using a different display resolution to you. Another factor is that if you *zoom* in on a raster image, the pixels just get bigger and bigger until you end up with a screen full of squares of color that are completely unrecognizable as the source image. Vector images though, can work independently of display because they just say 'I want a line from this point on the screen to that point on the screen' and the line will always be the same relative length and clarity, no matter what resolution you view the picture at. No matter how far you zoom into a vector, the image will still stay crisp and at full resolution.

So why would you ever want to use a raster? Well, raster formats are good for images with thousands of different colors. Can you imagine trying to describe a photograph in terms of vectors? It would be horribly complicated, and have a far bigger file size than the raster equivalent. Luckily Flash makes the most of both worlds: the vast majority of its drawings and animations are vector based, but when that extra richness that you can only get with a raster is needed, Flash will allow you to import a bitmap and use it in conjunction with the dominant vectors.

What's Significant about Flash 5?

If you've used a previous version of Flash, the first thing that you'll notice when you open up the program is that the basic interface has changed. Macromedia has implemented a new common interface across its product line to help users seamlessly move between applications, and to make learning a new application that little bit easier.

There are also a couple of new tools on the toolbar. Both of these tools deal with Bezier curves to give the user more precise control over the direction and shape of their curves. Other new features include the ability to import MP3 sound files and an option to customize the appearance and functionality of the interface - allowing you to bring the tools you use most to the fore and so increase your workflow.

The biggest enhancement, though, is invisible at first. Flash now contains a hugely powerful but easy to use programming language called **ActionScript**. ActionScript was one of the major innovations in Flash 4, but the version of ActionScript in Flash 5 is virtually unrecognizable - it has been extended, refined, and supercharged. Flash 5 ActionScript has now become a much deeper and more professional tool allowing you to add mind-blowing effects to your sites but keep that minimal file size. You can use ActionScript to program flexibility and complexity into your Flash web sites and to pass information backwards and forwards between the movie and the web server with greater ease. Although only taking your first tentative Flash steps with this book, you may eventually use this feature to produce a truly interactive site with content that's rich and dynamic.

A by-product of ActionScript becoming more advanced is that it's become more complicated for the novice user. However, there's no reason to be intimidated by it. Although it's far too big a topic for us to cover definitively in a book of this size and scope, you'll learn the essentials of using ActionScript in four dedicated chapters which will allow you to build your knowledge as you explore Flash further. As ever, we're aiming to give you an accessible, secure foundation.

Flash 5 is a much more mature product than previous versions of Flash have been. At the end of its life Flash 4 had reached saturation point: the main feature set was complete and working perfectly, and the creators could now spend time fine tuning it and adding features requested by the users. This is a great time to be learning Flash.

Our Aims and Philosophy in this Book

As its title suggests, the aim of this book is to give you a solid, extensible foundation in Flash design, implementation and programming. We believe that Flash is too complex a tool to cover definitively from scratch in 1000 pages, let alone 500. We're aiming to give a rock-steady foundation: not a trivial overview of each and every feature of the interface and the package, but an in-depth treatment of the core aspects of using Flash.

We believe in creating a reliable foundation, enabling you to understand Flash more fully and absorb and internalize the material we cover. We're not going to list every menu option and cover every single ActionScript command in immense detail: we're going to concentrate on the real core of learning Flash successfully, taking you from zero knowledge of Flash through to being able to put up a web site you can be proud of.

Everyone knows that the best way to learn is to play and practice. It's no good someone just telling you what to do - to master Flash, you have to use it. This book follows that philosophy by providing examples and tutorials in every chapter, and on every topic we cover. It's another well known fact that although small examples are fun and they do help you learn, it's difficult to go away and apply those examples to the real world when you've finished the book. So, at the end of each chapter you'll be able to apply the things you've just learned to our **case study project**. Each case study is a distilled vial of information that, chapter by chapter, will build into an integrated, working interface for a web site:

The web site interface you'll create has animated buttons, a background soundtrack, and Flash-enabled content that pops up when the buttons are pressed. As it's gradually created, this real world example will reinforce the core skills you learn in this book.

We believe that by learning the Flash skills you need, in context, you'll build the knowledge and mental adaptability to fit your expanding knowledge and specialization into a structured and reliable framework.

How to Use this Book

To use this book, all you'll need is a copy of Flash and a computer to run it on. If you want to publish your Flash movies onto the Internet, you'll also need a connection and some web-space to publish them to. Your Internet Service Provider (ISP) will be able to sort this out for you if you have any problems.

The case study you'll create contains an animated intro, interactive buttons, examples of masking and morphing, and even a full soundtrack. It's modular nature means that you can easily go back and find the specific functionality that you're looking for and modify it or replace it with something completely different. If you want to use the buttons in a different web site, or if you want to use the soundtrack, but with music more suited to your tastes, you can easily flip to the relevant chapter for a recap on how to do it, and then just pull the desired part out of the one movie and incorporate it in the other.

You don't have to download anything to use this book, but we've supplied support files containing the sounds and images that we've used to allow you to recreate the worked examples exactly as they are in the book. The case study files, and all support material, can be found in the **Code** section of our web site at www.friendsofed.com. We'll point you at the relevant files in the chapters as necessary.

The case study project files are there so you can pick up the project at any stage in the book and work through it, or you can use them as backups if you've lost your files and don't want to have to recreate them all again. You may just want to check that your results are the same as ours. The files are arranged so that you have a pre-prepared project as input for a chapter: for example, if you wanted to start from chapter 5, you'd go into the appropriate folder and use the **for chapter5.fla** file, which would contain all of the work done on the case study in chapters 1 through 4. If you'd just finished the chapter 5 case study and wanted to check it against ours to make sure it looked right, you would use the **for chapter6.fla**.

We also have some optional sound files which can be downloaded if you want to try your hand at the sound compression material we cover in chapter 11. These (uncompressed) sound files are quite large, and could take a long time to download on some connections.

Support: we're here for you

If you have any questions about the book or about friends of ED, check out our web site: there are a range of contact e-mail addresses there, or you can just use feedback@friendsofed.com. There are also a host of other features up on the site: interviews with renowned designers, samples from our other books, and a message board where you can post your own questions, discussions and answers, or just take a back seat and look at what other designers are talking about. So, if you have any comments or problems, write us, it's what we're here for and we'd love to hear from you.

Layout Conventions used in this Book

We've tried to keep this book as clear and easy to follow as possible, so we've only used a few layout styles:

- When you first come across an important word it will be in **bold** type, then in normal type thereafter.

- We'll use a different font to emphasize **technical words**, **phrases that appear on the screen**, and **code**.

- Menu commands are written in the form **Menu > Sub-menu > Sub-menu**.

- When there's some information we think is really important, we'll highlight it like this:

> *This is very important stuff - don't skip it!*

- Worked exercises are laid out like this:

  1. Open up Flash.

  2. Start a new movie file, and save it as TestMovie.fla.

  3. Etc...

PCs and Macs

To keep the book as easy to read as possible, we've used PC commands as a default, so that every time you come across a mouse command you don't have to read something long-winded like, 'right-click on the PC or CTRL-click on the Mac'.

We've only written *both* instructions where there is a difference between the standard Mac substitute command, and the actual command required.

When we just say 'click' we mean *left*-click on the PC or simply *click* on the Mac. The common substitute commands are:

PC	Mac
Right-click	CTRL-click
CTRL-click	Apple-click
CTRL-Z (to undo)	Apple-Z
CTRL-Enter	Apple-Enter

OK, that's the preliminaries over: it's time to get down to work.

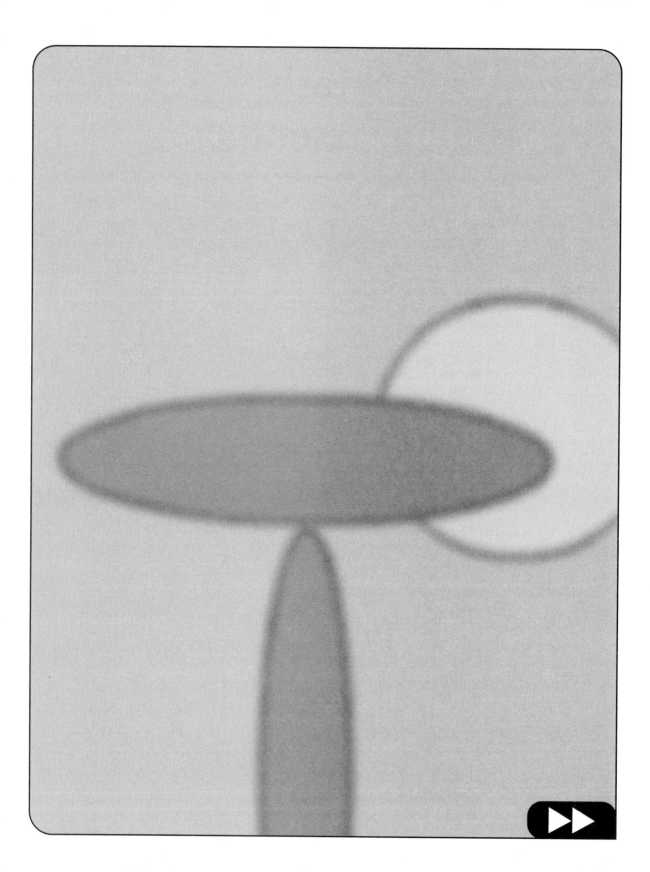

1 Flash Movie Essentials

What we'll cover in this chapter:

◆ The Flash **stage** - where you create your movies in Flash

◆ Manipulating the size of the stage, and changing your movie's overall background

◆ The **timeline**, which controls the playback of your movies

◆ **Frames**: these are essential for creating and arranging the content of your movie. You can think of a frame as representing a moment in time

◆ **Animation** - making content move

◆ **Layers,** which allow you to add depth to your movie, and help you keep track of complex content

◆ **Scenes**: we can create separate scenes that contain distinct chunks of our movie

▶

Flash is really two things; firstly, it's the standard file format for delivering interactive, visually-rich content and animation on the web - this is the .swf file format we talked about in the Introduction; and secondly, it's the actual authoring environment that lets you create and publish those .swf files. The Flash program you install on your computer is the gateway to state-of-the-art web content.

In this chapter we're going to introduce you to the authoring environment - the Flash 5 interface - and take you through the essentials of creating visual content in Flash and making it move. In doing this, we'll start building up a picture of the main components of a Flash movie, and see how they fit together.

Taking time to understand the core elements at the heart of the Flash movie will pay off later - you'll have a firm grasp of the foundations, and you'll be able to build effectively on these as you learn.

So...let's begin by looking at the first thing that most everybody wants to do when they open up their copy of Flash - create a movie and make interesting things happen on the screen.

The Authoring Environment

If you don't already have Flash 5 up and running, start it up now.

When you first open up Flash, you're presented with an array of screen elements: icons, menus, content preparation areas, toolbars, palettes and status bars:

> *Don't worry if your screen doesn't look exactly like ours when you start up Flash: if you've already opened Flash up before and played around with it you'll doubtless have altered the setup in some way.*

This is the feature-rich authoring environment that lets you create your Flash movies and export them so that they can be published on the web and accessed by the adoring multitude. It's Flash's studio, workshop and test track combined.

If you've never used a Macromedia product before, you might be intimidated by the unfamiliar interface the first time you open Flash - don't be: before long you'll be navigating the interface with ease. And there's an added bonus to learning the Flash 5 interface: the inception of the new Macromedia common interface means that once you're familiar with Flash, you'll have no trouble finding your way around other Macromedia programs such as Fireworks or Director.

There's a tremendous amount of detail and power tucked away in the Flash 5 interface, and at first it can seem a little daunting if you're new to the software. To avoid the sense of clutter, and in order to "turn down the volume" a little, let's clear some of the elements out of the way: so that we can concentrate on the bare essentials for a moment (but don't worry, you won't be missing a thing - we'll be explaining all of the core features during the course of this book).

Configuring the Authoring Environment

1. First, let's close down any floating palettes - called **panels** in Flash 5 - like the two that we've got shown on the right-hand side of the previous screenshot:

   These floating panels - and others like them - are used to help you modify and manipulate the content of your Flash movie once you've created that content. This content could be graphic images, pieces of animation, text or any number of things - but you can use the panels (and menu options) to alter their characteristics and the way that they behave.

   You can think of any element you create in your movie (such as pictures or text) as a discrete object: each of these objects has its own attributes, such as color, transparency and size, and you can use the panels to change these attributes. Additionally, changing panel settings can also alter the way that an object behaves. We'll be looking at all of these aspects as we progress through the book. At the moment though, we don't actually have any content to work with, so let's move these panels out of the way for reasons of clarity:

2. Click on each of the panels' 'close' boxes, or choose the **Window > Close All Panels** menu option. We'll come back to these panels later.

Next, we want to make sure that we can see all of the area where we're going to create the visual content in our Flash movie:

3. Click on the **Magnification** drop-down list box at the bottom left of the screen...

4. ...and choose the **Show Frame** option:

Notice that the white area in the center of the screen is now visible in its entirety:

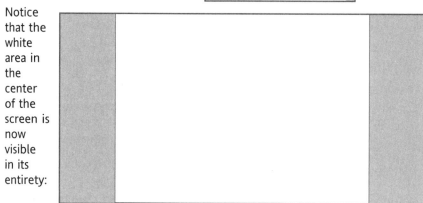

This white area is called the **Stage**, and it's where all the action in your movie takes place. The gray area around the stage is called the **Work Area**. Let's talk about these different areas a little.

The Stage

The stage can be likened to what a movie director can see in the viewfinder of a movie camera: what you see in the viewfinder is what will appear in the movie that the viewer watches in the theater. In the motion picture world, you can have action taking place on the film set (stage), and you can have actors waiting off stage, ready to make their entrance and come into shot.

At different times in the movie, different people and objects will be visible on the stage and, consequently, 'in shot'. The stage in Flash works on the same principle: at any given point in your Flash movie, the things that are on the stage are what the viewer will see when the movie is rendered in their browser. Another thing to consider is that the movie set can be much larger than the camera's field of view, and the camera can move around and seek out previously hidden corners.

If you want the end-user to see something in the Flash movie that plays in their browser, then that something has to be visible on the stage area when you create the movie. This also means that movie content can move onto the stage from the 'wings': for example, an animated actor could enter stage left, walk across the stage, and exit stage right. In the Flash authoring environment, any visual element that moves beyond the boundaries of the stage winds up in the **work area**.

The Work Area

The **work area** surrounds the stage. You can place content in the work area, but only content that actually appears on (or moves across) the stage will show up in the finished movie that the user watches. So, when you're designing your movie, you need to think about whether the visual elements it contains will spring into existence directly on the stage, or whether they're going to wait in the wings and then move onto the stage at some point.

Another example of this would be a car that starts its journey in the work area to the left of the stage, moves across the stage (and into the viewer's sight), and then accelerates off into the work area on the right:

Stage   Work Area

While the content is on the stage, the viewer sees it in the browser. When it's 'in the wings', it's invisible to the viewer.

What we've done so far is use the Magnification box to change our view of the stage **in the authoring environment**. Any changes we make by zooming in and out and making the stage look bigger or smaller in the authoring environment will **not** be applied to the finished movie seen by the end user. These magnification changes are just to help us see things more clearly when we're creating and modifying our movie.

To alter the size and proportions of our finished movie once it's displayed in the user's browser, we need to change the **properties** of the stage itself.

Changing the Size of the Stage

When you're planning your Flash movie, you should consider how much browser real-estate you want the finished movie to take up - you'll need to decide what size you want the movie's window to be, based on factors such as what kind of content you're displaying, what else will appear alongside the movie in the host page, and so on. When you've made that size decision, you can alter the size of the stage to match your plan. Here's how...

You can view the stage's current dimensions by opening up the **Movie Properties** dialog box. This dialog box is where you make global changes to the **properties** (or *characteristics*) that affect the whole movie.

To view your current movie's global characteristics, right-click either on the white stage area or on the surrounding gray work area and select **Movie Properties** from the menu that appears. You'll be presented with this dialog box:

You can also bring up the **Movie Properties** dialog box using the **Modify > Movie** menu option.

You can see here that the default **Dimension**s of the stage are 550 pixels wide by 400 pixels high. When you change the dimensions of your stage, Flash will always measure them from the top left-hand corner. For example, if you change the width of your movie to be 600 pixels and the height to be 450 pixels, Flash will simply add another 50 pixels to the right hand side of the stage, and 50 to the bottom:

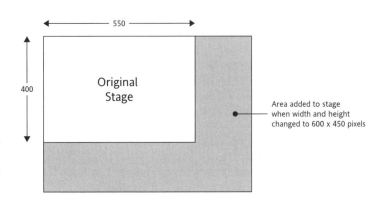

If, like us, your brain doesn't translate pixel-speak too easily, you can always change the units of measurement that Flash uses throughout the entire movie by picking a different option from the **Ruler Units** drop-down box:

Whichever option you choose here will be applied across this whole movie until you change it to be something different.

> *Remember that when you set the **Dimensions** of the stage in this dialog box, you are directly affecting the size of the window that your Flash movie will be displayed in inside the user's browser. It's good practice to think about this before you start creating your visual content on the stage. You can always change the size of the stage as and when you like, but the more planning you do, the smoother your movie creation process is likely to be!*

Note that the **Match: Printer** and **Match: Contents** options will automatically change the size of the stage if you select them: **Match: Printer** will set the stage size to reflect the default paper size for your default printer, and **Match: Contents** will change the stage so that it is large enough to contain all of the content elements that you've created (even those that spill over into the work area outside the stage).

As you can see, there are a number of other global properties that you can change for the whole movie: we'll be covering all of the important ones as they come up in the course of building our example movies in this book. At this stage, let's just observe that the **Frame Rate** property influences the playback speed and smoothness of your movie. The default frame rate is 12 fps (**frames per second**), which will be fine for most of the movies that you'll produce.

The next movie property we want to concentrate on here is the **Background Color** option. This is the option that you use to change the overall background color your movie has when it's rendered in the user's browser.

Changing the Movie's Background Color

Probably one of the most frequently asked beginner questions in Flash is: "how do I change the background color?"

Again, the background color is something you should probably think about when you're *planning* your movie. The kind of questions you might ask yourself are: What size will the display window be in the browser? Will the movie take up the whole display in the browser? Do I need to stick to a color scheme that matches the rest of the site that my Flash movie will appear in?

When you're in the Movie Properties box, you can change the background color simply by clicking on the **Background Color** box...

Background Color:

...and selecting a color of your choice. The only drawback is that the movie has to be the same color **throughout the entire movie**. You can't change the color in different parts of the movie.

Another thing you need to think about in this context is the background color of the web page that your movie will appear in. If your finished movie is embedded in an HTML page, the choice you make for the background color of the movie is important. By default, Flash will take the background movie color you specify here and use it as the background color of the HTML page that your movie appears in.

> *There are a number of different options that you can use when you're exporting your finished movie for publishing on the web. We'll talk about the built-in publishing features of Flash in more depth later in this book.*

For now, let's start on a little movie project that we'll be working on over the next couple of chapters: this will be a simple movie that will get you practicing your Flash skills - and it'll also give you the chance to start expressing your creativity in the Flash authoring environment.

The Movie Background at Midnight

Our test movie is set at night. The cicadas are doing their thing, there's a cool breeze, the moon is up, and there's the faint aroma of fresh mushrooms rising from our garden mushroom patch. We're going to start creating that scene inside of Flash.

The background for our little movie scenario is going to be the night sky, so we need to choose a suitable background color to reflect that.

1. If you don't already have it open, go into the **Movie Properties** dialog box (**Modify > Movie**). Knowing that mushrooms only grow while we're asleep, select a deep midnight blue from the **Background Color** box:

You'll notice that when you move the cursor over each color, its identity is displayed using a '#' followed by a **hexadecimal** value (made up of numbers and letters). These hexadecimal (hex) values are the same ones that people use when writing HTML web pages, and each combination of numbers and letters represents a unique, universally recognized color. This makes it very easy for you to match your background and host web page colors if you want to.

2. Click OK to confirm your color choice and return to the stage.

Saving Global Movie Settings

The values you set for this particular movie in the **Movie Properties** dialog box are saved away when you click on the OK button. If you want these settings to be applied to all of your Flash movies, click on the **Save Default** button: Flash will then assume that you want to use these settings whenever you subsequently create a new movie. You can obviously change these default settings as and when you need to.

Having set the global properties for our movie, the next step is to start creating some content. We're going to do that here by walking through a basic creation/modification/animation scenario in the context of our nighttime movie: this will familiarize you with some essential techniques and give you the chance to stretch those creative muscles.

In introducing you to the creation/modification/animation process, we need to talk about two absolutely critical features of the Flash authoring environment: the **Timeline**, and **Frames**.

The Timeline

The **Timeline** is one of the vital parts of the Flash interface, and one of the most important things to understand as you learn Flash.

When a web surfer visits your site and your movie starts to play, Flash 'interrogates' the timeline encoded in the .swf file and 'reads off' what should be displayed in the user's browser. The relationship between your movie's content and the timeline is absolutely vital in coordinating the end effect that the viewer sees.

You've already seen that the Flash stage has height and width: the Flash movie also has another critical dimension - **time**. Although Flash movies can have a high degree of user interaction and change the way that they run based on choices that the user makes, the essential experience of seeing a Flash movie is that it **starts** when you open a web page or click on a link, and it **finishes** when the movie has run right through, or when you exit the web page that the Flash movie lives in.

What the user sees in their browser between the start and end points of the movie is determined by the **content** that you create in your movie, and by how you use the timeline to **organize** that content. The length of your movie's timeline will control how long the movie runs for, and how content changes in the movie over time. As the movie's author, you control all of this by using the Flash timeline in conjunction with the content you create.

To help you visualize this, picture a simple movie scenario: imagine a time-lapse nature movie that shows a mushroom growing in slow motion. At the **start** of the movie, you'd have the tiny head of a mushroom poking up from the soil, and at the **end** of the movie, you'd see a full-grown mushroom, standing tall above the grass:

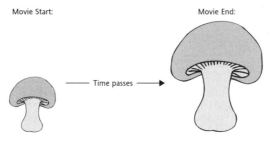

Clearly, your movie won't just consist of those two images, and your movie won't just jump from 'tiny stalk' to 'fully grown' instantaneously: in between the those two points, time passes, and your mushroom moves through the intermediate stages of growth until it attains its full-grown state. In between the start and end-points of the time-lapse movie will be a whole series of images that represent the mushroom at the different stages of its development:

In the real world, mushrooms have a natural growth rate, which is determined by mushroom DNA or by divine guidance (depending on who you ask). In a Flash movie, you have to *imitate* the effect of time passing - and that's where the timeline comes in: to create the effect of time passing, you need a start point, an end point, and some space in between that represents the passage of time. The timeline lets you do this, and gives you complete control over the length of your movie, the speed that it plays at, and what you see on the screen at each point in time. How? By using **Frames**.

Frames

Take a look at the timeline in the Flash authoring environment:

Now concentrate on the right-most part of the screenshot:

You can see that the top-most part of the timeline (the all-gray part) is divided up into numbered segments, and that there are corresponding divisions in the next line down, consisting of groups of four white rectangles separated by single gray rectangles.

Each of these little boxes on the second line down represents a **frame**, and the numbers on the top line give us a frame number reference: frame 1 on the left, through to frame 45 (and beyond) on the right. Your movie can be 1 frame long, or it can be thousands of frames long. The length of your movie is determined by the number of frames of content that you create.

The red rectangle with the line coming out of it on the timeline is called the **playhead**.

The Playhead

The playhead indicates where you currently are in your movie. You can click on the playhead and drag it back and forth along the timeline and the stage will change to show the contents in the selected frame. At the moment, of course, we don't have any images or objects on the stage, but as we start to add content you'll see how you can spool through your movie using the playhead.

The playhead lets us anticipate what will be seen when the movie plays back in the browser: when we position the playhead over a frame, we see what will be displayed on the screen at that point during playback.

Our movie begins in frame 1. By default, when it loads into the user's browser, our movie will start at frame 1 and play through the rest of the frames in sequence until the end point. Each successive frame on the timeline represents a moment in time, a moment that will be played back when our movie runs.

At the moment, all of the frames in the timeline shown here are empty - that's because we haven't created any content yet. If we were to play back our nighttime movie now (by pressing **F12**), we'd just see a block of color displayed in the browser window. This is Flash displaying the background color of the movie that we set using the **Movie**

Properties dialog box. To make our movie more interesting, we have to add content at various points along the timeline so that they can play back in the browser. This is where frames come in.

By placing content in frames at different points along the timeline, we imitate the passing of time, make animations, and generally make things happen in our movie: just like that time-lapsed mushroom movie we mentioned earlier, we can create start and end points and show all of the intermediate stages in between. When the movie plays, it looks at each frame on the timeline and renders what it finds there in the user's browser. To achieve the effect of content appearing and disappearing, animating and morphing, Flash provides us with different types of frame that we can use.

To see the nature and effects of the different types of frame that Flash gives us, we first have to get some content onto the stage. So without further ado, it's time to start drawing.

Making Mushrooms

What we're going to do here is create a mushroom that will live out its life under the midnight sky that we created as our background earlier.

1. First of all, click on the **Snap to Objects** button on the main toolbar:

    Snap to Objects

    > On the Mac, you'll need to use the **View > Snap to Objects** menu option.

    > If you don't see the main toolbar on your PC, use the **Window > Toolbars > Main** menu option to display it. You can dock the toolbars in Flash 5 in the same way as you can in other packages.

    The button will appear to be 'depressed' when you've turned the option on.

    Turning on **Snap to Objects** invokes Flash's ability to help us make our drawings more precise: this option will automatically 'snap' the drawing cursor to certain points as Flash anticipates what you're trying to do. For example, when you turn snapping on and draw with the oval tool, Flash will jump to a perfect circle when you get close to it, but with snapping off, it will let you draw the oval to whatever dimensions you want. Whether you use this snapping feature or not is entirely dependent on personal preference and what you're trying to achieve: if you're drawing perfect circles it makes sense to leave it on, but for most freehand drawings it is easier to leave it off. Experiment and see what works best for you in different circumstances.

Next, we need to select the drawing tool that we'll use to draw our initial mushroom. All the drawing tools are accessed in the Flash **Toolbox**. We'll be detailing more aspects of the Toolbox and its contents in the next chapter, but we'll start making use of some of its features as we work through this example.

2. The Toolbox is located (by default) on the left-hand side of the authoring environment. If you hold the mouse cursor over any of the tool buttons in the Toolbox, a **tool tip** will pop up with a description of the tool that the button represents:

The letter in brackets next to the tool's name is the shortcut key for that particular tool. In this case, pressing 'O' will select the Oval tool.

3. Click on the Oval Tool. Each of the tools will be covered fully in the next chapter, but we'll dip into them now as we set about creating some content.

Now we need to select a color for the outline of the shape that we're going to draw.

4. Click on the **Stroke Color** box:

This will open a palette from which you can pick a color for the outline (**stroke**) of the object that you're drawing. Similarly, the **Fill Color** box allows you to select the color that you want to use to fill the area **inside** the outline. By default, many of the objects that you draw using tools from the toolbox have an outline and a filled interior. You can control and modify these outlines and fills to a very fine degree, as you'll see as we progress through this book.

5. Set the stroke color to a dark brown.

6. Next, click on the **Fill Color** box and set the fill color to a lighter, mushroom-like brown.

7. Now for the actual drawing. At the bottom of the stage, about half way along, click and drag with the Oval tool to make a small stalk for your mushroom:

8. Now, using the same click and drag action, draw a flatter, larger oval just above the stalk. Make sure that there's a gap - a small one - between the two ovals:

This larger oval will be the cap of your baby mushroom.

9. If you look at the timeline now, you'll notice that the first frame has changed:

If you look closely at the second line down, you'll see that this frame is now shaded a darker gray, and that it contains a little black circle. Why is that?

Well, in a new movie like ours, Flash always assumes that we want the action to start in frame 1. So, when we started drawing on the stage, Flash thought:

"Aha, they're drawing an oval. This is the first piece of content that they're creating for this movie, so I'll put this drawing in frame 1 - thats where the movie will start, after all."

So Flash has created the starting point for our movie, based on the drawing that we've made. This is the first fixed point in time for our movie - the first image in a sequence of images that we want to display changing over time. If you like, this is the first snapshot in a sequence that we want to show to the user.

Flash uses a particular type of frame to store fixed points in time that hold visual (or other) content: this type of frame is called a **keyframe**.

Keyframes

A keyframe indicates that something important happens at the point in the timeline where the keyframe is located: for example, we display some content, or we make something disappear, or we make a transition from one piece of content to another. Keyframes are markers in time, indicating start and end points for different pieces of action.

Essentially, a keyframe says to Flash, "there's something significant here". Your Flash movies will consist of a series of keyframes spaced out along the timeline, with each keyframe flagging up the start and end points of distinct pieces of content that are to be displayed in the user's browser.

Think back to the time-lapsed nature movie that we discussed earlier. Remember how we said that the start and end points of that movie would be the baby mushroom and the full-grown mushroom?

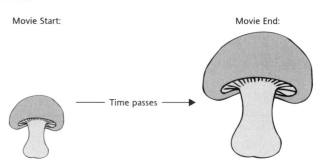

In Flash, those start and end points are defined by **keyframes**. We'd need a keyframe in frame 1 that contained the baby mushroom image, and a keyframe in a later frame (say frame 15) containing the image of the fully developed mushroom:

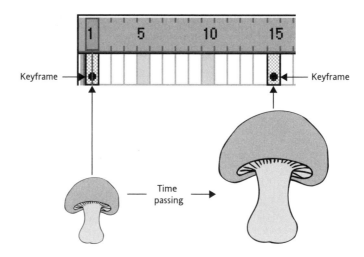

These two keyframes will tell Flash that we have images of our mushroom in two different states: 'starting to grow', and 'finished growing'. Once we have those two keyframes in place, we can get Flash to help us create and animate the intermediate growth states for the mushroom that should exist between the start and end images. We'll be looking at how to do that in more detail very shortly. For the moment, remember this:

> *If something significant changes on screen in your movie, there'll probably be a keyframe involved. Keyframes are the 'key' to making things happen.*

Much more on frames in a moment. First, a bit of housekeeping...

Saving your Movie

It's good practice to save your work often - just in case your dog eats it or the computer crashes and burns. The way to save your embryonic Flash movie is the same way that you would in most other programs

1. Click on **File > Save** in the main menu.

    You'll be prompted with a dialog box asking where you want to save the movie, and what name you would like to give it.

2. Choose (or create) a suitably named folder to save your work into, and then type '**Mushroom**' into the File name box and click Save:

Flash will automatically save the movie that you're working on as an .fla file, which is the extension used for Flash authoring files.

Remember that there's a distinction between the file that you work on in the authoring environment (the .fla file) and the file that's loaded and played (the .swf file) when a surfer visits your site: as an author, you create and modify your content inside the .fla, and the .swf is created when you publish your movie. The publishing process takes all of the drawings and other content that you created in your .fla file and compresses and encodes them into the .swf format. The .swf file is much smaller and more compact than its parent .fla file, and is thus much quicker and more efficient for the end user to download.

Now that we've got our example movie safely saved away, we can continue our exploration of frames.

We've already drawn a couple of ovals in frame 1: these represent our baby mushroom - the starting point for our movie. If we were to play the movie now, we'd see a static image of our baby mushroom in the browser (you can try this by pressing **F12**. This will open up your default browser and render your movie - you'll need to close the browser or click back into your Flash 5 window once you've finished viewing your masterpiece).

The reason that we see this static image is that we have only created a single frame with any content in - the movie has nowhere else to go except this single keyframe. When Flash plays back the movie and looks at the timeline, it only finds this single keyframe. Flash's default publishing settings tell it to **loop the playback** of our movie, so what we're seeing in the browser is the same single frame, being shown over and over again as Flash repeatedly loops through the timeline. Flash will continue to do this until we close the browser or move onto another web page.

Next, we're going to see how to add an **end** point for our 'mushroom growth' movie, and how to create the sequence of images that imitate the passage of time and show the mushroom growing. This will mean that we'll have a proper movie to play rather than a single-frame loop.

Making the Movie Really Move

We've already seen that keyframes mark the beginning and end points of pieces of action in our movie. In this sense, Flash can be compared to traditional animated cartoons. In traditional 'toons, the animator would plan out the action sequence that they wanted to create - for example, a car driving from one side of the screen to the other. They would create the background for the action - maybe a desert setting with some distant mountains - and this background would typically remain static.

Next, the animator would create their start and end images of the car: the car on the left of the screen, and the car on the right of the screen. Clearly, you'd also need to have a series of intermediate images that showed the car in progress across the desert. Each image would be drawn onto a separate sheet of transparent acetate. The plan would be to use a movie camera to photograph the start, intermediate and end images against the static background to create a number of different frames of film. Running the frames in sequence would show the car in motion against the static background.

This was a time-consuming business, and cartoon production companies didn't want to tie up their star animators in slaving over frame after frame of minutely-changing action. The solution was to get the lead animators to create the key images - start and end points, and important transitional images - and then use specialized 'in-betweeners' to sit down and draw up the images that came in between the keyframes that the expert animator had created. These in-between frames were critical to ensuring that the cartoon action was smooth and convincing.

In Flash, we do things similarly. We can create keyframes that define significant stages in the action that we want to show, and then get Flash to generate the in-between frames that link the keyframes together. This saves us a lot of time and effort in creating the transitional frames, and is an important factor in making Flash the successful animation package that it has become. (Note that you can mimic the traditional animation method in Flash if you wish, by hand-drawing each frame individually. This can be a powerful way to express yourself and create great animation, but it's really too big a subject to tackle. Maybe in another book...)

Let's get back to our mushroom movie. Currently, we have that single starting keyframe containing the baby mushroom. Next, we want to create a keyframe holding the fully-grown version, and then get Flash to create all the in-between frames that show the mushroom growing over time - let's work through that in an exercise now.

Working with Frames

As we've said already, a keyframe marks a significant change in your movie. In order to create the image showing our mushroom when it's fully grown, we need to add a keyframe to the timeline. This will tell Flash that we have some important new content that it needs to be aware of.

To insert a new keyframe in to the timeline, you simply click in the timeline at the position where you want to add your keyframe. Once you've selected the frame position, you can then choose the **Insert > Keyframe** menu option, or use the keyboard shortcut *F6*, and a new keyframe will appear.

It might occur to you to ask, "how far along the timeline should I put my second keyframe?" The answer to this depends on how long you want your piece of action to last. The thing to remember here is the **frame rate** setting that we saw in the **Movie Properties** dialog box. Remember we said that the 12 frames per second default rate was about right for most basic movies? This **frame rate** setting means that **for every 12 frames our movie takes up on the timeline, there will be one second of action when the movie plays back**. So, the math is fairly simple: estimate how long you want the action to last in seconds, and multiply the number of seconds by the frame rate. You can always change the position of the keyframes later on if you need to tweak the timing of different pieces of action.

Let's make that mushroom grow.

1. Click on frame 14 of your mushroom movie and press **F6** to insert a keyframe.

You'll see immediately that the timeline has changed:

Frame 14 now has a black circle in it and a black border, and all the frames between frames 1 and 14 have turned gray. Additionally, there's a small white rectangle in frame 14, and the playhead has jumped to frame 14. Let's take a look at what all this means:

- The black border around frame 14 indicates that this is a keyframe. We're going to use this keyframe to hold some content that's different from the frames that precede it.

- The white rectangle in frame 13 tells us that this is the last frame before a new keyframe, and that all of the frames to the left of this rectangle contain the same content as the **previous** keyframe - in this case, frame 1. The frames are grayed to show you that they contain the same content as frame 1- every frame in the black bordered box running from frame 1 through frame 13 contains the same image of the baby mushroom that we created in frame 1. If you move the cursor over the grayed frames, you'll see a label pop up saying 'Static':

Again, this indicates that these frames all contain the same static image as frame 1.

- The black circle in the keyframe at frame 14 indicates that this frame contains some content. But how come? We didn't add any content to this frame yet, did we? What's happened is that Flash has carried over the content from the previous keyframe (frame 1). This is the default behavior when you add a new keyframe. This feature can be very useful, as you'll see in a moment. There's one other thing to note here: when you move the playhead backwards and forwards through your movie, the current frame number is also indicated in the area just underneath the timeline:

So far, then, we've got an opening keyframe (frame 1), followed by some intermediate frames (frames 2 - 13), and a new keyframe (frame 14) that will soon contain the image of our fully-grown mushroom.

All of the frames from 2 to 13 now 'belong' to the keyframe in frame 1, and reflect what is in it. If you changed the image in frame 1, the following 'slave' frames (2 - 13) would change to reflect the new picture. Frame 14 would remain as it is, however, as we've told Flash that we want this frame to be self-contained so that it can contain new content.

2. Click anywhere on the timeline between the two keyframes. You'll see that frames 1 through 13 turn black:

This shows you that these frames all hold the same content - they're all dependent on the content in the keyframe at frame 1. You can't alter the content of frames 2 through 13 by editing them directly - you can only change their contents *indirectly* by amending what's in frame 1. You can only directly edit content that's in a keyframe.

3. Deselect the black-highlighted frames by clicking away from them. Next, hold down the Control key (*Ctrl*) and click again between the keyframes. This time only the frame that you clicked on is selected:

4. Use the **Insert > Frame** menu option or press the *F5* key twice to insert two new frames into the timeline at the position where you just clicked with the mouse. This will add two frames to the timeline, and these new frames will inherit the contents from the preceding keyframe (frame 1).

Using the playhead to move through your movie you can see that it is now 16 frames long, and each of the frames contains the same picture of a mushroom. We promise that your mushroom will grow soon, but first there are a few more tricks we can perform with frames.

5. Control-click between the keyframes again to select a single frame.

    This time, rather than inserting 'slave' frames, we're going to insert a blank keyframe. A **blank keyframe** is just what its name suggests, a keyframe that has no content in it. It is, however, independent of the content of the keyframe that precedes it.

6. Use the **Insert > Blank Keyframe** menu or press the *F7* key to convert one of the normal frames in your timeline into a blank keyframe. You can tell it is a blank keyframe by the black line that divides it from the previous frames, and the way all of the frames after it are now white:

    The white frames in frames 8 through 13 are all dependent on the blank keyframe that we just inserted. Note that the keyframe at frame 7 does not have a black circle in it - this is because it doesn't yet have any content.

7. If you now scroll through your movie using the playhead, you'll see that all of the dependent frames after the blank keyframe are also blank, reflecting the fact that the keyframe before them was empty. Blank keyframes are useful for stopping animations or dividing different pieces of content that exist on the same layer (stay tuned, there's more on layers later).

    You'll also see that the keyframe at frame 14 still has the baby mushroom image in it. That's because it inherited the content of frame 1 when we created it. However, there is no link between the inherited image and the current (possibly amended) content of frame 1 - frame 14's keyframe is completely independent.

8. We don't actually want half of the frames in our movie to be blank, so somehow we'll have to get rid of that blank keyframe and its dependent frames. There are two ways to do this: you can either delete the blank keyframe or convert it into a normal frame. We're going to do the latter - the advantage of this is that the movie's length remains the same.

9. Click on the blank keyframe and use the **Insert > Clear Keyframe** menu command. This menu option name is a little confusing - what we're actually doing here is converting the keyframe to a normal frame - we're not actually *inserting* anything as such. The result of doing this is that the white frames become shaded again, and if you run the movie through now, you'll see that they've all been refilled with your baby mushroom picture.

So you now have 16 frames in your movie, all filled with exactly the same mushroom image. We only wanted the movie to last for 15 frames because it's a nice round number, so you'll have to remove one of those frames now...

10. Control-click to select a single frame anywhere between the two keyframes and use the **Insert > Remove Frames** menu to delete the highlighted frame. You should now be left with two keyframes on your timeline (in frames 1 and 15), and a set of identical normal frames between the keyframes containing the same image of your mushroom that you created in frame 1.

The 'normal' frames that separate out the keyframes may appear to be plain and boring at the moment, but don't dismiss them: they're the Flash equivalent of pawns on a chessboard or foot soldiers in an army - not as glamorous as the other elements, but just as important.

> *In Flash there are three different methods for adding, converting, and deleting frames, each with its own advantages and disadvantages. The first, and most 'formal' method is to use the **Insert** menu. This menu, found on the main menu bar, contains all of the manipulation actions associated with frames. The second, and probably most commonly used method is to use the keyboard shortcuts that mimic the **Insert** menu options. The major problem with this is that you have to learn them first, although this is something that most people pick up quite quickly through use. The third method is to right-click on the relevant frame in the timeline to highlight it, and then to select the appropriate command from the context-sensitive menu that appears. Throughout the tutorial sections in this book, we'll use a mixture of these methods. There is no single 'best' method - whichever one you find easiest is the one that you should use.*

As promised, let's make our mushroom live and...well, breathe.

Making the Mushroom Grow

Frame 15 is going to be the final frame of our movie, which means that we need to populate it with the content that represents the final growth stage of our mushroom. Let's add the fully-grown mushroom image to the keyframe in frame 15. What we want to do is have our mushroom grow from the baby form in frame 1 to an adult version in frame 15.

1. Start by clicking on frame 15 in the timeline. Notice that when you click on the frame the whole mushroom (the two ovals we drew earlier) is already

selected. Remember, these ovals were inherited from the keyframe in frame 1, so they are identical in shape and position to the mushroom in frame 1. This in turn means that we don't have to worry about positioning the image of the mushroom in frame 15 - it's in exactly the same place as it in frame 1 - this will make our animation easier to perform.

> *A related, and very useful feature in Flash is the ability to copy (or cut) and paste content into exactly the same location on the stage. This is particularly useful when you want to paste images or other components into other keyframes or onto other layers and still have them occupy the same coordinates on the stage as the original image. To achieve this, you copy (or cut) the original component, and then use the **Edit > Paste in Place** menu option. This way you are sure to place your object exactly where you want it. We guarantee that you'll find this feature immensely useful in your Flash career.*

2. Click on the Arrow tool in the top-left corner of the Toolbox, and then click on the background of the stage to deselect the mushroom.

3. Now double-click in the middle of the cap of your mushroom: this will select both the stroke and the fill. If you had only clicked once in the middle of the cap, you would only have selected the fill.

4. Next, click on the mushroom cap and drag it up to where you want the cap of your full-grown mushroom to be:

> *If you hold down the **Shift** key while you drag, Flash will help you drag the mushroom cap upwards in a straight line (provided that you've turned on the **Snap to Objects** option).*

5. Double-click on the stalk (the lower oval) to select it, and then press **Backspace**. This will delete the baby version of the stalk from frame 15 (although the stalk is still intact in frames 1 through 14).

Our next task is to create the fully-grown version of the mushroom stalk.

6. Click on the Oval tool in the Toolbox again, and draw a long thin oval from the bottom of the cap of your mushroom down to the bottom of the stage, again ensuring that there's a small gap left between the edges of the two ovals. This is your adult mushroom stalk:

> *If you need to move your new stalk when you've drawn it, select the Arrow tool, double-click on the stalk, and drag it to the desired position. If things go wrong, there's always the 'undo' option to fall back on (**Ctrl-Z**).*

7. OK. Press the Enter key to preview your movie. Hmm...not particularly convincing, is it? We're getting the same picture for 14 frames, and then a sudden jump to a fully-grown fungus. What we really want is a smooth transition from 'button' mushroom to 'big mushroom', and Flash can do this for us. You're about to see how Flash can perform as underpaid, unappreciated 'in-betweener'.

8. Click somewhere in-between the two keyframes on the timeline to select the first keyframe and all of the normal frames that depend on it:

What we're going to do now is change the behavior of these frames. We're going to tell Flash that we want to create an animation that smoothly transforms the small mushroom in frame 1 into the fully-grown version that we've just created in frame 15. Our ability to do this is entirely dependent on the existence of our two keyframes: the keyframes define the two different states of the mushroom, and we're asking Flash to create all of the in-between frames that will represent the growth of the mushroom. Let's do that.

9. Right-click on the frames you've got selected in the timeline. From the context-sensitive menu that pops up, choose the **Panels > Frame** option. This will open a panel with the Frame tab at the front - the Frame tab will let us change the properties of the selected frames:

From here, we're going to give these frames a label, and create our growth animation.

In Flash, animation is called tweening. This might seem an odd name, until you realize that it's short for 'in-betweening', or the process of creating the transitional frames that go in-between the keyframes.

10. Click inside the **Label** box and give your frames a label that identifies them - we've called ours 'Mushroom Growth'.

Using labels makes it easier to identify specific bits of action inside a large and complex movie. If, as we have suggested, you keep objects on separate layers, and name those layers, then you should not need to use as many labels. They will come in useful later on when we start to deal with actions, but this will be discussed in greater detail when we come to it.

11. Now click on the arrow next to the Tweening box, and select **Shape** from the drop-down menu. This will automatically create a **shape tween**: Flash will decide that we want the stalk in frame one to morph into the stalk in frame 15, and that we want the cap in frame 1 to morph into the cap in frame 15, and it will automatically generate the in-between images in frames 2 through 14 that will produce this effect.

12. Click on the playhead and notice that the tweened frames on the timeline have now been colored green by Flash, indicating a shape tween, and that there is an arrow pointing from Frame 1 to Frame 15 this indicates the length of the tween. Finally, Flash has added our label to the tweened

frames, and appended a little red flag to draw our attention to it:

(For clarity, we've removed the label from subsequent screenshots.)

13. Slowly drag the playhead back to Frame 1, noticing that Flash has automatically filled in all of the animation frames between 1 and 15. Now press **Enter** to preview the movie, and the mushroom will steadily grow to its full-size.

14. Save your happy-grow-lucky mushroom.

We've spent some time looking at frames in Flash, and started to see how they can help us achieve the effects that we're after in our movies. What we'll do next is introduce you to another vital element of Flash authoring files - **layers**.

Layers

Whereas the timeline and its frames help us organize and manipulate content over time, layers help us add depth to the movie, and allow us to separate out pieces of content and action that would otherwise get tangled up. If you had to place all of your movie content on a single layer, it would be horrendously difficult to achieve anything complicated. By separating out the action onto different layers, you can create much more convincing and complex movies, and make full use of the flexibility and power that Flash's timeline gives you. Multiple layers mean that your movies can have a host of different elements on the stage, all acting completely independently of each other.

A traditional animator would have a different set of sheets of acetate for each part of their cartoon. For example, the background forest would be on one set of sheets, Red Riding-Hood would be happily skipping on another set, and the Big Bad Wolf would be stalking her from yet another set. By keeping the parts separate, the animator had much greater control over the individual aspects of their cartoon. It meant that if there was a mistake, or something needed to be altered, the animator could change just one set - say, adding an evil twinkle to the Wolf's eye - without having to redraw the forest or Miss Riding-Hood as well. Another benefit of having separate animations on different sets of acetate is that they can be reused later in the cartoon, or indeed in a completely different cartoon, so while Jack and Jill are running up the hill in cartoon two, cartoon one's Little Red Riding-Hood can be happily skipping along below them without having to be redrawn. The content on the different layers is independent and portable.

In Flash, layers are shown to the left of the timeline. Each new Flash movie comes with a single layer by default:

Insert Layer button

Delete Layer button

This layer - **Layer 1** - is the default layer that we've been working with in our mushroom movie so far.

In Flash, layers are the equivalent of those separate sheets of acetate containing different visual components. Layers make movies easier to alter, and allow for much greater richness of content. Let's take a look at what layers allow us to do in our sample movie.

Working with Layers

It's good practice to keep each element of your movie on a separate layer for ease of editing and for neatness. We'll see how this works in this exercise.

1. The **active layer** in Flash is the highlighted layer with the pencil icon next to its name: this pencil icon indicates that this is the layer that you have currently selected to work on.

2. Click on the **Insert Layer** button. Flash will create a new layer above **Layer 1** and call it **Layer 2**.

3. Notice that Flash has automatically made **Layer 2** 15 frames long to match the length of **Layer 1**. If you look at any of these frames though, they will still all be empty:

   Flash always calls a new layer 'Layer n' where n is the next number up from the last layer that you created. This means that even if you subsequently deleted a layer, Flash would still increment the next layer's number as if the deleted layer still existed. For example, if you deleted **Layer 2** and then added another layer, it would still be called **Layer 3** even though there was no **Layer 2**. Luckily, the good people at Macromedia understand just how confused you are at the moment, so instead of trying to work out which layer is which, they've given us the ability to uniquely name each - which means that we can forget about the whole numbers shebang, and work with meaningful, descriptive layer names instead. Giving your movie's layers names is another good habit to get into, and it will save you a lot of heartache.

4. Double-click on the name '**Layer 1**' in the timeline. When you double-click it, it will become editable, allowing you to change the name of the layer:

5. Type 'mushroom' and press *Enter*.

6. We want **Layer 2** to contain a picture of the moon in front of our night-sky background, so double-click where it says '**Layer 2**' type '**moon**' and press *Enter*. We now have our two layers meaningfully named and we can instantly infer what's on each of them.

7. Click on the Oval tool. Our moon will be a full one, so we'll use this tool to create the celestial body.

8. Click on the **Default Colors** button under the two color boxes:

Default Colors

This button will reset the colors to a black stroke with a white fill.

9. Still on the 'moon' layer, use the playhead to go to the final frame of the movie, and then draw a circle (remember, you can hold down the Shift key to help you draw a perfect circle) over the top of the right-hand side of your fully-grown mushroom cap:

If you look at the timeline, you'll notice that Flash has automatically created a keyframe at frame 1 of the 'moon' layer, and that it's also populated all of the frames on this layer with the image of the moon. This is a handy effect, as we want the moon to be visible in the sky throughout our movie. If we'd wanted the moon to appear in the movie from frame 15 onwards (and not before), we'd have needed to create a keyframe at frame 15 in the 'moon' layer.

10. Press *Enter* to play your movie:

Flash has zipped through the timeline and displayed the content of both layers for us.

But something looks slightly wrong, doesn't it? The mushroom seems to be further away than the moon, and bigger, too. If we're going to get the perspective right, then you'll need to put the moon *behind* the mushroom. We need to get the layers' stacking order right.

The higher up a layer appears in the layer list on the left of the timeline, the closer the contents of that layer appear to you on the

screen. So to get your mushroom in front of the moon, you just have to move its layer above the moon's layer in the layer list. Let's do that now.

11. Click on the name of the 'mushroom' layer in the layer list and drag it above the 'moon' layer. You'll see a shaded bar appear while you're dragging the layer:

   This indicates where the layer will go when you release the mouse.

12. Now when you play your movie, the mushroom should rise in front of the moon. Perspective has been returned, and the tale of the very big mushroom and the very small moon has been consigned once more to legend.

   Deleting a layer is as easy as adding a layer - it only takes the click of a button. To delete a layer, you'd just click on the layer to highlight it, and then click on the **Delete Layer** button, which is indicated by the trash can icon underneath the layer listing. You should note that Flash will not let you delete **all** the layers in a movie: there must always be at least one layer left. If you're trying to delete everything from a movie and start again, it's easier to close the current movie and start a new one.

To conclude our look at layers, let's talk about the different **layer modes** that are available to us.

Layer Modes

Layer modes define how you view and affect specific layers in the authoring environment. There are three layer modes in Flash and, by default, they're all turned 'off'. The three modes are controlled by clicking on the icons in the three columns after the layer name, and the status of the modes for a particular layer is indicated by the two dots and the square next to that layer's name:

The first column controls showing and hiding a layer, the second controls locking and unlocking a layer, and the third column is used for viewing the contents of that layer as outlines. Let's take a look at how these different modes interact in the authoring environment, and see what benefits they give us.

Working with Layer Modes

With all three of the layer mode selector icons in the 'off' position, the authoring environment will behave exactly as it has done so far: if you were to start drawing a circle with the oval tool right now, it would appear as normal on the currently selected (active) layer. Let's see what happens when we start switching the layer modes 'on'.

1. In the 'mushroom' layer, click on the dot underneath the picture of the eye.

    Three things will happen:

    *   As we've hidden the layer, its contents will will disappear from the stage in the authoring environment

    *   A red cross will replace the dot in the eye column, reminding us that this layer is currently hidden

    *   The pencil icon will have
        a red line struck through
        it, indicating that the
        contents of the hidden
        layer cannot be edited.
        If you try to draw on

        the stage now, you'll find that the cursor has changed to a pencil with a warning circle next to it.

The warning circle tells us that the currently selected tool cannot be used at the moment. The logic here is that if you *were* able to draw on the hidden layer, you'd be able to unwittingly draw all over the content that you'd created so carefully already. Flash is protecting you from yourself.

If you were to actually click on
the stage with the Oval tool,
you'd get an error message:

Hiding layers is very helpful
when you need to concentrate
on some content on a particular layer and you don't want to have the contents of other layers obstructing your view. For example, in the final frame of your mushroom movie, the mushroom covers part of the moon. If you wanted to draw a face on your moon it would be hard to see what you were doing because the mushroom would be in the way. By hiding the 'mushroom' layer, you can see the whole of the moon, select the moon layer and draw

away to your heart's content. You could then click on the cross in the eye column and the 'mushroom' layer would be visible again.

2. Click on the cross in the eye column to return everything to normal. Now click on the dot in the 'lock' column. A small padlock will replace the dot, and the pencil will again have a line through it. This time, though, although the layer is locked and you cannot draw or select objects on it, the mushroom will still be visible.

Locking layers allows you to work with objects above or below them without accidentally selecting anything in the locked layers. This is useful when you're drawing or modifying on one layer and you want to see the contents of the other layers to keep things in context. Locking the surrounding layers means you can draw and edit confidently, secure in the knowledge that you won't mess anything up on the other layers.

The final mode allows you to display all objects on a layer as **outlines only**, rather than as filled shapes:

3. Unlock the 'mushroom' layer by clicking on the small padlock across from the layer name. Now click on the colored box to the right - the mushroom will be reduced to just an outline. The outline takes its color from the color of the box that you just clicked on. Each layer will have its own dedicated outline color (automatically allocated by Flash), so you can easily make out which objects belong to which layer.

4. Click on the outline button on the 'moon' layer, and (on your monitor, at least!) you'll see that the moon's outline is a different color to the mushroom's.

Outline mode is useful for helping you get a grip on exactly what's in your movie across all layers. Things start to get complicated when you have lots of different things on lots of layers and you can't quite see what is going on. Outline mode lets you step back from the

jumble and get a clear view. Outline mode is also helpful in previewing your movie, as Flash finds animating outlines easier to render than fully-filled shapes, meaning that the movie preview displays quicker.

You can easily change the layer mode for **all** of the layers by using the icons at the top of each of the columns. So, to turn outline mode **off** for both of our movie's layers, just click on the black box next to the eye and the lock. This will instantly return your mushroom and moon to their full-color glory.

If you're working with a lot of layers and want to lock every layer except the layer you're currently working on, it is easiest to click on the **Lock/Unlock All Layers** button to lock every layer, and then click on the small padlock on the layer that you want to use to just unlock that layer. The same principle applies to the show/hide feature invoked via the eye icon.

Layer modes only affect how you see the layers as you are constructing them: they have no affect on the final movie that you create, so layers that are hidden in the authoring environment will be visible in the final movie. Similarly, layers that are in outline mode will be seen in full color when they're rendered in the browser.

Now let's move on to the last Flash concept that we want to introduce into this chapter - **scenes**.

Scenes

Scenes are used to organize your movie into sections, sections that you can view as independent pieces of the whole movie. The ability to have a multi-scene movie allows you to break up your content up into logical chunks and helps you organize things efficiently.

Flash movies can be large or small, simple or complex. Small, simple movies can usually be contained in a single scene with no problem, but when you're talking about a large movie with many components, or a movie that has long animations or multiple navigation elements, then multiple scenes can be the way to go.

You can think of scenes as an extension of your timeline, giving you the facility to break up the action and continue from one scene to another. The benefit to you as an author is that your authoring files are more manageable, and the benefit to the user can be a more navigable movie. Many developers simply use separate scenes for their preloader (an element of a Flash movie that downloads movie components in advance of their being used), the introduction, and the main movie.

Some developers also use separate scenes in the same way as traditional designers use HTML pages on their sites - 1 scene is equivalent to 1 HTML page: this can be a useful model when you're designing a whole site in Flash - you can create a front page for your site, and then jump to different scenes (pages) depending on which buttons the user presses. We'll discuss this design approach in depth in a later chapter.

Each new Flash movie starts out with one default scene, named Scene 1. You can tell what scene you are currently in by looking at the scene name directly above your layers:

You can add and delete scenes as you wish, using the **Insert > Scene** and **Insert > Remove Scene** menu options. You can see the names of all of your scenes by opening up the **Scenes** panel. You do this via the **Window > Panels > Scene** menu option:

Here, you can use the buttons to manipulate scenes, and you can also drag scenes to change the order of playback. Usefully, you can also double-click on any scene in the **Scene** panel and give it a meaningful name. Once again, this is useful for bringing clarity to your movie authoring files.

Delete scene

Duplicate scene   Add scene

By default, Flash will always play the scenes in the sequence in which the scenes are listed in the **Scenes** panel, so make sure that you keep the right scenes in the right order here. However, you can also use Flash ActionScript to jump from scene to scene and play them in different sequences.

Another way to swap between scenes in the authoring environment is to click on the scenes button at the top and click on the scene you want to edit in the drop-down list:

And there's yet another way of navigating between your movie's different scenes in the authoring environment: the Movie Explorer.

The Movie Explorer

The Movie Explorer is a new feature in Flash 5, and it gives you the ability to browse your way through your whole movie at different levels of detail. You can open up the Movie Explorer by choosing the **Window > Movie Explorer** menu option or by clicking on the Show Movie Explorer button in the Launcher bar at the bottom right of the Flash window:

The Movie Explorer window looks like this:

As you can see from this view of our mushroom movie, the Movie Explorer can reveal the contents of your movie to you in depth, in terms of its component scenes, layers, and keyframes (provided that you've chosen the relevant options from the **Show** buttons along the top): You can click on any node in this displayed hierarchy and be taken to that point in the movie. This is a really powerful way of helping you navigate through your movies - especially as your movies grow in size and scope. We'll be seeing more of the Movie Explorer as we progress through the book.

For now, though, let's just recap where we've been before we move on to the next chapter.

Summary

In this chapter, we've introduced you to the Flash authoring environment and demonstrated some of the essential elements of Flash movie creation.

We saw that:

◆   We create movie content on the stage, which has a surrounding work area

◆ The content we add to the stage is displayed in the viewer's browser when the movie plays back

◆ Our movie is a series of points in time: these are played back in sequence as the playhead moves along the **timeline**

◆ We use **keyframes** to hold new or changed content, and to indicate to Flash that something significant is happening. Keyframes are separated by 'normal' **frames** that influence how long the action between keyframes lasts

◆ **Layers** add depth and manageability to your movies

◆ **Scenes** allow us to separate our movies into distinct chunks

◆ The **Movie Explorer** lets us navigate through our entire movie and browse through its content

In the next chapter, we're going to look in more depth at the built-in Flash tools that let us create movie content. As we've already seen, these tools live in the Flash Toolbox.

Home

Clients

Contact

Services

2 The Flash Toolbox

What we'll cover in this chapter:

◆ The Flash **Toolbox**: where we find Flash's integral drawing and manipulation tools, and what they're capable of

◆ How to use these tools to create and amend movie content: images and text

◆ Precision drawing and fine-tuning with Bezier curves

In the previous chapter, we took a look at the key structures contained in every Flash movie - the stage, the timeline, keyframes, frames and layers. In this chapter, we're going to start exploring Flash's built-in facilities for creating and manipulating movie content.

To do this, we'll examine each of Flash's drawing and editing tools in the context of enhancing our mushroom movie: these tools are the integral means that Flash gives us for drawing pictures, creating text, and manipulating these and other visual elements on the stage.

All of these built-in content creation tools are accessed via the Flash Toolbox.

The Toolbox

The Toolbox is where you'll find all of Flash's drawing and editing tools. Using these tools in conjunction with Flash's panels, you'll have at your disposal everything you need to design and manipulate the visual components and building blocks of your movie.

By default, the Toolbox is situated on the left-hand side of the screen when you open up Flash for the first time, but you can move it around or hide it, just like any other window. The Toolbox window itself is subdivided into four sections - **Tools**, **View**, **Colors** and **Options**:

- The **Tools** section is where all of the basic design and manipulation options are found. These tools can be used to draw pictures, create text elements, select objects and move them around the stage - amongst other things.

- The **View** section contains tools for two main functions: zooming in and out on the stage, and changing the stage's position on the screen. These changes of view and position only apply to screen display in the authoring environment where you're creating the movie - any changes you make to the view here don't have any effect on the way that the finished movie itself is rendered in the user's browser. You might, for example, wish to shift the stage around on screen so that you can see other screen elements - such as open panels - more clearly.

- The **Colors** section is used to control the color of the **stroke** (line) or **fill** of an object. For instance, if you wanted to have a blue circle with a black outline, you'd choose those options in the Colors section. The topmost tool in the Colors section determines the stroke color, and the tool below it (the one with the paint bucket icon) controls the object's fill color. Reading from left to right, the three remaining tools in the Colors section are responsible for: setting the stroke and fill colors to black and white; switching off the stroke or fill (depending on which of them is selected); and swapping back and forth between black stroke/white fill and white stroke/black fill.

- The **Options** section is where you can change the properties of the currently selected tool. For example, you can change the size and shape of the Paintbrush tool to make different kinds of brush marks. You can't modify the characteristics of every tool in the toolbox, so don't worry if this section appears blank for some tools.

If you're working in Windows, you'll see that the modifiers in the Options section are duplicated in the main Toolbar at the top of the screen:

These options become visible on the Windows Toolbar once you've selected an object on the screen using the Arrow tool. We'll be looking at how to use these modifiers as we progress through the book.

> *Remember that you'll need to have the main toolbar activated - otherwise, you won't see these options.*

You've already used the Arrow and the Oval tools to help create your prototype mushroom in the previous chapter, and in this section you'll be amending and expanding your movie to incorporate the effects of all of the other tools. By the end of this chapter, you'll have a working knowledge of all of the basic tools, and have a sense of how to apply them to achieve the results you want.

Let's start with the Arrow tool, which is used for manipulating visual elements of the movie.

The Arrow Tool

The Arrow tool is maybe the most important tool in Flash, and probably the one that you'll use most often when creating and amending visual content on the stage.

Essentially, the Arrow tool is used to select objects on the stage for editing, and to move and place those selected objects just where we want them. The Arrow tool has a few little quirks that are important to understand. Let's take a look at them now.

Using the Arrow Tool for Selection and Manipulation

Here, we're just going to examine the basics of using the Arrow tool. To do this, we'll need something drawn on our stage.

1. First up, open a new movie, click on the Oval tool in the Toolbox...

2. ...and select a black stroke, and a fill color of your choice. To choose a color for strokes and fills, simply click on the relevant color selector box to bring up the color palette and make your choice:

3. Next, click on the stage and hold down the mouse button, dragging the mouse so that you draw a nice big circle on the stage:

(Remember that holding down the **Shift** key while you drag will result in a perfect circle).

4. Now select the Arrow tool by clicking on its icon in the Toolbar:

When we select the Arrow tool, its five associated modifiers appear in the **Options** section of the Toolbox:

These modifiers can be applied to the objects that we select with the Arrow tool - we'll be seeing how to use each of these later.

5. Now that you've selected the Arrow tool, the next thing to do is point at the center of the big circle you've drawn:

Note that when you move the Arrow tool over the center of the circle, the cursor turn into a bold cross with arrows on each of its arms: this indicates that you're hovering over an object that can be selected and moved simply by clicking and dragging.

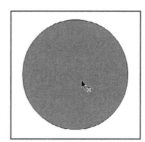

6. Click on the colored part of the circle (it'll be highlighted as soon as you click on it) and drag it off to the side. Then release the mouse button:

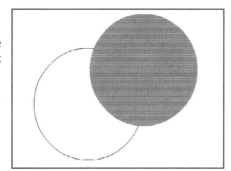

You'll see that what's happened here is that we've separated the fill part of the shape from its enclosing line (stroke) - the circle has become two separate objects.

Note that, by default, the enclosed shapes you draw using the tools in the toolbox will consist of an outline and a fill. You can choose to have 'no outline' or 'no fill' by selecting the Stroke Color or Fill Color box in the Toolbox...

...and then clicking on the **No Color** selector:

This will put a red slash through the color box, indicating that color for that drawing element (stroke or fill) is switched 'off':

It's easy to accidentally separate the stroke and fill elements of a shape when using the Arrow tool as a selection device, and it points up the need to take care when selecting objects.

Furthermore, if we now click away from the highlighted disk of color, then click on it and drag it again...

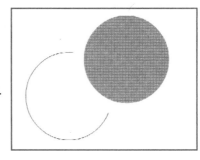

...you can see that it's taken a bite out of the original stroke that used to surround the circle. Dang.

So, what's the solution to this? Well, we can always undo the change we just made using ***Ctrl-Z***, and then try again. A less haphazard way to avoid separating an object into its component pieces is to make sure that you select both the colored fill and the surrounding stroke before moving the object. The way to achieve this is to double-click on the object that you want to move - this will select its stroke and its fill. By double-clicking on a shape like this, you ensure that you can drag it around as a single entity.

Another solution is to **group** the components together so that they are treated as a single shape. To do this, you can choose one of two methods: you can double-click on your shape with the Arrow tool (thus selecting both the fill and the stroke) and choose the **Modify > Group** menu option; or you can select the Arrow tool and then use it to draw a rectangle around the shapes that you want to group together:

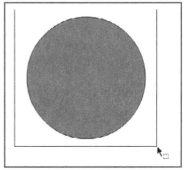

Again, this will select both the stroke and the fill, and you can use the same **Modify > Group** option to group them together.

Whichever of these two methods you use, the result will be the same: your objects will be grouped together - in this case, the two objects being the circle's surrounding stroke and color fill.

Grouped objects, when selected, will be highlighted by a colored line that indicates that they are a group. (The color of this line is determined by the global **Highlight Color** setting that you choose via the **General** tab of the **Edit > Preferences** menu.)

To separate grouped items back into their component parts, select the group, then choose the **Modify > Ungroup** menu option.

And there's another common mishap that can befall us when we're using the Arrow tool to select and move objects. Take a look at this...

Yes, it's that familiar circle, drawn once again using the Oval tool - this time with a green fill (honest) and a black stroke.

Now, let's suppose that I want to use the Arrow tool to select the circle so that I can move it. I remember that I need to select both the fill and the stroke, so I decide to use the Arrow tool to draw a selection box. I click and drag the mouse to draw the box...

But, sadly, I've misjudged the starting position for my drag, and I've accidentally missed the top of the circle. However, I decide to persevere. At the end of the drag, I release the mouse button, then click on the center of the circle and try to drag it away to the right...

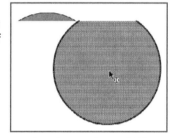

Hmm...not *quite* what I wanted. Flash thinks that I want to *carve up* my circle rather than move it as a single entity. Again, this problem can be avoided by grouping the stroke and fill segments. Take care - those selection boxes can be sharp!

We've looked at the selection and moving of objects, both here, and in the last chapter when we constructed our first mushroom-oriented Flash movie. The Arrow has one other important use, though - it can help us change the shape of objects by dragging their outlines. Let's take a look at this functionality next.

Extending your Mushroom's Cap

What we're going to do here is modify the mushroom-based movie that we started work on in the previous chapter.

1. Open Mushroom.fla from the end of the last chapter.

2. Click on your keyframe in frame 15 of the 'mushroom' layer.

3. Choose the Arrow tool from the Toolbox once more.

4. Click on the stage, away from the drawn shapes, to ensure that you've got nothing selected.

5. Now position the point of the arrow cursor on the edge of the mushroom cap - that is, touching the line around the filled shape:

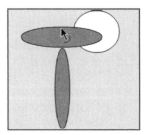

You'll notice that when the arrow point touches the line, the cursor changes to an arrow with a curved line underneath it:

This change of cursor indicates that you are now in a position to click and drag a point on a line, thus changing the shape of that line. A cursor with a right angle underneath the pointer, like this...

... means that you are in a position where you can drag a corner.

6. Now click on the line and drag it upwards to create a domed, more 'natural-looking' cap to our mushroom. Notice that when you release the mouse button, the fill expands to flood the modified shape with color:

OK, our little bit of genetic modification is complete.

7. Play the movie. You'll see that Flash has automatically modified all the frames in-between the keyframes so that the animation shows the smooth growth of our newly amended mushroom cap. Flash is great at making life easy for us in this respect: if we change the start or end points of our animation - the keyframes - then Flash will recalculate all of the in-between images, without even asking us.

Next, let's take a look at a tool that lets us really close in on the objects in our movie and see them in fine detail - the Zoom tool.

The Zoom Tool

Here's the Zoom tool in the Toolbox, along with its related modifiers in the Options section:

The Zoom tool is very easy to use: clicking on the screen with the **Enlarge** option selected will zoom in on the screen, and clicking with the **Reduce** option selected will zoom out. Simple.

Once you've selected your zoom 'in' or 'out' mode, you can temporarily switch from one state to the other by holding down the **ALT** key. When you click on the screen with this key depressed, the zoom will operate in the opposite direction from what's selected in the Options section: this saves you having to keep changing the mode in the Options box whenever you want to zoom in and out.

With the Zoom tool selected, you can also drag a box around an area, and Flash will enlarge that area to fill the screen.

Zooming in and out on the Moon

1. Still in your Mushroom.fla file, hide the mushroom layer by clicking on the dot in the eye column next to its name:

2. Now use the Zoom tool to enlarge the moon until it fills the screen. Look at the edge of the moon and notice that the quality of the image doesn't degrade as you zoom in, however much you increase the magnification. This is one of the wonders of working with vector graphics - you never lose any detail.

    Also, note that any changes in magnification you make inside of the .fla file don't affect the finished movie: the zoom features are just there to help you when you're creating your movie.

The next tool we're going to look at is also a relatively simple one - the Hand tool.

The Hand Tool

The Hand tool is used for moving around the segment of the stage that's displayed on your screen. It's most useful when you're zoomed right in and you're not able to see the entire movie all at once. Remember that any changes in view you make in the authoring environment will not have any effect on the display of your finished movie.

Using the Hand tool, move around your zoomed-in movie, making sure that you finish up with the moon in the middle again. You can achieve the same effect using the scroll bars below and to the right of the stage, but the Hand tool feels somehow more controlled and intuitive.

Now let's zoom in on our next Toolbox component - the Oval tool.

The Oval Tool

You've already used the Oval tool to draw the mushroom and the moon in Chapter 1, where we saw the option of pressing the Shift key when you're dragging to automatically 'snap' the oval so that it becomes a perfect circle. We'll use the Oval tool again here to enhance our moonscape.

Making Craters with the Oval Tool

1. With the Moon filling the screen to ensure precision, use the Oval tool to draw a number of craters on the surface of the moon. You can draw them as ovals or as perfect circles - it's your call:

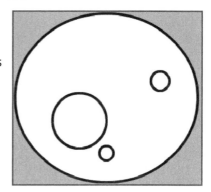

2. Now zoom back out to 100% and unhide the mushroom layer to view the current state of the picture - the night, the moonlight, and a groovy mushroom.

OK, that's enough admiration of our handiwork for the moment - let's move on to the next tool.

□ The Rectangle Tool

The Rectangle tool, as the name suggests, is used for drawing squares and rectangles.

Round Rectangle Radius

It operates virtually identically to the Oval tool in the way that shapes can be created by selecting the tool, then clicking on the stage and dragging the shape to an appropriate size. Similarly, pressing the *Shift* key while drawing will snap the rectangle to a perfect square.

As you can see in the screenshot above, the Rectangle tool has a modifier in the Options section - the grandly named **Round Rectangle Radius** modifier. Translated into simpler terms, this modifier controls the extent to which the corners of the rectangle you're drawing are rounded off.

Let's put the Rectangle tool to work in our mushroom movie.

Making a Rectangular Signpost

We're going to create a sign that'll stand at the edge of the mushroom patch.

1. Create a new layer in your Mushroom.fla movie and name it '**Signpost**'.

2. Next, click on the Rectangle tool, then on the Round Rectangle Radius modifier, and enter the figure **15** into the **Rectangle Settings** dialog box that pops up:

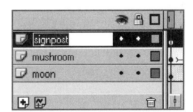

You can also bring up the **Rectangle Settings** box by double-clicking on the Rectangle tool in the Toolbox.

3. Click on **OK**.

By entering the number 15, we're telling Flash that we want to round off the corners of the rectangle by a factor of 15 *points*.

4. Draw a rectangle on the left-hand side of the picture, a little higher than the moon. This will be your sign board in the movie foreground:

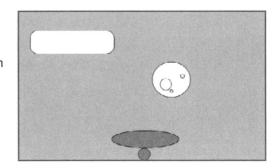

We'll be enhancing our sign soon. In fact, almost immediately, using the Line tool.

✏️ The Line Tool

The Line tool is used for drawing lines: yup, it really is as easy as it sounds.

To use the Line tool, you select it, and then just click (and hold) on the start point of your line, then drag the mouse and release on the end point. To work with the Line tool really effectively though, we need to use the Stroke panel - this will enable us to closely control the characteristics of the line that we draw. Let's look at that in a short exercise.

Making a Post with the Line Tool

1. Click on the **Show Info** icon (the left-most in the list) in the **Launcher** bar at the bottom-right of the screen:

2. A panel will open up with the **Info** tab selected:

    This tab gives us precise information about the currently selected object (or the object over which the cursor is currently positioned): its width and height, position, color (the RGB values) and the Alpha (intensity) level.

3. Click on the panel's **Stroke** tab to display the modifiers that can be applied to your strokes - lines - in Flash:

Stroke Style

Stroke Width

Stroke Color

Stroke Preview

These modifiers will also work in conjunction with the other drawing tools: this means that you can alter the characteristics of the outlines of your ovals and rectangles after you've drawn them.

Next, you're going to use the Line tool to draw a post to support your signboard.

4. Click on the downward-pointing arrow to the right of the **Stroke Width** box:

A slider will pop up - this controls the width of your line. (You can also type a precise width into the box if you prefer - the maximum width being **10**.)

5. Choose the thickest stroke you can by moving the slider to the top of its range - this will result in a size 10 line. You'll also see that the example line in the bottom box has now become thicker:

6. To fix your size choice click anywhere else on the panel.

7. Now click on the Stroke panel's Color box to bring up the standard palette, and select a dark woody brown for the post. Again, notice that the line in the example box has changed to the color that you selected.

8. Click on the Snap button (the magnet) in the main Toolbar (Windows), or choose the **View > Snap to Objects** menu option (Mac).

    Doing this will ensure that when your line gets close to a perfect vertical or horizontal orientation, the line will automatically 'snap' to the vertical or horizontal. When you draw your line, you'll see that there's a small circle at the end of the line while you're dragging the mouse, and that when the line snaps this circle grows bolder to signal to you that you've reached the desired angle. When you're in 'Snap to Objects' mode, you can also hold down the Alt key while you're dragging: this will snap when your line attains a 45-degree angle.

9. OK, back to our example. Click and drag a line from the bottom of your sign to the edge of the stage (which is where the ground is on our mushroom patch), snap the line to the vertical, and release the mouse to fix the line. Don't worry if the end of the line sticks out over the edge of the stage. Remember, only things that appear on the stage will be seen in the final movie.

    Here's our movie content so far:

Let's make some more modifications to the scene, this time using the Paint Bucket tool.

The Paint Bucket Tool

Gap Size

Lock Fill ── ── Transform Fill

The Paint Bucket, also commonly known as the 'Fill' tool is used for filling in empty shapes or for changing the fill color of existing shapes.

We'll talk about all of these modifiers later in the book when we come to use them 'in anger'. For the moment, let's stick with the core functionality of the Paint Bucket tool.

The Paint Bucket tool is used in conjunction with the Toolbox's color palette. You select the Paint Bucket tool and pick a color from the color palette, clicking on the area you want to fill with that color.

Let's do that now in the context of our mushroom world.

Filling the Moon with Color

1. Select a pale yellow color from the color palette - we're going to paint the moon.

2. Click on the Paint Bucket tool, then click once on the main section of the moon: it will instantly be filled with the pale yellow that you selected.

    Every cursor has a point, called a **hotspot**, that tells the computer *exactly* where you're clicking on the screen. The hotspot for the Paint Bucket tool is the end of the paint spilling out of the can:

3. Select a slightly darker yellow and fill the craters in the same way that you re-colored the lunar surface. If you find it hard to click exactly on a small crater, try zooming in so that you have a larger area to hit with your Paint Bucket's hotspot.

OK, we've now transformed the surface of the moon - not bad going for just a few minutes work. But, relentlessly, we have to move on to the next tool - the Ink Bottle.

The Ink Bottle Tool

The Ink Bottle works hand in hand with the Paint Bucket. Where the Paint Bucket changes *fills*, the Ink Bottle does the same for *lines*. The hotspot for the Ink Bottle is at the tip of the spilled ink. Let's use it to alter the nature of our signboard's supporting post.

Changing Lines with the Ink Bottle

Here, you're going to transmute your signpost from a wooden model to a metal version.

1. Select the Ink Bottle tool, and then choose a gray hue from the Stroke Color palette.

2. Click on your post, and it will instantly change to the gray that you selected. Wood to metal in one click - superb. If only those mediaeval alchemists had known about Flash - their lives would have been *so* much easier.

You can also use the Stroke panel to alter the style and thickness of a line, and then apply it with the Ink Bottle.

Having seen a couple of ways of applying changes to different objects on our stage, let's now look at how we can 'copy' characteristics from one object to another. The tool we use to do this is the Dropper.

 The Dropper Tool

This tool is used to 'suck up' the colors and styles of fills (or lines) from objects that you've already created. When you use the Dropper to pick up an object's attributes, Flash will then automatically switch over to the tool that you'll use to apply these attributes to another object. That is, if you pick up a *fill* style, Flash will flip over to the Paint Bucket tool, and if you pick up a *line/stroke* style, Flash will take you to the Ink Bottle.

The Dropper tool can also be used to pick up bitmaps and gradients, and we'll cover these uses in detail later.

Now let's apply the Dropper tool to our example movie.

Picking Colors from Lines and Fills

What we want to do here is change our signpost so that it mirrors the attributes of our yellowish moon. This will give us a nice tonal continuity.

1. Click on the Dropper tool and move it over the yellow-filled surface of the moon. Notice that a little picture of a paintbrush appears next to the cursor: this indicates that if we were to click here, we'd be picking up a fill style: When the cursor is held over a stroke rather than a fill, a little pencil icon appears, as is shown below.

2. Click on the pale yellow moon. The Dropper will immediately swap over to the Paint Bucket tool. Notice that the fill color in the Toolbox has now changed to the color you've just selected.

3. Now click on the middle of your signboard and fill it with the same pale yellow as the moon.

4. Select the Dropper tool again, but this time click on the gray line that you drew for your signpost's supporting strut. Look at the Stroke panel: not only has the Dropper selected the color, but it's also picked up the Stroke width from the post - in this case, 10. If you were to click on the line around the sign now, it would become the same thickness as your signpost.

5. Instead, though, change the line thickness in the Stroke panel to **3**, and then click on the sign's outline. It will immediately become a medium-width line the same color as your signpost:

OK, we've now got a nicely-proportioned sign at the edge of our mushroom patch. What's next? Well, I guess the sign should probably *communicate something*. How about some text to tell people that we don't want their big boots all over our precious mushrooms? For that, we need the Text tool.

The Text Tool

The Text tool in Flash is used in conjunction with the Character panels. Together, they allow text entry and editing in your Flash movie. In Flash 5, text fields can also be used as hyperlinks - more on this later.

Giving your Sign Character

First, we'll define how our text should look.

1. Create a new layer and call it 'text'.

2. Click on the Show Character button on the Launcher bar (the one with the capital A on it). This will open the Character panel - make sure that the Character tab is selected:

The options displayed on this panel are similar to those in a word processing program, and many of them will probably be familiar to you. Just for the record, the options that you have here are:

Font - The name of the font you want to use. Note that Flash previews the fonts when you open the font list:

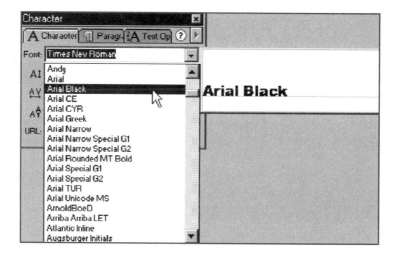

Font Size - This is the size, in points, that you want your font to be.

Tracking - This inserts a uniform gap of your chosen size between each of the characters.

Kern - 'Kerning' is the gap left between pairs of characters. Most fonts will have built-in kerning so that the gaps between certain characters will be different sizes: for example, the gap between an A and a D will be larger than that between an A and a V. The default is to use the font's built-in kerning, and in most cases you will want to leave this on.

Baseline Shift - This is where you can choose to display the font as subscript or superscript.

URL - If you enter a web address in this box, the text in your exported movie will act as a hyperlink to the web site specified by that address.

The **Bold** and **Italic** modifiers will make the text either bold or italic, and the **Color** button will open up the standard Flash color palette so that you can choose the text color.

3. Select the Text tool and click on the pale yellow fill of the signboard:

A small text box appears with a blinking cursor at the text insertion point. Don't worry if your insertion point is not in exactly the right place - we'll be able to position the text precisely later by selecting the text box with the Arrow tool and relocating it.

4. In the Character panel, choose a font that you like the look of (we've used Arial Black), and choose a font size that will fit nicely on your sign. Notice that as you move the Font Size slider up and down, the text box on your stage is automatically resized: this guide will help you to choose how large a text size you should choose to fit on your sign.

5. Set the color of your font to black.

6. Finally, you can type some text into your text box. To maintain the sanctity of our mushroom, we chose to write 'Keep Out' on the sign, but you can write whatever you like (provided that it fits!).

7. Click on the Arrow tool.

The white box around the text will disappear to be replaced by a thin, colored highlight (this will be the color that you have set as your default Highlight Color on the General tab of the Edit > Preferences menu). You can now pick up this text with the Arrow cursor and move it around until you are happy with its position on the sign:

8. To go back and edit the text again, just click on the text with the Text tool.

Also note that in Flash, there is no text modifier that will underline text. If you want to have underlined text in Flash, you will have to manually draw a line underneath it. Maybe in Flash 6...

We've now got a number of elements that we created using straight lines, ovals, rectangles and text. Next, let's live on the edge a little and try some freehand drawing. For that, we can start with a pencil.

The Pencil Tool

The Pencil tool is used to draw freeform lines.

Pencil Mode ——→

This tool uses the Stroke panel to set its different characteristics (i.e. Stroke width, style and color). The Pencil tool also has one modifier in the Options section of the Toolbox - the Pencil Mode modifier. This sole modifier is an important one, though - it controls how the line behaves when we draw by clicking and dragging with the mouse.

Clicking on this modifier reveals that there are three Pencil modes to choose from:

Let's see how these work, in the context of adding some foliage to our mushroom patch.

Penciling in Some Grass

Here, we're going to add a little local color to our mushroom movie.

1. Save away your Mushroom.fla movie and create a new movie by clicking on the New button on the main toolbar, or by using the **File > New** menu option. This will open a fresh, blank white movie in Flash.

   Don't worry about not being able to see your Mushroom movie any more - it's still there, as you can see by choosing the **Window** menu option: the resulting pop-up window will reveal the list of currently open movie files at the bottom.

2. Using the Pencil tool, draw a series of similar lines with the different Pencil Modes and notice the results.

- **Straighten** mode will flatten out some of the curves in your line. Another feature of this tool is that it will automatically complete simple shapes that you draw. For example, if you draw a rough circle with straighten mode on, Flash will snap it to a perfect circle:

 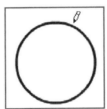

- **Smooth** mode will refine the curves in your hand-drawn shapes, rounding out kinks and generally softening awkward shapes. It's a good mode to use if your freehand drawing is a little shaky, as it will neaten the lines and make them look more professional.

- **Ink** mode is the basic pencil mode. If you want to draw something on the screen and have it come out *exactly* the way that you drew it, this is the mode to use. In this mode, you'll notice that Flash does seem to smooth the lines a little bit: this is just a result of the process of converting the line from the raster line that it uses while you're drawing to the vector version that it will actually store and render.

3. Close the movie that you've been using to experiment with pencil modes: choose *not* to save it (unless you really did like it), and you will be returned to your mushroom movie.

4.   Create a new layer, and call it 'grass'.

5.   With the Pencil tool selected, choose a nice grassy green from the Stroke palette, then click on the Ink mode modifier so that you can draw truly freehand.

6.   Scribble some rough lines around the base of your sign. Don't worry if they look a bit messy, as these will be tufts of grass at the bottom of your signpost:

7.   Save your movie again.

Now for the Brush tool.

 ## The Brush Tool

The Brush tool is very similar to the pencil tool, but instead of drawing lines, you're painting fills. Every time you use the Brush tool on your movie, you're simply painting a fill with no enclosing border line.

The Brush tool has four options:

- **Brush Mode** controls the way that your brush strokes are painted. This option has five additional modifiers:

    - **Paint Normal** will paint over anything else that's on the screen (provided it's on the same layer as the one you're drawing on, of course)

    - **Paint Fills** will only paint fills, and leave lines as they are - in place, and visible through the fill that you just painted

    - **Paint Behind** will only paint on blank areas of the current layer: any objects on that layer will not be painted over

    - **Paint Selection** will only paint on selected areas of the screen, those are areas that have been highlighted with the arrow tool

    - **Paint Inside** is the tool you always needed when you had those coloring in books as a kid.

When you start painting, Flash will ignore any marks you paint when your brush crosses a line:

- The **Brush Size** option changes the width and spread of the brush strokes

- The **Brush Shape** option opens a menu containing a selection of different shapes to paint with - round, flat, and so on

- The **Lock Fill** button works in the same way as the button of the same name under the Paint Bucket tool, and its use will be covered in a later section

Having seen how to paint, let's see how to erase our mistakes...

The Eraser Tool

The Eraser tool is similar in operation to the Brush tool - it just erases rather than paints. It has three modifiers: **Eraser Mode**, **Eraser Shape** and **Faucet**.

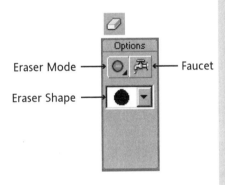

- The **Eraser Mode** button has five modifiers. These are the same as those for the Brush Mode button on the Brush tool, and they behave in the same way.

- The **Eraser Shape** button lets you change the shape of the eraser brush.

- The **Faucet** button changes the Eraser tool so that it will erase an entire fill or line at once: in this mode, you just touch the Eraser tool hotspot to the target line or fill, and the whole thing is erased.

Next, let's take a look at a rather interesting tool that's new to Flash 5 - the Pen tool.

The Pen Tool

The principles embodied in the Pen tool are an example of how high level science and math can have unforeseen spin-offs. The space race gave us microprocessors and non-stick pans, but a less well-known spin-off comes from the automobile industry of the 1970s: designers had just started using CAD/CAM packages to design cars, but there was a problem - the computers couldn't draw squiggly lines. They could do straight lines and simple curves, but they couldn't come up with a way to draw squiggles. Squiggly lines are difficult because the equations that define them - unlike those for straight lines or regular curves - are extremely complex.

Bezier Curves

The solution to this problem was a special kind of curve called a **Bezier**, named after Pierre Bezier a mathematician. Monsieur Bezier's curve is used in all sorts of computer applications today, from designing curved cars to displaying postscript fonts.

The difference between a Bezier and a normal curve is that a normal curve is made up of points. A Bezier curve, on the other hand, is made up of points that include two additional pieces of data that we will call *direction* and *speed*.

Bezier curves are drawn using the Pen tool, lets see how the Pen tool works in practice.

Working with Bezier Curves

1. Open up a fresh Flash movie to experiment inside.

2. Select the Pen tool, making sure you have a fill color and line color of your choice selected. The cursor will change into a pen nib with a little cross next to it:

3. Next, click and hold with the mouse, and drag away in the general direction you want the curve to go:

   You'll see a line start to appear as you drag. This line consists of three points; one at the center and one on each end, so there's a kind of bow tie look to the line. The center point of this line is where our finished curve will start from.

4. Don't let the bow tie get too big, and once you're happy with it, release the mouse. You've now created the starting point of the curve.

5. Now position the mouse pointer at another point on the screen that you want your curve to pass through. In the same way as you did before, drag out another bow tie, keeping the mouse button down as you position the bow tie:

   Notice that as you drag the second bow tie around, the curve between the two center points of the bow ties changes in real-time. The way it changes is pretty difficult to describe in words, but once you have seen it, it somehow looks totally natural: the direction of the bow tie defines what *direction* the curve goes in, and the *length* of the bow tie affects its curvature.

   A good way to think of it is that the bow ties represent the position (via the center point of the bow tie) and the speed (via the length of the bow tie) of a car trying to move in a straight line between the two points. As it gets faster (bow ties get bigger) the car travels in a curved path. Some of you may recognize the bow tie as the car's *velocity vector*, but the rest of us will just be having fun making the squiggle dance about to care too much about the math. In fact, practicing drawing the curves using the bow ties is the best way to get the feel of what's happening - sometimes words are just too much!

6. Keep adding bow ties to form a roughly puddle-shaped squiggle as shown here, creating something that looks just a tiny bit like the USA:

As you put the pen near the original starting point of the first bow tie (or near any point on a line that would make a closed area), the pen tool changes to show an 'O' where it was previously an 'X':

This is Flash's way of saying that the next point you add will create a closed shape. This sounds a little complicated, but just try it. As with most everything associated with Beziers, it's actually easier to do than to explain!

Sometimes, when you're constructing shapes with the Pen tool, you don't want a shape composed completely of curves, but rather a mixture of curves and sharp corners. If you want to create a corner rather than another curve, you simply click on the stage with the Pen tool rather than clicking and dragging. This will give you a mix of curves and straight lines:

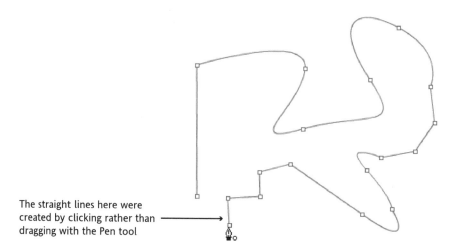

The straight lines here were created by clicking rather than dragging with the Pen tool

Once you've used the Pen tool to create your basic Bezier shape, you can edit it with the **Subselect** tool.

The Subselect Tool

This tool is certainly worth getting to know: it allows you to select and alter specific points on a curve, which means that you can have far greater control over modifying the curves that you've created.

If you choose the Subselect tool from the Toolbox and click the mouse on one of your pre-drawn Beziers, you'll see that a skeleton-like structure is shown inside your shape. This shows you the start and end points of the curves, and the shape of the curves that underlie the displayed drawing:

> *You might have to zoom right in to see this clearly - it's easier to see this if you have a big fat line like the one in this screenshot.*

And there's more: if you click on one of the little 'nodes' on the skeleton, the Bezier bow ties will appear...

...allowing you to modify the curves with precision and confidence.

There's another application of the Subselect tool that's extremely useful - you can use it to modify shapes that weren't drawn with the Pen tool, too.

Go into your mushroom movie, choose the Subselect tool, and then click on the outline stroke of the moon image:

Although it's difficult to see outside of the authoring environment, the same skeleton and node structure appears. Click on a node, and those familiar bow ties spring into view again:

This reveals that all the shapes you've drawn using Flash's drawing tools are implicitly composed of Beziers that you can modify. Once again, this shows that these integral tools are can be used precisely and powerfully. By dragging the bow ties, you can rework shapes:

This facility is useful, way beyond converting the moon to an ectoplasmic form.

Beziers and Animation

One thing about Beziers that doesn't become apparent until you play around with them is that they're not just a fancy drawing tool: they can be used to simulate real world movements much better than standard curves. For example, imagine a tennis ball hitting a net. When the ball makes contact with the net, the ball's weight and momentum will drag the net with it, changing the net's shape. If you draw your net with Beziers, the fine control we have with the bow ties lets us regulate a significant parameter - the *tension* of the net.

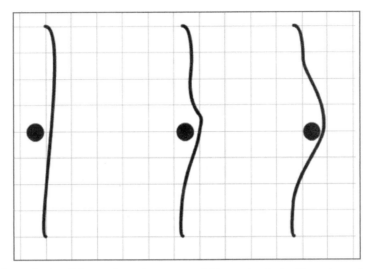

As you'll learn in detail later, these images could be animated with a *shape tween*. The Bezier curve bow ties can be used to 'set the tension' of the net, and therefore show its acceleration. Acceleration is a fundamental attribute of good animation, since it's the direct result of forces acting on the shape - which is what animation should try and express. With Beziers we can animate the effects of these forces more easily.

The use of Beziers for *animation* rather than just for shape creation opens up a whole new facet to expressive animation. If you stop thinking 'tennis net' and start thinking 'eyebrows and mouths' for example, you can begin to see how these curves could help you animate a face as its expression changes. Why not have a play and give it a try?

In this chapter we've taken a long look at some of the more important aspects of Flash's integral tools. We haven't covered every option, but we'll be looking at some of the other tool uses as we progress through this book.

Case Study

As a final exercise in this chapter, let's start building our case-study web site. We'll be using this throughout the book to implement the things we discuss in each chapter, and this will help us see the Flash components we're learning about in context.

Case Study Exercise: Background and Base Elements

Let's start this exercise by creating our simple background to our movie. First, we'll set up our movie's global properties.

1. Create a new Flash movie. Bring up the **Movie Properties** window and ensure that the dimensions of the movie's stage are set to 550 x 400 pixels. Set the background color to a nice deep red - maroon, maybe. This will give us a nice rich backdrop for our movie.

2. Change the name of the movie's default single layer to '**background**'.

3. Save your movie with a suitable name.

4. Now use the Oval tool to draw a big circle **with no outer line** and just a black fill. Make sure that the circle takes up a large portion of the movie stage:

5. Now zoom out a little and move the circle into the top left corner so that only a section of it is overlapping the stage:

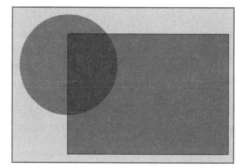

6. Using the Arrow tool, click and drag to select the areas of the circle that extend past the movie stage, and delete them:

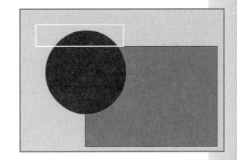

7. After deleting both areas, you should now have the remaining fragment of the circle in the upper left hand corner of your movie:

This will be the background for the movie that will run in our example web site. Now we need to start creating the content that will sit in front of that background and act as the interface that the viewer sees.

8. Add a new layer called '**Elements**'. This is where we're going to draw just a few base words and objects that we'll develop further as we add to our movie in later chapters.

9. To start building your content, use the Text tool to create four separate pieces of text:

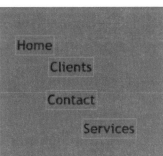

- Home

- Clients

- Contact

- Services

Don't worry about their position for the moment.

10. Use the Arrow tool to drag a box around all four of the text boxes you've just created.

11. With all four boxes selected, open up the **Character** panel:

12. As shown in the screenshot above, set the text boxes' font to **Arial**, and the size to **14**pt. Make the font bold, and choose a light gray color to contrast your maroon background.

We only have one component left to draw for the moment. We're going to create the basis for a button that we'll be developing later.

13. Create a small perfect circle with a red fill and no stroke. Make sure that the red you choose contrasts with the background red:

14. Open up the **Info** panel and ensure that the **Info** tab is selected.

15. Select your perfect circle and make sure that it is 35 pixels across. You can do this by keying the correct dimensions into the **Info** panel's width and height boxes:

Make sure that your movie's Ruler Units are set to pixels for this task! Remember that this setting is in the Movie Properties dialog box.

That's all for our case study in this chapter. This might seem very simple so far, but as you work through the final case study exercise in each chapter you'll see the concepts and content build bit by bit. This is the way any Flash movie is built: first you have an idea, then you create your building blocks that you need for your movie, and then you splice them all together.

Summary

In this chapter, we walked through some of the main features of the Toolbox, using the different tools to add and amend movie content. We'll continue to do this in depth throughout the book.

We saw that:

◆ Drawn shapes in Flash consist of **strokes** and **fills**, which can be moved and modified separately

◆ Flash's drawing tools have modifiers that control how drawn elements look and respond

◆ We can use tools (such as the Ink Bottle and Paint Bucket) with their modifiers to change the attributes (color, width etc) of strokes and fills

◆ We can also use **panels** (such as the **Stroke** panel) to change the characteristics of drawn objects

◆ We can create text fields and customize them using the **Character** panel

◆ The Pen tool allows us to draw precise and amendable **Bezier curves**

◆ With the Subselect tool, we can select and alter the curves and lines that make up any drawn shape in Flash

Now that we've seen how to create simple shapes and text in Flash, let's look at how we can convert them into reusable components. These reusable movie content components are the subject of our next chapter - **Symbols**.

Services

Services

Clients		Graphic
Contact		Graphic
Home		Graphic

Services

3 Flash Symbols and Libraries

What we'll cover in this chapter:

◆ **Symbols** - what they are, why they're useful, how to create them, and how to store and reuse movie content elements in the **library**

◆ The different kinds of symbol:

   ◆ **Graphic Symbols** (static images)

   ◆ **Button Symbols** (providers of interactivity)

   ◆ **Movie Clip Symbols** (independent, self-contained movie components that free you from the linear tyranny of your movie's main timeline)

In Flash, a **symbol** is a particular kind of movie *content* component - a piece of self-contained content that you can save away and reuse time and time again. Symbols add life and richness to your movies by loosening up the rigidity of everything having to happen along the movie's main timeline. Now that you know how to get around the stage and main timeline, and you have a working knowledge of the toolbox, you can begin to really make Flash come to life. **Symbols are a vital part of making great Flash movies**.

Typically, you create symbols when you know that you're going to have particular elements that you'll use repeatedly in a movie or in a number of movies, or when you want to encapsulate a little piece of action or animation and use it independently of what's going on in the rest of the movie - and you can *share* the saved symbols from one movie in your other movies, too.

Using stored symbols rather than uniquely-created content for every element in your movie has at least three advantages: firstly, symbols allow you to create far more interesting, flexible and extensible movies; secondly, it gives you the benefits of mass-production and reusable components; and thirdly, it helps you keep your movie file size small and the end-user happy and attentive to your site.

In this chapter you'll learn about the three types of symbol that Flash employs, and create and use an example of each. The more complicated aspects of critical symbols will also be covered in more detail when we come to use them later in the book. Here, we'll give you a solid grounding in the basics of symbols that will stand you in good stead.

Symbol Essentials

A **symbol** at its most basic level is a 'thing' in Flash that you can use time and time again. That 'thing' could be a simple picture, an interactive button, or even an entire mini-movie that runs within your main movie. You can convert your existing movie content into symbols, or you can create symbols from scratch - either way, you will be saving the completed symbol away so that you can use it again later in your movies.

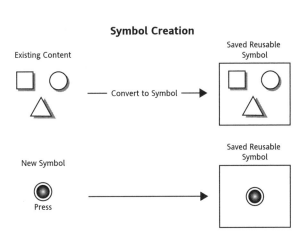

Symbol Creation

Existing Content

Saved Reusable Symbol

—— Convert to Symbol ——→

New Symbol

Press

Saved Reusable Symbol

Every time you create a new symbol in Flash, it's added to a **Library** that's attached to your .fla authoring file. The Library is where all of the reusable symbols are stored for the movie that you're working on:

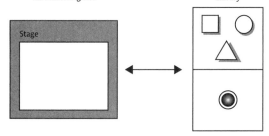

Whenever you use one of these saved symbols in your movie, you open up the library, select the symbol that you want to add, and drag it onto your stage. The original symbol remains in the library, however - Flash creates a 'copy' of the stored symbol and renders it on the stage for you. The stored symbol kept in the library is like a *template* that Flash uses to create a brand new copy of the saved symbol. When you create a new, individual copy of a stored symbol on your stage, it's known as an **instance** of that stored symbol.

Each new instance is a unique object - an exact copy of the stored symbol that the instance is based on. There's also a default link between the symbol and its instances: if you amend the underlying symbol, these amendments ripple through to the instances, too. However, you can change the properties (tint, size and so on) of individual instances without affecting the underlying symbol.

One way of picturing the relationship between the stored symbol and the copy (or copies) of it that you create on the stage is to think about that familiar kitchen tool - the cookie cutter. A cookie cutter is designed to turn out multiple copies of cookies that are the same size and shape. The cookie cutter is a template for mass-production of identical objects:

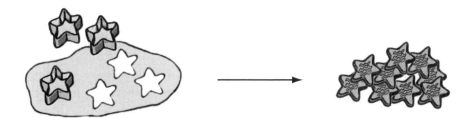

You apply the cookie cutter to the cookie dough and produce identical cookies every time. In Flash, the stored symbol is the cookie cutter, and the instance copied onto the stage is the identical individual cookie derived from the cookie cutter. With cookies, you can add toppings to specific cookies, and in Flash you can change the characteristics of individual instances via the **Instance** panel.

One of the beauties of creating instances of symbols is that you can then customize each instance on the stage individually. For example, suppose you need a series of buttons in your movie that the user can click on to navigate through your web site. Rather than create the same button 15 separate times, you can just create one button symbol in your library, and then customize each instance of the button on your main movie stage.

Let's start creating some symbols and see how to implement them in practice.

Symbol Types

When we create symbols in Flash, we have three basic types to choose from:

- **Graphic symbols**

- **Button symbols**

- **Movie Clip symbols**

Each type of symbol has different capabilities and levels of complexity, and the type of symbol we decide to create will be based on our judgment of what we want that symbol to do - how we want it to **behave**. For example, if we just want to reuse a static graphic that's essentially inanimate, the graphic symbol is the best fit. For a symbol that embodies some animation and maybe some sound, we choose to create a movie clip symbol. Each of the different symbol types has its own *range* of possible behaviors - from the simple graphic symbol on up to the potentially very complex movie clip symbol.

All three types of symbol are created by two alternative methods: either by converting an *existing* drawing or other object (such as a text field) into a symbol, or by creating a *new* symbol from scratch. You'll use both of these methods to construct symbols of all three types in the following examples.

Let's begin with the simplest kind of symbol - the graphic symbol.

Graphic Symbols

A graphic symbol is a symbol whose content remains static. Although graphic symbols are not as feature-rich as button or movie clip symbols, they're no less important. They are used for static images throughout your movie so if you know that you are going to use an object over and over again, but don't need it to be interactive or animated, then a graphic symbol is your best bet.

Let's create a simple graphic symbol now.

Creating a Graphic Symbol

Here, we're going to create a new symbol from scratch.

1. Open Flash and create a new movie by clicking on the **File > New** menu.

2. Click on the **Insert > New Symbol** menu option. The **Symbol Properties** dialog box will appear:

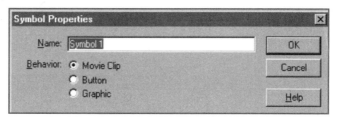

This is where we choose the **type** of symbol that we want to create. Notice that Flash labels the different categories of symbol using the term **Behavior** - as we've seen, this is because each type of symbol has it's own repertoire of behaviors. The default symbol in this symbol creation dialog box is a movie clip - but on this occasion we want a graphic symbol.

3. Change the behavior of the symbol to a graphic by clicking on the bottom-most radio button - next to the word '**Graphic**'.

4. Next, change the name from '**Symbol 1**' to '**Graphic Symbol**' by deleting the existing text in the Name field and typing your own, and press **OK**.

We've told Flash that we want to create a new graphic symbol, and we've assigned this symbol a name. This is the name that the symbol will be stored under in the library.

To actually create our symbol, Flash has whisked us away to a separate editing window: after pressing the **OK** button, we're no longer looking at the main stage. Instead, we're in the edit window for our newly-named Graphic Symbol.

Flash indicates this to us by highlighting the name of our symbol above the timeline, next to the name of our movie's default first scene.

The fact that our new symbol's name is highlighted here means that we are now in **Edit Symbols** mode. When you create a new symbol, or convert an existing shape to a symbol, you don't modify it on the main stage - you can only alter the symbol's content in Edit Symbols mode.

You'll see that even in Edit Symbols mode, the timeline and layer list are displayed. This is very important: it shows you that each symbol has its own internal layers and timeline. So, if you added extra layers while inside Edit Symbols mode, this would only affect that one symbol, not the entire movie.

Notice also that, inside Edit Symbols mode, there's a small black cross displayed in the middle of the stage. This is called a **Registration Point**, and it defines where Flash considers the center of the symbol to be.

> *It can sometimes be a bit confusing to see whether you are in Edit Symbols mode or normal editing mode, and the only way to really be sure is by checking above your timeline to see if the symbol name appears there: if it does, you're definitely in Edit Symbols mode, and if it doesn't, you're not.*

5. Click on the icon for **Scene 1** (next to the name of your graphic symbol, just above the timeline).

    We're now back in normal edit mode, and we're looking at the stage and the main timeline.

    But wait a minute - where has our new symbol gone? There's no longer a reference to it displayed above the timeline.

    To see our new symbol again, we need to open up the **library**. Flash has automatically created a place to store our new symbol in the library that's associated with this authoring file.

6. Open up the library by using the **Window > Library** menu option, and take a look at the window that pops up:

There's the entry for our new graphic symbol - in the white box at the bottom. The small icon with the circle, square, and triangle on it next to the name is the visual identifier for a graphic symbol. We'll be discussing the library in more detail soon. For now, let's get on with creating our graphic symbol.

7. Double-click on the icon next to our new symbol's name in the **Library** window. This will take us back into Edit Symbols mode, where we can work on the actual content of our symbol.

8. Back in Edit Symbols mode (you'll have a blank screen with the registration point in the center), select the Text tool.

9. Using the **Character** panel, select your favorite font in any size and color. Now click on the stage and type the words, '**Graphic Symbol**':

10. Click on the Arrow tool. The text will automatically show a blue rectangle around it, indicating that it is selected. Click on the **Show Info** button in the Launcher bar to open the **Info** panel:

    The **X** and **Y** boxes contain the coordinates of your text in relation to the center of the screen - where the registration point is currently found.

11. Click on the center square of the grid on the **Info** panel and change the **X** and **Y** coordinate values to **0.0** by highlighting each of them, typing '**0**', then pressing **Enter**.

    After you've done this for both of the coordinates, your symbol should be in the exact center of the screen.

12. Click on the '**Scene 1**' tab above the timeline to return you to normal editing mode (or use the **Edit > Edit Movie** menu option).

    Notice that there's no sign of your text anywhere on the stage. This is because although you've constructed the symbol in the library, you've yet to go to the library and create a copy of the symbol on the stage itself.

13. If it's not still open, open
    up your library by using the
    Window > Library option.
    Your library will appear on
    your screen again with one
    thing in it - your graphic
    symbol:

The library works like a mini file browser. You can use it to find symbols and
use them, or to create new symbols, or delete symbols you no longer need.

14. Click the *New Symbol* button: this has the same effect as using the **Insert >
    New Symbol** menu.

15. In the resulting Symbol Properties dialog box, type '**Circle**' into the **Name**
    field, select the **Graphic** behavior type, then press **OK**.

    You'll automatically be taken into Edit Symbols mode again, and this time
    you're editing the new **Circle** symbol.

16. Use the Oval tool to draw a circle in the middle of
    the stage:

Notice that your new symbol has been added to the library, and that you're
getting a preview of the symbol in the preview pane.

Let's see what else we can do with the library window.

Working with the Library

The **New Folder** button allows you to create folders in your library as a means of organizing your symbols.

1. In the library window, click on the **New Folder** button (second from the left at the bottom of the window): a new folder will appear in your library with its (so far generic) name highlighted:

2. Double-click on the new folder's name, type '**Circle Folder**' as the name, and press **Enter.**

    Flash automatically sorts the contents of the library into alphabetical order, so your new folder will suddenly jump above the graphic symbol.

3. Now click on your **Circle** symbol in the library and drag and drop it onto the **Circle Folder** icon. As you'd expect from a file browser program, the **Circle** symbol is now located inside the new folder:

    You can tell it's inside the folder by the level of indentation.

4. Double-click on the **Circle Folder**'s icon: it will change to a 'closed' folder and your circle will disappear. Double-click on it again and it will re-open. Double-clicking on the name of the folder now will allow you to rename it - if you do this by mistake, just press **Enter** to leave it as it is.

5. With the folder open, click on the **Circle** symbol to highlight it and then click on the **Properties** button in the library:

This will open the **Symbol Properties** dialog box, from where you can rename your symbol or change its behavior - that is, its *type*:

6. Click **Cancel** to exit the dialog box without making any changes.

7. With the **Circle** symbol still selected, click on the *Delete* button in the library.

You'll be prompted with a dialog box asking whether you *really* want to delete the circle:

Flash always gives you this prompt, as you cannot undo deleting something from the library: once it's gone, it's gone, and the only way to get it back is to load a previously saved version of the file, or just bite the bullet and draw it again.

8. Click Delete to get rid of the circle symbol, and delete the folder in the same way.

You will now be back where you started with just the single original **Graphic Symbol** in the library. Let's put an **instance** of this symbol on our stage.

9. Click on the **Scene 1** tab to get you back to the main stage.

10. To get an **instance** of your symbol onto the stage, just click and drag the name of your symbol out of the library and release it on the stage. Don't

worry about placing things too precisely - you can always move the symbol around again later.

You'll now have a single instance of your symbol on the stage.

11. To illustrate how easy it is to re-use symbols, drag out another couple of instances of the **Graphic Symbol** symbol and put them anywhere you like on the stage:

That's a lot easier isn't it? Notice that we've got three instances on the stage, and that they're all displaying a little cross, indicating that they're symbols.

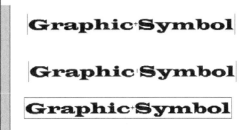

Perhaps the best thing of all here is that even though we now have *three* images on the stage, they still only take up the space of *one* picture in the final .fla file: this is because the instances of the symbol on the stage are really just 'coordinates' telling Flash where to put a copy of the content of the master symbol stored in the library.

OK, we've got our instances of the symbol on the stage - what if we decide that we want to change the symbol in the library that they're based on?

Modifying Symbols

When you change the symbol defined and stored in your library, all of the *instances* of that symbol on your stage will change as well.

Modifying a Symbol in the Library

1. Select the **Graphic Symbol** in the library, and then double-click on its picture in the preview window. This will take you into Edit Symbols mode.

2. Select the symbol on the (Edit Symbols) stage and then change its color by using the Fill Color palette in the Toolbox. Pick something obviously different from the original color.

3. Now when you click on the **Scene 1** tab above the timeline and return to the main stage, you'll notice that *all* of the instances of your graphic symbol have changed to the same color as the master in the library.

This is clearly a very powerful feature, meaning that you can redesign and amend significant parts of your movie without having to edit each and every symbol throughout the movie - you can just change the symbol in the library that the individual instances are based on.

Let's now experiment with the second, and slightly more complex type of symbol - the **button symbol**.

Button Symbols

Buttons are essential features of any interactive web site, and they're the key to any good menu or site navigation interface. Why? Because we're all tuned-in to clicking on buttons and having them do things for us - it's almost an unconscious action. And using buttons is such an obvious thing that we're often not aware of doing it when we're interacting with a web site or software application. However, if you ever go to a site whose navigation architecture doesn't provide you with buttons, you'll quickly become aware just how vital they are.

It's amazingly easy to create buttons in Flash and include them in our movies, and they're one of the components that take Flash from being a great animation package to being a web application development tool. Flash buttons are irresistibly important because they let you into the world of true interactivity, where your site visitor can control their experience. Whether it's jumping from movie to movie or kicking off a series of complex actions, buttons can be the way in. In Flash, button symbols embody the behaviors that open up the interactive world.

To get us started with buttons we'll build a simple button and take you through a button's basic features and capabilities. Later in the book we'll be doing some extremely interesting and important things with buttons.

Creating a Button Symbol

Let's create that button symbol. First, we need a shape to convert to a symbol.

1. In the same movie where you created your graphic symbol, select the Oval tool and draw a circle with a stroke and fill of your choice. We've made our circle 120 pixels across so that we can create a big hefty button.

2. Select the circle and change it into a symbol, either by using the **Insert > Convert to Symbol** menu option or by pressing the *F8* shortcut. (Incidentally, why this 'convert' option comes under the **Insert** rather than the **Modify** menu is one of the many mysteries of Flash, and something that just has to be learnt and accepted. Suggestions on a postcard please...)

3. In the **Symbol Properties** dialog box, choose the **Button** behavior type. Name your button '**Button Symbol**' and press **OK**:

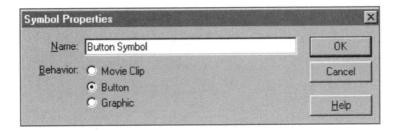

You should notice three things: your circle on the stage will now have a bounding box around it, indicating that it's now a symbol; the new symbol will appear in your library; and, if you bring up the Info panel, you'll see the symbol's name displayed next to a 'pointy finger over a rectangle' icon - this is the icon for a button symbol:

The circle that you drew on the stage has now become an instance of the new symbol in the library.

4. Double-click on the instance of your button symbol on the stage, and you'll be taken into Edit Symbols mode again.

This time, however, a few things have changed. Because you already had three instances of your graphic symbol on the stage these are still shown, but they're now 'dimmed down' so you can tell they're not part of the symbol that you're currently editing.

5. You may also have noticed that your timeline has changed:

Whenever you create or edit a button symbol you will see this button-specific style of timeline. This

timeline is only visible in Edit Symbols mode, and every button symbol has this same kind of special internal timeline: it's this timeline that controls how the button will behave when we interact with it.

> *A button symbol's internal timeline is 'nested' inside the symbol. When Flash comes across an instance (copy) of the symbol on the stage, it is aware of the button's timeline, but the button only does anything when the user interacts with it.*

Every button timeline has only four frames, each of which controls a different aspect of the button's behavior. The names above the four frames - **Up**, **Over**, **Down** and **Hit** - refer to the four possible conditions that a button can find itself in. These conditions are called **button states**.

Button States

The states of a button are defined in the four frames of the button's timeline. Each frame describes what the button will look like and what it will **do** when the button is in that state.

So what does each state represent?

- **Up** state - What the button will look like in its 'static' state: that is, when the button is sitting there in the movie interface, waiting for a user to come and interact with it

- **Over** state - What the button will look like when the user runs their mouse over it

- **Down** state - What the button will look like when the user clicks on it

- **Hit** state - This is a special state that you can't see in your finished movie: the *hit* state defines the part of the button that is actually clickable. Think of it as a target for the mouse to hit: hitting this target will make the button work. Make sure that whatever part of the button you want people to be able to click is defined in the hit state. It doesn't have to be pretty, but it's important to clearly define the hit state.

OK, let's see how these states work by defining them for our circular button symbol.

Making your Button Work

At the moment, your button is just a single-state, lifeless circle that might as well be a static graphic symbol. What your button needs is that extra something that makes a button a button - interactivity. And we define this interactivity in the four frames of the button's timeline.

Notice that only one of the frames on the button's timeline is actually a **keyframe** - the first frame, which represents the button's Up state - the other three frames are currently blank:

This is because Flash automatically populated the button's Up state when we created the button symbol: Flash assumed that we wanted to display the circle we'd drawn when the button is in its Up state. We can edit this keyframe and change the image that's displayed if we want to.

To create the other three states for the button, we first need to convert the three blank frames in the timeline into keyframes: remember, a keyframe is what defines a significant change to piece of Flash content. By defining these keyframes and their content, we're telling Flash how we want our button to behave.

1. Click individually on each of the three blank frames in the button timeline and press **F6** to insert a keyframe. You should now have a full timeline:

2. Click on the **Over** state in the timeline. Your button will automatically be selected.

3. Open the Fill Color palette from the Toolbox and select a different color from the original button symbol color. The color of your button will automatically change to reflect your new choice.

4. Now select the **Down** state keyframe in the timeline and change it to another different color in the same way. Leave the **Hit** state as it is for now.

5. Test your movie by using the **Control > Test Movie** menu.

    This will open a new window showing what your finished movie will look like when it's rendered in the web browser. There will be a few graphic symbols floating around, but just ignore them for now: your attention should be focused on your wondrously interactive new-born button.

6. Move your mouse over the button...

    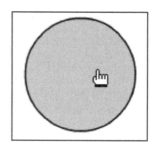

    ...and it changes color. This color is the color you defined for the **Over** state.

7. Now click on the button. While you hold the mouse button down, the button will display the color defined in the **Down** state keyframe.

    You have just created your first button and taken your first steps towards interactivity. It was pretty easy, wasn't it? But remember, what you're learning here about button states is the basic foundation on which you can build an infinitely complex universe of interactivity.

8. Close the Test Movie window using the **File > Close** menu, and you'll be returned to the Edit Symbols mode where you left it.

    At the moment, we haven't explicitly defined a different Hit state for our button: Flash is currently using the image from the preceding keyframe to define the Hit state. Let's be more explicit...

9. Click on the **Hit** state keyframe on the timeline and use the Rectangle tool draw a big rectangle (any color you like) around your button:

10. Now go into the Test Movie window again.

    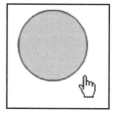

    This time, even though everything looks the same, when you run the mouse over your button you'll see it change color before you get to the actual button itself:

This is because you defined the (invisible to the user) **Hit** state as a larger area than the (visible) button. You may be wondering why you would ever want to do this - normally you wouldn't, but there is one case where this technique is incredibly useful: when you want to use a piece of text as a button.

Making Buttons From Text

1. Click on the **Scene 1** tab above the timeline to get back to the main stage.

2. Using the Text tool, find a clear part of your stage and type '**Hello**' in any font and color.

3. Click on the Arrow tool to select your text, and then convert it to a button symbol, naming it '**Hello**'.

4. Insert a keyframe into each of the button states as you did before, and test your movie.

    This time when you move your mouse over the text, it seems to flicker on and off. This is because the Hit state of the button is defined, by default, as the actual text itself - the gaps between the letters and the 'holes' in the letters don't respond to the mouse. If all text buttons were like this, nobody would be able to use them, and this is where the hit state comes in.

5. Go back to Edit Symbols mode and click on the **Hit** state keyframe. Using the Rectangle tool, drag out a rectangle (make sure it has a fill) that just covers all of your text:

    Don't worry about not being able to see your text any more in the authoring environment. As you saw before, the **Hit** state image is invisible in the displayed movie.

6. Test your movie again. As your mouse moves over the text it stays highlighted: this is because there is now an (invisible) border around the text, which means that the whole of the text is now defined as the **Hit** area.

7. Close the Test Movie window, and then click on the scene tab to return to the main stage.

    There's an easy way to see, and edit, all of the symbols in your movie. There are two buttons on the top right of your timeline:

If you've chosen to include the Macromedia Generator extensions when you installed Flash, you'll see three buttons here. We're not going to deal with Generator here, as it's beyond the scope of this book.

If you click on the *Edit Symbols* button, a drop-down menu will appear with a list of all of the symbols available to you in your movie's library:

When you click on one of the named symbols, you'll instantly be taken to the editing mode for that symbol. Try it with your three symbols and see. You can go back to the main stage by either clicking on the scene tab as you've done before, or by clicking on the **Edit Scene** button and then selecting **Scene 1** in the menu that pops up.

Now let's take an initial look at the third type of symbol in Flash - the **movie clip symbol**. As we progress through the book, we'll be using movie clips more and more.

Movie Clip Symbols

The movie clip symbol is the third and final member of the Flash symbols set. Movie clip symbols - usually referred to as 'movie clips' - are vitally important components in Flash movies. The simplest explanation of movie clips is that they are 'a movie within a movie': you can use them to create entirely self-contained pieces of action that you want to run independently of the rest of the things on the main timeline. Movie clips can have multiple layers, just like the main timeline, and contain many graphical, animation and sound components. An example of a typical movie clip would be a clip that encapsulated a logo and some background music: you can have the music playing and the logo fading in and out repeatedly throughout your whole main movie while other action changes around it.

Like the button symbol, a movie clip symbol has its own internal timeline. However, a movie clip's timeline is not just limited to the four standard frames. As we progress through this book, you'll find that movie clips are truly flexible and multi-talented members of the Flash team.

Movie clips can be very complicated things, containing all manner of actions and animations. In this section we'll just introduce the basics of what movie clips are and how to use them.

Creating a Movie Clip Symbol

1. Your stage will be getting pretty cluttered now, so close the current movie and create a fresh, new one.

2. On the main stage, use the Rectangle tool and draw a square - any color you like. Select the square and convert it to a symbol. Make sure the symbol's behavior is set to the **Movie Clip** type. Name the new symbol '**Square Clip**':

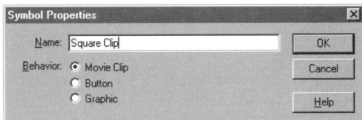

3. Now double-click on the square with the Arrow tool to get into Edit Symbols mode.

   Notice the timeline inside your new movie clip. This timeline works just like your normal one above the stage in the main movie. The difference is that your movie clip symbol's timeline only applies to what happens inside the symbol itself: any action and animation that you create using this timeline will be encapsulated inside this movie clip. You can do anything that you would normally do in your main movie inside a movie clip, letting you create completely self-contained units of movie content that you can then add to your main movie by dragging the movie clip symbol onto the main stage.

   Let's make a quick shape tween as an example.

4. Still inside your new movie clip, click on frame 20 and press **F6** to insert a keyframe.

5. Now click outside the square in frame 20 to deselect it, and use the Arrow tool to pull out the sides and make an irregular shape to your taste:

   Now that we've got two keyframes with distinct content in them, let's animate the shape tween.

6. Bring up the **Instance** panel's **Frame** tab and use it to create a shape tween between the two keyframes (just as we did with our mushroom movie in chapter 1).

7. Now click on the **Scene** tab above the timeline to get back to the main stage.

8. Open your library if it's not already displayed: there'll be one thing in it - your square clip:

    The strange blue sunburst next to the symbol's name is the icon that identifies movie clip symbols.

9. Click on the icon for the **Square Clip**.

    You'll see that there are two interesting features in the top-right of the preview window:

    These two VCR-type controls are used to preview your movie clip inside the library window (these controls are also available when you select a button symbol in the Library). If you click on the 'play' button, your movie clip will start playing in the preview

    Stop Movie Clip   Play Movie Clip

    window. You can use the 'stop' control to halt playback if it's a long movie clip.

10. Drag a couple of copies of your square clip from the library onto the stage.

11. Press *Enter* to preview your movie - nothing will happen. This is because movie clips are not rendered in preview mode.

If you want to see your movie clips play, you have to use the **Control > Test Movie** menu, or the *F12* key to publish your movie. If you do this you'll see your animations happily, er, animating. Movie clips can do so much more than this though, but you'll have to wait until the later chapters before you can find how just how powerful they really are.

12. Save your movie as Movie Clip.fla.

13. Close down the Movie Clip.fla movie.

Movie Clips and the Main Timeline

When you drag an instance of a movie clip symbol on to your stage, you bring with it all of the action that you've added to the movie clip's timeline. When Flash finds the instance of the symbol in a keyframe on the main timeline, it digs down into the symbol and plays the content that it finds encapsulated in the symbol's internal timeline. Simultaneously, Flash continues along the main movie's timeline, rendering any content that it finds there. In this context, you can think of movie clips as separate 'loops' that get started off and are then left to run their course while the main movie's playhead continues along the main timeline. Your movie clip is still integrated with the main movie, though - it shares the host movie's frame rate and background color, for example.

Another way of thinking about movie clips is that they're the 'children' of the main movie. The main 'parent' timeline plays in sequence, and periodically in its life - when it comes across a movie clip symbol in a keyframe - it'll spawn a movie clip. Once Flash has given life to the movie clip, that movie clip enjoys an independent life of its own while the main timeline continues separately.

Imagine a movie where we create a static background layer (a gradient) that lasts for fifty frames:

When we test our movie, we see the static image displayed for fifty frames, and then the movie loops and starts again. Now suppose that we create a keyframe at frame 10 and insert a 'morphing square' movie clip from our library into it:

Next, we could add a 'morphing triangle' movie clip in a new keyframe at frame 25:

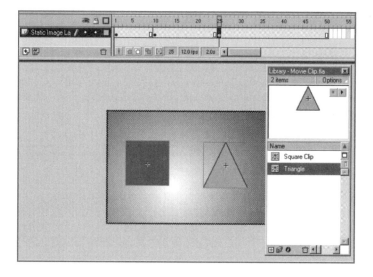

When we test our movie now, we'll find that the static background will display for a few frames and then, when the playhead hits the keyframe at frame 10, the morphing square movie clip will be triggered. The main movie playhead will continue along the main timeline until it encounters the morphing triangle at frame 25, whereupon it will kick off that movie clip before continuing to display the static background until frame 50 - the end of the movie. It's very important to remember that launching these movie clips doesn't pause or stop the playback of the main timeline: all three playback elements (the main timeline, plus the two internal movie clip timelines) play back simultaneously:

'Morphing square' movie clip starts in frame 10

'Morphing triangle' movie clip starts in frame 25

A movie clip has a 'mind of its own': its behavior is embedded in its internal timeline. However, the parent timeline can still have the authority to tell the child movie clip what to do: it can use ActionScript commands to tell the movie clip to stop, start, change position and so on. We'll see this in practice once we've learned some ActionScript.

So far, we've dealt exclusively with symbols in the library that's attached to the specific movie that we've been working on. But Flash also gives us the facility to reuse symbols from other movies' libraries.

Sharing Symbols

Let's take a quick peek at this facility.

Using Symbols from other Movies

1. Create a new movie file.

2. Now open up the new movie's library window. As you might expect, it's currently an empty library:

3. Go to the **File** menu and choose the **Open as Library** option.

4. In the resulting dialog box, navigate to the folder where you stored your Movie Clip.fla file and select it:

5. Once you've clicked on the **Open** button, take another look at your library window:

You now have the symbol from that movie available to use in your new movie. This means that you can build up a collection of common symbols and share them between different movies - another labor-saving device from Flash! Flash 5 also implements a new feature whereby people can also share libraries across networks and even over the web, but this is a little beyond the scope of this present book.

Finally in this chapter, let's implement some of the things that we've just discussed in our case study project.

Case Study

In this exercise you'll take the file you started working on in the previous chapter, convert all the components in it to symbols, and add some new symbols too. You'll also manipulate a few of your objects and use techniques you've learned in this chapter.

Case Study Exercise: Creating Symbols

1. Open up the case study movie that you created at the end of the previous chapter.

    Currently, you have your background on one layer, which is totally finished. You also have a red circle, and some text elements. Let's convert these elements to symbols.

2. Select the **Home** text box:

3. Convert this text box to a graphic symbol, ensuring that you choose the **Graphic** behavior in the dialog box. Name this graphic symbol '**Home**'.

4. Now use the same process to convert the rest of your text boxes into the graphic symbols, naming each one according to the text content. When you're finished you should have four graphic symbols in your library - **Clients**, **Contact**, **Home** and **Services**:

    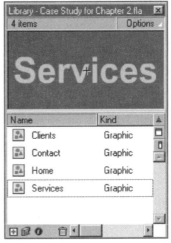

    Next, we're going to create a new symbol that represents a 'mail us' button.

5. Create a new symbol via the **Insert > New Symbol** menu option. Name the symbol '**Email us**' and make sure you choose **Button** as the behavior type.

6. In the Edit Symbol window for the **Email us** button, add keyframes to all four of the button state frames.

7. Select the Up state keyframe and use the Text tool to type this phrase on the stage:

Use the Character panel to make this text white, and then align the text so that it's centered on the crosshair that you see on the stage in Edit Symbols mode:

Remember that you can get your content centered by entering zeroes into the **X** and **Y** coordinate boxes of the Info panel as shown here.

8. Now select the Over state keyframe. Select the Email text in this keyframe and change the font color to a hot pink.

9. Select the Down state keyframe, and amend the text color to a lighter pink.

10. Now for the Hit state. Use the Rectangle tool to draw a box around your text and fill it in with any color you like:

Recall that we need to do this to make the whole area of the text an active Hit area.

11. Now that we're done editing this button, drag an instance of it on to the main stage and test the movie, ensuring that all your button states work as intended.

We'll be bringing this button to life later in the book, once we've learned a little more about some of Flash's more sophisticated features.

Now we'll add a new folder to this movie's library - this will help us manage our content more efficiently as our movie grows.

12. In the library window, click on the New Folder button and name the resulting folder '**Main Buttons**':

13. Now select the four graphic symbols and drag them into the **Main Buttons** folder:

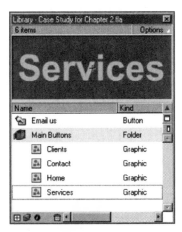

14. Now you can go back to your main movie stage and delete your text symbols from the stage. This doesn't actually delete them from your movie as we have them safely stored away in the library. We'll be retrieving them from the library later as we enhance our case study web site.

Summary

In this chapter, we've taken a preliminary look at the nature, creation and storage of symbols in Flash.

We saw that:

- **Symbols** are self-contained pieces of movie content that we can create once and then use many times in our movies

- When we create a copy of a symbol on the stage, it's called an **instance**

- Symbols are stored in a **library**, and we can organize the library and use it to share symbols between different movies

- Symbols have their own '**internal timeline**', which allows them to work independently from the main movie's timeline:

    - **Graphic symbols** effectively have just a single frame, and a static image in their internal timeline

    - **Button symbols** have a standard four-frame internal timeline. This timeline encodes the different button states

    - **Movie clip symbols** are the multitalented superstars of the symbols world. Their internal timelines are infinitely customizable. You can embed the same kind of multilayered graphics and sound content in movie clips symbols that you can on the movie's main timeline

We'll be seeing much more of symbols and their use later in this book. In the next chapter, we're going to examine the features that Flash gives us to help us manage and arrange multiple pieces of content on the stage.

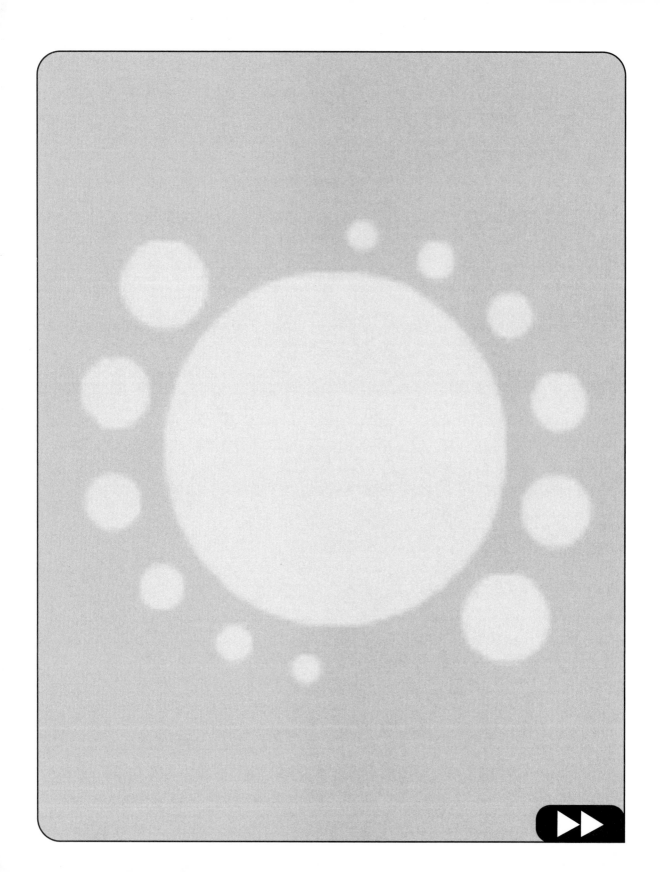

4 Managing Content on the Stage

What we'll cover in this chapter:

- Precision content assembly and placement on the (three-dimensional) Flash stage

- **Grouping objects** for consistency and convenience

- Using **grids**, **rulers**, **guides** and **alignment tools** to place objects exactly where you want them

- **Transforming objects** with control and confidence

- **Stacking** multiple objects inside a layer

In this chapter we're going to examine the tools and facilities that Flash gives us for aligning and arranging objects on the stage. In doing so, we'll be working on the stage in three dimensions: width, height, and depth.

When you're creating movies that only have a couple of visual components, arrangement and alignment is not so much of an issue, but if you're building larger-scale movies, or if you want to make your movies look more elegant and effective, you need to ensure that the components in your movie are effectively and harmoniously set out. Additionally, when your movies are growing in size and complexity, you need ways of grouping content elements together so that maintenance and amendments are easier to make. Flash provides us with plenty of tools in these respects, and getting a grip on these tools will save you a lot of pain and frustration.

Let's begin by seeing how Flash can ease the burden of moving things around and editing them while maintaining proportions and relative positions.

Grouping Objects and Editing Groups

You've already seen how useful grouping can be when you're manipulating single objects, preventing you from cutting objects in half or picking up just the fill. Here, we'll look more closely at grouping and the benefits that it brings. You can think of grouping as an easy way to organize and manipulate multiple objects.

Grouping Multiple Objects

1. Open a new movie.

2. Using the Rectangle tool, draw a squarish shape anywhere on your stage. Now draw a smaller circle on a nearby part of the stage with the Oval tool.

3. Now use the Arrow tool to drag a box around both objects to select them, then group them using the **Modify > Group** menu. Now when you move one of the objects, the other will move with it, staying in exactly the same position relative to the other object:

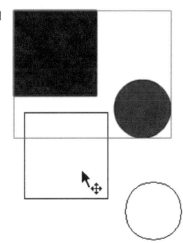

This is clearly a useful feature when you're dealing with large numbers of objects and you don't want to move them around individually by hand, and it'll help you maintain the design and look of your movie when you're maintaining it.

You can group lines, fills, buttons, graphics, movie clips, text – in fact pretty much anything that you can put on the movie stage. A sure sign to tell whether an object is part of a group or not is the thin colored highlighting line that appears around the outer edges of grouped objects. As a default, this is pale blue, but you can change the highlight color using the **Edit >**
Preferences menu option and amending the **Highlight Color** option on the **General** tab:

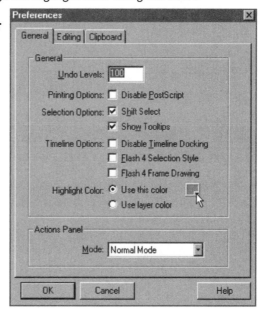

It's also extremely easy to ungroup objects in Flash and have them go back to their original individual states.

4. Click on your grouped shapes with the Arrow tool to select them and use the **Modify > Ungroup** option. They will now be returned to two distinct objects with their own separate lines and fills.

5. Use the Line tool to draw a triangle on your stage and fill it with color.

6. Now drag a box around all three of your objects with the Arrow tool and group them all together.

    It would be a laborious process if, every time you wanted to edit a specific line or fill within a group, you had to ungroup it, edit it, and then group it again. Flash gets around this by having an '**edit group**' mode. This mode is used to add, subtract, or change elements in groups.

Editing a Group of Objects

1. To enter Edit Group mode, simply double-click on your group, or select the group on the stage and use the **Edit > Edit Selected** menu.

2. Once you're in Edit Group mode you'll notice something has changed above your timeline. In the same place where the symbol name was displayed in Edit Symbols mode, it now says '**Group**' with an icon next to it similar to that of a graphic symbol:

   This is Flash's visual cue to let you know that you're currently editing a group of objects. Another visual cue is that when you're in Edit Group mode, all of the objects on the stage apart from the group you're editing will be 'dimmed down' and inaccessible.

3. In Edit Group mode, deform your triangle using the Arrow tool and move it to somewhere else on the stage:

4. Return to the main stage by using the same method as you would from Edit Symbols mode - by clicking on the **Scene 1** button next to the group icon.

   Back on the main stage, everything is still grouped together and moves as one object, but your 'once-was-a-triangle' shape is now happily sitting in its new position in the group.

   There's no limit to the amount of groups you can have in Flash. In fact, you can have *symbols* within groups, groups within *groups*, and even groups within symbols within groups - the possibilities are endless.

Groups within Groups

'Nested' groups are easily manageable from within the Flash interface.

A Hierarchy of Nested Groups

1. Double-click on your square-circle-triangle group to enter Edit Group mode.

2. Once inside Edit Group mode, double-click on your once-was-a-triangle to select its component lines and fill, and then group *them* using the **Modify > Group** menu option.

    Now when you double-click on your newly-grouped once-was-a-triangle shape, you'll be taken to another Edit Group mode - inside the previous group. You can tell you've gone one level deeper by looking at the tabs above your timeline:

    To return to the last group you were working in, just click on the group tab to the left of the one you are currently in. This can all be a bit confusing at times, but as long as you keep an eye on the tabs above the timeline, you should be able to work out where you are. If in doubt, return to the main stage and work your way back through your nested groups to reach the one you wanted.

3. Click on the **Scene 1** tab to return to your main stage. From here, click on your group of objects and use the **Modify > Ungroup** command to ungroup them. Notice that there's still a highlight box around your once-was-a-triangle:

    This is because ungrouping only affects the specific level of the group that you currently have selected - groups nested inside that level are not affected.

4. Click on a blank space on your stage to deselect your objects, and then click on your once-was-a-triangle to select *that*.

5. Press *Delete* to erase this shape, and note that even though you cannot *edit* the contents of the group directly from the main stage, you can still *delete* the entire group and all of its contents.

To prevent accidentally deleting or moving a group, you can **lock** it. This is similar to locking a layer, but it only affects the one group on that layer, allowing you to carry on editing the rest of the layer's contents. You can also lock symbols in the same way.

6. Double-click on your circle on the stage and group it.

7. Use the **Modify > Arrange > Lock** menu to lock your group on the stage.

   If you try to select the circle group now to ungroup it, you'll find that, no matter what method you try, you cannot select the circle. If you drag a box around both the circle and the square with the Arrow tool, only the square will be selected.

8. To unlock the circle, use the **Modify > Arrange > Unlock All** menu.

   Your circle is unlocked, and you can happily select it and ungroup it.

> *This menu option will unlock all the locked symbols and groups on the stage so that you can select and edit them as you need to. Unfortunately, there's no way to unlock locked objects individually - it's an all or nothing option.*

Now that you know how to create and manage groups and symbols, how can you get them lined up neatly and evenly on the stage? You could always do it by eye of course, but Flash gives you a couple of quicker and more precise methods. Let's start out with the most basic way - using the built in **grid** and **rulers**.

The Grid

By default, the grid in Flash gives you a background of fine-lined squares that you can use to guide the placement and alignment of objects.

Using the Grid

1. To access the grid in Flash, use the **View > Grid > Show Grid** menu. The stage will now have a series of grid lines across it:

2. Turn on Flash's **grid snapping** feature by clicking on **View > Grid > Snap to Grid**.

3. Select your square, making sure you select both the fill and the stroke. Carefully click on the center of your square and drag it - it will 'snap' to a grid line when it gets near one:

If you miss the middle of the square when you click and drag, the square won't snap to the grid and you'll be able to move it around freely. It can be deceptively difficult to find the middle of an object, and the only solution to this is to try, try again. When you click in the center of an object and drag it, a small black ring appears next to the cursor: this is called the **Snapping Ring**. When you drag an object close to a grid line, the ring will jump to the grid line and become larger and darker:

The snapping ring snaps to any gridline, but is *easiest* to snap to the grid at an intersection - where vertical and horizontal gridlines meet.

Experiment by moving your square around the stage with snapping turned on and off, and see the different effects. Also, try zooming in and moving the object again: notice that it gets easier to position things precisely the more 'zoomed in' you are. The trade off for this is that you won't be able to see your whole image. The best solution here is to experiment until you find a happy medium - this will, of course, be different for each movie you work on.

When you're aligning your shapes, you won't always want to do so by dragging the shape at the center. Flash caters for this by allowing you to drag the shapes by their *corners* as well. When you're dragging shapes by the corners a similar snapping ring appears:

These are the default behaviors of the grid. Flash also gives you the ability to customize the grid and its settings to suit your every need.

Changing the Grid Settings

1. Open the **Grid** dialog box by using the **View > Grid > Edit Grid** menu:

From here, you can change the spacing and the color of your grid lines.

It can be useful to change the grid color if the current grid lines are merging into the color of your movie background, or even if you just prefer another color aesthetically. The units of measurement will be the same movie-wide values that we saw how to set in the **Modify Movie** dialog box.

The **Snap accuracy** option allows you to alter how close the snapping ring has to be to something before it will snap to it. So, if you find those lines are just too 'sticky', you can set it to **Must be close**, on the other hand if you want to be seriously snap-happy (sorry) you can set it to **Always snap** and never be left with those middle of nowhere blues again. Again, you can experiment with these settings at different levels of zoom.

The option to **Save Default** is the same as that on the **Modify Movie** box - using this will apply these values to all of the Flash movies that you create.

2. When you're finished, close the dialog box by clicking **OK**. To turn off the grid, go to the **View > Grid** menu again, there'll be a tick next to the **Show Grid** option, indicating that it is currently turned on:

3. Click on the **Show Grid** option and the tick will disappear along with the grid lines. Try moving your square around: you'll find that even though the grid is

no longer visible, your square will still snap to it if the **Snap to Grid** option is on. To stop this you have to go into the **View > Grid** menu again and click on the **Snap to Grid** option.

As you might expect, the grid is not shown in your final movie. If you *wanted* to see a grid effect in your finished movie, you'd have to draw one yourself: this could be easily accomplished by drawing over the grid in the authoring environment on the farthest back layer using the Line tool with snapping turned on for precision.

Flash has yet more ways of making drawing and alignment easier. Among these are **rulers** and **guides**.

Rulers and Guides

Guides are a great new feature of Flash 5 and, in conjunction with Flash's rulers, they give you a powerful, customizable and easy-to-use set of alignment tools. Let's see these in action.

Using Rulers and Guides

1. Use the **View > Rulers** menu command to display Flash's rulers. As soon as you do this, a pair of vertically- and horizontally-oriented rulers will appear around the stage:

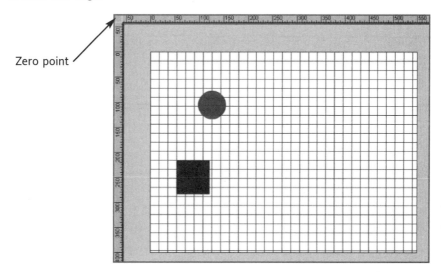

Zero point

These rulers are marked out in the units currently defined in the **Movie Properties** dialog box.

The **zero point** for your rulers - where everything is measured from - is always at the top left-hand corner of your stage.

2. Using the Hand tool, move the stage around and notice how the zero point moves with it.

   Rulers are not just handy for alignment: they're also useful for seeing how big your object is and how all of the changes that you are making are affecting it.

3. Grab hold of your square with the Arrow tool and move it around the stage, taking a look at your rulers as you do so. You'll see two black lines on each ruler that shift position as your shape moves. These lines indicate the dimensions and position of your shape on the stage:

Shape position/size indicators

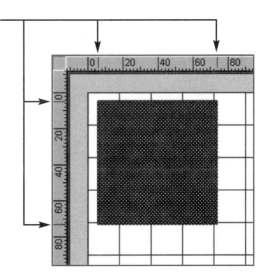

These lines mark the shape at its widest point, so if you have a big irregular weird shape, Flash will put an invisible bounding box around it at its very edges and use these for reference:

Another feature of rulers is that you might have seen in other packages is the ability to drag **guides** out of them. Guides are basically reference lines to help you with shape alignment, and the great thing about them is that - unlike grids and rulers, which are in a fixed position - you put guides wherever you like, and add as many as you like. This means that no matter where an object is or what shape it is, you can always use a guide to help you line it up precisely with another shape.

4. Click anywhere on the ruler at the top of the stage and drag a horizontal guide down on to the stage:

(We've turned off our grid so that you can see the guides more clearly in the screenshot.)

5. Release the mouse anywhere on the stage to fix the guide at that point. The color of the guide defaults to a rather lurid green, but it can be altered via the **View > Guides > Edit Guides** menu. To get a vertical guide, just drag out a line from the left-hand ruler in the same way:

A guide's position is never set in stone. Whenever you move your mouse over a guide, the cursor will change:

When the cursor looks like this, you can pick up your guide and move it elsewhere, and you can even drag it right off the stage to get rid of it altogether.

6. Click on your horizontal to pick it up, drag it to the bottom of your square, and release it to anchor it there:

In the same way that we can get shapes to snap to the grid, we can snap objects to guides, too.

7. Make sure that this snapping functionality is active by going to the **View > Guides** menu and ensuring that the **Snap to Guides** option is turned on.

8. Now click in the center of your circle and drag it until it snaps to the guide. Your circle will now be perfectly lined up with the bottom of your square:

One more circle and we've got us a wagon...

To get rid of your guideline, just click on it the same way you did to move it, and drag it all the way back onto the top ruler and release it. Dropping it anywhere on the ruler will do.

If you have a number of guides on the stage and you want to get rid of them all at once, you can use the **View > Guides > Edit Guides** menu and click on the **Clear All** button in the resultant dialog box:

The **Lock Guides** option here will fix all current guides in place, meaning that you will not be able to move them after dropping them in place. This is useful when you're working with a lot with guides for precise placement purposes, and you don't want to pick them up by accident when you're moving other objects around.

As your movies become more complex, multi-layered and sophisticated, you'll find guides increasingly useful, particularly as they are visible through all the layers of a movie. But, as with a lot of things, Flash offers more than one way to align objects.

Alignment

There's a place in Flash that acts as a hub for a number of alignment features: the **Align** panel.

The Align Panel

With the Align panel you can fine-tune the position of multiple objects on the stage by aligning them, spacing them evenly, and even sizing them to ensure they all have exactly the same dimensions.

You access these features via the **Window > Panels > Align** menu, or (in Windows), by clicking on the **Align** button on the main toolbar:

Align tool

This will open up the **Align** panel:

Alignment options →

Distribution options →

Size matching options →

Align to Stage option

Spacing options

In this panel you can see all the different alignment options that you have. The seventeen options that take up the bulk of the panel work, by default, on the objects that you have selected on the stage, aligning them *in relation to each other*. If you turn the **To Stage** modifier on and then use the alignment buttons, the selected objects will be aligned *relative to the stage*:

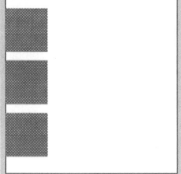

The key to using each of the options is to look at the thin black *line* on each button and its positions relative to the *objects* shown on the button. This line dictates how the objects will be aligned. For example, look at the first group of alignment buttons at the top-left of the panel:

In the first button, the black line is to the *left* of the objects, meaning that the objects will all be aligned along their left-hand edges. The next button along will align your objects by their *centers*, and the third button will align them along their *right*-hand edges.

As you'd expect, if you hold the mouse cursor over any of the buttons, a tool tip will appear helping you check out the basic function of the button:

The best way to get a grip on using the Align panel is through practice and application. We'll look at representative examples of the buttons in each of the categories.

Aligning Objects

Let's start by aligning objects in relation to each other with the basic alignment buttons. Make sure the **To Stage** modifier is turned off.

The **Align** options consist of two sets of three buttons: one set for aligning horizontally, and the other for vertical alignment:

Horizontal   Vertical
alignment   alignment

1.   In a new movie, draw three new objects: a square, a circle, and a triangle. Make the objects different sizes, similar to what's shown here:

2.   Select each shape individually and group each one so that you have three separately grouped objects (this will make them easier to move around and manipulate).

When aligning objects, Flash puts a box around the object or group of objects marking its boundaries, and then uses this to align by. You see this highlighted box for a grouped object or a symbol when you select it. Flash uses the center of this highlighting box as the notional center of the object or group. This can be a bit confusing at first, because we humans tend to credit two-dimensional drawn objects with real-world characteristics - giving them weight and volume, for example. In contrast, your cold-hearted computer sees these objects as just a collection of pixels on the screen.

For example, the center of this (grouped) shape is marked by the cross:

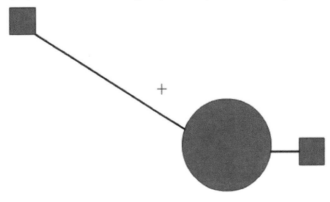

Which is probably not where you expected it to be. To show why Flash put the center-point there, look at the same object with the bounding box around it:

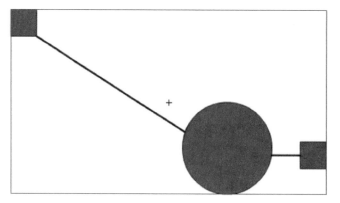

You can clearly see now that the cross is in the center of the box, which Flash treats as the center of the whole object.

3. Arrange all three of your grouped objects on the stage on a rough, unevenly spaced diagonal:

4. Select all of your objects together by dragging a box around them with the Arrow tool.

5. Now click on the **Align left** edge button (the one at top-left on the **Align** panel) and your objects will immediately reposition themselves by aligning with the left-hand edge of the left-most object - in this case, the square:

If you had selected the **Align right edge** button, they would all have lined up along the right-hand edge of the *triangle*.

The **Distribute** options will ensure that there's an equal distance between the respective edges of the objects.

6. For example, with all three of your objects still selected, click on the **Distribute left edge** button. Your objects will now rearrange themselves like so:

7. To clearly see the effect that this has had, make sure that rulers are turned on, and then drag guides out to each of the left hand edges of the objects:

Now, you can clearly see that Flash has spaced the objects with equal distances between each of their left-hand edges.

8. Remove your guides either by dragging them individually off the stage, or by choosing the **View > Guides > Edit Guides** menu and clicking on the **Clear All** button.

9. Now turn your attention back to the **Align** panel and click on the **Match width** button (bottom-left in the **Align** panel). Your circle and triangle will suddenly grow in size:

The **Match Size** options work by making all of your selected objects the size of the *largest* one in the selection. So by clicking on the **Match Width** button, you have made all of your objects the same width as your square. To ensure all objects on your stage are exactly the same dimensions, just click on the **Match width and height** button, and in the blink of an eye Flash will do the job for you. An example of when this comes in very handy is when you're drawing buttons and you want each button a different *shape*, but the same *size* in relation to the others.

The two **Space** options at the bottom-right of the **Align** panel will ensure that the *gaps* between the objects are the same size. This means, for example that you can precisely arrange a set of buttons so that they look just right. Compare the left-hand set of buttons with the evenly-spaced selection on the right:

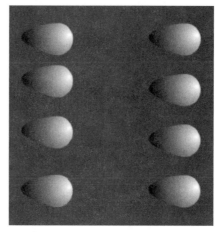

Although the differences in spacing are subtle in isolation, an accumulation of unevenly-spaced objects in your movies can quickly make things look rough and sketchy.

10. Back in your movie, click on the **Space evenly vertically** button. This is another option where using guides can help to clarify exactly what Flash has done:

You can clearly see from here that the space between each of the objects is now the same size.

The final option left on the **Align** panel is the **To Stage** button on the right-hand side:

This is a global switch that will affect all of the other options on the Align panel. As you have already seen, so far Flash has used one of the other objects to align the others to, for example the largest object for matching size, the leftmost object for aligning to the left and so on. When **To Stage** is turned on, Flash uses the stage to align the objects to instead, so aligning to the left will align the objects to the left of the stage, and matching size will match the objects to the full size of the stage. You could use this latter option to size an imported graphic image to match the dimensions of the stage - for example, if you wanted to use the image as a background layer.

11. Clear all of your guides away, then click on the **To Stage** button to highlight it.

12. Now click on the **Match Width** button. All of your objects will be resized horizontally to mirror the width of the stage:

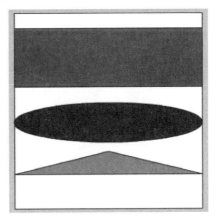

As you've seen from this series of examples, the different alignment buttons can drastically affect the way that your objects appear on the stage. You can also see how much easier it can be to use these tools to do the job rather than attempting to align and match everything by eye.

Next, we're going to look at ways of manipulating objects by precisely changing their size, rotation, and orientation. Flash calls these kind of changes **transformations**.

Transforming Objects

In Chapter 2 we introduced several tools and menus associated with drawing objects, all of which were found in the Flash Toolbox. Here, we're going to show you some basic ways to manipulate those objects on the stage through different forms of scaling and rotation. In Flash, these features are collected together under the Transform menu.

The Transform Menu

Transformation simply means changing an object by scaling (resizing) it, rotating it, or flipping it. All of these options are found under the **Modify > Transform** menu:

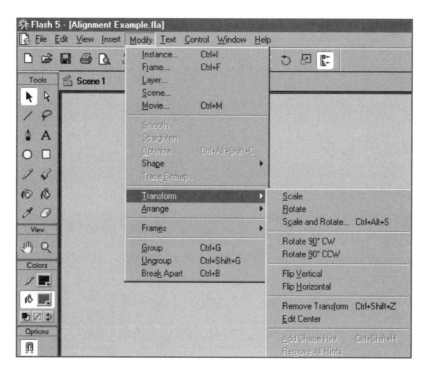

Let's start by looking at scaling objects.

Engineering a Giant Mouse

1. Start a new movie in Flash.

    Flash comes with a library of pre-built basic symbols that you can use in your movies. These can be found under the **Window > Common Libraries** menu.

2. Choose the **Window > Common Libraries** option and select the **Graphics** option from this menu.

3. This will open up a library containing a number of sub folders and graphic symbols, one of which is called '**Mouse**':

4. Drag an instance of this mouse symbol onto your stage and close the library.

5. Click on the mouse instance to select it - it's now ready for its transformation. (We'd like to reassure you that no real mice were harmed during the creation of this example.)

6. Click on the **Modify > Transform > Scale** menu. Eight white squares will appear around your mouse:

    These squares are called **handle**s, and they're used to scale objects by grabbing them with the mouse pointer and dragging them.

The corner handles will change both the height and the width of the object together, maintaining the object's shape and proportions, whereas the 'edge' handles in between will stretch or squeeze the shape in one dimension only: horizontally or vertically. Note that you can also get access to these handles by clicking on the **Scale** button in the **Options** section of the Toolbox (provided that you've already selected an object):

7. Click on the right-hand middle handle and pull it to the right. You'll see the outline of your mouse increasing in size:

When you release the mouse (no pun intended) it's fixed in the proportions that you stretched it into:

Note that when you stretched the mouse using the 'horizontal scale' handle, the mouse scaled up on both sides of its centerline. This is how symbols behave when you scale them, but hand-drawn shapes behave slightly differently.

8. Draw a square on your stage, then go to **View > View Rulers** and drag out a guide from the left-hand ruler and place it at the square's centerline (or thereabouts):

9. Now select the square, activate the scaling handles, and pull the right-hand middle handle out to the right:

You can see from this that the right-hand side of the square has scaled-up, whereas the left-hand half has remained the same.

The same effect occurs whichever handle you choose: drawn shapes are scaled directionally, whereas symbols scale so that their shape is kept in proportion.

10. Return your stretched square back to its original perfect square shape. Now convert to a graphic symbol (any name you like) and then perform the same scaling operation using the right-hand middle handle:

This time, as you can see, the square (now a symbol) has scaled up proportionally on both sides of its centerline.

Let's get back to our mouse.

11. To restore the poor mouse to a state of respectability, click on its top-middle handle and drag it up until you reach what you think are about the right proportions for an average small rodent. You should now have a large, and vaguely normal-looking mouse on your stage.

12. Click on the **Modify > Transform > Rotate** command, or click on the Rotate button in the Toolbox: the chain of squares around the mouse will now be replaced by a chain of circles:

13. Move the mouse (y'know, your electronic one...) over one of the 'corner' circles. The cursor will change, giving you four arrows which indicate that these are the points you should drag from to rotate the object:

Moving the mouse over the 'edge' circles displays a double-headed arrow, indicating **skewing**:

14. **Skewing** is the name given to a particular way of distorting a shape. To visualize what skewing is, imagine that your shapes - a circle and a triangle, let's say - are surrounded by invisible bounding boxes:

When you skew the shape using skew handles, you're changing the shape of that bounding box by changing it into a parallelogram. When you finish skewing and release the handles, your shape maps itself to fit into that new parallelogram:

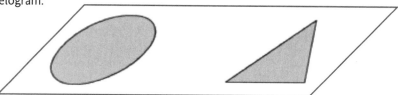

This will all become clearer when you try it yourself.

15. Select your mighty mouse and activate the skewing handles.

16. Click on the top middle-handle and drag it as far as it will go to the right, then release it. The mouse will now look as if it's leaning forward to get at a particularly tasty-looking piece of cheese:

If this isn't twisted enough for you, you can always repeat the procedure from the newly-skewed state to get an even stranger-looking mouse.

You can also apply precise levels of skewing by bringing up the **Transform** panel:

As you can see, this also has boxes that you can use to scale and rotate your objects by precise amounts.

Let's perform one last experiment on our mouse. I think it'll enjoy this one.

17. With the rotation handles active, click on the top-right corner handle and drag it down. You will see the mouse begin to spin:

By dragging any of these corner handles, you can spin the mouse around and around its center to your heart's delight. Release the mouse when you think it's quite dizzy enough.

18. Click on the **Modify > Transform** menu and choose the **Scale and Rotate** option.

This will open the Scale and Rotate dialog box:

From here you can enter numbers to precisely perform the same two tasks you did earlier. We don't think it's as much *fun* as the previous methods, but it does mean that if you need to apply exactly the same transformation to a number of objects, you can do it quickly and easily.

19. Type '**200**' into the **Scale** field. This number will affect both the width and the height of your object.

20. Now type '**180**' into the **Rotate** field. In this box, *positive* numbers will rotate your shape clockwise, and *negative* numbers will rotate it counter-clockwise.

21. Click on **OK**. Your mouse will now be twice the size it was, and at the opposite angle to whatever you left it at previously:

22. Reopen the **Scale** and **Rotate** dialog box.

You'll see that it has the same **200** and **180** figures that you last entered into it. This is designed to help you when you're applying the same transformation over and over again - you don't have to keep entering the same numbers over and over.

23. Click OK, and your mouse will almost be ready to take over the world (albeit at a peculiar angle).

The **Modify > Transform > Remove Transform** command is not one to be used by the unwary. This command will remove every single transformation that you have ever applied to your shape. Not just the last one or two, but every one. If you only want to remove the last change you made, then use the **Edit > Undo** command.

The **Remove Transform** command really will wipe the slate clean. In this case though, this is what we want to do - we owe it to the poor mouse to remove all of the bizarre transformations that we've been putting it through.

24. Select the **Modify > Transform > Remove Transform** option from the menu and return the mouse to the state that nature intended.

The **Rotate 90° CW** (clockwise) and **Rotate 90° CCW** (counter-clockwise) options on the **Transform** menu are just shortcuts for commonly used rotations. They will give the same results as entering **90** or **-90** respectively into the rotate field of the **Scale and Rotate** dialog box:

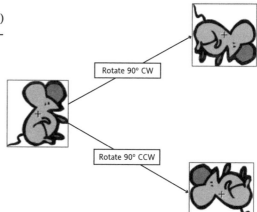

Rotate 90° CW

Rotate 90° CCW

25. The two **Flip** options do just what you'd expect them to... they flip your object. Click on the **Flip Vertical** command, your mouse will now stand on its head:

26. If you now click on the **Flip Horizontal** option, your break-dancing mouse will spin on its head to face the other way. It's now in exactly the opposite state to how it was when we started.

    Close your movie and let our cooperative rodent scurry away home - heck, you might even want to give the little fella a round of applause.

    We've looked at a range of ways to manipulate objects in two dimensions, based around the options found on the Align panel and in the **Modify > Transform** menu. Let's turn now to the third dimension and look at how Flash implements the **stacking** of objects.

Stacking Order

In Chapter 1 you were introduced to **layers** and how they function in a background/foreground relationship. For example, when your mushroom was growing behind the moon, you simply pulled the moon layer underneath the mushroom layer, and hey-presto the mushroom grew in correct perspective. There's a similar effect within individual layers, too: Flash's default behavior is to give objects that are on the same layer a 'front to back' order - this is called the **stacking order**.

Only symbols or grouped objects can be stacked in Flash. All other objects - such as hand-drawn shapes - will 'fall down' to the lowest possible level of the layer: they'll be stuck right at the back. You can see this effect when you hand-draw two or more shapes on the stage. If, for example, you draw a rectangle and a circle on the stage...

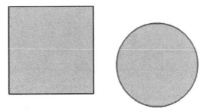

...they'll both be occupying the same plane. If you drag the circle onto the rectangle and then click away somewhere on the stage, Flash will assume that you want to merge these shapes on this plane:

The overlapping areas of these shapes now share the same piece of stage real estate. If you click on the arc of the circle inside the shape...

...and delete it, the two shapes have now become a single, fused entity, with all the lines and fills on the 'floor' of the layer:

This is why drawn shapes 'eat each other' when they overlay each other and are then shifted around - their component lines and fills are all trying to occupy the same space at the back of the layer.

In contrast to this 'hand-drawn object' behavior, however, Flash assumes that we want to be able to move symbols and groups backwards and forwards in relation to the base of the layer. To facilitate this, Flash assigns each new group or symbol that's added to the stage on a particular layer a 'stack position' that determines how far up from the floor it sits. Flash assigns these positions based on the order in which the symbols or groups are added to the stage: this means that every time you create a new symbol or group, it's placed on top of the ones that were already there.

Let's look at this principle in action.

Shuffling a Deck of Cards

1. Start a new movie, and set the movie background color to a warm, casino style baize green.

2. Click on the Rectangle tool and set the **Corner Radius** modifier to **15**: we want to create round-edged rectangles that'll represent playing cards.

3. Now click on the **Show Info** button on the Launcher bar to open the **Info** panel, and click on the panel's **Stroke** tab. From here, set the stroke width to 2 and close the panel.

4. Next, set the stroke and fill colors to black and white by clicking on the **Default Colors** button in the Toolbox:

5. Now that everything is ready, draw a playing card-shaped rectangle on the stage:

6. Select the whole shape (fill and stroke) and convert it into a graphic symbol. Call the symbol '**Card Base**':

We now have a blank card that we can use for all of the cards that we'll show on the stage.

What we need to do next is create four cards on the stage - the Jack, Queen, King and Ace. Each card will use the same **Card Base** symbol as its background, but will have a different letter on top of that background to indicate its seniority - J, Q, K, or A. We can easily do this by adding separate text boxes that we'll place on top of each instance of the card base.

7. Open up the **Character** panel. From here, select an appropriate font and color.

8. Next, select the **Text** tool from the Toolbox and click in the middle of your card - this will help you judge what size the font should be:

(Make sure you don't actually go into Edit Symbols mode on the **Card Base** instance: all we want to do is create a text box that'll *float above* the symbol instance.)

9. Use the **Character** panel to set the font size to something that will look good on your card.

10. Type a capital 'J' for 'Jack' and use the **Align** panel to center your text in the card:

The simplest way to achieve this centering is to select the symbol instance *and* the text box by dragging a box round them with the Arrow tool, and then click on both the **Align vertical centers** and **Align horizontal centers** buttons on the **Align** panel.

11. Finally, make sure you have the card and the text both selected and use the **Modify > Group** command to group them. Your symbol instance and its unique text identifier are now tied together.

12. Now use the same process to drag out three more instances of the Card Base symbol. Add the '**Q**', '**K**', and '**A**' to these other three cards, **in that order**. Don't forget to group each pair of symbols and text boxes!

When you've finished, you should have four cards on your stage looking like this:

13. Now drag each of your cards to the left so they overlap each other:

Notice that the Jack, which you created and grouped first, is at the bottom of the stack, and the Ace, which you created and grouped last, is at the top. The Queen and King are in the correct sequence, too, so the stacking order is currently J, Q, K, A. Flash has faithfully created a stacking order for the cards based on the sequence that we created them in.

You can change the stacking order of these cards by using the options brought up by using the **Modify > Arrange** menu:

Bring to Front	Ctrl+Shift+Up
Bring Forward	Ctrl+Up
Send Backward	Ctrl+Down
Send to Back	Ctrl+Shift+Down
Lock	Ctrl+Alt+L
Unlock All	Ctrl+Alt+Shift+L

14. Click on your King card to select it, and use the **Bring to Front** command from the **Modify > Arrange** menu. Your King will now jump to the top of the stack, so that the stacking order (from back to front) is changed to J, Q, A, K:

15. Now click on the Jack and use the **Modify > Arrange > Bring Forward** menu option.

The **Bring Forward** option pulls the selected object up one level in the stacking order, so the Jack will immediately be brought forward one space, and jump in front of the Queen.

16. To test the Jack's position in relation to the other cards, pick it up and drag it between the King and the Queen:

OK - that shows us that it's in front of the Queen.

Now drag the Jack across between the King and the Ace:

You will notice it is behind *both* of them. As we expected, the order is now Q, J, A, K.

17. Click on the Ace and use the **Modify > Arrange > Send Backward** menu. The Ace will now be moved backwards one level, and jump behind the Jack:

18. Drag the Ace up next to the Jack, between the Queen and the King.

The Jack will now be in front of the Queen, but behind the King:

The order is now Q, A, J, K.

19. Finally, click on the King and use the **Modify > Arrange > Send to Back** menu. This will put the King all the way to the bottom of the stack:

Leaving the final order as K, Q, A, J.

This exercise illustrates that you can manipulate the stacking order of symbols and groups to a very fine degree, which can be of real help when you're putting together complicated objects and pieces of content.

There will be times when you're building something on your stage and you'll find that one component disappears behind another one: having a grasp of stacking order means that you'll be able to understand why it disappeared, and how to get it back.

One final point to bear in mind: Flash gives you two main ways of operating in the third (depth) dimension - **layers**, and the **stacking order** within layers. With experience, you'll develop your own strategies for combining these two options, but one rule of thumb is that if you're going to have lots of separate overlapping objects, it's usually best to have them on different layers. The stacking order is particularly useful when you're constructing individual objects and groups of objects that'll always be kept together.

Case Study

In this chapter's final exercise, we'll be creating another component for our Flash movie/ web site. Using the 'red dot' graphic we created when we looked at the Toolbox in Chapter 2, we'll start developing a 'spinner' that'll enhance the appearance of our buttons in the finished movie. The effect we're after is a *Close Encounters*-like light show around each button. The first stage of this is to create the basic graphic, which we'll do here. We'll be enhancing this component in later chapters.

This is the finished basic graphic that we want to create:

Building the Spinner Foundation

1. Open up your 'case study' movie from wherever you saved it last.

2. Select the 'red dot' graphic on the main stage, copy it, and paste a copy back onto the stage:

3. Select the new circle you just pasted, and go to the **Modify > Transform > Scale and Rotate** menu option. We're just going to alter the size of the circle here.

4. In the **Scale and Rotate** dialog box, specify a scaling ratio of **30%** and press **Enter**. This will make your new circle drastically smaller.

5. Now place the smaller circle in orbit around the original circle (you might want to zoom in and turn on the grid to make placement easier and more precise):

6. Now select the smaller circle and copy and paste *that*. Use **Modify > Transform > Scale and Rotate** once again (or use the **Transform** panel) to scale this copy to **80%**. You should now have a new circle that's slightly smaller then the last one, placed like this:

7. Repeat these steps of copying and pasting the last circle you created and scaling it down by **80%** *four* more times. You should then have six circles from largest to smallest hugging the side of your central circle:

8. Now select all six new circles and copy and paste them:

9. With the six copies still selected, transform them by selecting the **Modify > Transform > Flip Vertical** menu option, followed closely by **Modify > Transform > Flip Horizontal**.

10. Now just line the six transformed circles up opposite their counterparts on the other side of the central circle and you're done:

Summary

In this chapter, we've introduced ourselves to the integral Flash facilities that help us arrange and align objects. These features are intimately linked with the ability to arrange content in space on the Flash stage in the three dimensions of width, height and depth.

We saw that:

◆ **We can group objects** together to maintain their relative proportions and still have access to them for editing

◆ **We can nest groups** within groups and symbols within groups and so on, giving us the ability to create hierarchies of precisely arranged, related objects

◆ Flash's **grids**, **rulers** and **guides** help us draw with a steady hand and sure eye

◆ Flash's **Alignment** panel, and the **Transform** menu/panel allow precision placement and transformation of objects

◆ Each Flash movie layer has an implicit **stacking order** for symbols and grouped objects, which we can manipulate *explicitly*

The focus in this chapter has been on working with multiple objects and seeing how to arrange them. In the next chapter, we're going to drill down inside of some objects and see how to use color to enrich content and effects.

5 Enhancing your Appearance

What we'll cover in this chapter:

- *How Flash **renders color***

- *Creating and saving custom colors*

- *How **gradients** work, and how to use them effectively as **fills** on drawn objects*

- ***Manipulating** object fills*

- *The essentials of importing and **using bitmaps***

In this chapter, we're going to see how Flash allows us to customize the objects that we create by fine-tuning their colors and fill styles. We'll see how Flash handles color, and how you can ensure that Flash's color features are working smart for you. Additionally, we'll take a quick look at how to import bitmaps and manipulate them in Flash, and we'll have some short digressions along the way, too. This is a long chapter, with a lot of worked examples, but stick with it: by the end, you'll be handling Flash's color features with much greater confidence.

Variety, they say, is the spice of life, and colors, fills and gradients are the extra paprika on the already tongue-tingling dish that is Flash. If you've used any of the many graphics programs that are available today, you'll be instantly at home with Flash's color creation methods. If, on the other hand, you're new to the world of swatches and radial gradients, don't worry: by the end of this chapter you'll be whistling along to "*R-G-B, as easy as 1-2-3*" while using the Alpha slider to open new windows into your movies.

It's never going to be entirely satisfactory discussing colors in a book printed in black and white, but with a little bit of imagination, and by working through the exercises with Flash open beside you, you'll get through without any problems.

Let's begin by talking about computerized color in general terms - then we'll see how Flash does it.

A Color Background

Color on a computer monitor, as on a TV, is rendered using a mixture of three discrete components of colored **light**: some red light, some green light and some blue light - hence **RGB**. When you're working with paint on a blank white canvas, you know that you need to add colored paint to make the painting. And you've probably also discovered that if you add red, blue and green paint together in the right quantities and mix them up, you end up with a murky black.

When you're dealing with colored *light* rather than colored *paint*, however, the opposite applies: with light, if there's no color present, everything is black, and if we add all the colors of light together at the right strength, we get white light:

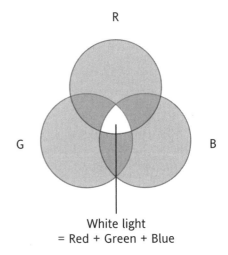

White light
= Red + Green + Blue

The three different color elements can be combined in an infinite variety of mixtures and strengths: just blue light on its own will give us a blue screen, whereas if we add a little green to that blue, we'll see the color change.

Each unique color that a computer monitor displays is composed of different proportions of red, green and blue. Furthermore, these unique colors can be described *numerically* by values that specify the amount of R, G and B that we want to display - these values determine the color that we see on the screen, and it's these numbers that tell the computer what to show. On a computer, these numbers are expressed in base 16, otherwise known as **hexadecimal** or **hex** for short.

In base 10, which we use every day for counting, our numbers fall into familiar columns: the right-most figure in a number is the number of 'units' (ones), the next column is the number of 'tens', the next is 'hundreds' and so on:

100s	10s	1s	Base 10
4	7	9	= 479

In hex, a different model applies. The right-hand figure in a number is still expressing the number of 'units', but the next column along is telling you how many *16s* there are in the number, etc.:

256s	16s	1s	Base 16 (HEX)
0	1	F	= 31

Because the second column from the right starts at 16, the 'units' column has to go up to 15, but still be expressed as a single digit. This is achieved by using letters rather than numbers: in the 'units' column, you count from **0** to **9** as in normal base 10, but the numbers from **10** through **15** are expressed as the letters **A** through **F**. So, **A** in hex is equal to 10 in base 10, **B** is **11**, and all the way up to **F**, which is **15**. After that, the units column goes back to 0, and the 16s column increments to 1. Thus, the figure 10 in hex means "1 lot of 16, and zero units".

Back to our colors. Remember we said that they're expressed in hex. Each unique color is the result of combining the three base colors, and each unique color has a six-digit identifier. In this six digit number, there are two digits for each of the base colors: the first two digits describe the amount of red present, the next two the green, and the last two the level of blue light. This means that black - the absence of any color of light - is expressed as 000000. That's 00 (hex) of red, 00 of green, and 00 of blue:

	Red	Green	Blue
Black =	00	00	00

Now, the largest number that can be expressed in two digits in hex is **FF**, which means (15 x 16) + (15 x 1), a total of 255. So a color whose number was **FF0000** would be 255 parts of red, zero parts of green, and zero parts of blue - which means that some red would be displayed on the screen. The opposite of this is white, which is a mix of all the colors at full strength, so pure white in hex is FFFFFF. Play around with the hex values of each base color component in a six-digit identifier, and you're creating different colors. In fact, the different combinations possible with this hex numbering system give us access to a range of over 16 million colors. Enough, I'm sure you'll agree, for most people to find one that they like - even if you can't find a shirt that matches it.

Right now, you're probably thinking, 'This chapter said it was about color, and all I've had so far is a math lesson.' and you'd be right. Hopefully though, this brief digression will help you to understand how Flash sees color, and from there, how you can best manipulate it to get the effect you want.

Let's start to take this theoretical knowledge and see how it's implemented in Flash. A good place to start is with custom colors: this is where Flash lets us create our own mixtures of the base colors that we can use and save.

Custom Colors in Flash

Bored with seeing the same colors everywhere you look? Want to make your whites whiter than white? Then you need...the **Mixer** panel:

This is where we can get Flash to mix us up *just* the color that we're looking for. This panel has two tabs: **Mixer** and **Swatches**.

On the **Mixer** tab, we can enter the precise RGB values that we want our strokes and fills to have, and then apply these colors to the objects in our movies. The **Swatch** tab shows us the predefined colors that we have available to choose. (A *swatch* is the name given to a single color, and a group of swatches together is called a *palette*.)

Here's an exercise to take us through the process of creating our own custom colors.

Creating Custom Colors with the Mixer Panel

1. Open the **Mixer** panel, either by clicking on its button on the launcher bar, or from the **Window > Panels** menu, and then click on the **Swatches** tab:

The colors shown in the top part of the **Swatch** panel make up the 216 **web-safe colors**, and this is the default palette used by Flash. These 'web-safe' colors are guaranteed to work on any computer using *any* browser running anywhere in the world, which means that if you always want your work to render perfectly on any old or superceded browser, exactly as you designed it, then these are the colors to use.

If you're not sure about using a particular custom color you've created, then the best thing to do is to test your movies and web pages in as many different browsers as you think is necessary: ultimately, there's a trade-off here between how certain you want to be that your page looks tip-top *everywhere*, and the time and effort that it takes to test *everything*. For most people, testing their movies and sites on up-to-date versions of Internet Explorer and Netscape is the norm.

2. Click on the **Mixer** tab:

In this tab you'll see the familiar Stroke and Fill Color boxes in the same layout as you find in the Toolbox.

Also, on the right-hand side, there are four input boxes: three where you can change the RGB value combinations for the current color (using a value of 1 - 255 for each base color), and one where you can set the **Alpha** value. *Alpha* is essentially another word for **transparency**: 100% Alpha is solid opaque color, 0% is fully transparent, and anything between will give an appropriately intermediate degree of transparency. Alpha is commonly used to make objects fade in and out of movies, or to create 'windows' in objects so that you can see through them. How to use alpha in your movies will be more fully explored in the next chapter, when we look at animation in more detail.

The final tool on the **Mixer** tab is the **Color Selector** bar along the bottom. This is a quick, visual way to choose a color. You just click anywhere on the bar, and that color (with its RGB values) will automatically be selected.

3. Click on the Fill Color selection box - the current color palette will appear:

Preview Box

Basic Colors

Hex Edit Text Box

No Color

Color Picker

Color Palette

Gradients

On the very top row of this color selection box (above all the available colors, and to the right of the preview box showing the currently selected color) there's a box showing the *hex value* of that color:

#000000

It can be extremely useful to know the hex value, as it means that you can match the color of your Flash movie to that of the host web page, and vice-versa, since web page colors are also defined in hex.

4. Click on the **Color Picker** button - the one at the top-right of the color palette, with the rainbow-hued disk on it. Doing this will open the **Color** window, where we can create a custom color:

This is where all of your alchemical color mixing takes place. To the left of the window is a set of basic, solid colors, which you can use as starting points. Your attention though, was no doubt already drawn to that lush, blush-drenched window pane on the right, the one that looks like a piece of blotting paper used to mop up a spilt rainbow. This window, with the luminance slider next to it, contains all of the colors that you can use in your movies.

> *For our Mac-using audience, the preceding picture and description will have been extremely confusing. The Mac's color picker, you will no doubt have noticed, is very different in appearance to the PC version pictured above, but it works in almost exactly the same way.*

In HLS mode, pictured here, a color wheel takes the place of the blush-drenched window and the slider underneath it controls lightness rather than luminance. If you want to adjust the RGB values of your color, you simply click on the RGB Picker icon in the menu on the left. The color picking options available to the Mac user are more sophisticated than those on the PC, and are beyond the scope of this chapter. What the Mac doesn't have, however, is the ability to create multiple custom colors in one visit to the picker - you'll have to mix your new colors one at a time.

The black cross in the color window marks your currently selected color.

5. Click in the color window and drag the mouse around. You'll notice that everything seems to change at once, the colors in the luminance slider shift like a tie-dyed chameleon, and the RGB values rush frantically to keep up with your waving mouse.

6. Release your mouse-finger and let the chameleon take a rest.

It's time to explain some more of those numbers. Next to the RGB values are three boxes containing the **Hue**, **Saturation**, and **Luminance** (HSL) of the current color:

These three terms are just another way to describe color. The hue is the actual color, and it's a relative of the RGB settings, but with a smaller range.

7. Click and drag your mouse carefully left and right, perfectly horizontally across the color window, and you'll see that only the hue setting will change.

8. If you move the mouse vertically up and down the window, only the saturation value will change.

> On the Mac, hue is determined by the angle you select on the color wheel, while saturation changes as you move nearer or further away from the hub of the wheel. If you move your cursor along the radius of the color wheel towards the center, the saturation setting will decrease from 100 at the rim to 0 at the hub, but the hue setting will stay the same.

The saturation determines the *amount* of that color, so now imagine you've got a tin of white paint, and you've chosen the pigment (hue) that you're going to add to this paint. The amount of saturation is determined by how much you put in: if you only put a little in, you'll have a very pale color, and if you put the whole lot in you'll have a very deep rich color, even though you're still using the same pigment.

The final value here is the luminance (sometimes called brightness - hence HSB - and called lightness on the Mac), which is the *amount of light* in the color. So far, you've chosen your original pigment (hue), and you've mixed it into your white base to get the depth of color (saturation) you wanted, and now you paint it onto a big sheet of glass. You then place a light behind the glass: this light determines the *luminance*. If you use a small, dim light, then the color will be a dark, gloomy shade, but if you position a huge arc light behind the glass, the color will become so painfully bright that there will only be a negligible difference between it and white. The luminance value is controlled from the slider bar on the left of the color window:

9. Choose a color from the vast spectrum available to you.

10. When you've chosen a color, check the color preview box to ensure that you

have the color you want. You may think this is obvious, but it's very easy to choose a color from the color window and leave the luminance set to 0, which will mean that everything comes out as black!

11. Finally, when you're sure everything is right, click on the **Add to Custom Colors** button at the bottom of the window.

    Your color will now become a swatch in one of the **Custom color** boxes on the far left. These boxes serve as a temporary storage area for your swatches: next time you want to use your swatch, you can come back to this window and it'll be there waiting for you.

> *Beware though, next time you open the* **Color** *window. If you select a color from the spectrum and add it to your custom colors, Flash will automatically overwrite the color in the top-left of your custom color boxes:*

By default, Flash will always save your color into this first box, even if it's currently filled with the perfect peach tone that you took hours to perfect. The only way to specify which box your new color goes into is to click on the specific custom color box you want to use, then select your color from the spectrum, and finally add the color to the box.

12. Click OK to close the Color window, and notice that your custom color is currently selected in the Fill Color box.

13. If you were now to use the Oval tool to draw a circle, it would be filled with your beautiful custom color. (Go on, try it... you know you want to...)

> *It's important to remember one thing when you're creating custom colors: Flash does not automatically save them permanently for you. If you close Flash and reopen it again, all of your carefully constructed colors will be gone from the custom color boxes.*

So the question arises - just how the heck do I make my custom colors *persist?*

Persistent Custom Colors

Saving custom colors in Flash is, unfortunately, quite a long-winded process. Once you've created your color, and defined it as a swatch in a **Custom Color** box, you must then add it to the main color palette, and finally save this as a color table.

Let's see how.

Saving Custom Colors Permanently

1. Make sure the **Mixer** panel is open with the **Mixer** tab selected. Also make sure that the swatch that you want to add is displayed as the currently selected fill or stroke color: this means you need to ensure your chosen custom color box is selected when you close the **Color** window where you chose it from the spectrum.

2. Click on the small arrow on the top-right of the **Mixer** panel, and take a look at the resulting drop-down menu:

This menu contains four entries: three optional ways of displaying color values numerically - RGB, HSB, and Hex - and one for adding a swatch to a palette. This is the one that we want to use here.

3. Click on the **Add Swatch** option.

4. Now, when you open up your color palette on the **Mixer** panel, you'll see your new swatch in a fresh row at the bottom of the palette:

New Swatch

You can now easily select your new color from this palette.

Once you've added all of your new swatches to the bottom of the palette, you still need to save it away so that it'll be available to you in the future.

5. Select the **Swatches** tab, then click on the arrow to access the drop-down menu for
this tab:

This menu contains all of the commands for dealing with swatches and palettes. For the moment, let's just focus on a couple of these options - **Save Colors**, and **Add Colors**.

6. Click on the **Save Colors** option, which will open up the **Export Color Swatch** dialog box. This dialog box will allow us to save our current colors away into a permanent file - a **color** set - that Flash can always access in the future:

Flash's default location for these files is in the **Color Sets** folder, which lives inside your Macromedia\Flash 5 folder. The *exact* location of this folder on your machine will depend on where you installed the Flash program to - typically it's at **C:\Program Files\Macromedia\Flash 5\Color Sets** on a PC, and in your **[Hard Drive] > Applications > Macromedia Flash 5** folder on a Mac.

7. Navigate to where you'd like to keep your swatches, give your color set a name, and then click **Save**. Your swatches will now be saved in a Flash color set (.clr) file.

The files that are already in this folder are the ready-made palettes that come with Flash, each one designed to cater for a specific set of requirements. To load these into Flash while you're creating a movie, use the **Add Colors** option from the **Swatches** tab's drop-down menu. Once loaded, you can use the slider button at the edge of the **Swatches** panel to scroll through the newly-available colors:

Note that Flash's default behavior is to open up the standard color set whenever it restarts. If you want to access your self-created color set again, just open the drop-down menu from the **Swatches** tab and click on the **Add Colors** command. This will open the **Import Color Swatch** dialog box, from where you can select the specific color set that you want to use to enrich your palette.

There are many different ways of creating and describing color, but a detailed analysis of them is beyond the scope of this book. If you're interested in learning more, there are plenty of resources around just waiting to be discovered, ranging from the Internet to your local library. The best thing you can do is experiment and see how the different values affect the final color. It's up to you to decide which method you prefer from RGB or HSL, but remember that your color will be rendered in Flash, and on the web, as an **RGB** value.

Here and now, our next step is to look at color and gradients.

Gradient Color

The ability to create custom colors is great, and the only problem with them is that no matter how much work you put in picking and choosing your color values, you still end up with a single flat color. This is where **gradients** come in. Gradients are distinct color features that we can apply to our objects' fills.

A gradient consists of a smooth change from one color to another. In Flash, gradients can be simple and 'pure', with a starting color and an end color, or they can be more complex, with up to eight different colors: in complex gradients, intermediate colors create distinct 'steps' in the gradient, giving the effect of a richer and more complicated spectrum:

Simple gradients:

start color (white) | gradient transition | end color (black)

Complex gradients:

transitional colors | transitional colors | transitional colors

start color | intermediate color | intermediate color | end color

These different types of gradients allow for some pretty spectacular effects, especially when you tween transitions from gradient to gradient. Just for now though, we'll start with the basics.

This next screenshot shows a simple gradient, which runs from from white to black:

This is an example of a **linear gradient**, so named because the gradient runs in a straight line from the first color (white, on the left) to the second color (black, on the right). With linear gradients, you just define the start and end colors (and any intermediate ones, if you want a more complex effect), and Flash works out the intermediate colors between the defined colors. Flash has a number of pre-defined linear gradients in its palette, but we can also mix our own too, as you'll see shortly.

The other type of gradient is a **radial gradient**:

Radial gradients have their 'starting' color at the center, and their 'finishing' color at the outside. The gradient radiates out from the center to the edge. Again, Flash has some standard radial gradients but, once again, we have infinite customization features at our fingertips.

The choice about which gradient to use for a given task is entirely down to your personal taste: there's no right or wrong gradient type, just use the one that you think looks the best for what you're trying to do.

Gradients are really just smooth transitions of color between two (or more) distinct colors. If you've ever tried to create a gradient on paper with colored pencils or paint, you'll know how difficult it can be to get the effect right. Thankfully, Flash gives us a little studio and palette where we can create, preview, and amend gradients to our heart's content.

Making the Gradient

To work with gradients, you need to use the Mixer panel and the Info panel. A little counter-intuitively, Flash keeps the controls that influence gradient creation in two separate places: the gradient-setting controls are found under the Fill tab of the Info panel, and the controls for fine-tuning individual colors are on the Mixer panel, as you've already seen.

Creating and Modifying Gradients

1. If the **Mixer** and **Fill** panels aren't currently open, bring them up now from the **Window > Panels** menu, or from the Launcher bar.

    You'll probably already have noticed some boxes at the bottom of the color palette that don't look like the other solid colors:

    These are Flash's predefined gradients. There are five basic (two-color) gradients and two more complicated ones.

    Gradients

2. Click on the **Swatches** tab of the **Mixer** panel to open up the palette. From here, click on the black and white linear gradient, at the bottom on the far left, to select it.

   Notice that as you select the gradient, the Fill tab automatically changes to reflect this choice:

   We've now chosen the gradient style that we want to use - a simple, linear, black and white gradient. We can now either use this as the fill on a new or existing object, or we can customize it as we're going to do here.

   Let's ensure that we don't *overwrite* the default linear gradient.

3. Click on the little 'save' icon in the bottom-right corner of the **Fill** tab. This will add a new gradient at the right-hand end of the list:

   You can also create new gradients by clicking on the arrow on the **Fill** tab and using the drop-down menu to choose the **Add Gradient** command:

   We now have our very own gradient to tinker with.

4. Click on the new gradient's box at the bottom of the **Swatches** panel to ensure that this is the one you're working on. The currently selected gradient box will have a white outline around it:

As we've selected a linear gradient to work on, we see the gradient controls in the **Fill** tab:

Fill Style

Gradient Preview

Save

Gradient Range

The most important of these is the long bar across the middle with the white paint pot hanging from the left-hand side, and a black paint pot hanging from the right. This bar shows the **range** of your gradient - that is, its start and end points.

5. Click on the white paint pot and drag it along to the middle of the bar:

The gradient in the little preview window on the left will now be half bleached-out, with only a smudge of black creeping in from the right-hand side. We've effectively told Flash 'I want everything to the left of the white paint pot to be white. Start the gradient where the white paint pot is, and use the black as the end point'. Notice also that the gradient box in the Swatches

panel has also changed to
reflect your alteration:

6. Now click on the black paint pot and drag
   it past the white pot in the middle,
   all the way over to the left-hand side
   where the white paint pot used to be:

   Your gradient has now been reversed: it
   now consists of a small black stripe on the
   left, with a large white mass to its right.

   Now we can start adding to the basic gradient and make it a little more
   interesting. To do this, we have to add some intermediate color stages to the
   range bar.

7. Click below the gradient range bar to the
   right of your current white paint
   pot, and another pot will appear just
   below where you clicked:

   Because we clicked underneath a white part of the gradient, this new paint
   pot will inherit that color. If we'd clicked in a black area, we'd have got a
   black paint pot.

8. Click in the same way under the gray
   gradient between the black and the white
   pots:

Again, your new paint pot will be filled with the same gray as the color immediately above it in the gradient bar. Notice that the currently selected paint pot has a black pointer at the top, and that the body of each paint pot indicates what color that pot represents. Furthermore, the color box to the right of the range bar shows us what color is in that paint pot at the moment.

We can now change the color content of our paint pots and thus customize the gradient still further.

9. Click on the color box on the right of the range bar to open up the color palette.

10. From here pick a color - say, a pure blue. As soon as you click on the color, the current paint pot will be filled with it and the gradient bar will change to reflect its new Technicolor glory.

> *Warning: When you're mixing a gradient, it's tempting to try and use the Swatches tab to pick the color. Don't do it. If you do, Flash will think you want to use a solid color instead of a gradient, and it'll take you out of the gradient selection on the Fill tab. If you do this by mistake, just click on the Fill Style drop-down box and re-select the gradient type you were editing, and your gradient colors should still be there, exactly how you left them.*

11. Click on the paint pot on the far right and, using the color box by the range bar again, change its color to red.

Your gradient should now flow from black on the left to blue, with a very thin white bar in the middle, which rapidly fades into red on the right:

Now that you've created your gradient, how do you use it? Easy. It's now your selected fill for any objects that you draw, and if you click on the Paint Bucket tool you can use it to fill existing objects.

12. Draw a square with the Rectangle tool, and you should see something much like this, but in glowing color:

Radial gradients are created in exactly the same way.

13. Go back to the fill panel and select **Radial Gradient** from the drop-down **Fill Style** menu:

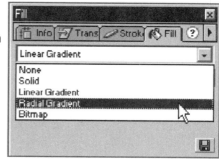

Note that Flash has retained the colors that you defined on the range bar, but that they've now been mapped onto a radial gradient with what was the left-most color (black) in the center of the gradient, and the rightmost color (red) on the outside.

14. Draw another square next to the last one:

From this, you can clearly see the relationship between linear and radial gradient: they're both based on a spread of colors that we defined on the range bar, and the way that this range is displayed depends upon the left-right arrangement of those colors. We can alter the way that the gradients display by shifting the relative positions of the paint pots on the range bar.

15. To save your gradient permanently, use the same technique we used in the previous exercise: bring up the menu using the arrow on the Swatches panel and save (or overwrite) your customized color set. **Make sure you don't overwrite any of Flash's default color sets.**

If your gradient boxes get messed up (as they sometimes can, while you're experimenting), you can always revert to your saved color set (using the Add Color option from the Swatches panel menu), or reload Flash's default colors:

Now that you have an initial understanding of gradients, let's have a look at how they can be used to create light effects in your movies.

Light and Shade with Gradients

By combining simple gradients with drawn shapes, it's easy to create convincing light effects, simulating shadow, shade, and implicit light sources. In reality of course, we won't be building true 3D light-sourced objects (you need other packages to create those), but we *can* fabricate an adequate enough illusion to fool the eye. These effects can add real interest and depth to your movies.

Let's explore this by constructing a shaded sphere.

Using Gradients to Create a Shaded Sphere

1. Open up a new movie.

2. Start by selecting your Oval tool, then click on the Fill Color box and pick the green radial gradient from the bottom of the palette:

Green radial gradient

Because we want the sphere to look like a realistic three-dimensional object, we need to remove the stroke line from around the edge.

3. Click on the Stroke button in the Toolbox, and then click on the **No Color** button, either at the top of the palette, or in the Toolbox:

Now you're ready to draw your circle.

4. Use the Oval tool with the *Shift* key held down to keep it perfectly symmetrical. You should now have a black sphere with a green center:

To bring the sphere to life you need to adjust the position of the green center 'light' on your sphere. Traditionally, spheres are lit from the top left, and this has become such a widely accepted convention that if the lighting is anywhere else, it just doesn't look right.

5. Reposition the center of the fill - the point from which the gradient radiates - using your Paint bucket tool. Imagine that the tip of the bucket is your light source, and click in the top-left hand side of your circle to readjust this source. You'll end up with a passable sphere like this:

And that's it, your very own 3D sphere, just waiting to be moved around on the stage and morphed into something else. From this basic technique, it's easy to make more complicated shapes with multiple gradients. Maybe a festive egg...

...or a metal cube made from two skewed rectangles:

Warning: Just like custom colors, custom gradients are not permanently saved when Flash is closed. To save them, you must go through the same process that you did for custom colors. First add the gradient to the palette by clicking on the disk icon on the Fill tab. Then click on the **Save Colors** *command on the drop-down menu on the* **Swatches** *tab of the* **Mixer** *panel.*

We've seen how to make a basic shape look three-dimensional with a standard gradient. Flash also has some features that let you finesse the gradient effects you apply to your objects.

Applying Gradients to Objects and Modifying Them

It's all well and good being able to make a perfect linear gradient for your shape, but what if your shape itself isn't perfectly linear? For example, a linear gradient looks fine on a square, but on a skewed parallelogram, the standard gradient doesn't really enhance the impression of a real object with the light falling on it:

Luckily, Flash provides ways of changing your gradient to suit your shape.

The simplest and most painstaking way of applying the gradient in a non-standard way is achieved with the Paint Bucket tool.

If you draw a filled rectangle on the stage after selecting a linear gradient for the fill, you get a dandy-looking gradient:

The only problem is that all of your rectangles drawn with the basic gradient as a fill will look the same. You can change this, however. If you select the Paint Bucket with the standard linear gradient as the fill, and then *click and drag* the mouse to apply the fill to the shape, you can simulate light coming from a different direction:

The angle that you drag at will make the gradient flow from a different starting point. This method is one of trial and error - experiment and see the effects you can get with different types of gradient.

Flash - you're not going to be surprised - also has more precise methods of manipulating gradients. Remember those two buttons at the bottom of the Paint Bucket tool that you briefly cast your eye over in the Toolbox chapter?

These two buttons are your keys to modifying gradients professionally. In this next exercise, you'll find out how to fit a gradient to a skewed parallelogram, and see the methods you can use to alter gradients in a controlled manner once they're on the stage.

Scaling and Rotating Linear Gradients

First of all, you have to create your parallelogram.

1. Use the Rectangle tool to draw a square with a black border, but no fill. Skew your square using the **Modify > Transform** menu, or by using the Arrow tool, the Rotate button and the drag handles via the Toolbox:

2. Now fill the new shape with a linear gradient. We've used a custom gradient
    consisting of two black paint pots at each end of the gradient bar, and a white
    one in the middle:

The effect we're trying to achieve with this shape is to make it look like a
length of metal pipe. It looks like a piece of metal, but more like a flat
lozenge than a tube. Let's see if we can model it better.

3. With the Paint Bucket tool selected, click on the **Transform Fill** button in the
    bottom right of the tool options:

Your cursor will change to an arrow with a gradient filled rectangle next to it.
This indicates that you're in **Transform Fill** mode:

4. Click on the gradient that's filling your skewed shape. Two blue lines will
    appear around your shape, along with a circle in the center, and a square and
    a circle on the right-hand side:

These are the handles used to move and transform your gradient, and you can think of them as the **Scale** and **Rotate** commands rolled into one. When you move your mouse over each one, it will change to a different cursor depending on its function: the Center point is a cross with arrow heads on each end; the Resize handle is a two headed arrow; and the Rotate handle is indicated by curved arrows around in a circle.

Each of these handles controls a different aspect of the gradient that's filling the parallelogram.

5. Click on the Center point and drag it to the left-hand side.

When you release the mouse, the gradient will be centered around this new point. Notice also that the lines at either side of your shape moved as well. These bounding lines act as a quick guide to seeing the position, size and angle of your gradient:

6. Next, click and drag the Rotate handle down until the gradient is on a similar slant to the sides of your skewed square:

The gradient looks a little too big now, and to our eye it seems to be bleaching the shape a bit. We can get around this by squeezing the gradient to fit into the shape better.

7. Click on the Resize handle, and move it in until you achieve your desired effect - a strip of metal pipe in low light:

And there you have it, a gradient that you've fitted perfectly into your skewed parallelogram.

From here, it's surely only a matter of time before you start building that Flash oil refinery...

Radial gradients are also amenable to our creative sleight of hand.

Modifying a Radial Gradient

When dealing with a radial gradient you have four parameters to transform the fill, rather than the linear gradient's three. The majority of them are the same, but their implementation can appear very different on a radial gradient.

1. Still working on your skewed parallelogram, click on the gradient fill with the Arrow tool to select it, then use the **Fill** panel to convert the linear gradient to a radial one:

2. Now choose the Paint Bucket tool, select the Transform Fill option, and then click on the gradient to select it:

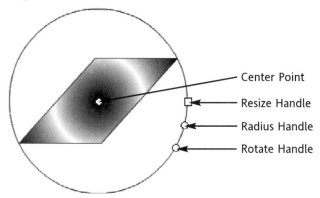

Center Point

Resize Handle

Radius Handle

Rotate Handle

The circle around the radial gradient is the equivalent of the two bounding lines that were on either side of the linear gradient. This marks the shape and the limits of your gradient.

3. Click on the Rotate handle (the bottom circle) and drag it around.

Notice that nothing seems to happen when you release it. This is because you're rotating a circle, and as you know, no matter how much you spin a circle, it will always remain the same. You're probably thinking, "So what's the point of having a Rotate handle then, if it doesn't do anything?" And if it didn't do anything, you'd be perfectly right to think such a thing, but luckily it does. The secret is to change the *shape* of your gradient first, so that it's no longer a perfect circle.

4. Click on the Resize handle and drag it in towards the center of the shape:

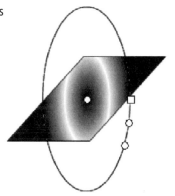

Your gradient will now be elliptical, but at a funny angle to the rest of your shape.

5. Now's the time to use the Rotate handle to spin the gradient so it fits nicely into your parallelogram:

Now for the Radius handle (we'll leave the Center point handle aside, as we want to keep our ellipse centered in our shape). The Radius handle is similar to the Resize handle, but rather than squashing or stretching the shape, it resizes the circle uniformly.

6. Click on it and drag it towards the center a little. Your gradient will shrink, but retain the same proportions:

You've now used all of the gradient tools, bar one. So far you've only been able to give gradients to individual shapes, and then modify those, but imagine what you could do if you could apply your gradient evenly to a number of different objects spread out over the entire stage? That's just what the **Lock Fill** option gives us.

Locking Fills

By locking the fill, you can make a gradient span across multiple shapes. That is, you can get the effect of a series of cut-out shapes that reveal a common underlying background, almost as if you were opening up little windows to reveal a big picture behind them:

Here's how to use the Lock Fill feature.

Locking a Fill

1. Start off by selecting a gradient from the **Swatches** tab. We've used the black and white linear gradient for clarity, but feel free to experiment with something a little more adventurous.

2. Now use the Rectangle tool to draw a long, thin rectangle across the stage from left to right:

3. Next, change the Rectangle tool's fill to **No Color** and draw six small squares underneath your original rectangle:

4. Select the Dropper tool from the Toolbox, then click on your big gradient filled rectangle. This will tell Flash to use this particular gradient (and its orientation on the page) as a fill for other objects.

   Flash will automatically change the cursor to a paint bucket with a small padlock next to it, the sign for - you've guessed it - a locked fill:

5. Finally, click on each of the squares to fill them with the gradient:

   See how the gradient stretches across the six squares as if they were a continuation of the fill in the big rectangle? Flash is intelligent enough to work out the continuation of the gradient beyond the original shape and map it onto the new shapes. This can be a very powerful way to achieve symmetry across your gradients.

We have spent all of our time so far talking about ways of drawing images directly in Flash, but it's also possible to create images in external programs and then import those into Flash for manipulation and use. One of the most common image types that you might want to bring into Flash is a *bitmap*.

Using Bitmap Images in Flash

A **bitmap** image (otherwise known as a **raster** image) is a generic name for an image that's defined in terms of thousands of individual *pixels*. Typical bitmap formats include JPGs, BMPs, GIFs and TIFs, the difference between them being the particular ways they store the image data. Bitmaps are usually used for complicated images like photographs or paintings, where every single pixel can make a difference in the finished picture. The problem with bitmaps is that the image file has to describe each and every pixel that the image is composed of, which often results in a large file, in turn meaning long download times. (Some 'lossy' bitmap formats such as JPG can compress images by describing blocks of similar color, rather than every pixel, but at the expense of picture quality.)

A **vector** file, on the other hand, will describe an image in terms of mathematical expressions - e.g. the start and end points of a line. It's this fact that allows vector files to compress a lot of graphical information into a small space. Mathematical line description is great for simple shapes, but it's more difficult to try to describe the Mona Lisa in terms of vectors.

The first thing to remember when you're considering using bitmaps in Flash is that Flash is not designed as a bitmap program. To get the best performance in your movies, it's always preferable to create everything inside Flash using the drawing tools provided, or to use vector graphics imported from other software applications. In this way, Flash can optimize the file to ensure it is the smallest (and therefore the quickest) download possible. It's possible to create a 'flipbook' style movie by using a sequence of imported bitmaps, but this will create such a huge file, and take so long to download, that most people will have moved on to the next site before the first couple of frames of your movie have loaded!

There'll be times when you've got a nice logo that you've created in a paint program, and you're tempted to just pull it into Flash and then animate it. Although you can do this, in the long run you're better off doing it from scratch in Flash. It may not look exactly the same, but the benefits of smaller size and higher speed will probably outweigh the small graphical differences. So, the first rule of thumb when using bitmaps is - think carefully about the tradeoff between file size and the benefit that the bitmaps will bring to your movie.

So, a couple more rules of thumb. Use bitmaps when:

- You need to have photos or lifelike images

- You need to have screenshots

- You need to have pictures of drawings or artwork

For anything else, draw it inside Flash or another vector program.

> *Warning: Don't forget that the web safe color rule that applies to the colors you use in Flash also applies to the colors of any images that you import into Flash. If you want your image to be guaranteed to display correctly on all computers, you should use the 216-color palette throughout all of the stages of your movie's creation. This means that when you find an image to import, it's best to change its colors in a graphics-editing program first to make sure it will display as you want it to, and then bring the image into Flash.*

OK. You've considered all the warnings, you've tried your best to draw your picture in Flash, but you've come to the decision that you're just going to have to import a bitmap image into Flash... So how do you do it?

Working with Bitmaps

1. Inside a new movie, Click on the **File > Import** command to open the **Import** dialog box.

2. Navigate to a .bmp file image on your computer, the Mac will import this file using QuickTime, click yes when prompted (you can download the example we've used here from this book's support section on our web site):

3. Open the file.

4. Your file will be imported into Flash and placed both on the stage as an object, and in the library

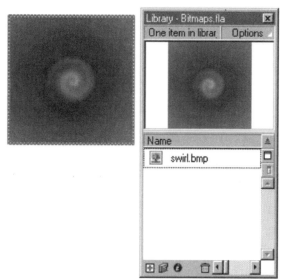

Warning: Flash uses the original image stored in the library as reference-point, so if you delete this, it can cause problems with your Flash movie. Even if you break apart the image and convert it to a graphic symbol, it will still be inexorably linked to the original bitmap.

Once you've imported the image into Flash, there are a couple of methods that you can use to modify it.

5. Right-click (or **Control**-click on a Mac) on the bitmap symbol in the bottom pane of the library window.

This will open a context-sensitive menu with a list of commands that can affect your image:

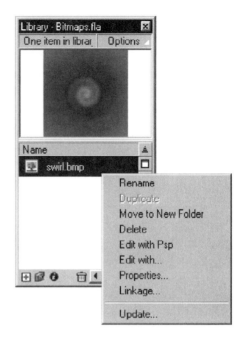

The commands that we're concerned with are the **Edit** with commands. The first of these (**Edit with Psp** here, or **Edit with Picture Viewer** on Mac) will open up the default image-editing program that Windows has associated with that file type. The second **Edit with...** option will open a dialog box, from where you can choose a program to edit your image in. Both of these commands will open the bitmap within the selected editing program. When you've finished editing the bitmap, save it and close the program to return to Flash, and you'll find that the image in the library will have been updated to reflect any changes you've made.

The second method of altering bitmaps is to modify them *within Flash itself*. At the moment, the bitmap on the stage is an instance of the symbol in your library.

6. Double-click on the instance on the stage: you might be expecting to be taken into an 'Edit Bitmaps mode', but instead, nothing happens.

To alter a bitmap inside Flash, you first have to **break it apart**.

7. Click on the **Modify > Break Apart** menu option.

Your bitmap image has now become a *shape*, with no outline, and filled with the image from the library. This shape can be modified as any other shape can be in Flash: you can draw on it, cut bits out of it and scale or rotate it.

8.   Click on the Lasso tool, and you'll see three options for it at the bottom of the Toolbox:

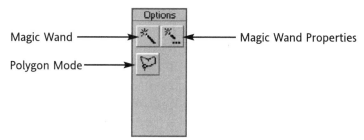

Magic Wand ⟶ ⟵ Magic Wand Properties

Polygon Mode ⟶

The two important options in the bitmap-editing context are the Magic Wand and the Magic Wand Properties. The Magic Wand is used to select a *specific color* in the image, which means that if you had a picture of a sky with clouds, and you only wanted to select the sky and *not* the clouds, you'd use the Magic Wand tool. With this tool, you could just select the blue areas and ignore the gray and white clouds.

9.   Select the Magic Wand option, then click on the far top-left corner of your broken-apart image. A small section of the image will be selected:

Selected area ⟶

This is because Flash has *only* selected the sections of the image whose pixels are a very close color match to the original pixel you clicked on.

10.   Now click on the Magic Wand Properties option, and a dialog box will appear:

From here, you can alter the settings for the Magic Wand tool.

The **Threshold** box defines the amount of *deviance* Flash can make from the clicked-on color when it determines the 'matching pixels' to include in its selection. In our cloudy sky example, if your sky ranged from a deep blue to lighter gray-blue, then just using the Magic Wand on its default settings would only select a small piece of the sky. A setting of **10** will only allow Flash to select 10 shades of blue different from the one that you clicked on. By putting a larger number into this box, you're allowing Flash to select a greater portion of the sky.

11. Type '**20**' into the **Threshold** box.

12. Click off the stage to deselect the corner of the image, and click again with the Magic Wand in the same place on the image as last time:

Now you can see that Flash has selected a much greater part of the image. If you were to increase the **Threshold** number again, Flash would select an even bigger portion.

The other option in the Magic Wand Properties box is for **Smoothing**. This controls the amount Flash will smooth the boundaries of the selection:

The **Pixels** setting means Flash will not smooth the boundaries at all, and that only a very tight range of color will be selected. The other 'granularity' options range all the way up to **Smooth**, which does as its name suggests - smoothes out the differences between bordering colors.

If you're trying to select a very specific area of color, then you should set this to **Pixels** with a low **Threshold** (1-2), and if you're trying to select a large area with variable color, then set **Smoothing** to **Smooth** and choose a high **Threshold** figure.

You've already played with solid and gradient fills in objects, but you can also fill objects using **bitmap** images. Using bitmaps to fill shapes in your movie can give some very interesting results, just so long as you always bear in mind that wherever bitmaps are involved, a larger file size is sure to follow.

Using Bitmaps as Fills

1. Working with the same imported bitmap image as before, use the Arrow tool to pull out and deform the sides of the shape, and increase its size:

You'll see that your image has automatically been used to 'tile' the background of the altered shape. Whenever you draw a shape that's bigger than the actual bitmap image, Flash will tile the bitmap to fill the shape's outline.

2. Click on your shape with the Dropper tool. If you look at the fill color in the toolbar now:

You'll see that there's a small copy of your image inside the box, which means that the current fill color is actually your bitmap image!

3. To really demonstrate this, draw a simple rectangle on the stage next to your other shape:

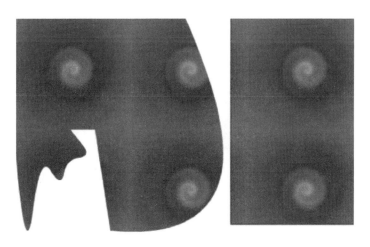

The new shape will be filled with the bitmap, showing a continuation of the tiling that was apparent when we stretched our original shape. This is because the bitmap image is effectively acting as a locked fill on the stage, just as we saw earlier with our gradient locked fill.

Another useful way to manipulate bitmaps in Flash is to use the **Trace Bitmap** command.

Tracing Bitmaps

Tracing a bitmap converts it from a bitmap image into a series of vectors. Although this sounds like a good thing, giving you bitmap detail with vector scalability, the results, in practice, can leave a lot to be desired. You'll need to experiment with this feature and make a judgment about the benefits it has. Let's walk through an example of bitmap tracing.

Tracing Bitmaps

1. Delete what's on your stage at the moment, and drag another two instances of your bitmap image out from the library and on to the clear stage.

2. Select the first bitmap instance and click on the **Modify > Trace Bitmap** command.

You'll see this dialog box:

The settings are as follows:

*   **Color Threshold** - This works on the same principle as the **Threshold** setting in the Magic Wand Properties box: a higher number means that Flash will include a greater number of colors as 'matching', which means that your final (traced) image will decompose into fewer vector shapes.

*   **Minimum Area** - This defines the minimum size (in pixels) that an area can be, while still being considered 'a shape'. The more detailed that you

want your final image to be, the smaller you should make this number, remembering of course that 'more shapes' means 'bigger file size'.

- **Curve Fit** - This is similar to **Smoothing** in the Magic Wand Properties box. Setting this to **Pixels** here will ensure that the resulting traced curves will stay faithful to the original bitmap, while setting it to **Very Smooth** will let Flash round out the curves in its selection. The smoother a line is, the fewer vectors Flash needs to define it, and so the smaller the file size.

- **Corner Threshold** - This performs the same task as **Curve Fit**, but it deals with how far a line must bend before Flash breaks it into two lines with an angular corner. The fewer corners in the image, the smaller the file size.

3. Leave the settings as the defaults shown in the screenshot, and press OK. Flash will now convert the first bitmap instance into a group of vectors using the settings you provided. You'll get a result like this:

You can see that this isn't *particularly* faithful to the original bitmap. Let's try and trace an image that's a little closer to the original.

4. Click on your second bitmap instance, and open up the **Trace Bitmap** dialog box again.

5. This time, set the values to **10**, **2**, **Pixels**, and **Many Corners** respectively and press **OK**:

We think you'll agree that this looks virtually identical to the original bitmap. Unfortunately, the price you pay for this accuracy is it will give you an enormous file. You'll see just how big this file is when you come to **optimize** it in a moment.

Optimizing Bitmaps

Optimizing minimizes the amount of corners in an image and smoothes out the lines to give a smaller, but less precise picture. You can optimize any shape that you've drawn, but it comes in particularly useful when dealing with traced bitmaps.

Optimizing the Traced Bitmap

1. Highlight the whole of your first bitmap image instance and use the **Modify > Optimize** menu option to open the **Optimize Curves** dialog box:

2. Change the settings to those in the screenshot by dragging the **Smoothing** bar to the far right and checking the **Use multiple passes** box. By doing this, you're ensuring that Flash will optimize the curves as much as possible, and create the smallest file it can.

3. Click **OK**:

You'll see a report window, showing the number of curves that Flash was able to optimize.

If you look at your image on the stage now, you'll see that it is a lot spikier than it was before, because Flash has converted all the pixilated smoothness into vector precision. By keeping the **Smoothing** slider at a lower setting, you can keep the image more faithful to the original, but at the expense of optimization.

4. Do the same thing with your second (more accurately traced) image, using the same settings as before:

Now you can see how tracing bitmaps accurately can leave you with a huge number of curves, which all add up in the final file size. Whereas with the first image there were only 64 curves, in the second there were 5839, and even after optimization there are still 1507 curves. The final image though, is not too shabby a reproduction of the original, and at a considerably smaller size:

The original bitmap image is on the left, the highly optimized vector image is in the middle, and the accurately traced and optimized vector image is on the right. Again, you're on the horns of that old 'size vs. quality' dilemma - and only you can make the ultimate decision about whether those extra k are worth it.

> The **Trace Bitmap** tool will not always give the best results, and can leave you with very large files. It is sometimes more useful to import the bitmap onto one layer, lock it, and then physically trace it using the Pencil tool on another layer, and deleting the original when you're finished.

Next, we'll now focus on another type of bitmap image - the GIF file, and see how Flash treats these when it imports them.

Importing GIFs into Flash

The GIF (Graphic Interchange Format) file is one of the most commonly used image types on the Internet. What makes them so special is that not only can they be compressed to produce relatively small images, but they can also include animations and single color transparency. When you import a GIF into Flash, you can retain these attributes.

Let's see how, starting with the GIF transparency idea.

Transparent GIFs

GIF transparency is not as powerful as Flash's Alpha setting. Whereas with Alpha you can have a range of partial transparencies from 'completely opaque' through to totally transparent, with a GIF, the transparency can only be 'on' or 'off'. However, reusing transparent GIFs in Flash can still be a useful feature to exploit.

Using Transparent GIFs

1. Open a new movie.

2. In the **File > Import** menu, navigate your way to a transparent GIF that you have on your computer, or use the downloadable transparent.gif file from this book's support area on the **friends of ED** web site. You should have a red square on your screen with a circular hole in the middle:

The hole in the middle is the transparent area of the GIF.

3. Draw a line across the stage, and right across the image, using the Paintbrush tool. The line will pass behind the image, but it will still be visible through the hole:

4. Move the GIF around on the stage. Wherever you put it, you should still be able to see the painted line behind it through the hole.

   Remember that there's not actually a gap in the image, such as you'd get if you drew a vector rectangle with Flash's Rectangle tool and then used the Oval tool to cut a vector circle out of the middle. The hole in the GIF is more akin to a window: there's still a solid piece of image there - it's just that it's completely transparent.

5. To test this, click on the part of the line that you can see through the window. If there was a gap here, you'd expect to be able to select the line, but instead, you'll find that the GIF is selected, even though it looks like there is nothing actually there.

The next type of GIF to look at is an animated one.

Animated GIFs

An animated GIF is basically just a collection of static images that play one after the other at a specified speed. You can import these into Flash and incorporate them into the main timeline or into a movie clip's timeline.

Using Animated GIFs

1. Start a new movie, and use the **File > Import** command to locate an animated GIF and bring it into Flash. Again, we've provided a file on the website that you can use - animated.gif.

2. When you bring an animated GIF into Flash, you'll notice that your timeline changes:

Flash creates a new keyframe for each frame in your animated GIF, and the number of normal frames between each keyframe on the timeline is dependent upon the delay specified *inside* the GIF. For example, our original GIF has six frames, and a delay of 1/2 a second between each frame. This gives a total running time of three seconds (6 x 1/2 = 3).

In Flash, each keyframe is followed by five 'keyframe-dependent' frames on the timeline, meaning that each of the GIF frames is displayed for six Flash frames. The movie is playing at the default twelve frames per second, so each set of six frames will take 1/2 a second to display. This is the same as it was in the GIF, as is the total time, thirty-six (frames) divided by twelve (fps) = three seconds.

3. Each of the keyframes reproduces each of the GIF frames as bitmaps within that frame. Open up your library:

You'll see that there are six bitmap images within it, one for each frame of the GIF. The first one is named after the filename of the GIF, and the following images are just named '**Bitmap**' followed by a number. If you're going to be using animated GIFs in Flash, it is helpful for your reference to create a folder in your library for the GIF and store all of its frames within that folder.

It's also possible to create a similar effect by importing a sequence of images into Flash. So if you have a number of images named slide1.gif, slide2.gif, slide3.gif etc... in the same directory, and you import the first one, then Flash will ask you if you want to import the rest of these as a sequence of images.

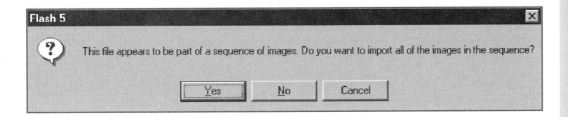

If you answer 'Yes' to this, Flash will import your sequence of images as keyframes, one after another in a straight line.

We'll now look at importing files from other Macromedia products, and get a glimpse of the extended integration between them.

Importing Files from Freehand and Fireworks

One of the great things about Flash 5 is that it is better integrated with other Macromedia products such as Freehand and Fireworks. Here we will give you just a basic overview of how to import files from these programs.

Importing Fireworks files is a very simple process. Simply use the **File > Import** menu and then select **PNG Image** from the menu. You'll then be prompted with a dialog box like this:

When importing your Fireworks file, it's wise to retain the default settings that Flash gives you in the dialog box - this will give you the best rendering of the imported image.

With **Import Editable Objects** checked, Flash will import the separate parts of the Fireworks image as separate objects on your stage. It will allow you to edit your text and images as if they are in vector format. The three check boxes below this option will allow you to tell Flash whether to import any images, text or guides respectively contained in the Fireworks file. Flash will import each of the separate elements on a different layer, or keep the layer structure that was found in the original file.

If you choose to check the '**Flatten Image**' box, all of the graphics and text inside the file will be flattened into one bitmap graphic when you import it into Flash. This means that you won't be able to edit each of the items separately.

The same basic process also applies to importing Freehand files, use **File > Import** but select Freehand from the drop-down menu. Once you've selected a file, you'll see a different dialog window appear from the Fireworks import box:

As you can see you have many more options for Freehand files. Freehand is also a vector program, but instead of creating images for the web, it is mostly used for designing for print.

With Freehand you have the ability to have multiple pages. Flash will allow you to import these pages as separate scenes with one page in each scene, or it can simply import them into their own individual frames.

You can also tell Flash how you want the layers of Freehand to import. If you want to keep everything exactly the same as you had it in Freehand, then just keep the **Layers** radio button checked, or you can have Flash flatten out the Freehand file, but the problem with this is that none of your text or artwork will then be editable, just like with Fireworks.

In the Freehand Import dialog window, you can specify which pages of the Freehand file you want to import, and you also have a few extra options to import layers that you had hidden in Freehand, as well as your background layer. You can also make sure that any text that was in the file is imported as text, and is therefore still editable.

It's recommended that you keep the default settings here as well, as this way all of your artwork is editable once imported (unless it wasn't vector artwork to begin with in Freehand) and is easy to manipulate in case a mistake is made.

Importing and Using Vector Clipart

Clipart has had a wonderful history in print art, presentations and web pages, so it should come as no surprise that it can be used in Flash as well. The greatest thing about clipart though, is that, unlike bitmaps, most of it is already in vector format, and so can be easily imported and used in Flash.

The best type of file, and easiest for Flash to import, is a **WMF** file (Windows Metafile). These files can be easily imported into Flash through the **File > Import** menu and then because they are already vectors, they are easily manipulated once inside Flash.

WMFs are usually imported as groups, so if you want to start editing them, you can either edit each group separately, or highlight the whole image and use the **Modify > Ungroup** option to convert them all into lines and fills. There are sometimes lines and fills behind others in clipart files, which can add up to unnecessary file size. To ensure this is not the case, ungroup the whole image, and deselect the object to let Flash merge the visible objects together, and discard the hidden ones.

Don't be afraid to use clipart in your Flash movies. Some people don't like the way clipart looks, but keep in mind that you can use clipart as a building block for your own art, as you can edit it to the look and feel of your own web site.

Images are not the only visual elements that Flash can handle though: it can also use your system fonts and some modification tools to give your movies that extra personal zing.

Fonts and Typefaces

It comes as a surprise to some people just how much of a difference a font can make. Fonts are so much more than just boring 'clothes' for words: they can define a web site, and a bad choice of font can easily put people off from viewing your movie or staying at your site. Building up a font collection is a relatively easy task as the Internet holds many free font repositories, and there are hundreds of font collections on CD that can be found lurking in computer store bargain bins.

> *Warning: A lot of people don't realize that fonts, like images, are usually copyrighted. If you find a font that you like and you want to use it on your site, or in your movies, it's always best to check the copyright on the font and get the permission, or buy a license, to use the font. The easiest way to get around this is to use system fonts that you know are copyright free, or just create your own, although this latter option is not as simple as it sounds!*

One of the advantages of Flash is that it's not as fussy as HTML when it comes to fonts. While HTML supports the standard fonts - Arial, Times New Roman and Courier (and a few other differing fonts on Macs and PCs) - if you use some more 'exotic' fonts in HTML, these will just be substituted for one of the standard types, robbing you of the effect that you sought after spending so long choosing the perfect typeface. It is possible to embed a font in an HTML document, but again, Macs and PCs differ in the fonts they use, and this also makes your files slower to completely download.

There are two ways to get over these obstacles in Flash. The first way is to convert the font to a graphic symbol, although this means that the text part of the object can no longer be edited or selected. The other method is to *embed the font within the movie*. Flash will automatically include embeddable fonts in your movies when you publish them from the FLA file.

Flash will also work with True type, Postscript Type 1, Bitmap fonts (Macintosh), and Device Fonts.

Working with Device Fonts

Of the four font types mentioned above, the first three are embedded into a Flash movie, bulking up its SWF file size. The fourth type, **device fonts**, will not be embedded, so the file size is much smaller. When you use a device font, Flash will search the computer that your movie is being played on for a suitable font, and then use that to display your text.

Flash comes with three device fonts, and you can identify a device font in your font list because the names start with an _ (underscore):

The standard device fonts are:

- sans (will display as similar to Arial or Helvetica)

- serif (will display as similar to Times Roman)

- typewriter (will display as similar to Courier)

Be sure to either select the font from your font list when you first use it, or have **Use Device Fonts** checked in the **Text Options** tab:

Working with Text

In Flash, you have many of the same commands at your disposal that you find in a word-processing program. We covered the **Character** panel earlier, but there are two more panels associated with text.

The **Paragraph** panel allows you to change the layout and justification of your text with tools that will be familiar to most computer users.

You can select an entire block and align all the text a certain way, or you can select certain lines within the text block and have them aligned and spaced differently.

You can change text to be any solid color and still remain as editable text, but to make any more complicated effects, the text must be broken apart and converted to graphics. This will increase file size, but it does mean you can give your text some pretty interesting effects:

We'll be looking at the **Text Options** panel later in the book, when we learn how to use text boxes for user input and interaction.

Finally in this chapter, let's work on our case study exercise.

Case Study

In the last chapter, we created the static image for our spinner, using a collection of little red circles. Here, we're going to further enhance our interface's graphics using the techniques that we covered in this chapter. We'll create the basis for some sexier buttons, and we'll make the spinner better, too.

Creating Beauteous Buttons

First, we need a nice graphic device to jazz up the interface a little. Here, we'll use a radial gradient on some circles to produce some convincing spheres that will act as focal points for our movie's buttons..

1. Open up your case study movie from the end of the last chapter.

Remember the spinner that created in the previous chapter's final exercise? Now we're going to convert its center main circle to a sphere.

2. Select the central red circle from your existing spinner graphic and copy and paste a new copy of it on to the stage.

3. Open up the **Mixer** tab and open up its **Fill Color** palette:

4. From here, select the red radial gradient from the bottom of the window:

5. Now go to the **Fill** tab to bring up the gradient range bar for your radial gradient. We're going to add some more colors to the gradient to make it more lively:

6. Click on the **Save** icon to create a new gradient, and make sure you click on this new gradient at the bottom of the **Swatches** panel (this'll ensure you don't overwrite the original red radial gradient).

7. Back on the **Fill** tab, add two new paint buckets on either side of the center point as you see here:

    Now we just need to tweak the colors on the bar.

8. To the farthest left, we want to change that red to white to simulate a light source. Select the left-most red paint bucket, then click the color palette to the right of the range bar and choose white to bleach out that paint bucket:

9. Now change the lighter red (the second-left paint bucket) to a full bright red color and move the bucket slightly to the left so that we can have more red in our fill:

10. Now select the Paint Bucket in the Toolbox and fill the copy of the circle that you pasted earlier with this gradient fill. Click on the top-left part of the circle for the best effect:

    We want to use this sphere later, so let's save it as a symbol in the library.

11. Convert the sphere to a graphic symbol and save it as '**Button Base**' in the library's **Main Buttons** folder:

Now that we have the button base, let's create four specific button symbols based on it in the library - one for each of the **Clients**, **Contact**, **Home** and **Services** buttons.

Creating the Four Buttons

1. In the library, right-click on the **Button Base** symbol to bring up the context-sensitive menu.

2. Click on the **Duplicate** option. In the resulting dialog box, make sure that the **Button** behavior option is selected, and name the copy **Clients Button**:

    It's important that you add the **Button** part to the name. Flash won't let us create symbols with the same name in the library.

3. Now repeat the duplication of the **Button Base** symbol three more times, creating three *more* buttons called:

    *   Contact Button

    *   Home Button

    *   Services Button

You'll now have all four new button symbols added to your library:

We've now got the spherical basis for each of the buttons that we'll finesse later in the book.

Now we're going to make the spinner look a little more interesting, too.

Enhancing the Spinner using Alpha Settings

All we're going to do here is change the **transparency** (Alpha settings) on each circle around the edge of the center circle.

1. If it's not still open, bring up the **Mixer** panel. This is where you'll be able to change the Alpha settings for the component circles of your spinner.

2. Select the largest circle on the edge of the main inner circle and set its Alpha to 70%:

3.   Now select the second largest circle and set the Alpha to 60%.

4.   Reduce all the others just like you did above, reducing the Alpha setting in 10% increments. By the time you've finished, the smallest circle should have an Alpha setting of 20%.

5.   Now perform the same steps for the small circles on the opposite side of the central circle: 70% Alpha for the large circle, 20% for the smallest.

6.   Select the main inner circle and delete it:

We're going to use the spinner in combination with the three-dimensional looking sphere we created a little while back, so we don't need the central guide circle any more.

Finally, we want to save the spinner as a symbol for reuse.

7.   Select all of the circles that make up the spinner at once, and convert them to a graphic symbol called '**Button Dots**' in the library's **Main Buttons** folder:

8.   Save your movie.

We'll be returning to this case study at the end of the next chapter.

Summary

In this chapter, we've examined some general Flash features, all of which are targeted at helping you make the objects in your movies look more effective.

We saw that:

- There's a palette of '**web-safe**' colors that we can always rely on to render properly in any browser in the known universe

- We can create our own **custom colors**, and have great control over their constituent colors

- We can use **hex** values to match and amend colors

- **Gradients** can bring flat objects to life, and we can create, modify and save our own customized gradients and color sets

- **Gradient fills** are infinitely 'tunable' once we've applied them to an object

- We can import, trace and optimize **bitmap images** for use in our movies - even though there can be a file size penalty to be aware of

In the next chapter, we're going to focus on animation and put more detail onto the sketch that we drew in the first chapter when we built that simple animated mushroom.

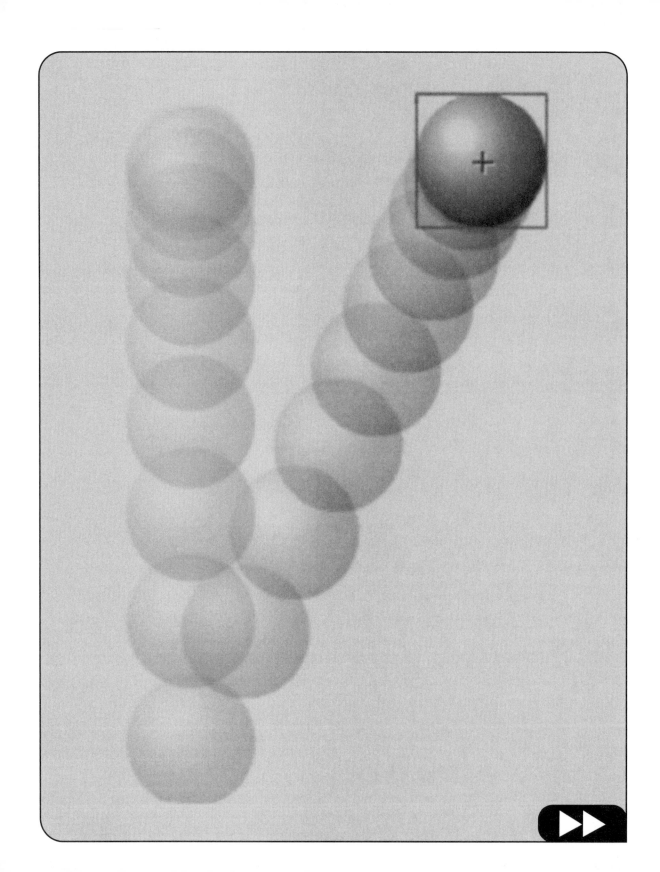

6 Motion Tweening

What we'll cover in this chapter:

♦ **Motion tweening** - the art of moving objects around in your movies and animating them convincingly

♦ How to scale, rotate, fade and change objects' color as they move

♦ Making objects appear to accelerate and decelerate using **easing**

♦ Using **onion skinning** to view multiple frames simultaneously - this helps you make convincing animations

♦ Creating **motion paths** for your moving objects to follow

▶

The five preceding chapters have immersed us in a number of different aspects of Flash: its basic layout, its tools, how it uses symbols, and color. We're now going to start combining these different elements in some more sophisticated ways, giving you plenty of opportunity to test things out and - of course - practice, practice, practice. This is a big chapter, and an important one - as well as learning about motion tweens, we'll also apply all that we've learned so far in a substantial case study exercise.

The next step we're going to take is to return to the subject of animation, which we touched upon briefly in the first chapter when we encountered an animatronic mushroom.

Animation Revisited

As you'll no doubt recall from the first chapter, Flash animation is based on the simple principle of representing change over time. When Flash 'tweens', it draws the frames 'in-between' two significant moments of action, which are themselves defined by the contents of keyframes. The replayed sequence of 'keyframe, in-between frames, keyframe' is the essence of a Flash animation.

There are really two different types of animation in Flash: the **shape tween** that we used to make our mushroom grow, and the **motion tween**. A *shape* tween is a *morphing* operation, where the original object is *transmogrified* into a different object, and a motion tween is the representation of an object *moving* around the stage:

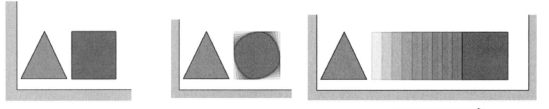

Shape Tween:

Motion Tween:

square morphs into circle over time

square migrates across the stage over time

In this chapter, we're going to focus on motion tweens, and in the next chapter we'll look at shape tweening in more detail.

Motion Tweening

Motion tweening, put simply, is moving an object from Point A on the stage to Point B on the stage. Motion tweens will only work on symbols or grouped shapes.

Here's an example:

Simple Movement with Motion Tweening

1. In a fresh movie, draw a square, select the fill and the outline together, and group them. Place the grouped shape on the left-hand side of the stage.

2. In the timeline, insert a keyframe at frame **30** (*F6*).

3. In the new keyframe (click on the frame in the timeline if it's not currently selected), move the grouped shape to the far *right*-hand side of the stage:

4. Now go back to the timeline and click on any frame between 1 and 29.

5. Bring up the **Frame** tab of the Instance panel and select **Motion** from the **Tweening** drop-down menu:

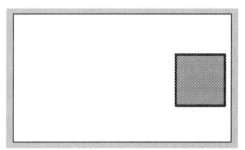

Notice that Flash has drawn an arrow-headed line from frame 1 to frame 29 and colored in the frames:

As with our shape tween in the first chapter, the arrow indicates the length of the tween frame 1 through frame 29. Here, the tweened frames are colored blue to indicate a motion tween.

If you see a *dotted* line instead of the arrow-headed version, it means that there is a motion tween between the frames, but it's not executing properly:

This is an indication that there's something wrong with the events in the timeline, meaning that Flash can't construct the tween successfully.

You may, for example, be trying to motion tween *ungrouped* shapes, which cannot be tweened. Alternatively, make sure that you haven't added extra keyframes or objects that are disrupting the motion, and if you still can't see where you've gone wrong, don't be afraid to delete the whole layer and start over from scratch.

6. Test the movie and watch the object move from the left to the right.

    You might be thinking that you want the objects in your animations to do more than just move from A to B. You might even be thinking that this plain vanilla motion tween looks kind of wooden and mechanical. Well, through using some of the more sophisticated features of motion tweening you can make your objects change size, spin round, move in complex patterns, and move more convincingly. Let's look at these features now.

Scaling Objects in Motion Tweens

The first thing we're going to do is scale our object - change its size - as it moves across the stage. Scaling an object using a motion tween is not the same as the shape tweening, or morphing, that we did in the first chapter when we made the mushroom grow. In a scaled shape tween, the shape itself remains the same: only its size changes.

Tweening Simultaneous Motion and Scaling

1. In the same movie that we've just been working on, click on frame 1 on the timeline.

2. If it's not already displayed on the screen, bring up the **Frame** panel now.

    Notice that the tween **Scale** field is already checked.

This is always checked by default and there is no real reason to uncheck it. **Tween scaling** will allow you to progressively change the size of your object over the duration of your animation. With tween scaling turned off in our current test movie, the square would remain at its original size for 29 frames, and then suddenly jump to its new size in frame 30. This will look very abrupt, and this is not the staccato effect we want here.

We know that the tween scaling option is turned on, so let's scale our tweened square so that it'll make use of the default tween scaling feature.

3. Go back to the stage and, still at frame 1, ensure the square is selected.

4. Bring up the scaling controls from the **Modify > Transform > Scale** menu, or use the **Scale** button in the Toolbox's **Options** pane.

    The selected object will now have a dotted box around it with six scaling selection handles:

5. Grab the lower right-hand corner handle and use it to scale the object down to about half its original size.

6. Now click on frame 30 on the timeline, where the motion tweened square is located at the right side of the stage. This time, scale the square *up* by about a half, using the bottom left handle to do the scaling.

7. Test the movie, and you'll see the square gradually grow larger from frame 1 to 30 as it passes across the stage.

8. To see exactly what the tween **Scale** option does for your animation, go back to frame 1 and turn it off in the **Frame** panel by unchecking the box. Now re-test the movie and notice the migrating square's sudden change in size when the playhead hits frame 30. With the tween scaling option turned *on*, Flash is doing all the hard work in 'joining the dots' of the animation, creating a relatively smooth and gradual motion and growth effect.

Motion tweening also allows us to spin objects round and round as they move on their path. Again, this is fairly straightforward. Here's how...

Motion and Rotation

1. On the **Frame** panel, turn tween scaling back on.

2. Now click on the arrow next to the **Rotate** box and take a look at the resulting menu:

You can chose to rotate an object clockwise, counterclockwise, or not at all. The value in the (currently grayed-out) box to the right of the **Rotate** menu controls how many times, if any, an object will rotate in the selected direction.

You'll see that you currently have no rotation selected - let's change that.

3. Click on frame 1 in the timeline and then select CW (clockwise) in the **Rotate** drop down menu. Change the number of times to be rotated from 0 to 3:

4. Test the movie again, and now you'll see the object rotates clockwise three times during its movement across the stage.

   This is OK for a start, but we can also customize the rotation to achieve a more interesting effect. For instance, we can change the *center point* around which the square rotates.

5. In the keyframe at frame 1, draw a box around the grouped square shape to select it, and then choose the **Modify > Transform > Edit Center** menu option.

   You'll see a thick cross appear in the center of the shape:

   This shows you the position of the currently-defined center point of the shape. This is the point that Flash will use as the center of rotation and, by default, Flash will always position the center-point slap bang in the middle of the object. This applies both to grouped shapes and to symbols.

6. Click on the thick cross and drag it to a different position on the square - we've put ours at the bottom-middle.

7. Play the movie again, and notice the difference in the movement. This time, the square seems to have some *weight* that's governing the rotating motion. Experiment with the center point in different locations, and see the effect that this has on your square's style.

For further variation, you can try placing the center point *outside* the square:

If you play your movie now, the square will rotate in bigger, weightier arcs. This makes us think about maybe animating some amusement park rides or martial arts equipment...

Back to reality. The ability to rotate objects about different center points helps us to imbue our objects with character and individuality - essentially, with characteristics that mimic how things move in the real world. This is one of the secrets of really convincing animation. Flash has other features to help us here. One of them is easing.

Easing

If you need another way to add a touch of real world physics to your Flash animation, you can use the **easing** feature on motion tweens to make an object move more naturally. Easing is essentially a way of controlling the apparent **acceleration** and **deceleration** of the motion-tweened object.

If you look just above the **Rotation** field on the **Frame** tab you'll see another field called **Easing**:

Easing is set to **0** by default. On this setting motion-tweened objects will move at a constant speed - as they have in the motion tweens we've created so far. By entering a figure in the **Easing** box, you can make your tweened objects start slowly and *accelerate* (**easing in**), or start quickly and *decelerate* (**easing out**).

Easing runs on a scale of -100 to 0 for Easing In and from 0 to 100 for Easing Out.

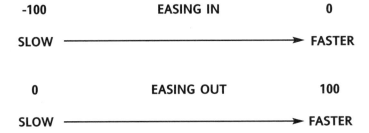

-100   **EASING IN**   **0**

SLOW ──────────────────────▶ FASTER

0   **EASING OUT**   **100**

SLOW ──────────────────────▶ FASTER

To illustrate how easing can be used effectively, we're going to create an animation of a bouncing ball.

Easing a Bouncing Ball

First, we need a ball...

1. Open a new movie. Rename its default layer 'Standard Ball'.

2. Using the Oval tool and a suitable radial gradient fill, create a small strokeless sphere on the 'Standard Ball' layer, and then covert it to a graphic symbol called 'Bad Ball'.

3. Place this ball at the top left of your stage:

4. Now add keyframes at frames 10 and 20.

5. Next, click on keyframe 10 and move the ball to the bottom of the stage. (Remember that by holding **Shift** you can ensure the ball will drop in a straight line.) If you click on keyframe 20 you'll see the ball is still at the top of the stage. We now have three positions for the ball:

    -   'top of the drop' (frame 1)

    -   'bottom of the drop' (frame 10)

    -   'top of the bounce' (frame 20)

    The next step is to animate the bounce.

6. Add a motion tween between frames 1 to 10, and then another between frames 10 to 20. These two tweens animate the fall and the bounce of the ball respectively.

    > *You can select both sections by clicking on the timeline between frames 1 and 10, holding down the Shift key, and then clicking on the timeline between frames 10 and 20. With both sets of frames selected, you can add both motion tweens at once from the Instance panel's Frame tab.*

    Whichever way you add the two motion tweens, your timeline should now look like this:

7. Test your movie.

    You'll see that it kind of drops and bounces - but the movement is to uniform to *really* resemble a bouncing ball, isn't it?

    Let's add another ball to our animation - and try and make it act more realistically under the influence of gravity.

8. Add a new layer to your movie and rename it 'Eased Ball'.

9. Create a new graphic symbol on this new layer, consisting of another sphere: a different color to the last one, but about the same size. Call this symbol 'Good Ball'.

10. On the new layer, repeat the steps you took with the previous ball: click on keyframe 1 and place your new ball at the top of the stage next to the original

ball; create keyframes at frames 10 and 20; move the new ball to the bottom of the stage at keyframe 10, and then add two motion tweens to make it bounce.

11. Test your movie and verify that both balls drop and bounce in the same way:

Now we can add some easing to the second ball.

12. Making sure you're working on the 'Eased Ball' layer, select keyframe 1 and use the box on the **Frame** tab to set the easing to -100 (that's 'minus' 100). You can do this with the slider or by keying the value in. This easing value will only apply to the first motion tween on the timeline.

    Remember, this is the most extreme 'easing in' value: the ball will start slowly and accelerate as it approaches frame 10 - the 'bottom of the stage position'. This will make the ball appear to accelerate as it falls to the bottom of the stage.

13. At keyframe 10, set the easing (out) value to **100** - the maximum. This will make the ball *accelerate* out of the bounce, and *slow down* as it reaches the top of the bounce.

14. Test your movie.

    The 'Good Ball' will now look more like a real ball - speeding up as it falls (easing in) and slowing down as it rises (easing out). This is a good way of mimicking the effects of gravity on animated objects: you just need to think how the object would behave in the real world, and add the appropriate easing to the motion tween.

> *Remember: ease in to speed up, ease out to slow down.*

It's also important to note that you can only specify easing values *once* on any single motion tween. To make an object speed up *and* slow down, as in the example above, *two* motion tweens are needed. Each motion tween has its own easing setting, so for every change of speed you want your object to have you *must* create a separate motion tween.

> *Another thing to keep in mind when practicing your animations is that if you want two or more objects to move simultaneously they have to be on separate layers. For example: you can't have two circles in layer 1 with one moving from top to bottom and the other moving from bottom to top: to achieve this, each circle should be in its own layer, with its own separate motion tween. Two objects can move on the same layer provided that each has its own tween at separate points on the timeline.*

Next, we're going to look at some editing options that Flash uses to help us when we're creating tweens.

Fine Tuning Your Animations

When you want to make minor corrections to your animation, or get a sense of the flow and direction of the animated frames, it can be a great help to be able to view more than one frame at once. Flash's **Onion Skin** tool allows you to do just this - and there's also a feature that lets you *edit* more than one frame at a time.

Onion Skins

Using onion skins allows you to work as if you were drawing each frame on a sheet of tracing paper and piling them on top of each other as you worked. The term 'onion skin' comes from the days when traditional cel-based animators used transparent onion paper to ensure that the frame they were drawing followed on correctly from the previous one. Being able to see the outlines of the previous drawing through the semi-transparent paper meant that they could better gauge changes of position, acceleration, and so on over time.

In Flash, onion-skinning is freed from the tyranny of shuffling paper sheets, and wrapped up instead inside a couple of buttons in the bottom left corner of your timeline:

Onion Skin   Onion Skin   Edit Multiple   Modify Onion
              Outlines   Frames   Markers

You may never have used them before, but they'll prove to be very useful as your Flash career develops.

So how is onion skinning used? Well, go back to your animation of the two bouncing balls. If you click on the onion skin button, the transitional world of the motion tween will start to reveal itself:

There're a couple of things to notice here.

Firstly, as the playhead is on frame 1, we see both balls in all their glory, clearly defined at the top of the drop. But we can also see the ghostly presence of each of the balls at subsequent stages of the drop. Note that the appearance of each ball is slightly different in the ghosted frames: this is because one has easing and the other one does not.

The second important thing to notice is the change up on the timeline - two little markers have appeared, and they're spanning frames 1 to 3:

Onion Markers

The onion markers define the number of frames that will be ghosted in around the frame that the playhead is currently on.

If you click on the right-most marker and drag it off to frame 20, you'll see that you now get a preview of *all* of the movie's frames:

By clicking and dragging the markers, you can alter the range of onion-skinned frames.

If you find that the density of ghosted frames in the onion-skinned view is affecting the clarity of your vision, it's possible to just view the ghosted *outlines* of the animated frames. You get access to this feature by clicking on the **Onion Skin Outlines** button:

You can see here that for the eased version of the ball, there's a cluster of tightly-packed frames at the top of the drop, and only a few at the bottom of the bounce. To see things even more clearly, turn off the **Onion Skin Outlines** option, click on frame 20 and drag the 'finish position' version of the ball away to the right:

Now you can see the uninterrupted flight of the ball without the 'down' and 'up' legs being superimposed on each other. Note also that Flash has automatically recalculated and re-rendered all the in-between frames. If you test the movie now, you'll see that moving the 'final position' image has resulted in a new flight path: onion skinning is an excellent way of seeing just what effect your amendments will have on the finished movie.

Let's just consider those clusters of frames again. The density of frames shown by the onion skinning is greater at the start of the drop and at the top of the bounce, and smaller at the bottom of the bounce. This is because when we apply the easing option, Flash uses a tighter time-clustering of frames to simulate slow motion, and a looser clustering to represent high speed. This can be a little counter-intuitive at first, until you realize that the apparent speed of an object is determined by a combination of the number of frames *and* the frame rate. The more frames it takes for an object to move, the slower the apparent motion will be on the screen. When your brain 'sees' only a few images within a fixed timeframe, it 'fills in the blanks' and figures that the object must be moving *fast*. If your brain gets the chance to register more images (frames) in that fixed timeframe, it figures "I'm seeing a lot of intermediate images here. This object must be moving *slow*."

Let's get an overview of the other onion skinning options we have.

The **Modify Onion Markers** button...

...allows you to alter the way your markers and onion skins appear on the timeline and the stage. If you want the markers to always be shown on the timeline (even when you aren't using onion skins) then select **Always Show Markers** from the **Modify Onion Markers** menu:

The **Anchor Onion** option, when checked, simply prevents your markers from moving as you move the playhead. This means that you only see the frames of your movie that are *within* the markers as you move the playhead. If this option is *not* checked and you move the playhead along the timeline, the markers move with the playhead to show you the onion skins in the section you are viewing.

Selecting the **Onion 2**, **Onion 5**, or **Onion All** from the menu moves the markers to show varying numbers of onion skinned frames. For example, **Onion 2** will show you the frame you're on, plus *two* onion skinned frames on either side.

It's important to note that the onion skin effect does *not* export with your movie, and is never seen by the end user. If you want to create an onion skin effect for the user then you have to manually create it frame by frame (sorry about that...).

Onion skinning allows us to *view* multiple frames simultaneously, but Flash also has a feature that lets us *edit* multiple frames.

Editing Multiple Frames

Being able to edit several frames all at once can be extremely useful - provided that you take care!

Imagine that you decide that everything on your bouncing ball animation needs to be moved to the right to accommodate another graphical element on the left of the stage. Thanks to the **Edit Multiple Frames** feature this can be done in one hit rather than having to alter every single frame.

In your bouncing balls movie, click on the **Edit Multiple Frames** button:

Now adjust your onion skin markers so that all the *frames* in your animation are selected:

Making sure that none of the objects on the stage are currently selected, use the **Edit > Select All** menu option to select everything on the stage.

Both of the balls, at all phases of their existence, will now be selected:

Note that if you'd chosen the **Edit > Select All** menu option *without* having first chosen the **Edit Multiple Frames** tool, only the objects in the current keyframe would have been selected. Using **Edit Multiple Frames**, we pick up *everything* within the bounds of the onion markers.

Now you can drag *all* of the selected content across the stage to its new position:

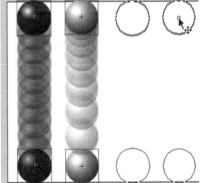

This option can save you real pain, as it means that you don't have to worry about precisely repositioning everything frame by frame. Another example of getting Flash to do our work for us.

Motion tweening is not just limited to controlling the movement of objects. It can also be used to make them fade in, fade out and change color. Let's see how.

Motion Tweening Effects

If you want to make an object slowly disappear and reappear, there are two ways you can do it in the motion tweening context: changing an object's **alpha** value, or changing its **tint**. *Alpha*, as we've mentioned before, is really 'transparency', and *tint* affects an object's color characteristics.

Each of these two attributes possess different qualities and it's really your call on which one you use and when. Let's work through examples with both of them, starting with alpha, and then you can decide for yourself.

Fading with Alpha

1. In a shiny new movie, create a new graphic symbol - we've used a simple filled square here. Make sure your movie's background color is set to white.

2. Place the graphic symbol on the stage in the default keyframe at frame 1, and then insert new keyframes at frame 15 and frame 30:

3. Click on frame 15, select the symbol, and go to the **Effect** tab on the **Instance** panel.

Here, hidden away in the drop-down list, are the different effects that you can apply to your symbol instance on the stage:

4. Select **Alpha** from the pull-down menu, and then set the Alpha slider to **0%**. This setting will render the symbol instance totally transparent in the keyframe at frame 15:

5. Now simply add two separate motion tweens from frames 1 to 15, and frames 15 to 30 respectively:

When you test your movie you'll see the object fade out and fade in. All that's happening here is that we're gradually increasing and decreasing the square's level of transparency. When we get to frame 15, where the transparency is 100% (invisible), we're looking clean through the square and seeing the movie background. Our square doesn't actually turn white. The tween from frames 15 to 30 fades the square back up, gradually obscuring the movie background again.

Now we'll achieve the same end result again, but using the tint approach.

Fading with Tint

Use the same movie you created in the previous exercise, retaining the white movie background.

1. Insert a new layer.

2. Place a second instance of your graphic symbol on the stage at frame 1 in the new layer, and again insert keyframes at frame 15 and frame 30.

3. At keyframe 15 select the second symbol and open the **Effect** tab again.

4. This time, select Tint from the pull-down menu.

   Unlike alpha, tint has a percentage value *and* RGB values. With tint, you're effectively overlaying an opaque layer of color on top of the object's existing color. The parameters of the **Tint** effect control the actual color used and its opacity.

5. Set the tint's opacity value to 100% and choose white from the **Tint Color** box.

When you choose white, notice that the RGB values are all set to equal 255, indicating that all the constituent colors of (electronic) white are present at full strength. Each of the three R, G and B boxes has their own slider, which lets you control the amount of each base color in the tint color, and if you prefer to use Hex values to select your colors you can open up the palette and type in the appropriate value in the Hex field.

By setting our values to 100% and 'white', we're saying to Flash "at this frame, I want an overlay of pure white that's completely opaque over the top of the symbol":

6. Now simply add motion tweens from frames 1 to 15 and frames 15 to 30.

7. Play the movie.

Again, you'll see the object fade out and in as previous page, just as before, but this time the mechanism underlying this effect is different. The *alpha* effect literally makes the object disappear by decreasing its opacity and making it transparent, while the *tint* effect changes the color of the object itself. The great thing about alpha fades is that you don't have to make sure that the color of your object changes to match the background - the background color shows through naturally. However, the trade off is that this process is more CPU intensive - it's harder for computers to process, and is a bit slower. Using tint is a little more involved because of the need to alter the color settings, especially if you have multicolored objects and backgrounds.

Alpha is the easy way out as far as fading is concerned, but tint also allows you to change the colors of your objects during your animation.

Animating a Color Change

Let's take a look at how to change the color of an object during a motion tween.

Changing Object Color mid-Tween

In this example, we'll move an object (some text) across the stage and change its color as it moves.

1. In a new movie, start by creating some text to apply the color effect to. You can use any font, but a large blocky sans serif font (Arial Black, here, at 48 points) will best illustrate the effect. Use black for the text color:

   FLASH

2. Select the text on the stage and convert it into a graphic symbol. Remember, only symbols (movie clips, buttons and graphics) and grouped objects can be motion tweened.

3. Place the symbol on the stage at frame 1 (if it isn't already there) and create three more keyframes at frames 10, 20 and 30:

4. At keyframe 10, select the symbol and bring up the **Effect** tab.

5. Select **Tint** from the drop down menu and change the tint amount to 100%. Then, using the color selection palette, change the color to red.

6. Repeat this procedure at keyframe 20, but selecting *green* as the tint, and at keyframe 30, this time selecting *blue* as the color. Now your text should be red at keyframe 10, green at keyframe 20 and blue at keyframe 30, and if you test the movie you'll see it change color in jumps.

7. Last but not least, add three motion tweens to the timeline: between frames 1 and 10, 10 and 20, and 20 and 30:

8. Now if you test your movie you should see your text undergo a chameleon-like constant color-change.

Now you could try clicking on each of the keyframes in succession and dragging each particular instance to a different position on the stage (doing this with onion skinning turned on will give you some groovy psychedelic effects). If you do this and then play the movie, you can see the basis for some more experimentation, and this also shows that the tint (and alpha) effects can be combined with *actual* motion around the stage.

There's something else of real significance here: although we only had a single copy of the graphic symbol containing our text on the stage, we were able to change its color in three different keyframes, using the **Tint** option on the **Effect** tab. What's more, we're able to drag each of the different colored versions of the text around on the stage independently. The reason that we can do this is that each different colored version of the text in the different keyframes is effectively treated as a separate *instance* of the graphic symbol: all of the instances have the original symbol as their *base*, but each instance has *properties* that we can change independently of the underlying symbol. We've already seen how you can change individual instance's tint and alpha, but you can also scale, skew, and rotate instances - all without affecting the underlying symbol. If you edit the underlying symbol in Edit Symbols mode, however, these changes will ripple through to *all* of the instances - although any instance *properties* you've set (tint, alpha etc.) will be retained:

This facility gives us a tremendous amount of flexibility and power in the way that we use symbols.

So, you can now make your objects grow, shrink, spin round, speed up, slow down, disappear and change color - but they're still all moving in straight lines. This chapter promised to get your objects moving in complex patterns like curves, loops and zigzags. To add these features to your animation, you need to learn to use motion guides.

Motion Guides

A motion guide is basically a path that you draw for an object to follow during a motion tween. The motion guide is invisible outside of the authoring environment, and it sits on a special layer underneath the object you're tweening. How do they work? Well, let's create a motion guide of our own and see.

Using Motion Guides

1. Before you start creating, make sure the 'snap' feature is on by going to the **View > Snap to Objects** menu and making sure that the option is checked: we want our drawn object to snap crisply to an underlying motion guide.

2. Create a simple new graphic symbol of any type - this'll be the object that we motion tween. We've used a small fish:

3. Insert your symbol into the default keyframe at frame 1 and rename the default layer '**Fish**'.

4. Next, select frame 30 and insert a new keyframe.

5. Now make sure you've got the 'Fish' layer selected, and use the **Insert > Motion Guide** menu option to create a guide layer or, alternatively, click on the Add Guide Layer button at the bottom of the layers window:

   The motion guide layer will automatically appear above the current layer, and it will inherit the name of the layer that it's a guide for, prefixing this with the helpful word 'Guide' and a tiny icon of a bouncing ball - the signifier for a guide layer:

So, the motion guide has its own layer, and it's on this layer that we will draw the motion path that we want our object to follow. A motion path simply consists of a drawn line.

6. Click on the guide layer to select it, and then use the Pencil tool to draw the path that you want your object to follow. Draw the path at the location on the stage where the action will take place - although you can always move it later if you want to.

The motion path itself can be any length or shape you like: up, down, side to side, zigzag, curves, loops - just so long as it's a continuous line with no gaps. You don't have to use the Pencil tool - the Line tool, Pen tool, Brush tool, and even unfilled rectangles and circles can all act as motion guide shapes. The important thing is that you have a *line* on the guide layer.

We've used a simple line to start with:

Remember that you don't need to worry about the color of the path because it will not be seen in the final exported movie. Also, you can treat the line just like any other object: you can resize it, trim it, skew it and so forth once you've selected it on the guide layer.

Now for the exciting part: making the object travel along the motion guide. To do this, you need to snap the object to the start and end points of the motion path - that's why we've got two keyframes: one for where the guided motion tween will start, and one at the end of the action.

7. Lock the guide layer so that you don't accidentally click on the guide line.

8. In the first frame on the 'Fish' layer, grab the graphic symbol instance at its center and drag it over to the left end of the motion guide.

As you'd expect with snapping turned on, the 'dragging circle' at the symbol's center point will 'pop' when it's snapping to the line:

9. In the second keyframe at frame 30, pick up the fish and drag it to the right-hand end of the motion path and drop it when it snaps.

   You now have the fish attached to the line in the desired start and end positions. Now all we have to do is make the movement happen!

10. Still on the object layer, select a frame between 1 and 30 and add a motion tween. Then test your movie and watch your object move along the motion path.

Although motion guides are fairly simple to create, getting the object to snap correctly to the guide takes time to get used to and not getting the object snapped properly is a common problem. So practice and don't get discouraged.

> *The motion guide must be the same length as the timeline for the object that's being guided.*

For example: if the animation is 30 frames long, the guide layer's timeline has to be 30 frames long too. In this exercise you inserted a keyframe at frame 30 on the object layer and then added the motion guide layer. Flash automatically added 30 frames to the guide layer to match the 'Fish' layer that the guide layer was spawned from: Flash is intelligent enough to look at the contents of the layer and work out where to put the keyframes in the guide layer - provided that you decide how long the actual animation will take and mark its boundaries first.

Adding keyframes to the 'Fish' layer *after* creating the motion guide will obviously alter the length of the animation. For example: if we created a new movie and drew an object on the stage in the default keyframe at frame 1, and then immediately added a motion guide layer, the guide layer will only be 1 frame long. If we were then to add a keyframe at frame 30 on the 'object' layer, that layer would be 30 frames long, but the motion guide would remain at a measly 1 frame long. The resulting problem is that the motion guide itself will not exist in frame 30!

You can get around this problem by adding frames to the guide layer, but it's much easier to plan things out, create the animation layer, and then let Flash create an appropriate guide layer when you ask it to.

Motion path effects can produce some really wild results, especially when combined with the other effects we discussed earlier in the chapter. Once you've got the basic idea nailed down, experiment with different color combinations, timeline lengths, and differently-shaped motion paths. The possibilities are endless.

Case Study

In the previous chapters we've been gradually building some components for our Flash web site: you should already have some components in the library - four spherical buttons and a button base, some alpha-faded dots, an 'e-mail us' button, and some graphic symbols containing text:

Now, let's get busy putting some animation into the movie, and marrying all that animation to the objects that we've created previously in the case study movie. If you're feeling weary at this stage, now would probably be a good time to stretch your legs or get a cup of your favorite beverage: the case study exercises in this chapter are quite extensive, and will require some concentration. In these exercises, we're going to be putting together everything we've discussed so far - symbols, motion tweens, motion guides - the whole lot. In doing so, we're going to build some powerful functionality for our case study's web site movie.

First, we're going to create a movie clip that we can use with each of the buttons in our movie: this movie clip will be an animated version of the spinner. We'll create the spinner animation once, and then use it on multiple buttons. When the user runs the mouse over the buttons in the finished movie, this movie clip will play: the spinner graphic will rotate around the button and some button text will pop up and fade out.

Animating the Spinner

1. In your saved Case Study movie, create a new movie clip symbol in the library, and call it '**Spinner**'.

2. At the keyframe in frame 1 of the new movie clip symbol, insert the '**button dots**' graphic symbol you created in the previous chapter:

3. Now insert a new keyframe at frame 20 in the movie clip.

4. Next, add a motion tween between frames 1 and 20. When you add the tween, use the **Frame** tab to set the **Rotate** option to clockwise (**CW**), and type 1 into the **times** box:

On testing this, you should see the dots rotate clockwise once over the 20 frame period.

Next, we're going to start assembling the animated part of the first of our buttons - the **Home** button, which will itself be a movie clip that we embed in the main movie. We'll build this clip using the **Spinner** movie clip symbol and some new components.

Creating the 'Home' Button

1. Create a new movie clip symbol and call it '**Home mc**'. The mc stands for 'movie clip', a common naming convention amongst Flash designers.

2. Rename the movie clip's default layer '**Spinner**' - this is where we'll embed the spinner animation for our button.

3. At frame 1 on the **Spinner** layer, insert the '**Spinner**' movie clip from the library. Ensure that you place the **Spinner** movie clip at the center point of the **Home mc** clip: use the little crosses to guide you.

4. Now add a keyframe at frame 10 so that the spinner animation plays throughout the length of the **Home mc** clip:

In the screenshot here, you can see that we're in Edit Symbols mode inside the **Home mc** clip. The center point cross for the embedded **Spinner** movie clip is shown slightly offset from the cross belonging to the host **Home mc** clip. An instance of the **Spinner** movie clip is now embedded inside the **Home mc** movie clip. When the **Home mc** clip plays, the **Spinner** clip will play inside it.

5. Now add a new layer to the **Home mc** clip, and call it 'Text'. This is the layer where we'll place the basic text that'll appear next to the button.

6. Make sure you have frame 1 of the new **Text** layer selected. From the library, drag out the '**Home**' graphic symbol we created a couple of chapters back, and which consists of some text. Place the **Home** graphic symbol on the **Text** layer at frame 1, positioning it just to the left of the **Spinner** movie clip instance:

7. Click on frame 1 of this **Text** layer and copy it via your favored method (menu, keystrokes, whatever) - we're going to use the same text for a motion tween and fade effect.

8. Add a third layer called 'Text Fade' to house the fading text effect.

9. Click on the keyframe at frame 1 in the new layer, and use the **Edit > Paste in Place** menu option to paste the previously copied frame into it. We want the text in the motion tween to start in the same place as the text on the **Text** layer.

10. Now insert a keyframe at frame 10 of the **Text fade** layer, and move the **Home** graphic in this keyframe to the left, so that it's almost clear of the same word on the **Text** layer:

11. Make sure you have the graphic symbol instance in frame 10 of the **Text Fade** layer selected, then bring up the **Effect** tab and set the instance's alpha to 0%.

    Nearly there - phew!

12. Add a motion tween between frames 1 and 10 of the **Text Fade** layer.

13. While you're still in Edit Symbols mode inside the Home mc clip, press the *Enter* key to preview the clip. You'll see the text on the **Text Fade** layer slip out from under the fixed text on the **Text** layer, fading to nothing as it goes.

14. Now go back into the main movie by clicking on the **Scene 1** icon above the timeline.

15. Back in the main movie, drag an instance of the new **Home mc** movie clip out onto the stage and press *F12* to preview the movie.

When the movie previews, you'll see the **Home mc** clip play, including the animated **Spinner** movie clip that we embedded *inside* **Home mc**. The spinner will spin, and the text will move and fade. This was a tricky little task, but we think you'll agree that the effect is a good one:

Essentially, what we've done in the last two exercises is make a movie clip that embodies part of the animated graphical display that we want for all of our movie's buttons, and we also built the specific animation component for the **Home** button.

Next, we need to create that customized animation functionality for our remaining three buttons - **Clients**, **Contact** and **Services**. The good news is, we don't have to create each one from scratch: we can reuse all the work we just did (sigh of relief...).

Creating Movie Clip Animations for the Remaining Buttons

1. In your case study movie's library, right-click on the **Home mc** movie clip.

2. In the context-sensitive menu, click on the **Duplicate** option, just like you did when you duplicated the spherical button bases in the last chapter. When the dialog box pops up, duplicate the symbol as a movie clip, and call it **Clients mc**.

3. Now do the same thing twice more, creating two additional movie clips called **Contact mc** and **Services mc** respectively.

You'll now have four animated movie clips, one for each of the buttons:

We now have the four distinct movie clip animations we need, but there's a hitch: as these were all duplicated from the **Home mc** clip, they all have identical content - the three layers of animated spinner, fixed text, and fade text. So we need to amend each clip so that the text in each one matches that button's purpose.

It may also have occurred to you that there's another problem: the text inside each of those movie clips says 'Home', and it comes from the graphic symbol that we created way back, when we first started work on our case study's symbols:

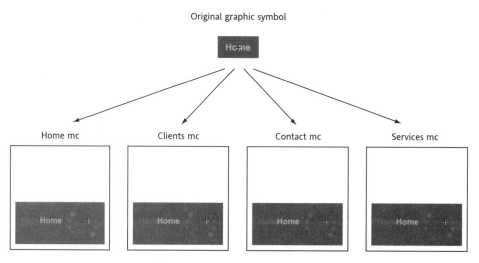

If we edit any instance of the 'Home' text graphic symbol inside each of the four movie clips, we'll be changing the *original* graphic symbol too, and this change will ripple through to all of the other instances of the graphic symbol inside the other movie clips. We need a way to get around this, and - fortunately - Flash has an immensely useful tool to help us here - we can dig down inside a symbol and 'swap' one embedded symbol for another. This means that we can replace the 'Home' text graphic symbol with the appropriate text graphic symbol for that specific button.

Changing Embedded Symbols

Let's start with the **Clients mc** movie clip symbol.

1. Open up your **Clients mc** movie clip in Edit Symbols mode.

2. Select the **Text** layer, and the instance of the **Home** text graphic symbol in keyframe 1 should be highlighted:

3. Now bring up the **Instance** panel.

    Take a close look at the bottom of the panel, and you'll see an icon with a couple of shapes and arrows on it:

    Swap Symbol button

    This is the button that you'll come to love. By clicking on it, we can get Flash to show us a list of the existing symbols in our movie's library. When we select a symbol from the list, Flash will substitute it for the symbol that's currently selected on the stage, freeing us from any worries about altering underlying symbol content. We can swap embedded symbols in and out of our movie freely and cleanly.

4. With the 'Home' graphic symbol instance still selected, click on the **Swap Symbol** button on the Instance tab. You'll see a list box pop up:

    In the center is the scrollable list of all the symbols in our current library, with a black dot and a highlight associated with the symbol that's currently selected on the stage. There's also a thumbnail of the symbol at the top-left.

As we're inside the **Clients mc** movie clip, we want to replace the 'Home' text with the **Clients** graphic symbol.

5. Click on the **Clients** symbol in the list box, check that the preview shows the text you want, and then click on **OK**.

    You'll see that the Home text on the Text layer has been replaced by the text contained in the Clients graphic symbol we just swapped in:

    This looks really fuzzy because there's still an instance of the **Home** text sitting in the same position on the **Text Fade** layer. We need to fix that too.

6. Click on the **Text Fade** layer in the layer window. This will select the **Text** graphic symbol instance in the first keyframe for you (you might find it easier to see if you hide the **Text** layer!).

7. Use the **Swap Symbol** button again and choose the **Clients** graphic symbol from the list box once more.

    We've now replaced two instances of the text, but there's a third instance lurking at the end of the motion tween on the **Text Fade** layer.

8. Click on the keyframe in frame 10 of the **Text Fade** layer. This will select the final text instance, which has **0%** alpha:

9. Use the **Swap Symbol** button again and pull in a third instance of the **Clients** graphic. Note that this instance will inherit the instance properties of the symbol that we just swapped out, and will still have zero alpha.

10. We're done with the text replacement for the **Clients mc** movie clip. Make sure all three layers in the movie clip are visible, then press the *Enter* key to preview the clip. You'll see that it now animates the word **Clients** instead of **Home** - exactly what we wanted.

11. Now repeat the graphic symbol replacement process for the remaining two button movie clips - **Contact mc** and **Services mc**, replacing the **Home** text with the appropriate **Contact** or **Services** graphic symbols. Remember that the key thing to do is to use the Swap Symbol button to replace all three instances of the Home text in each movie clip.

Next, we really see all of this hard graft starting to come together. We're going to embed the customized movie clips we just worked on inside the four spherical button symbols.

Movie Clips Marry Buttons

The effect that we want for our buttons is this: when the user rolls their mouse over the central sphere, the text and spinner animation springs into action, highlighting what the button does. Let's do it.

1. Open up your **Home Button** symbol for editing. At the moment, this button only consists of a red sphere with a single Up state:

2. Rename the button's default layer as **Main Button** - this is where the sphere lives.

3. To bring the button to life, add a new layer to it called **Movie Clip** and move it down underneath the **Main Button** layer:

This layer is where the animated movie clip will go.

4. In the **Main Button** layer, select the **Over** state frame and add a keyframe to it.

5. Select the **Movie Clip** layer and add a keyframe to its **Over** state frame.

6. Now drag an instance of the **Home mc** movie clip out of the library and place it on the stage in the **Movie Clip** layer so that the spinner lines up nicely around the outside of the sphere:

This arrangement means that when the mouse goes over the button in the final movie, the animated movie clip will play. When the mouse *isn't* over the button, only the sphere will be visible.

7. Click out of Edit Symbols mode and back into the main movie. Drag an instance of your newly-enhanced **Home Button** onto the stage, deleting any old instances you have lying around on the stage. In the authoring environment, all that lovely animation is inert, so preview the movie by pressing *F12*.

8. When the movie previews, move the mouse over the button and you'll be rewarded with the animation springing to life.

9. Now repeat these steps by editing the **Clients**, **Contact** and **Services** buttons. In each case:

- Add a new layer to the button, call it **Movie Clip**, and move it below the **Main Button** layer

- Add a keyframe to the **Over** state on the **Main Button** layer

- Add a keyframe to the **Movie Clip** layer's **Over** state

- Drag the relevant movie clip out of the library and line it up over the sphere

- Close the button symbol

Now we need to create a new movie clip called '**Information**'. This is where all of your information about our web site's services, contacts, and clients will reside. Ultimately, the user will be able to access the relevant information by clicking on one of the buttons - but we'll need to learn some ActionScript before we can enable that. For now, we're just going to build the basic movie component that'll eventually be accessed when the user clicks on the the **Services** button.

Creating the Information Movie Clip

1. Create a new movie clip symbol called **Information**.

2. Create two layers in this movie clip called
   Titles and **Info**:

3. At frame 20 of the **Titles** layer, add a new keyframe.

4. On the stage in this keyframe, create a text box with the word '**SERVICES**' in
   and then draw a line underneath the
   box. Use any color combo that you like,
   but make the text about 20 point:

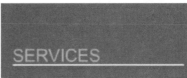

   You don't need to convert this to a symbol as it's always going to be the same
   static content.

5. Now insert a keyframe at frame 25 so that the word display extends across
   the five frames.

6. At frame 20 in the **Info** layer, create a new keyframe and type out the text
   (about 15 point) as shown in the
   screenshot below and line it up
   under the **Services** text:

7. Select the text you just wrote and convert it to a graphic symbol called
   '**Services Text**'.

8. Still on the **Info** layer, select frame 25 and create a new keyframe. This will
   extend the life of the graphic symbol as far as that frame.

9. Select the instance of the **Services Text** symbol at frame 20, open up the
   Effect panel, and reduce the alpha value to **0%**.

> **10.** Add a motion tween between frames 20 and 25 on the **Info** layer. When this part of the movie clip plays in the finished movie, the **Services** text will fade in.

We've now built just about all the pieces of this movie that will use motion tweens. We only have one more task to complete in this chapter that will really pull the movie into shape and start to show you how all the visual components fit together. What we'll do next is create motion guides for our four buttons to run along.

Building the Button's Motion Guides

The effect we want in the finished movie is for the main buttons to roll down onto the screen and line up along the edge of the black part-circle that we created way back:

With that in mind, let's begin!

> **1.** On the main movie stage, add a new layer and call it '**Button - Contact**'. Not surprisingly, this is where our **Contact** button is going to reside.
>
> **2.** On frame 1 in this new layer, drag out your recently turbocharged **Contact Button** symbol and position it in the work area above the movie stage, roughly lined up with the curve of the part-circle:
>
>
>
> Starting the buttons' motion off in the work area will make them look like they're 'falling' into the movie when it's finally exported for viewing.
>
> **3.** Insert a keyframe on the same layer at frame 30. Add a keyframe at frame 30 of the **Background** layer too so that the background persists for the appropriate period.
>
> **4.** Back on the **Button - Contac**t layer, select the **Contact Button** instance at frame 30 and use the **Modify > Transform > Scale and Rotate** menu option to scale the button down by **65%**:

5. Still at frame 30, move the miniaturized button down onto the stage and locate it on the edge of the black circle:

6. Select any frame on the **Button - Contact** layer and use the **Frame** tab to add a motion tween between the button start and end positions. Set the easing to **100%** out:

You might be baffled by one piece of Flash authoring environment behavior: if you come back to this motion tween in the future and want to amend it, you'll find that clicking on the frames where the tween happens will also select the static frames that follow it:

The way to select just the tweened frames is to hold down the Control key, click on the first frame you want and then drag the cursor to the last frame you want to select.

If you play this animation now, you'll see your button come down from outside the movie and slowly fall into place towards the bottom of the black circle. However, we want our moving buttons to follow the outer edge of the circle - which is where a motion guide will help.

7. Add a motion guide layer to the **Button - Contact** layer:

8. Select the guide layer and use a tool of your choice from the Toolbox to draw a path that follows the edge of the circle.

    Try using it in a bright neon color so you can see it better. We used the Circle tool to draw an unfilled circle that matched the curve, and then snipped off the irrelevant parts:

9. Make sure snapping is turned on, and then drag the instance of the symbol in frame 1 and snap it to the motion guide:

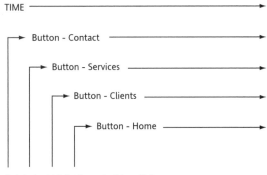

    Now do the same thing at frame 30 and snap the button instance to the line somewhere near the bottom of the black circle.

    If you test the movie now, you'll see the button animates down the edge of the background and slows up until it stops. A nice effect.

    Now we have to duplicate this effect for the remaining three buttons. The overall effect we want in the finished movie is the four buttons rolling down the edge of the circle onto the stage, and then sitting there waiting for the user to roll their mouse over them. To do this, we want to stagger the times when each button starts its journey onto the stage: we start the **Contact** button rolling, wait a while, then start off the **Services** button, and so on:

    It's quite simple to achieve this in Flash - we just put each button on a separate layer and start its motion tweened entrance a few frames later than its predecessor.

TIME ——————————————————————→

→ Button - Contact ————————————→

→ Button - Services ——————————→

→ Button - Clients ——————→

→ Button - Home ——————→

Point at which buttons start to roll down

Animating the Remaining Buttons

Adding these staggered tweens is going to spread the action out along the timeline, so let's make sure that our background lasts long enough to support the action.

1. Use *Control-Click* to select a centrally-placed frame on the **Background** layer, and then insert 30 frames so that the end keyframe winds up in frame 60:

The only problem now is that our **Contact** button will animate and be visible until frame 30, and then it'll disappear, leaving a vast expanse of background with nothing on it. When the movie gets to frame 60 it'll loop back to the beginning and the sequence will start again.

2. To make the button persist on the stage, click on frame 60 in the **Button - Contact** layer and use *F5* to add a frame there. Flash will fill in the frames between 30 and 60 with static images of the button:

The button will now animate into its position at the end of the motion tween (frame 30) and then sit there waiting until the movie loops. You don't need to extend the guide layer, as that only needs to be around for as long as the motion tween sequence lasts.

Now for the layers, keyframes and symbols for the next button - the **Services** button.

3. Click on the top-most guide layer in the layer window and add a new layer called **Button - Services**.

4. Add a keyframe to the **Button - Services** layer at frame 10, and drag an instance of the **Services Button** symbol out of the library, placing it in the work area just above the black part-circle.

5. ***Control-Click*** on frame 40 in the same layer and add another keyframe. In this frame, drag the **Services** button instance to a point just above the **Contact** button, and to its right:

6. Next, add a guide layer for your **Button - Services** layer, and add a keyframe to it at frame 10.

7. Now draw a motion guide around the edge of the black circle again. We copied the motion guide from the **Button - Contact** layer's guide layer, and then used **Edit > Paste in Place** to paste it into the **Services** button's guide layer.

8. Go and grab the instance of the **Services** button that you left sitting in the work area, and drag it until it snaps to the motion guide in frame 10:

9. In frame 40 of the **Button - Services** layer, drag the button instance and snap it to the guide just above the first button:

10. Add a motion tween for the **Services** button between frames 10 and 40, with easing out at 100%.

11. Finally for this button, click on the 'final position' instance of the **Services** button at frame 40 and use the **Modify > Transform > Scale and Rotate** dialog box to scale it down by a factor of **75%**.

OK, we're done on the Services and Contact buttons. If you preview your movie using F12, you'll see the buttons roll down in staggered succession. Time for another coffee before we finish off the last two buttons...

Finishing the Clients and Home Buttons

This exercise is a reprise of the previous one, so we'll run through it a little quicker.

1. Add another layer above the **Services** button's guide layer - call it **Button - Clients**.

2. Now insert a keyframe into the layer at frame 20 and drag an instance of the **Clients Button** symbol out of the library and into the work area at the top of the stage.

3. *Control-Click* at frame 50, add a keyframe, and drag the button instance down beside the black part-circle.

4. Add a guide layer, insert a keyframe at frame 20, and then draw (or copy and paste) the now familiar motion guide.

5. Snap the button to the guide at frames 20 and 50, finishing up with the button a little way up from the **Services** button:

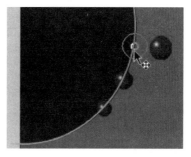

6. Add the motion tween between frames 20 and 50 on the object layer, with 100% easing out again, and scale the instance in frame 50 down to **85%**.

    Now for the last button - the **Home** button. Then you can eat.

7. Add a final layer above the **Clients** button's guide layer and name it **Button - Home**.

8. Now add a keyframe to the layer at frame 30. Pull an instance of the **Home Button** symbol out of the library and drop it on the work area just above the stage.

9. *Control-Click* at frame 60, insert a keyframe, and drag the **Home** button instance down alongside the others.

10. Add a guide layer, with a new keyframe at frame 30, and create the standard motion guide.

11. Snap the button to the guide at frames 30 and 60, resulting in a satisfying four button line-up like this:

12. And finally, create the motion tween between frames 30 and 60, and add the usual full out easing.

You're done! Thanks for sticking with it.

If you play the movie it will roll those buttons down and then loop - we'll fix this looping with a little bit of ActionScript later. If you leave the mouse in the path of the rolling buttons, you'll see each button's Over state trigger the animated movie clips that we embedded in the buttons - the spinner and the text fade.

Summary

We've traveled quite a distance in this chapter, passing through the varied landscape of motion tweening, and ending up in a country where multi-layer motion tweens containing movie clips embedded in symbols happen simultaneously. These case study exercises were important because they started to weld together all the elements that we've seen in the book so far. And they were great practice, too.

In this chapter, we saw that:

◆ **Motion tweening** can move objects around the stage, and we can use **motion paths** to guide the objects and **onion skins** to see multiple frames in the animation

◆ We can alter objects as they move: we can **fade** them into the background, change their **tint**, and scale and rotate them

◆ Using **easing**, we can simulate **acceleration** and **deceleration** for more convincing animation

In the case study:

◆ We saw how to **embed a motion tween inside a symbol**, creating a movie clip that we can reuse elsewhere as often as we like

◆ We created movie clips for each of our four buttons, each one containing a customized animation

◆ We learned how to **swap out symbols** that are embedded inside other movie clip symbols

◆ We built our animated buttons and tweened them onto the stage in staggered steps

Take a rest after all that hard work.

In the next - shorter - chapter, we're going to have some fun with motion tweening's sibling: **shape tweening**.

About our Company

General information about your company.

Home

7 Shape Tweening

What we'll cover in this chapter:

- ◆ **Shape tweening**: morphing shapes into something new, rich and strange, either standing still or moving around

- ◆ **Morphing text** into shapes and vice-versa

- ◆ Using shape hints to override Flash's default shape tweening behavior

Now that you've seen what motion tweening can do and experienced the power of Flash as an animation workhorse, it's time to climb the next rung on the ladder. So far, you can move a shape around the stage, but it will still be the same shape at the end of the animation. By the close of this chapter, you'll be able start the race with a tortoise and finish it with a hare, though Darwinians might not be too happy with what happens in between.

Shape Tweens

Shape tweening is similar in concept to its motion tween counterpart, and it's just as easy, but the results are often more impressive.

The basic idea is that at point A in time you have one object, and at a later point B you have another object: between the two points you have a gradual shape-shifting transformation from object A to object B. Like this, for example:

You've already encountered shape tweening in the first chapter of the book, where you made a mushroom grow, and in this chapter you'll be expanding and adding detail to that knowledge, and fleshing out the whys and hows of shape tweening.

How Shape Tweens Work

Shape tweens work just like motion tweens, in the sense that you provide a start point in one keyframe and a finish point in another, and Flash fills the intervening frames. And like motion tweens, it's advisable to only have one shape tween going on at any time on a layer - this way, you get more predictable results and less mayhem on the stage. Of course, if you want to shape tween multiple objects into one object at the same time, the objects will have to be on the same layer. It's really a question of necessity: if you need your tweens to interact with each other, they'll need to be on the same layer, but if they don't interact, then keep them on separate layers.

The most important thing to remember when creating shape tweens is that, unlike motion tweens, shape tweens must involve **shapes** and *not* groups or symbols. For a shape tween to work, it must be able to change the basic attributes - the stroke and fill - so that it can morph the original shape into something else. The simplest way to ensure that all of the elements you want to shape tween are 'shape tweenable' is to select all of the objects and use the **Modify > Break Apart** command to ensure they're broken down into their constituent elements.

Let's play.

Squaring the Circle

We'll set up a basic shape tween to start off with, and then play around with it to understand the finer points of tweening. The two simplest objects in Flash are squares and circles, so we might as well use these in our first example.

1. Create a new movie, and draw a circle in frame 1.

2. Click on frame 15, and press **F6** to insert a keyframe. You'll now have 15 frames full of nothing but a circle.

3. In the keyframe at frame 15, draw a large, filled square over the top of the circle:

If you want to position the square more...*squarely* over the circle once you've drawn it and released the mouse, don't forget that you can always turn on the 'show layer as outlines' option in the layer window.

You've now got your beginning and end keyframes, and all you need to do is tell Flash to morph from one shape to the other over time by putting a shape tween between the two keyframes.

4. Click on the timeline anywhere between the two keyframes, then open the **Frame** panel and select **Shape** from the drop down **Tweening** menu:

5. Select the Arrow tool, and then click on a blank part of the timeline to deselect your other frames. You can now see that the frames are colored *pale green* and have a solid arrow on them:

If you click on the **Onion Skin Outline** button just below the timeline and arrange the onion skin markers to encompass all 15 frames, you'll see a rather beautiful rendering of the shape tween:

All of this indicates that you've got a functional shape tween on your hands.

6. Press **F12** to preview the movie in your web browser. You'll see the circle smoothly transforming into a square. It's as easy as that.

   At the moment, the animation loops back to the beginning when the playhead hits frame 16, meaning that your smoothly morphed square suddenly jumps back to being a circle again in a fraction of a second. Ugly. To correct this, you need to create some extra frames that will facilitate the smooth return of the square back to the circular starting image - this will make the animation loop much smoother.

7. Click on frame 1: your circle should automatically be selected for you. Now copy it into your computer's clipboard using your preferred method, and...

8. ...click on frame 30.

9. Next, press **F7** to insert a *blank* keyframe. It's important that it's blank: we don't want this frame to inherit the image of the square from the previous keyframe.

10. Now use **Edit > Paste in Place** to put the copied circle in exactly the same place in frame 30 as it was in frame 1.

11. Finally, click between frames 15 and 30 on the timeline to select them, and use the **Frame** panel to create a shape tween:

Now when you press **F12** to preview your movie, you'll see a smooth transition from circle to square and back to a circle again. It's strangely mesmerizing to just sit and watch this simple shape beating out its regular morphing rhythm, but if we're going to get any further you'll just have to close that browser window down and return to the Flash interface.

12. Click in the keyframe in frame 15, and drag your square a little way off to side. Now press **F12** to preview your movie, and you'll see the circle will move as it tweens into the square, then move back as it returns to being a circle.

You might be wondering: "Hey! If we can still get motion effects on a shape using a *shape* tween, what's the point of a *motion* tween?" The simple answer is 'computing power' - it takes more power to perform a shape tween than it does to perform a motion tween. Running a lot of shape tweens will noticeably slow down the computer, but running the same amount of motion tweens will run a lot smoother. Don't forget that you can only have one type of tween in the same frame on the same layer, so you can't combine them. It's a question of judgment really - use motion tweens whenever you're just *moving* an object, and shape tweens whenever you want an object to change in some way as it moves.

Here's a simple chart, comparing when you would want to use each type of tween:

Shape Tweens	Motion Tweens
Tweening shapes into different shapes	Moving groups or symbols without altering them
Changing the color of objects	Changing the transparency of objects as they animate
Moving objects while altering them	When you need to use a motion guide

Now we have the very basics of shape tweening under our belt, let's get a little more sophisticated, and introduce some text-based tweens.

Common Tweening Text Effects

In the following exercises we'll be tweening pieces of text so that they transform themselves into different pieces of text, and morphing shapes into text.

The main thing to bear in mind when working with text is that to be able to tween it, you must first break it apart to convert it into a graphic. This means that you can no longer edit it as if it were a text field, so ensure that the text is exactly how you want it to be before you break it apart.

The first tween that we'll practice is the text-to-text tween.

Text to Text Tweening

This animation starts off with one word and uses shape tweening to change it into a different word.

1. Create a new movie, and in frame 1, use the Text tool in conjunction with the **Character** panel to write a big chunky '**This is my firs**t', on the left side of the stage:

This is my first

We've used Arial Black at 36 point.

2. Now, select frame 30 and create a new keyframe.

3. Highlight the text with the Text tool and delete it, then type '**text 2 text tween...**' into the box, and move it to the right hand side of the stage:

text 2 text tween...

4. Use the Arrow tool to select the text box that that you just created (you *don't* want to be inside of the box and selecting the text by dragging), and use the **Modify > Break Apart** command to convert it to a graphic.

5. Now do the same thing to the text in frame 1.

6. Click between the two keyframes on the timeline, and use the **Frame** panel to create a shape tween.

7. Now if you preview your movie you'll see the first words morph into the second while moving across the stage...

We said earlier that shape tweens will only work on 'raw' shapes that have been reduced to their constituent lines and fills. If you've already created a symbol to use in your movie, and you want to animate it, you can, providing that you first break it apart. Let's see how this works.

Shape to Text Tweening

In this example, we'll work through reproducing the tween we saw an image of right at the start of the chapter - where five squares morphed into the word 'Flash'.

1. Open a new movie and draw a *strokeless* black square on the stage - make the square about three quarters of an inch (2 cm) across.

2. Convert your square to a graphic symbol called '**Square**'.

3. Drag another four instances of your square from out of the library to make a total of five - one for each letter in the name of the world's greatest piece of software.

4. Use the **Align** panel to align your squares and space them evenly across the stage:

5. Now use the **Modify > Break Apart** command to convert your squares back into their component fills.

6. Insert a keyframe in frame 20. This keyframe will inherit the broken-apart squares from the first keyframe.

    Now we want to create the letters that spell out the word Flash - one letter to fit in each square.

    There are two ways to fit the letters over the squares. The longest, but most precise, way, would be to type each letter separately into its own text box, and then modify and break apart each letter individually. The second method is to write the word as one piece of text, then modify its size and spacing to fit over the squares. Because we're using a simple tween, we can get away with using the second of these options. If you were designing a more complicated tween, it would probably be better to treat each letter individually.

7. Use the Text tool to write '**FLASH**' on the stage. Choose a color that contrasts nicely to black. We've used 60 point Westminster for a retro, 1970s feel.

8. Select the text box with the Arrow tool and move it so that it's over the top of the squares, at the left hand side:

9. Use the Arrow tool to select the text box again, and then use the **Tracking** box's slider on the **Character** panel to adjust the text spacing so that the letters are over the black boxes:

The Tracking box is the third one up from the bottom - the one with **50** in it.

Don't worry about getting things *too* precise: just so long as the letters are roughly in the right place things will be OK.

10. Click away from the text box to deselect it.

11. Now double-click on each of the black boxes behind the letters and delete them:

    This will leave you with just the word '**FLASH**' on the stage.

12. Now that the boxes are out of the way and we can see clearly, highlight the text and change its color to black.

    We've finished working with the text *as text* now, and it's time to break it up.

13. Select the text with the Arrow tool and use the **Modify > Break Apart** menu to convert it to a graphic.

14. Everything is now ready for tweening, so click between the keyframes on the timeline and use the Frame panel to add a shape tween. Your tween should now work perfectly when you preview your movie.

If some of the animations look a little odd to you - like the way that the 'A' square transforms into the A - don't worry: we'll be looking at ways to tweak these little gremlins later in the chapter.

First though, we'll look at ways of making your shape-tweened animations more enjoyable for your viewers. For the most control here, you really need to use some of the ActionScript that we'll be encountering later in the book, but here are a few simple methods you can use right away...

Making Your Tweens Look More Natural

Whether you move a morphing object across the stage or keep it stationary as it changes from shape to shape, there's one slight drawback about using only two keyframes: the object starts immediately into its tween from frame 1. This can be a problem. For instance, with a text tween, the user usually needs to see what the text says before it starts to change into the next word, or shape.

In our previous example, the text was only whole in the final keyframe, which means that it was only perfectly readable for one tweltfh of a second - not really long enough for the average person to read. The way to change this is to add a 'buffer zone' of frames - which just contain the tween-free text - to the beginning or end of the tween. The static images in these frames will mean that Flash appears to pause over the static text.

Creating a More Subtle Shape Tween

We'll carry on using the same example as in the previous exercise, but we'll make one small change to it before adding the buffer zone - we'll make it go backwards.

1. Click on the layer name in the timeline to highlight everything that's on that layer:

2. Now use the **Modify > Frames > Reverse** command to reverse the order of the selected frames. You'll now find that your movie starts off with the word '**FLASH**', then tweens into the five squares. We've done this to make the changes that you're about to apply stand out more clearly.

3. Select all of the frames again, and this time click on them and drag them across the timeline until the last frame is in frame 30, then release them:

    Notice that as you click and drag, the cursor turns into a little fist, gripping the frames in transit to keep them together...

You'll be left with ten empty frames at the beginning of your movie. Your animation will start at frame 11 and run normally through to frame 30:

4. Click on the first keyframe of your movie (now in frame 11), to automatically select all of the text that's in it.

5. Next, copy this text to your computer's clipboard by using the **Edit > Copy** command (or any alternative method you like).

6. Lastly, click in frame 1, and use the **Edit > Paste in Place** command to paste your text into the frame in the exact position as was in frame 11.

7. Now preview your movie. The text will stay on screen for about a second, then tween into the five squares. It's now easier to read the text before it starts to change into the shapes. Obviously, if you had more text, you'd want to have a longer buffer zone to allow people more time to read it.

Now that we have covered different shape tweens, let's spice things up a bit by looking at **changing color** while tweening.

Adding Color to the Mix

Just like the 'tint' feature does in motion tweens, you can also add color to your shape tweens. In the previous chapter you made text fade through different colors by using the tint effect, and in the following example you'll be expanding your '**FLASH**' animation to include color.

Coloring your Shape Tweens

1. Still using the movie from the last example, click on the layer name again to select *all* of the movie's frames.

2. Click and drag them, as you did before, so that the final frame is now at frame 50.

3. Click on your first keyframe (now in frame 21) to select all of the text, and **Edit > Copy** it to the clipboard.

4. Now click on frame 1 of your movie, and use the **Edit > Paste in Place** command to put the copied text on the stage:

5. Next, move the playhead to frame 10 and use **F7** to insert a blank keyframe. Then paste your text in place on *this* keyframe in the same way as you did the last one.
    You now have your basic structure set up and ready to tween. The only thing left to add now is color.

6. Click back in frame 1 so that everything on the stage in that frame is selected, and change the color in your fill color box to red. The text on your stage will change to reflect this.

7. Now do the same for the keyframes in frames 10 and 21, but using the colors green and blue respectively.

8. The last thing to do is to create shape tweens between each of the keyframes to make your timeline a lean green tweening machine:

9. Now if you preview your movie, you'll see your text waltz along the spectrum before settling for black and tweening into the five squares.

10. As an added touch to show the power of Flash, click in frame 50 to select your squares and change the fill color to yellow. When you preview your movie you will now see the final animation changing shape *and* color at the same time.

So how do we get even closer control? With **shape tween modifiers**, of course!

Shape Tween Modifiers

As with most of Flash's expansive toolkit, shape morphing has modifiers and helpers you can use to tweak your tween. The place to look is on the **Frame** panel, under **Easing** and **Blend**.

In shape tweens, **easing** acts in exactly the same way as it does with motion tweens - it controls Flash's ability to speed up and slow down the action at the beginning or end of our animations.

Here's a quick reminder on the effects of easing:

- **Easing In** to a value of **-100%** will start the shape tween slowly and **accelerate** as it progresses towards the end of the tween.

- **Easing Out** to a value of **100%** will start the shape tween quickly and **slow down** as it progresses to the end of the tween.

Unlike motion tweens, shape tweens also offer the option of playing around with the *sharpness* of lines in your tween - the values for this are set in the **Blend** box on the **Frame** tab.

- A **Distributive** shape tween will create an animation where the intermediate stages of the tween are smooth and irregular with no straight lines.

- An **Angular** shape tween will create an animation where the intermediate stages of the tween *preserve* corners and straight lines.

An **Angular** blend is used to shape tween shapes with straight lines and corners, but if the shape has no corners Flash will revert to a **Distributive** blend.

Now that you know how to create and work with basic shape tweens, we'll turn to those promised tweaking methods that'll bring them that little bit closer to perfection.

One of the best enhancers available to us is the **shape hints** feature.

Shape Hints

Shape hints are used with shape tweening to give a higher degree of control in the morphing process. To apply shape hints you must select a frame that has shape tweening set on it. If it doesn't have shape tweening attached, Flash won't allow you to add hints.

Usually when you shape tween, Flash will automatically take the 'easiest' route to turn one shape into another, but this route will not always give the precise visual effect you're after. This is where shape hints come in: you can step in and override Flash's default 'as intelligent as it can get' tweening and finesse things to your taste. Shape hints can be a little complicated to implement in a complex movie, and they can give some spectacularly strange results when they go wrong, but with practice you can get a beautiful tween every time.

There's one other caveat: shape hints demand a lot more processing power than straightforward tweening. If you can get away with not using them, it's best to avoid them rather than risk your movie slowing down when running on less powerful computers.

Shape hints work by highlighting particular points on a shape, and telling Flash explicitly where those points should move to on a subsequent frame after a motion tween. Suppose you created a movie that had a square in frame 1 and a triangle in the same location in frame 15, and you wanted to shape tween one into the other:

Frame 1   Frame 15

If you get Flash to make the tween, it'll do something slightly counter-intuitive: Instead of pulling the top left- and right-hand corners of the square into the middle to from the point of the triangle, it'll instead twist the square through some weird contortions to perform the tween - as shown by the transformation lines in this ghosted tween:

Using shape hints, we can force Flash to pull the two top corners into the middle, giving us a slightly more intuitive tween:

You mark the specific points that you want to 'steer' in your *initial* shape, and you mark where you want them to end up in your final shape:

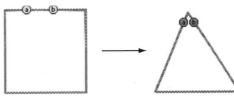

Start points   End points

Each hint is represented by a different letter so that you know which matches up with which. The only drawback to this is that you can only have a maximum of 26 shape hints, but this should be enough, and if you need any more, you should consider splitting your animation up onto different layers, as it is probably too complicated anyway. Let's see this in action.

Using Shape Hints to Control your Tween

1. Start a new movie, and draw a big yellow rectangle with a black outline on the stage. Use these kind of proportions:

2. Use the Line tool to draw two lines to make a triangle on one side of the image, and fill it with the same yellow:

3. Now select the part of the line that acts as the base of the triangle where it meets the rectangle, and delete it, leaving a shape like this:

4. Now draw a small blue circle inside the rectangle on the right-hand side, just above the triangle:

   This is the eye of your (admittedly basic) face.

5. Now click in frame 30 and press **F6** to insert a keyframe.

   We're going to make an animation of the face turning from 'looking to our right' to 'looking to our left', with the face looking at us in the middle of the tween. The first thing we need to do is to make the image in the final frame look in the opposite direction.

6. In the new keyframe at frame 30, use the **Modify > Transform > Flip Horizontal** command to turn it around.

7. Next, insert a shape tween across the timeline. You are now ready to preview your movie in all its glory...

...but seeing as this exercise is about fixing tweens that go wrong, you probably guessed something like this was going to happen. So now we have to go about fixing the tween.

8. Click on the first keyframe, and use the **Modify > Transform > Add Shape Hint** command. A little red circle with an '**a**' in it will appear like a beauty spot in the middle of the face:

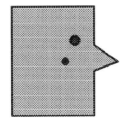

This is the first of your shape hints. Note that it's red at the moment.

Shape hints will appear by default in the center of the shape that you are tweening. Remember that the 'center' of the shape is defined by the invisible 'bounding box' around it, and is not always where you might think it should be.

9. It's easier to work with shape hints with snapping turned on, so make sure **Snap to Objects** is checked in the **View** menu.

10. Click on the shape hint and drag it onto the top left corner of the head:

It's still a red color.

Shape hints work best if you start with the top left-most point that you want to control, and then work counter-clockwise around the shape. They can produce some beautiful - but unexpected - results if you get them in the wrong order.

11. Now click on the keyframe in frame 30, and you'll find a corresponding 'a' shape hint (also red) there: we've added a shape hint to the start image, so Flash assumes we want one for the 'end' image too. Attach the shape hint in frame 30 to the top right-hand corner of the face.

Notice that the shape hint has turned green. This indicates that it's properly attached to the shape and that it's corresponding shape hint in the first frame is also attached properly. If you click back on the first frame, you'll see that it's turned yellow. This green-yellow signal means that shape hint '**a**' is locked on and ready to fire.

12. If you preview your movie now, you'll find that it's still not looking entirely natural. A few more shape hints will sort this out, so go back to your first keyframe and add another **three** shape hints. (the keyboard shortcut for this is *Ctrl-Shift-H*).

    If you ever find that the **Add Shape Hint** command is not available in the menu, go back to your keyframe and make sure everything on it is selected. Shape hints can only be added when the object that you're tweening is selected. If you ever lose sight of your shape hints, make sure that the **View > Show Shape Hints** menu is checked.

    When you add the three shape hints in succession, they'll all be added one on top of the other on the stage. This may seem a bit confusing at first, but you'll soon get used to it. The top-most hint will be '**d**' as that is the fourth one that you created.

13. Drag the three new shape hints out to the other three corners of the rectangle, working counter-clockwise from the first point:

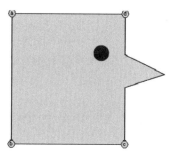

14. Now go to your end keyframe and drag the hints out from their little cluster in the center, but this time, reverse the relative left/right positions of the shape hints. The 'chin' shape hint in the first frame should still be on the 'chin' in the last frame, but it is on the other side of the stage because the face is turned around.

    Your finished shape should look like this in the last frame:

15. Preview your movie now, and the face should look as if it is turning from right to left. It's still not quite right though, as the eye seems to float through an out of body experience before returning to normality in the last frame. Ick. Guess what? Time for some more shape hints.

16. Go back to the first frame and add another couple of shape hints. Place the hints on either side of the eye:

17. Now go to the last frame and place the hints in the same relative (but horizontally flipped) positions on the final face:

18. If everything has worked correctly, your face should turn when you preview your movie. If you'd prefer the eye to blink as the tween flows, just add another couple of hints to the eye, one at the top and one at the bottom, the same in both keyframes. The face should now flip perfectly and wink at you cheekily.

    To remove shape hints you only need to grab and drag them off the stage, as you would do to get rid of a guide. Dragging the hint off the stage in any frame will affect both frames that the hints are in. The alternative method to dragging is to delete all the hints at once, and start again: this can be achieved via the **Modify > Transform > Remove All Hints** command.

Shape hints can be kind of confusing at first, but it's important to be aware of what they are, what they can do, and how you can use them to add more control to a shape tween if you need to. If you're dealing with a complex shape tween, and no amount of shape hints seems to help, you may want to try adding a 'staging post' frame for your animation half way through, with a keyframe containing the desired 'half-way through' image showing what the animation should look like at this point. You can then add two tweens, one on either side, to link the three keyframes. This makes it a little easier for Flash to follow and should give better results. This is more time consuming, but it may wind up easier than letting Flash decide how the tween will work, as well as saving you the hassle of adding and positioning multiple shape hints.

OK. We promised you a more restful chapter this time around, and we've delivered. Let's just do a small amount of work on our case study before we close down.

Case Study

In this next case study exercise, we're going to add some more content to the **Information** movie clip that we started work on in the last chapter. This movie clip will house the different information content that'll be displayed selectively, depending upon which buttons the user presses.

Here, we're going to create a title and brief descriptive text for one of these information displays, incorporating a shape tween.

More Information

1. Open up your ongoing case study .fla file and make sure you bring up the library window.

2. Double click the '**Information**' movie clip symbol in the library to take you into edit mode on it:

3. Currently, you should have two layers in this movie clip: **Titles** and **Info**:

4. Click on the **Info** layer and add a new layer between the existing two. Rename it '**Morphs**', and add a keyframe at frame 19:

5. Now select frame 1 of the **Morphs** layerand create a small black circle. Make it about 15 pixels across: remember that you can click on the circle and use the **Info** panel to type in the size values that you need:

6. Now copy and paste the original circle until you have twelve in a row, and use the **Alignment** panel to align them and get them evenly spaced. You might want to turn snapping off as you drag them close together before you use the alignment tools.

You should end up with something like this:

7. Line up the circles just above the movie clip's registration point - indicated by the cross hairs:

This is important because we want all the components of the Information movie clip to appear in the same place when they're displayed.

8. Use **Ctrl-Click** to select frame 19 of the **Morphs** layer.

9. Now select the Text tool and use it in combination with the **Character** panel to create some new text - "**About our Company**" - in a text box just above the circles. Try and match the text box to the width of the line of circles. Use a similar color to the one you used for the text on the other layers of this movie clip:

    We've used Arial at 25 point.

10. Now drag out two guides, one each from the vertical and horizontal rulers. Use them to mark the center point of the line of circles:

11. Still in frame 19, select all of the circles by drawing a box around them with the Arrow tool and delete them.

12. Now drag down the text box so that it sits over the same space where the circles were:

13. After you've placed the text to your satisfaction, use **Modify > Break Apart** command to, er, break it apart into its constituent lines and fills:

14. Select any frame between frames 1 and 19 on the **Morphs** layer and add a shape tween via the **Frame** panel.

Now we'll finish up by adding the description text that goes with this title. Remember that in the finished movie these snippets of information and their titles will be displayed when the user clicks on the relevant button.

15. In the **Info** layer below the **Morphs** layer, select frame 1 and create a new keyframe. Add a new keyframe at frame 19, too - we want the description text to last as long as the title's shape tween.

16. In the new keyframe, draw a suitably colored line below the circles - you might want to turn onion skinning on so that you can see the relationship between the line and the 'About our Company' title text that'll morph in:

17. Next, create some text saying '**General information about your company**.' below the line:

Make sure that the information text is below the crosshairs to the right. This is important in the end movie: it'll make sure everything is lined up nicely.

OK, that's all for the case study in this chapter.

Summary

In this chapter, we took a gentle canter around the world of shape tweening, adding another tool to our growing array.

We saw that:

◆ **Shape tweening** complements motion tweening. It enables us to morph shapes into other shapes, shapes into text, and more

◆ Shape tweens operate on **lines and fills** rather than the grouped shapes and symbols that motion tweens act upon

◆ We can combine shape tweening with color changes and movement

◆ **Shape hints** give us a fine degree of control over the way that a shape tween will work

In the next chapter, we're going to look at a technique that can add really engaging visual effects to your Flash movies, especially when used in conjunction with shape and motion tweens - **masking**.

FIGHTER PILOT

8

Masks and Masking

What we'll cover in this chapter:

◆ *Masks are a powerful feature in Flash that allow you to selectively show and hide content. You can create a mask and apply it to a layer so that only content 'underneath' the mask shows through. We'll explore their basic principles and see a range of different examples and applications*

This chapter introduces the use of **masks** in Flash. Masks act as a way of selectively showing and hiding content in a Flash movie, based on the position of the mask, which lives on a separate layer from the content that it's masking. Using masks, you can create great effects in your movies: illusions of depth, movement, illumination and more - as you'll see in this chapter.

Masks are strange creatures, but we think you'll find them indispensable once you grasp the techniques for using them. Some Flash designers don't seem to embrace the usefulness of masks, possibly because the effects you can create with them are more at home in animation than standard web site design. But, once you've seen the results that masks help you achieve, we think you may well be a convert.

What is a Mask?

Very early in this book, we discussed layers, and showed you how they can be used to simulate depth. If you're animating a character - let's call her Jane Doe - walking across the stage and behind a house, you'd put the house on a layer at the front of the movie, and Jane on a layer behind the house:

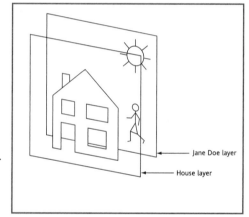

Jane Doe layer

House layer

As Jane walks across the area occupied by the house symbol, Flash knows that we want the house to stay in front because of the layer order that we've assigned. In effect, this will give the appearance that Jane has walked behind the house, and would create a sense of *depth* in the animation.

This effect can be achieved without masking, but suppose we wanted to show Jane walking around *inside* the house? That's more difficult, isn't it? You'd want Jane to be visible when she was behind an transparent part of the house front - the windows - and *invisible* when she was behind an opaque object such as a solid wall:

The requirement here is to make part of the front layer opaque, and part of it transparent. To do this in Flash, you need a mask.

When we create a mask, it's as if we lay a piece of card over our animation and block it all out. We then cut a window in the card and reveal a section of what's underneath. In Jane's case, we'd need to create a piece of card shaped like a solid-fronted house, and then cut holes in the card where the windows and doors should be:

Once we've cut out the holes, we can hold the card in front of the background animation of Jane walking across the stage. We can the either move the card - our 'mask' - around so that different sections of our animation are revealed, or make the objects in the animation pass across the holes, appearing and disappearing as they do.

That's the basic principle of masking in Flash - we just use electronic layers to create our masks, rather than card and scissors.

When else would you need to use a mask in Flash? Here are a few examples:

- When you need to show text scrolling from left to right across a TV screen. We'd only want the text to be visible when it was behind the area corresponding to the *screen*

- When you want to zoom into an area on a picture and keep the viewable area inside a constant-sized window. As the picture is magnified and gets bigger, we only want to show the zoomed area of the picture, and hide all other areas

- You want to simulate text being typed on the screen, making it appear, letter by letter, from left to right

None of these effects can be created using layers alone. In each case, we want to hide *part* of our object, and that's exactly what a mask will do.

To illustrate the use of masking, let's create an animation based on the first example listed above: text scrolling across a TV screen.

Putting on your Mask

First, we need our TV set.

1.   In a new movie, rename the default layer as 'TV'.

2.   In the default keyframe at frame 1, create your TV by drawing a shape that looks something like this:

Create the TV any way you like.

We made our (slightly retro) TV by drawing the basic shape with straight lines, then we bent the straight lines using the Arrow tool to give the impression that the TV is a freehand drawing, and added the antenna and some chunky control knobs. If you wanted to, you could use the Pen tool and the Subselect tool to create a Bezier-finessed masterpiece - it's really up to you. (Just make sure you end up with a TV that has a screen!)

A tip for drawing things in the cartoon style we've used here is to draw with thick black outlines, like Warner Brothers did in the psychedelic 60s.

3. Now use the Paint Bucket tool to fill your drawing with color:

In our example movie, we want our text to appear only on the TV's *screen*, so we need to create a mask that will only show the text when its position corresponds to an area inside the boundaries of the screen.

4. Add two new layers above the existing TV layer - **Broadcast** and **Mask**:

Mask will be our mask layer, and **Broadcast** will contain all the objects - the text - that we wish to show on the TV screen. The order of the layers is crucial, and must read **TV**, **Broadcast** and **Mask** from bottom to top.

Now for the clever part. Remember that the **Mask** layer is the piece of card that we'll use to hide and reveal the underlying **Broadcast** layer. We're going to cut a hole in our card that's the same shape as the screen of our TV, so that whatever we put on the **Broadcast** will only be visible when it is inside the TV screen.

5. Select the filled screen area of the TV - not the stroke. (You'll notice we've not made the TV into a symbol yet; this is so we can select the screen on its own):

6. Now copy the screen part into the clipboard with **Edit > Copy**.

The next thing to do is use this screen shape to create the masked area on the Mask layer.

7. Select the **Mask** layer and paste the screen in place with **Edit > Paste** in place.

8. Hide all the layers except for the **Mask** layer, and you should just see the pasted screen as shown here:

It's a good idea to make your mask areas a striking color so that you can easily differentiate them from other movie content. Black is a good color to choose if the movie background is white and vice versa. Let's make our mask black.

9. Select the Paint Bucket tool and fill the screen shape on the **Mask** layer with black:

Although it might seem counter-intuitive for a mask to be a solid filled color, trust us. Flash isn't constrained by the same laws of physics that stop light passing freely through a piece of card. So long as Flash knows the *shape* of the mask, we can make it any color we like - Flash just ignores the color and sees only the shape.

When this TV screen-shaped mask is being used, you'll be able to see anything on the underlying layer that falls *behind* the black area, and nothing that's in the areas outside the mask.

10. Lock the **Mask** layer so that you don't select anything on it by accident.

11. On the **TV** layer, select the whole of the TV and convert it into a new graphic symbol called **TV Symbol**.

> *Converting the TV set to a symbol is absolutely essential. Flash masks won't work unless your fills and lines have been converted to a symbol.*

12. Now lock the TV layer and unlock the **Mask** layer.

13. Select the screen-shaped mask on the **Mask** layer and convert it into a graphic symbol. Name it **Screen Mask**.

> *When you're working with masks on one layer, it's always a good idea to lock the layer containing the masked objects so that you can't inadvertently select both objects at once.*

Now we're going to tell Flash that we want our floating TV screen shape to act as a mask.

14. With the **Mask** layer selected go to **Modify > Layer** and click on the **Mask** radio button:

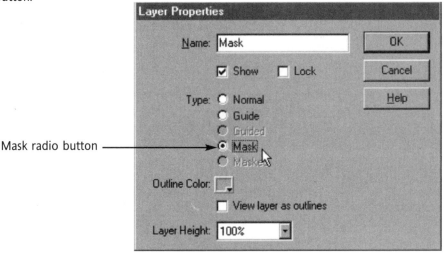

Mask radio button ───────────────────→

15. Leave all of the other values as the defaults, and click **OK**.

We've now converted the **Mask** layer so that it will act as a mask. All that Flash sees on this layer now is the screen shape that we want to use as the mask.

Notice that the **Mask** layer's appearance has changed in the layer window:

The little 'arrow' icon at the left identifies this layer as a 'mask' layer.

Now we have to tell Flash which layer we want the mask to be *applied to*.

16. Select the **Broadcast** layer and go to **Modify > Layer**. This time, select the **Masked** radio button to designate the Broadcast layer as the one that we want the TV screen shape to mask:

Masked radio button ——————→

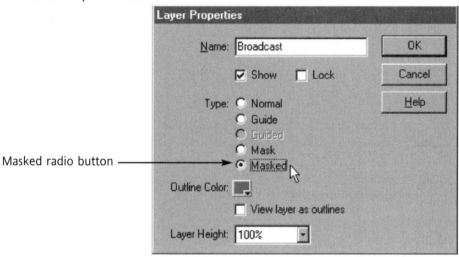

17. Click on **OK**.

Again, there's been a change in the layer window:

Note that the **Broadcast** layer now has an indented, 'bent arrow' icon attached to it. This is the indication that this layer has a mask applied to it.

Your layers now should look like this:

The little downward pointing arrow in Mask tells us we have created a mask, and the little ringed arrow in the Broadcast layer tells us that this is the layer we've placed our mask over the top of. The Broadcast layer is

the one that the screen shape on the Mask layer will apply to - hiding part of it from view.

> *It's vital to note that the layer, or layers, that you want to be partially hidden must be placed below the mask you've created.*

We won't see the effects of the mask layer yet because the **Broadcast** layer currently has nothing in it. Let's put a message on the TV.

The first thing we need to do is increase the length of our movie to give us enough time to read the text that'll shimmy across the TV screen.

18. Increase the movie length so that it lasts for a hundred frames. To do this, click on frame 2 and then drag the cursor *to the right* (as far as frame 100), and *down* to select all three layers. When you release the mouse, you'll have one hundred frames selected in all three of the layers:

If you ever want to see more frames in the timeline, you can click on the little **Frame View** button at the top-right of the timeline:

Frame view button

Clicking this button will bring up a menu:

If you click on **Small**, Flash will compress the frames displayed horizontally, and you'll see a greater number of frames in the timeline:

19. With all one hundred frames selected on all three layers, use the **Insert > Frame** menu option to increase the length of the movie.

20. Now for the content. In frame 1 of the **Broadcast** layer, use the Text tool to add the text '**Stay tuned to this channel...**' to the right of the TV, and at the same position vertically as the screen:

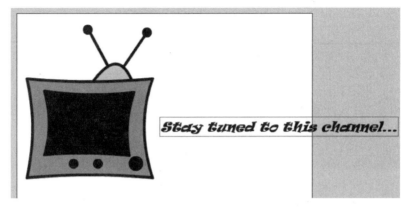

21. Break the text apart and convert it into a graphic symbol called **Text**.

Now we'll make the text move across the screen.

22. In the **Broadcast** layer add a keyframe in frame 100. With the new keyframe selected, move the text to the *left* of the TV to establish its end position after its scrolled across the screen:

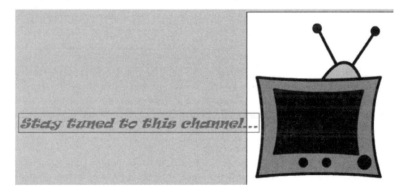

23. Now use the **Frame** panel to add a motion tween between frames 1 and 100 of the **Broadcast** layer:

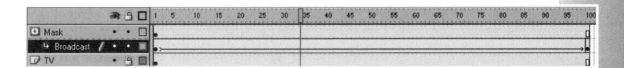

24. The last thing to do to make our mask work is to **lock** both the **Mask** layer *and* the **Broadcast** layer:

> *Flash will only show the effects of a mask when all the affected layers are locked. If you want your masks to work always lock all affected layers.*

25. Press *F12* to preview your movie.

    This is what you will see when you test your movie: the TV with the scrolling text appearing only on the screen where the mask is. With a little extra work, this would make a good loading page for someone's website...

You are now seeing how this can be a very powerful technique. The TV screen is a totally non-uniform shape, as is the rest of the TV. Simply by defining the area we wanted to display using a mask, we were able to achieve the complex effect we wanted with very little effort. The sequence of steps needs to be stuck to, but after a little more practice and experimentation, you'll be turning out masked movies of your own.

Remember that when you create a mask you have to specify the layer or layers that you want it to act upon. Only the sections of these layers that lie under the 'cut-out' shape(s) you draw on the mask layer will be visible in the finished movie.

Another thing to be aware of is that all the mask effects that we're creating here can be embedded inside movie clips and reused in all sorts of different ways. You can build great little animated masking effects, embed them in movie clips, and then use multiple copies of those movie clips to get all sorts of impressive action going on the stage.

OK, we've created a mask and tweened some text across it, to good effect. How about we see how to animate the *mask*? And how to mask several layers at once?

Animated Masks and Masking Multiple Layers

In contrast to the example we've just seen, you can also use masks and keep the background stationary while the mask itself is animated, selectively hiding and revealing different parts of your animation. We're going to learn how to do this now. We'll also see how one mask can be used to cover and reveal several layers at once by creating a spotlight effect on some text.

Moving the Mask

1. Create a new movie.

2. Change the global movie properties by right clicking on the stage or using the **Modify > Movie** menu.

3. In the **Movie Properties** dialog box, change the movie's background color to black. Now add some large bold white text in the center of the stage as shown here and rename the layer **Text**:

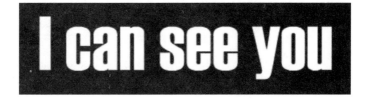

4. Add a new layer, and name it **Spotlight**. In this layer, draw a filled white circle that's a little bigger than the height of the text.

5. Convert the circle into a graphic symbol and name it **Spot**:

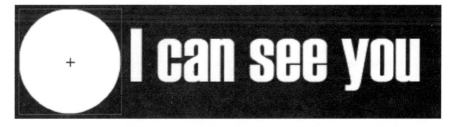

6. Make your animation 50 frames long in both layers by clicking, dragging, and inserting frames in the same way that you did in the last exercise.

7. Add a keyframe in frame 50 of the **Spotlight** layer. Your timeline should now look like this:

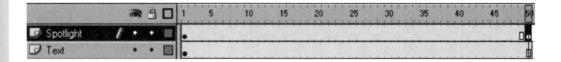

8. Move the instance of **Spot** at frame 50 to the far end of the text, after the '**u**', and create a motion tween between the two keyframes.

    The circle will now move over the text when you play your movie:

9. Finally, turn the **Spotlight** layer into a **mask** layer as you did earlier via the **Modify > Layer** menu, and then use the same menu to turn the **Text** layer into the **masked** layer.

10. Now lock both the layers and test the movie.

    There's a problem with the movie at the moment: we see the text revealed by the round shape of the spotlight as it travels along, but the circular shape of the spotlight doesn't really come across fully. That's because the background is totally black - a real spotlight would illuminate the background as well as the text. Let's remedy that.

    What we need to do is make the spotlight illuminate the background slightly. To do this, we'll draw a gray area behind the text on a new layer. This will be lit up in contrast to the text as the spot passes across it.

    You must do this exactly as shown, otherwise the **Spotlight** layer will not act as a mask to the new layer.

11. Select the **Text** layer and add a new layer by clicking on the little '**Add Layer**' button just below the layer titles. Name the new layer **Gray**:

We want **Gray** to be *behind* the text, so we must move it to the bottom of the stack of layers.

12. With **Gray** still selected, click and hold the cursor over it, and drag the layer to the bottom. Your timeline should now look like this:

Notice that both the layers **Gray** and **Text** have the little bent arrows on them, signifying that *both* will be masked by **Spotlight**. Flash has automatically made layer **Gray** a masked layer because of its adjacency to the mask layer when we created it.

13. Select **Gray** and draw a medium gray rectangle that covers the whole area that the circle will travel over:

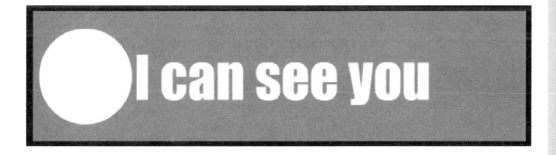

14. Lock all the layers again and test the movie.

You will now see what looks like an illuminated spotlight move from left to right, lighting up the darkness to reveal your text:

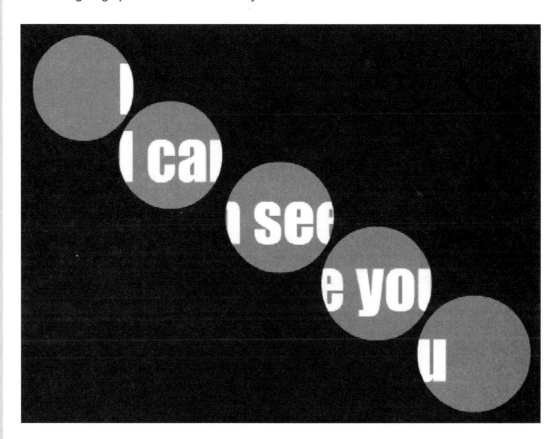

What's actually happening is that our circular 'window' is moving across white text on a gray background - but the effect is quite striking. How about adding more keyframes to the mask layer and more motion tweens, and creating a sweeping searchlight effect that moves up and down as well as from side to side. Or maybe a motion path that sweeps out in a spiral? Or a spotlight that starts small and grows bigger as the animation continues? Or...

We've only touched on the power of animated masks here. The number of effects that you can create with these features in Flash is limited only by your imagination. So practice, practice, practice....

Now let's look at some more text/mask combinations.

Using Masks with Text

Masks can be used particularly well with text. Text can act as the mask itself, as we'll see later, and an effect that can be easily simulated with masks is making words appear on the screen as if they were being typed. This is achieved by another method of animating the mask: instead of moving the mask around the stage, we *scale* it to make it grow - revealing more of the layer beneath it as it does so. Let's see...

Simulating Typed Text

1. In a new movie, rename the default layer to **Text**, and add a new layer above it called **Mask**.

2. Use the **Modify > Layer** menu to turn **Mask** into a *mask* layer, and **Text** into a *masked* layer:

3. Change the movie's background color to a hue of your choice, and then add some text in the **Text** layer:

> The ghostly font of 1974...

We've used a pale green on a dark green background - just in case there are any of you out there who are nostalgic for the days of corporate dumb terminals...

4. Now we want to make the text look as if it's being typed in letter by letter. In the **Mask** layer, create a long white rectangle that completely covers the text, and then convert it into a graphic symbol. Call the new symbol **Mask**:

Flash has turned the white rectangle into a symbol and the registration point - the black cross - has appeared in the middle. We're going to make the text gradually appear by scaling the white rectangle, and if we scale the rectangle with the registration point in the default position, then both ends are going to get shorter or longer, because scaling is done relevant to the registration point. To modify this default behavior, we're going to move the black cross to the left and move the symbol's registration point.

5. Select the symbol on the stage, then use the **Edit > Edit Symbols** menu to go into edit on the **Mask** symbol. Use the Arrow tool to pick up and drag the rectangle so that its left edge is in line with the registration point:

6. Go back to the stage by clicking on **Scene 1** at the top of the window and re-position the rectangle over the text:

7. Make the movie 50 frames long in both layers in the same way we did before, and then add a keyframe to the **Mask** layer at frame 50:

8. In frame 1 of the **Mask** layer, shorten the mask by going to **Modify > Transform > Scale** and dragging the right side of the rectangle way to the left so that it's too short to cover any of the text:

9. Add a motion tween between frames 1 and 50 on the **Mask** layer. This will create an animated mask that slowly reveals more and more text as it gets bigger. Remember that only the text that's *covered* by the mask will show up in the final movie - the rectangle growing is like a cut-out window on card gradually being torn open to reveal what's underneath.

10. Lock both layers and test your movie.

   Your text will gradually appear as the mask rectangle scales up out to the right.

   Don't worry that the mask will show *parts* of letters: the transition is usually too fast for the viewer to see that it isn't actually typing a word at a time, but revealing the words bit by bit. If it starts to look too obvious when you come to test the movie, simply shorten the motion tween by ten or so frames by going to **Insert > Remove Frames** - making sure that the playhead is not on a keyframe.

Now for another mean text-related masking technique.

A Text-Shaped Mask

One of the easiest ways to create instant masks is to use *text* as the mask. When using text in this way, it's a good idea to use a simple, heavy, bold and closely-spaced font: using this kind of font will mean that a larger proportion of the image behind your mask is shown. For this reason, the Haettenschweiler font shown here is a good choice:

Haettenschweiler.

Let's use this meaty-looking font as a mask in a practical example.

Masking with Text

In this effect, we'll create a color gradient and mask it using a piece of text.

1. Open a new movie and rename the default layer to '**text**'.

2. Now create a text box using a bold thick font, similar in length to this:

   We've used 80 point Haettenschweiler.

3. Create a new layer below **text** and call it **gradient**. In this layer, create a filled gradient that's taller than the text:

We've used a black and light color spectrum gradient, selected from the bottom of the (red-orange-yellow-green-blue-violet). You can select this pre-defined gradient from the bottom of the color palette.

4. Make sure that the **gradient** layer is underneath the **text** layer by dragging it there in the layer window:

5. We want to motion tween the rectangle, so convert it into a graphic symbol now.

6. Now make **text** into a *mask* layer and **gradient** into the layer that's being *masked*.

As always, the mask must be on top of whatever you want to hide. Change the layer order around if necessary *before* you try to make the mask.

7. Make your animation 50 frames long by clicking, dragging, and pressing *F5* in the now-familiar way.

8. At frame 50 in the **gradient** layer, add a keyframe. Move the gradient graphic symbol in this frame to the left:

9. Create a motion tween on the gradient layer to animate the movement of the rectangle. Your timeline should now look like this:

10. Lock both layers and test your movie. You'll see the text appear to cycle through the colors of the spectrum as the gradient moves past it:

   There's an additional cool modification you can make to this effect, and that's to add a *border* to the text. This will improve the effect because, as it stands, the lighter colors in the spectrum can make the outline of the text difficult to see on some screens.

11. Select the **text** layer and create a new layer above it. Call the new layer **text outline**:

12. Copy the text, then click on the **text** outline layer and paste the text onto this layer with a paste in place command (**Edit > Paste in place**).

13. With the text box on the **text** outline layer still selected, break the text apart with **Modify > Break apart**. Hide the other layers.

14. Change the stroke color to black and the stroke thickness to **1**:

15. Then, using the Ink Bottle tool, click on all the outlines in the text. To do this for the word '**spectrum**', you'll have to click on the *interior* outlines inside the '**p**' and the '**e**'. You might want to zoom in to get a better view while you're using the Ink Bottle.

16. Finally (with the text still selected), press your *Delete* key or go to **Edit > Clear** to delete filled areas of each letter leaving only the outline:

17. Test your movie. You'll see the color of your text change through all the colors of the rainbow once again, but this time with a more clearly defined outline:

Notice that layer **text outline** does not need to be locked for the mask effect to be seen, as it is not masking anything or being masked.

A really cool variant of this is to use a bitmap instead of a gradient. In a similar way to the computer 'typing' we simulated earlier, you can even use a bitmap to gradually fill your mask and reveal your text. Here's how...

Filling your Text with an Image

We're now going to use a bitmap image called **skyline** to slowly fill a text mask. This image is included in the downloadable files from the friends of ED website - or you can use any image of you own choice, of course.

1. Set up a new movie. Rename the default layer to **image** and add a second layer called **text** just above it.

2. Make **text** into the mask layer and **image** into the *masked* layer:

3. Now, on the **text** layer, create a text box containing the word or words that you want to make appear:

4. Bring the **skyline** bitmap (or your own image of choice) onto the **image** layer by selecting the layer and then using **File > Import** to navigate to the image in the dialog box:

5. Convert the imported image to a graphic symbol called **skyline object**.

6. Scale **skyline object** so that it's about the same height as your text, and place it on the stage so that its *right* edge is nearly at the *left* edge of your text:

7. Make your animation 50 frames long and insert a keyframe at frame 50 on the image layer:

8. At frame 50, move **skyline object** so that it's behind the text, and then create a motion tween:

9. Lock both layers and test your movie. Here's the effect you will see:

Because your bitmap is moving, you can get away with quite a low resolution quality, so the download time can actually be surprisingly quick. So if you keep the effect and the bitmap small, then the download time can be surprisingly quick. Be aware that an effect like this, combined with a large bitmap, can become quite slow on older computers if your text fills the full screen.

You can now create a layer that's a mask, and apply this mask to a layer, or layers, that are labeled as 'masked'. This is yet another powerful feature that you and your imagination can implement in conjunction with other techniques such as tweening, animated fades and so on.

The next section looks at a very different type of masking effect that we can use in Flash when we're working with bitmap images.

Masking Effects with Bitmaps

As Flash is a vector-based program, you might be a little skeptical about using bitmap images. However, there are some situations where bitmaps are unavoidable - here are some examples:

- When you're designing a website for an online catalogue and have to use photographic images

- When you're designing a sports webpage and find that all that grass and spectators in the photographs you're using are giving Flash a real headache tracing them

- When you want to add a picture of yourself on your home page, but find that if you try to trace the photograph the vector image is actually *bigger* than a JPEG at 50%

So, sometimes you're forced to use bitmaps, but you may well want them to *behave* like vectors. As we said at the start of the chapter, it's very simple to make a *vector* symbol appear to be behind or in front of another vector symbol, but what if we had to animate Jane Doe walking behind a *bitmap* image of a house on a white background? Jane would disappear behind the white edge of the bitmap before she reached the house.

Here's a related true story: a web designer came across this problem when they were given a brief by a client: the client wanted a drag and drop e-commerce front end where you could drag shirts, pants and bags from a rack and place them on a mannequin to see how they looked together. The client wasn't happy with the loss of quality that occurred when the bitmap pictures of the clothes were turned into vectors, but wanted the user to be able to layer the clothes onto the mannequin.

The web designer actually lost their job because they couldn't work out how to combine bitmaps with the clothes layering on the mannequin. The only way to allow all the different combinations of clothes to be put on the mannequin is to somehow 'cut the clothes out of their bitmaps' so they can be laid on top of each other. Now, how do you do that? Here's how.

Animating a Bitmap

The image of an airplane on the stage would suffer if it was converted into a vector because it has a lot of color and texture which would be lost:

But, in its current state, we can't make it pass in front of anything because its white background gets in the way.

When we created our mask layers earlier, we said it was like cutting a hole in a piece of card so we could see parts of our animation underneath. Imagine that the bitmap shown previously is a piece of card covering our animation. What we want to do is cut the plane out of the card and get rid of the white background. Once we've done that we can make an animation with the same impression of depth we achieved with vector images.

The airplane image is included in the downloadable files from our website's support area for this book.

Animating the Bitmap

1. Create a new movie and make the background color a nice sky blue. Rename the default layer as **Flightpath**.

2. Import the airplane bitmap (or a bitmap file of your choice) using the **File > Import** menu.

    When you import the bitmap, Flash automatically creates a library entry for it:

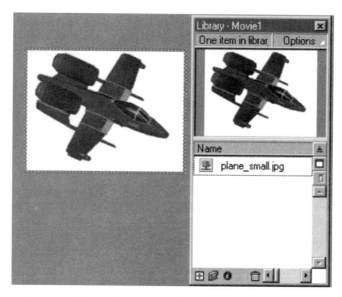

3. So that we can treat the image as if it were a vector, convert the bitmap to a graphic symbol and call it **vector plane**.

You'll now have *two* items in your library - one for the original bitmap image, and one for the symbol version, which has been converted to vectors:

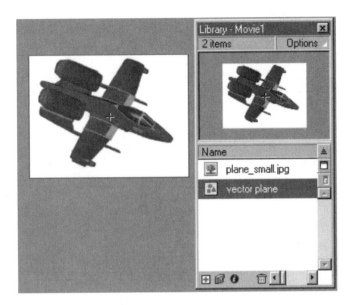

Now here comes the fun part: we're going to cut the plane out of its background by editing our new symbol.

4. Use the **Edit > Edit symbols** menu to go into edit mode on the vector plane symbol.

5. Select the plane and break it apart using **Modify > Break Apart**.

    For a vector-based program like Flash, this is an impressive function; it has 'opened up' the bitmap so you can edit it. Although you can't add pixels (there's no tool that allows you to do this), you can **delete** pixels using the eraser tool.

6. Using the Magic Wand and the Eraser tool, start to delete the white background areas inside the symbol. A good tip here is to use the Zoom tool as you get close to the edges of the airplane to give you better control.

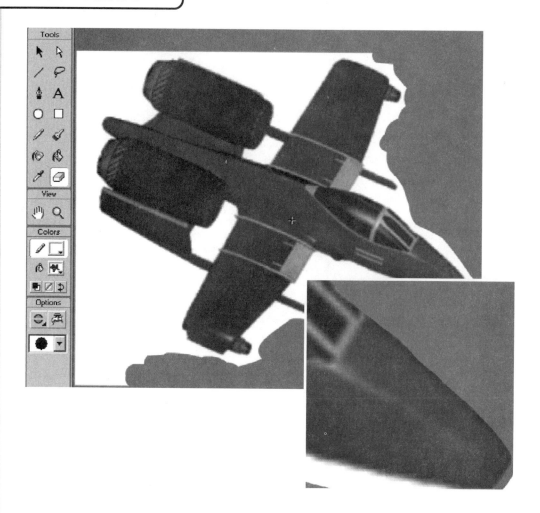

Notice that however much you zoom in the edges of the bitmap are not jagged - the bitmap seems to think it's a vector!

This can be a time consuming and tricky technique (although the Magic Wand sure helps!), but eventually you'll end up with something like this:

The symbol is now the shape of the airplane itself, and not the white-back grounded bitmap we started with.

The final thing we need to do is to control the file size of the bitmap, which underlies the vector version we've been working on.

7. Select the bitmap **plane_small** in the library and then, using the button at the top right of the library window, go to **Options > Properties**.

8. Un-check **Use** imported **JPEG** data and enter 30 in the **Quality** field. This will give you an overall file size of just 4k for the finished symbol.

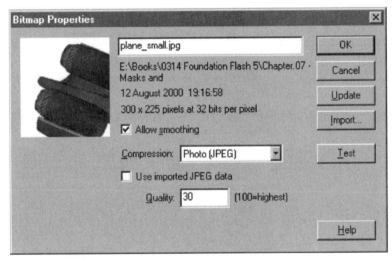

If we keep the file size small, Flash won't complain too much about the processing power required to move our symbol around, but it will have the level of detail and texture normally associated with a bitmap. Flash has internally created what's called a **vector mask** to cut out the background - no other program allows you to do this sort of thing. It can be a very powerful technique, and one you have to know to be able to take advantage of the particular niche of tasks where masking in Flash really starts to shine.

You can also use this technique using the PNG image file format, which supports masking channels, but you would have to create that 'masking channel enabled' file in a package outside of Flash. The method we've used in this exercise requires Flash only, and produces bitmaps without jagged edges. Also, because we're using JPEG compression from the Properties dialog box, we get finer control of the image file size.

> *A word of warning: at the heart of Flash is a real-time vector-rendering engine. This is not really set up to handle bitmaps (something Macromedia Director is more at home with). In practice, there don't tend to be any real problems as long as your bitmaps are either kept small or not moved around very much, so that the pixels do not show. A common trap that new Flash designers fall into is the over-use of bitmaps at the expense of vector symbols. So be happy, but realize the limitations of what Flash is actually designed to do.*

Back to our airplane.

9. Go back to the main stage and move your shiny new plane symbol to the top left corner.

10. Create a new layer, call it **text**, and place it below the **flightpath** layer:

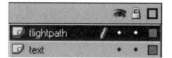

11. Create a text box on the **text** layer and type '**FIGHTER PILOT**' in white in the center of the stage:

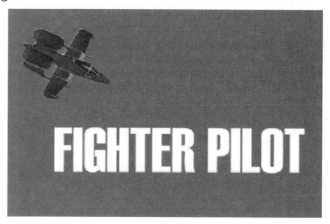

12. Make your animation 35 frames long in both layers, and insert a keyframe at frame 35 in the **flightpath** layer:

13. At keyframe 35 on the **flightpath** layer, move the plane to the bottom right of the stage.

14. Create a motion tween on the **flightpath** layer and test your movie:

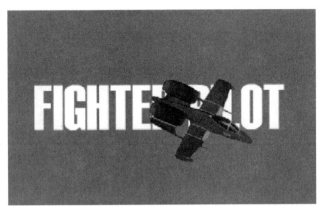

The plane should fly smoothly over the type, hiding and revealing sections of the text. We've produced what looks like a vector animation - but with a bitmap.

OK, that's it for the basic masking techniques. We think you'll agree that you can create some scintillating effects with them. The best way to learn more from here is to experiment and let your imagination run riot.

Case Study

There are a number of things we can do to our project with masking. The big black circle in the top left corner (the one that the buttons move around) could easily be replaced by a picture of your main product or trademark, or even a couple of smiling customers. As you already know, bitmaps tend not to be circular, so you would have to use masking to hide the bits of the bitmap which fell outside the circle.

Of course, you could use masking with vectors to create any number of effects to spice up the site, such as a ticker tape message (showing all the latest company headlines, etc) scrolling along part of the bottom of the site. You would then have to mask the text in the same way as we did with the TV earlier.

In actuality, we'll do something a little different for now: we'll create a simple text effect for the company client list. The client list will be one of the components of the **Information** movie clip that we've been working on before. The client list will show up when the user clicks on the **Clients** button, and we're going to use an animated mask to reveal the clients' names one by one.

Masking the Company Client List

1. Open up your case study movie.

2. Go into the **Information** movie clip by double clicking on it from the library window:

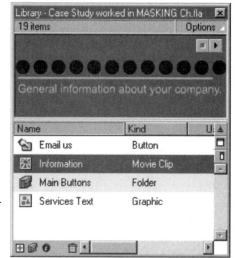

Notice that we've cleaned up our library by putting all of the buttons' movie clips into the **Main Buttons** sub-folder.

3. Create two new layers above the **Titles** layer, calling the top one '**Mask**' and the bottom one '**Masked Layer**':

Now we need to extend the movie clip's timeline so we can add our masking effect.

4. Create some space for the new effect by extending all the layers from frame 26 up to frame 45. Use that old 'click, drag across and down, and press *F5*' technique:

After inserting your frames, the timeline will look something like this:

We'll be adding your client list to **Masked Layer** - this list is what the mask will reveal. First, we need to make sure that the other components currently in the **Information** movie clip don't spill over into the display of client list.

5. To do this, ***Control-click*** on frame 26 in the **Titles** layer and insert a **blank** keyframe. You can do this via the **Insert > Blank keyframe** menu, or with *F7*, remember.

6. Now do the same for the **Info** layer.

7. Next, add another blank keyframe at frame 19 of the **Morphs** layer.

Your timeline will now look like this:

What we've doing is pooling all of the information content that'll be called from the movie's interactive buttons. The **Information** movie clip won't play all the way through sequentially: instead, Flash will jump to specific sections depending upon which button the user presses. *That's* why we're separating out the content on the timeline using these blank keyframes. Flash will jump into the Information clip, play a few frames of self-contained content, and then jump out again. This will be controlled with ActionScript, which we'll start examining in the next chapter.

We now have nothing in the movie clip from frame 26 onwards. A blank canvas on which to create our masking magic, no less.

Next, we'll add the title, underline, and information text for the client list.

8. Add a keyframe in the **Titles** layer at frame 30. This is where we're going to put the title for the client-related piece of self-contained content that can be jumped to on the timeline.

9. In frame 30 on the Titles layer, add the title '**CLIENTS**' in the same way that you previously added the **SERVICES** title in the last chapter:

   This consists of a text box, and a line drawn with the Line tool.

   Make sure that the **CLIENTS** title occupies the same space in relation to the registration point as the **SERVICES** title. There are number of different ways to do this: using the positional information on the Info panel; turning *onion skinning* on across frames 25 - 30; or copying the **SERVICES** title and underline from frame 25, pasting them *in place* in frame 30, and then amending the text and scaling the line.

10. Add a new keyframe in frame 30 of the new layer called **Masked Layer**.

11. In this keyframe, use a text box to type in the client list:

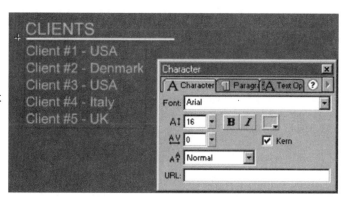

   This is the client list that we'll be applying the masking effect to. As you can see, we've used Arial 16 point.

   Your timeline now looks like this:

We want the client list text to start off as completely hidden, and reveal itself from the top downwards. It's easier to mask the final frame *first*, as this means that we can be sure the mask completely covers the text.

12. Add a new keyframe at frame 45 of the **Mask** layer and then add a black, strokeless rectangle that just covers all of the clients list text:

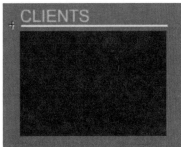

The black rectangle is our mask. Now, there are two ways we can go here: we can either make the mask a symbol and create a *motion* tween, or we can leave the mask as it is - just a fill - and use a shape tween. Just for variety, let's use a *shape* tween.

13. Select the black rectangle and copy it.

14. Create a new keyframe at frame 30 of the **Mask** layer and paste the rectangle *in place* in the new keyframe. This is the frame where the mask will start off from.

15. To get the mask into its start position, move the rectangle copy in frame 30 and move it *straight upwards*, clear of the client list, so that it will ultimately roll down without wobbling between frames 30 and 45.

    If your hands are not as steady as you'd like, use the arrow keys to nudge the rectangle. You do this by selecting the rectangle, and tapping the 'up' arrow key to move it to the correct position (you can also use *Shift* and the 'up' arrow for a bit more speed).

    Here's where to the rectangle should be in frame 30:

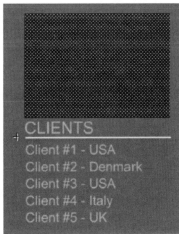

Remember that you don't have to worry about the mask rolling down over the title: only the content on the **Masked** layer will be affected by the mask.

16. With the keyframe at frame 30 still selected, use the **Frame** panel to add a shape tween.

Finally, we want to activate the mask.

17. Make **Mask** into a mask layer using the **Modify > Layer** menu and **Masked Layer** into a masked layer. Then lock both layers:

You can see the effect by going to frame 30 and pressing **Enter**. Make sure that the mask and mask layer are both locked as shown, otherwise the mask won't be active.

Now it's time to play. The reason we used a shape tween and not a motion tween is because there are now a number of different transitions you can try out. For example, rather than have the rectangle scroll down, you can have it appear in the center of the text as a small square and grow bigger. Simply delete the rectangle mask in frame 30 and replace it with a shape and size of your choice. There are endless variations to try here. Have fun!

Summary

We've seen here that masks in Flash can help achieve a range of pretty damned snazzy effects. You can make masks as simple or complex as you wish, and you can encapsulate masking functionality inside movie clip symbols.

We saw that:

◆ Masks are created on a special mask layer

◆ The mask layer is applied to a masked layer (or layers)

◆ The mask layer and all the layers it is being applied to must be locked for the mask effect to be seen

◆ A mask can consist of a shape (or shapes), text, lines - whatever you like, provided that it's a symbol

◆ Masks can be static or animated

Masks are useful for:

◆ Hiding and revealing selected parts of an animation

◆ Achieving a sense of depth

◆ Animating bitmap images as if they were vectors

In chapter 9, we're going to start on the next - very exciting - leg of our journey: we're going to start delving into the world of **ActionScript**.

CONTACT

+

Email: Support@friendsofED.com

friendsofED Ltd

29 S. La Salle St.

Suite 520

Chicago

IL 60603

USA

9 Actions and Interactions

What we'll cover in this chapter:

- Introduction to **interactivity** - the fundamentals of **interaction**, **events** and **event handlers** in Flash

- Introducing ActionScript - the programming language that makes Flash so powerful

- Creating interactive Flash sites with buttons and basic **ActionScript**:

    - **Animating** buttons

    - Adding **sound** to buttons

    - Invisible buttons

    - Attaching **ActionScript** to buttons and frames in the timeline to control the way the movie plays back, and to provide navigation features

▶

This chapter moves us along a significant way in our Flash journey. We're coming to the brow of a hill, and a whole new vista of Flash possibilities is going to open up before us, and there, bathed in sunlight, is the land of **ActionScript**.

ActionScript is what makes Flash a living, breathing, responsive program rather than just a brilliant linear animation tool. ActionScript is what enables Flash to be **interactive**.

Interactivity

Interactivity, in this context, means that your Flash movie, when it's running in the user's browser, *responds* to something that the user does, or *reacts* to pre-defined set of conditions. For example:

- Branching out of the movie's linear playback and playing a different movie clip when the user presses a button, or when the playhead hits a particular frame

- Saving the user's name and email address, which they've typed into a couple of text boxes

- Confirming the user's order when they've added things to their shopping cart in a Flash e-commerce site

- Playing different songs on a Flash jukebox

- Dragging around pieces of a puzzle in a Flash jigsaw

All of these examples rely on Flash's ability to respond to **events**. An *event* is simply something that *happens*. When you create an interactive movie, you plan the things that can happen, build an interface (buttons, text-entry boxes etc) that will allow the user to *make* those things - events - happen, and you create the ActionScript that will *handle* those events.

Events and Event Handlers

Walk along street

EVENT — Reach friend's building

EVENT HANDLER — Stop, turn right, walk up to door

In order for interaction to take place you need to have an **event** and an **event handler**. When you call on a friend, you walk along the street until you reach their building. When this 'reaching their building' event takes place, the 'I've reached their building' event *handler* in your brain responds by turning your steps towards their door. Something of significance - an event - has occurred, and a piece of processing has been carried out to handle it.

Now you push the doorbell or intercom button to let your friend know you've arrived. Your friend will then come to the door, look out of the window to see who's disturbed them, or grunt down the intercom.

Pressing that button was another event, and this time your friend responded to it - they 'handled' it, in that they were stimulated to *do something* by the buzzer sounding. From here you can discuss what you're going to do with your day - your extended interaction with your friend starts with the push of a button. If your friend had been out, or hadn't answered the door, your very own 'they're not there, I'll go to the mall' event handler would have kicked in. In the real world, events and event handling is complex - infinite, even. In Flash, you can control the environment more, and in your interactive movies you can plan for the anticipated range of events and handle them all.

And that, more or less, is everything that interaction is.

Let's examine one of the primary and most intuitive of tools that Flash gives us for interaction with the user - the **button**.

Buttons as Interactive Elements

In an interactive Flash movie, an *event* will be triggered by the mouse being clicked on, or dragged over, something on the screen - typically a button. The event *handler* here will be a set of instructions that we've attached to the button. These instructions will tell Flash exactly what we want it to do when the user clicks on that button and triggers the 'click' event. These instructions are written in Flash's internal programming language - **ActionScript**. ActionScript is really a set of instructions and structures that we can use to tie together all of the components in our movies so that they function as an integrated and coherent whole.

It's important to realise that a button on its own does not 'produce' interaction. A button placed in a movie has its default states - Up, Over, Down, and Hit - but they won't actually *do* anything interesting unless we explicitly tell them to. We've already seen that we can add keyframes to the button's internal timeline and change its display in each state, which makes the button more interesting to *look at*. But the button is still essentially 'dumb' - all it can do at the moment is *detect* events, such as when it's rolled over or pressed. To boost the button's intelligence we have to attach ActionScript to its different states: it's the ActionScript element that decides what to do when the button is pressed, and it's ActionScript that creates the interaction:

Basic button: - default look, four states, but all the same

Modified button: - each state defined in new keyframes

Intelligent button:

Use ActionScript to display preview image

Use ActionScript to take user to new page or movie

When you've attached the ActionScript to your button and added an instance of the button to your movie, the button will sit there, just itching for the user to interact with it.

In some programming languages - BASIC, for example - once your program starts, the program code is always running. In Flash, your 'program' - the ActionScript - is attached to a button, and will only run *when the button detects a particular action carried out by the user*. As your knowledge of Flash increases, you'll see why this is a much better way of creating user interfaces. One of the main features of advanced Flash sites is their use of buttons to start off lots of simple little sequences that, together, form a complex, fully animated and interactive user experience.

As we progress in the next couple of chapters, you'll see that a button in Flash can be much more than just a switch; as well as detecting simple things like mouse clicks to provide navigation, the button can be used to start whole *avalanches* of actions in motion.

Let's start with a simple button.

Creating a Simple Button

So, to create an interactive element in our movie, we need a button on the stage waiting to be pressed - giving us an event - and some ActionScript attached to it to handle the event and tell Flash what to do.

Before we look at attaching ActionScript that responds to mouse clicks, let's make sure we're getting the most out of our buttons by creating a simple button and slowly developing its abilities.

1. Create a new movie and rename the default layer as buttons.

2. Go to **View > Grid > Show Grid** and then **View > Grid > Snap to Grid** and ensure that both are checked - this will help us position our symbols on the stage more accurately.

3. Insert a new graphic symbol and name it **circle**. Make it a red circle with a black outline. Don't put your new symbol on the stage just yet:

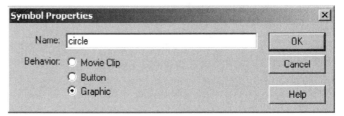

The reason we've created a graphic symbol before making it into a button is that we'll be using the circle many times within the button itself. By making the circle a symbol beforehand, we're allowing Flash to re-use the circle symbol, thus saving time and space.

4. Back on the main, stage, and in the library window, go to **Options > New Symbol** and create a new button symbol called button:

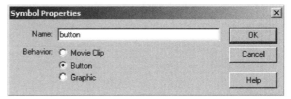

You'll now be inside the button symbol for editing, and you'll see a blank stage with button at the top. The timeline will contain the four button symbol states; **Up**, **Over**, **Down**, and **Hit**.

Remember the definitions of the four states of the button symbol:

- The **Up** state is how it looks in its original size and position

- **Over** is how it will look when the user's mouse passes over it

- **Down** is how it will look when it's clicked

- **Hit** contains filled spaces that denote the areas the user must be over to press the button

5. With the playhead on the Up state, click on the **circle** graphic symbol icon in the library and drag an instance of it onto the stage inside the button:

We're going to need to know the *exact* position of our symbol in the Up state - this is so that we can make the different visual renderings of the button's other states consistent. To do this, we'll use the **Info** panel to place it in the exact center of the stage.

6. Click on the central black box of the grid icon in the top right quadrant of the Info panel. With your circle symbol selected inside the button, enter **0.0** in the **X** and **Y** fields:

Only the Up frame of the button's timeline currently has a keyframe. To start bringing the other states to life, we need to add keyframes.

7. Add a blank keyframe to each of the other three states. You have now put an instance of the graphic symbol **circle** into each state of your button symbol:

In the finished movie, we want to make this button get bigger when it's rolled over, and smaller when it's pressed. We can do this by scaling the instance in each of the button's 'state' keyframes, and we're going to scale each one by a specific amount.

8. Bring up the **Transform** panel using **Windows > Panels > Transform**, and select the Over state in the button timeline.

9. Check the **Constrain** box in the **Transform** panel to maintain the proportions of the circle, and type 120% in either the horizontal or vertical scale fields.

10. Press the **Apply Transform** button or *Enter*. Make sure that the center position of the button stays in exactly the same place as in the Up state, otherwise the button will appear to move slightly when animated. You might need to drag the scaled version back to the central position - or you can use the **Info** panel again.

Also, don't make the Over state much bigger than the Hit state. You'll see why when you test the button: the parts of the Over state that are *outside* the Hit state won't respond to the mouse.

11. Now select the Down state and scale the circle instance there down to 80%.

Although it's not vital in this exercise, it's a good idea to make the Hit area a solid black object to avoid missing unfilled holes which, as explained earlier, could result in the button working erratically.

12. To do this, select the Hit state and go to the **Effect** panel. Select **Brightness** from the drop down menu and move the slider to -100%:

You can confirm that the Hit state circle has the same location and size as the Up state instance either by looking at all four states simultaneously using the onion skins tool, or by checking that the values in the Info panel match for each state.

13. Click on the **Scene 1** icon above the timeline and put an instance of the button symbol at the center of the stage by dragging it out of the library.

14. Test the movie. You'll notice that when the mouse goes over your button, it changes from a pointer to a hand icon and the button gets bigger. When you click and hold the button, it gets smaller:

That's the basic button defined. Time to accelerate its evolution into a more intelligent species of button.

Creating Animated Buttons

Flash allows us to define a *movie* as one of the button states. This feature allows us to create buttons that have complete animations within them. Let's create a simple animation and add it to the Over state of our button.

Putting a Movie into a Button

1. On the Edit Symbols stage, select the Over and Down states of the button from the previous exercise in turn, and press the Remove Transform button (or use **Modify >Transform > Remove Transform**). This will return both states' circle instances back to the same size as the Up state:

Now we'll create a simple movie that'll play when the user activates the button.

2. In the library window go to **Options > New Symbol** and create a new movie clip symbol called **circlemovie**.

3. In frame 1 of the new movie clip place an instance of the circle symbol at **X:0.0**, **Y:0.0** using the **Info** panel:

4. Add a keyframe at frame 10 and then use the **Transform** panel to reduce the size of the frame 10 circle instance to 40%:

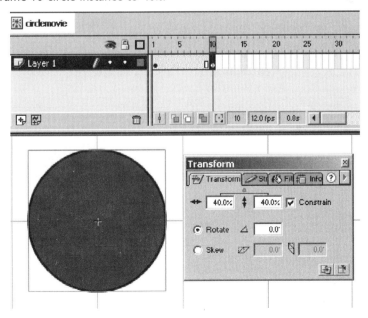

5. Add a motion tween at frame 1. If you turn on onion skinning between frames 1 and 10 you should see the button make the vaguely psychedelic pattern shown in the screenshot - simulating the way your button will shrink when its Over state is activated:

Once you've finished looking at the groovy pattern, click the onion skin mode button again to turn it back off.

We're now going to put our animated **circlemovie** symbol into the Over state of our **button** symbol - replacing the instance of the graphic symbol circle that's currently there.

6. To edit the **button** symbol, double click its icon in the library, and then select the Over state.

7. Select the **circle** symbol instance in the Over state and, using the **Info** panel, note its **W**, **H**, **X**, and **Y** attributes. Then delete the symbol.

Now we want to put an instance of our **circlemovie** animated movie clip in place of the **circle** symbol we just deleted.

8. Make sure that the playhead is on the Over state, and then drag an instance of **circlemovie** from the library and onto the stage.

9. Select the **circlemovie** instance on the stage and enter the attributes for **W, H, X,**and **Y** that you noted down from **circle** before: this way, we can ensure that it's in *exactly* the right place:

10. Now test the movie by pressing **F12**.

Notice that when your mouse goes over the button, you see a looping animation of a smoothly receding button.

Although the animation we have chosen here is not really *that* impressive, remember that you can have any number of animated effects embedded in a movie clip inside the button. All you have to make sure is that the first frame of the animation is the same size as the rest of the button states - from there, your over state button image could morph into a mushroom, a dog...anything you like. Also, note that you should never animate the button's Hit state (unless you *really* want to mess with the users mind!).

Although we now have a button with visual feedback, the button is still silent. Real buttons tend to click or squeak or ring. Let's add a sound.

Creating Buttons that Talk

The first thing we need is a sound file. It's beyond the scope of this chapter to specify the ins and outs of sound issues, so instead let's simply pull in an appropriate sound from the Internet.

Check out the Sound Sampling appendix at the back of this book for sites where you can download sounds. If you don't want to download from the internet right now, search your computer for an appropriate short sound clip - a .wav on the PC, and an .aiff file on the Mac.

Making our Button Buzz

The first thing to do is to get the sound into our movie's library.

1. To import your sound into the same button movie we've just worked on, use the **File > Import** menu and locate the appropriate file in the dialog box:

Once the sound file imports, your library window will look something like this:

You can hear the sound by pressing the play button on the top right.

Ideally, we would now edit the sound to optimize it, but we'll leave all that until our dedicated 'sound' chapter. Right now, what we need to do is attach the sound to the button.

2. Go into Edit Symbols mode on the **button** symbol.

3. Create a new layer called **sound** - this layer will be used to hold the sound our button will make.

4. Now add a blank keyframe to each of the button states.

5. Select the Down state on the **sound** layer:

This is the most usual button state to attach a sound to, and putting our sound here will make the button 'sound off' when it is pressed.

6. Open the **Sound** panel (**Window > Panels > Sound**) and click on the **Sound** drop-down menu - this will drop down to show you all the currently available sounds. Unimpressively, only the one you just imported will be there.

7. Select your sound. The **Sound** panel should now look something like the one shown here:

Look closely at the Down keyframe after you have done this. There's a tiny blue waveform shown on the keyframe to signify that a sound has now been attached there:

8. Test the movie. Hear your sound when you press the button? Yes? Then we're done!

9. Save your movie.

When you add sound to a button's Down state in the way that we've done here, you're adding sound to *all* instances of the button. This is a major advantage for adding sound to a previously silent website: if your website uses many instances of a single button symbol, you only need to add sound once for *all* your buttons to start making sounds.

When you attach sound to a button using ActionScript, it's only added to that particular *instance* of the button on the stage, and only that instance is affected. We're going to look at ActionScript properly right now.

Introducing ActionScript

Earlier, we likened clicking on a Flash button to what happens when we ring on someone's doorbell. Having a Flash button all by itself is like ringing the doorbell at a house where nobody's home, or where the wiring's been disconnected. The button we've just created looks pretty enough but, beyond the default state-related behavior that we've just explored, it doesn't actually trigger anything when you press it. It doesn't really *handle* the 'click' event: when we click on a button as a user, the sound or embedded animation that plays isn't what we're really concerned with - what we're really interested in is where that button's going to take us, or what it's going to make happen. We need to *wire the button up*.

By adding ActionScript we can make our buttons actually take us somewhere. ActionScript, remember, is exact instructions that Flash follows when responding to an event. ActionScript *is* the wiring.

To start demonstrating ActionScript's features, we're going to create a simple movie where Flash asks the user to pick one of two options, and then responds differently for each of the two possible responses. This implies a logical 'branching' in our movie rather than a straightforward linear playback: we'll present the user with two colored buttons and the user will press one of them, causing Flash to go to one of two possible places. This ability to branch and make alternative choices is an important principle in creating interactive movies.

Before we can add an ActionScript and make an interactive movie, we need to create a basic 'front end' for the user to interact with: this will contain buttons that access the different places the user can be taken to. We're going to set these up now.

Creating a Basic Front End

1. Carry on working with the button movie from the previous exercise.

2. Drag another instance of your **button** symbol from the library out onto the main stage - make sure you drag in the button symbol and **not** the graphic symbol.

3. Position the two button instances so they're next to each other in the center of the stage.

4. If it isn't open already, open the **Effects** panel. With one of your button instances highlighted, select **Tint** from the drop down menu and make the button blue by clicking on a blue part of the 'spectrum bar' at the bottom of the panel.

    You've just altered the properties of this specific instance of the **button** symbol: the underlying symbol has remained the same. Remember that each individual instance has a range of properties that we can change via the options in the **Effect** panel.

5. Repeat this **Tint** change for the other button, but make this one *pink*.

6. Create a new layer called **text** and use a text box to type '**pick your favorite color**' above the two buttons.

    Your stage should look like this:

pick your favorite color

Here, you've used the same button symbol twice, but made them look different by changing the color of the two instances. This is a timesaving trick used by many Flash web designers to help workflow when creating sites that have many different buttons on them. They just create one 'master' button and then change the appearance of each *instance*.

Now we need to set up two areas of our site that Flash will take us to when each button is pressed - one area for the pink button, and one for the blue button. We're going to put these areas in a separate scene from the default Scene 1 where we just created the front-end.

7. Bring up the **Scene** panel if it is not already open by going to **Window > Panel > Scene**. This will show you that you only have one scene at the moment, **Scene 1**.

8. Double click on the clapperboard icon of this scene - this will allow you to rename it. Call it **Scene 1 Buttons**.

9. Create a *new* scene by clicking on the + button at the bottom right of the panel. Call this scene **Scene 2 Choice**.

10. Click once on **Scene 2 Choice** to select it:

Inside the new scene, there'll only be one empty layer called **Layer1**. Don't worry, you haven't deleted everything! We're looking at our new scene, which is currently empty. You can check that you're actually in the new scene by looking at the top left of the timeline window, which will say **Scene 2 Choice**:

11. Rename the default layer in Scene 2 as **text**, and then add a new layer called **labels**.

12. Click in frame 2, and use the familiar 'click, drag, *F5*' trick to add frames to each layer to make the scene 30 frames long in total:

When the user presses any of the buttons in Scene 1, we want Flash to jump to particular points in Scene 2 - points which are related to whichever button the user chose:

Scene 1:

Scene 2:

We'll now label these points in Scene 2 so that they're properly signposted - which means that we can then use ActionScript to jump straight to them.

13. Select frame 1 in the **labels** Layer. Go to the **Frame** panel and type **pink** into the **Label** field:

What you've done here is specifically attach a label to frame 1 of the **labels** layer. With this label in place, you can use ActionScript to jump directly to this frame, in this scene, from anywhere else in the movie. That's a pretty powerful thing to be able to do - bypass the linear tyranny of the timeline and jump around inside the movie.

Notice that Flash has added a little flag in the timeline and is displaying the label name next to it:

We can use this label as a reference point for the pink button-related content that we want the user to be able to jump to.

Now we need to partition off this 'pink-labeled' section of the Scene 2 timeline from the part that we want to set aside for the stuff related to the *blue* button.

14. ***Control-click*** to select frame 15 in the same layer and add a new keyframe. Use the **Frame** panel's **Label** box to label the new keyframe **blue**:

Now, on the **text** layer, we're going to type the content the user will see when they press either of our two colored buttons. This is the content that's associated with the respective blue and pink parts of the timeline as marked by the labels.

15. Add a keyframe at frame 15 in the **text** layer and use a text box to type '**You selected blue!**' Center your text at the top of the stage.

16. In frame 1 of the **text** layer, type '**You selected pink!**' in the same place on the stage. You can use the onion skin tool to view both sentences at the same time if you want to place them precisely, or use the readings in the Info panel.

Your Scene 2 timeline should now look like this:

So, what we've done here is create two separate messages, each of which lives on its own separately-labeled section of the timeline in Scene 2. We know that we can use those labels as reference points that we can jump straight to using ActionScript.

Now we're ready to go back to Scene 1 and start getting our hands dirty by adding some ActionScript to do the jumping!

Attaching ActionScript to Timelines and Buttons

We now have a simple front end for the user to interface with and two alternative locations to move on to from the two buttons. However, when we play the movie at the moment, the playhead will zip through the movie in resolutely linear fashion: Scene 1 will go straight into Scene 2 and not give the user chance to choose a color. We need to shout: 'STOP!' at the end of Scene 1 so that the front end hangs around and gives the user time to ponder the alternatives and make their choice.

To do this we add an ActionScript **to a frame** in the timeline telling the movie to halt at a particular point: this will give the user all the time in the world to choose a button, and when they do we need to make sure Flash knows which part of Scene 2 to take them to. To do *this* we attach an ActionScript **to each button**. When we've added our ActionScript we'll have a fully working interactive movie.

To summarize:

- We can add ActionScript to a frame so that the ActionScript is triggered when the playhead reaches that frame

- We can attach ActionScript to a button so that the ActionScript is only triggered when the user clicks on the button. Here, the user triggers the event and the ActionScript handles it.

Let's add the ActionScript that'll hook up the front-end with the specific chunks of content in Scene 2.

Adding ActionScript to a Frame

1. Add a new layer to scene 1 called **halt**.

2. Select frame 1 in this layer and go to the **Window > Actions** menu option.

    Up pops up an interesting-looking window called **Frame Actions**:

    Don't worry. The reason this window looks a little daunting is that it's showing a whole *range* of ActionScript possibilities at the same time. The left-hand pane shows the available ActionScript elements, and the right-hand pane (currently empty) will display the specific elements that we've chosen to apply to this particular frame.

> *If your panel doesn't have the list of commands between Basic Actions and Actions like the one pictured, just click on the book icon next to Basic Actions to open it up.*

The open 'book' at the top contains all of Flash's **Basic Actions** - essentially, the relatively simple ones that were present in Flash 4. The other folders shown in the screenshot host the great riches that ActionScript has added in Flash 5.

For now, just remember that implementing ActionScript rests on your having an idea of what you want your movie to do, and then finding the particular

ActionScript element (or combination of elements) that'll let you achieve your aim - don't worry that you have to learn each and every element that's hidden away in this collection of little folders. ActionScript is a rich and powerful language in its Flash 5 incarnation, and you can go as far as you like with it. We'll go into more detail about the extended functions in the next chapter, and later in the book, but for now we're going to use this dialog box to give our movie a single, simple instruction.

The little blue circles you can now see below the **Basic Actions** icon are ActionScript **commands** or **actions**. These are the instructions we can give to our movie to tell it to do stuff and go places.

3. Double-click on the third command down, called Stop:

Two things happen.

Firstly, there's now a little **'a'** in the first frame of the **halt** layer. This signifies that this keyframe has a piece of ActionScript attached to it.

Secondly, a little bit of text has appeared in the right hand pane of the **Frame Actions** window. This is the piece of ActionScript itself - an ActionScript command telling frame 1 to do something when the playhead hits it.

What we've done so far is add a one line ActionScript command to the first frame of Scene 1, telling Flash to 'stop when you get to this frame'. Let's be clear about exactly how Flash will respond to this instruction: Flash will **not** turn off the animation - it'll merely *pause* it and wait to see what happens next. Our buttons will still be active, and all the visual content will remain on display in the user's browser. This Stop action is simply our way of saying 'keep those buttons on display where the user can see them'.

4. If you preview the movie now, your two buttons will be on permanent display, and if you move the mouse over them, they'll go through animated scaling behavior we built into the Over state.

We've used ActionScript to achieve our first objective of keeping the buttons up so that the viewer can choose their favorite color on the buttons.

What Flash needs to know *next* is where we want to take the user when they click on one of those buttons. To do this we're going to attach an ActionScript **to each button**. These pieces of ActionScript will hook up each button to its dedicated piece of content - we can use the labels to tell Flash and ActionScript *where* to go. But Flash also needs to know *when* to move to Scene 2.

Remember the **events** and **event handlers** that set off our 'visit a friend' interaction at the beginning of the chapter? Well, we want our interaction in this movie to start with the user doing something with their mouse on or near our button. What we're trying to detect here is called a **mouse event**. You can ask Flash (which acts as the event handler) to detect one or more types of mouse event. The most common ones are:

A **Press** event occurs when the user *clicks* on the button. You may think that this would be the event of choice to ask Flash to detect, but it actually causes Flash to race off and start doing new things as soon as the button is pressed. This doesn't leave any time for the user to see the button working - for instance, running the nice animation that we've built into the button.

Release is when the user *releases* the mouse button after a press, and it's what we use in the many situations because it allows us to see the button in its Down state.

A **Release Outside** event occurs when the user presses our button and then drags the mouse away from the button while keeping the mouse pressed. The event is triggered when the mouse is finally released. Why would you use this event? Well, you might use it when your buttons are very small and the user could inadvertently drag the mouse outside the button area before they release it. In this situation you could ask Flash to detect either Release *or* Release Outside.

The **Roll Over** and **Roll Out** events are used to detect whether or not the mouse is *over* a certain area. Buttons set up to detect these two events only don't usually look like buttons at all. For example, if you had a bitmap picture of the world and you wanted a bit of text at the bottom of the map to change to reflect which country the mouse was over, you would add a lot of country shaped buttons. Think of buttons asked to detect Roll Over and Roll Out events as 'mouse position sensors' rather than true buttons, and this class of mouse event will start to make more sense.

Notice that in the **Frame Actions** panel the last basic action - **On Mouse Event** - is currently grayed out. This is because we currently have a *frame* selected on the timeline. In a finished and published Flash movie, the mouse will only be able to generate mouse events on or around a **button**. Let's see how to attach actions to buttons now.

Adding ActionScript to a Button

1. Back in Scene 1, select the pink button with the Arrow tool.

   Notice that the title bar in the **Frame Actions** window has changed to **Object Actions** (telling us that we're tying this ActionScript to an object on the stage rather to a frame), and that **On Mouse Event** ActionScript element is now available in the pane on the left.

2. Double-click **On Mouse Event** in the left-hand frame:

   In the right hand pane, this ActionScript command appears:

   ```
   on (release) {
   }
   ```

This may look a bit too nerdy for some, but remember that you did not actually have to write it - Flash is generating the 'code' for you: you're just choosing the actions from the list on the left. When the code appears in the right-hand pane, Flash has recognized that you've attached it to the button in question.

The curly brackets at the end of the **on (release)** are a necessity of ActionScript's syntax, but the core part of the code is in the **on (release)** statement: this is now attached to our pink button, and it tells Flash "when the user clicks on me and releases the mouse button, I'm going to ask you to do something".

It's possible to type the code directly into the right-hand pane if you know the correct syntax to use. At the moment, we're using the ActionScript window in 'Normal' mode, but 'Expert' mode is available to you if you want to dispense with the tremendous amount of help that Flash gives you in Normal mode. You can switch between modes by clicking on the little right-facing arrow at the top of Actions

At the bottom of the window, where it says **Event**, you can choose *which* of the available mouse events you want Flash to detect. Try checking and unchecking the different fields to see how it affects the ActionScript in the right pane. Here, Flash is letting you make simple point and click choices that automatically alter the ActionScript attached to the button.

3. When you're done experimenting with the mouse event check boxes, make sure that you leave only the **Release** event checked.

   We now need to tell the event handler (Flash) exactly what to do when it detects the mouse being clicked and released over our pink button. This instruction will be appended to the **on (release)** code.

4. Double-click on the **Go To** action at the top of the list. This will add a new piece of code into the right-hand pane:

This is the default option for the Play ActionScript element. Essentially, the ActionScript we've assembled in the window is saying to Flash: "When the user release the mouse on this button, go and play some content that's stored elsewhere."

We now have to point Flash at that specific content.

5. Now look at the options that have appeared at the bottom of the **Object Actions** window:

These options help us make the choice about *exactly* where we're going to send Flash to find the content that we want it to play when the user clicks on the button. As we already know, we've created that content in Scene 2, and given each chunk of content labels.

6. Select the **Scene** drop down menu at the bottom of the **Object Actions** window and select **Scene 2 Choice**. (If you can't see the pull down menu tabs, make the window a bit wider).

Notice that this selection has now been incorporated into the **gotoAndPlay** statement:

7. Next, select the **Type** drop down menu.

This is where we specify more detail about the destination we're sending Flash to, and tells the event handler to go to either a specific *frame* in scene 2 or to a specific *label*.

8. Select **Frame Label**. The reason we're using *labels* is that if we were to change Scene 2, the frame numbers will change as we add or delete frames. By using a label, we're signposting the particular frame we are interested in, and this signpost will move with its frame as we add or delete frames on either side of it.

9. Tell the event handler which label in Scene 2 we want to go to by selecting the label **pink** from the **Frame** drop down menu:

10. Un-check the **Go to and Play** field at the bottom left of the window:

Notice that the second instruction in the right pane of the window is now **gotoAndStop**, not **gotoAndPlay**, and that the **'pink'** label is now inserted into the code:

This means Flash will stop when it gets to the new label, keeping the display of Scene 2's content on the screen.

> *It's important to note that the ActionScript is added to an instance of a button symbol on the stage, not the symbol itself in the library.*

11. Without closing the **Object Actions** window, select the blue button on the stage.

    The right pane of the **Objects Action** window will now be empty, as we haven't yet attached any actions to the blue button.

12. Repeat the steps you took to add the ActionScript to the pink button, this time telling the event handler to take the user to the blue label in **Scene 2**:

    • Add the On Mouse Event ActionScript element

    • Add the Go To element

- Uncheck the Go to and Play box

- Select the Scene, Type, and Frame in the drop-down boxes

13. When you're done, the **Object Actions** window for the blue button should look like this:

14. Test the movie (*Control-Enter*) and see if it's interactive!

When you click and release the mouse over one of the buttons your movie should take you to the appropriate part of scene 2. You'll notice that once you've made a selection you can't go back and try the other option. To do this you need to rewind your movie back to the start. This is done either by pressing the 'Rewind to Start' button on the **Controller** window (**Window > Toolbars >Controller**) that appears when you test your movie, or by going to the **Control > Rewind** menu option:

pick your favorite color

Rewind to Start Button

Although this interactive movie is very simple, the way we took the user to one of a choice of places depending on which button they pressed is the key to building website navigation. Instead of just two colored buttons, we could have used a whole menu of buttons, each taking us to a different part of the website.

What if our movie was actually part of a children's wear website, and we were asking the question because we wanted to know if the user's child was a boy or a girl? We could enable the user to jump from our movie to another Flash page that presented either boys' or girls' clothes.

Lets do it!

Linking your Movie to a URL

In this next exercise, we're going to use ActionScript to redirect the user to a different web page, with a specific URL, depending upon which button they press. Again, we're going to attach ActionScript to the buttons to achieve this.

Using ActionScript to Jump to a URL

Here, we're going to create two very simple drawings of a girl and a boy to display below the stereotypically color-gendered content in Scene 2 (i.e. pink for a girl and blue for a boy, like our buttons). We're then going to put an **invisible button** behind each drawing and use ActionScript to link the drawing to a web page when it's pressed:

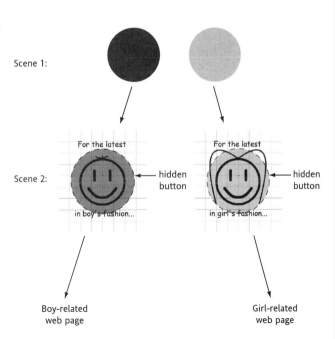

1. Continue using the same button-based movie.

2. Create two new graphic symbols called girl and boy, and in each one, draw an image of a girl and a boy respectively.

   We'll leave it to your own ingenuity and good taste to create your own boy and girl drawings, but make sure you include a line of text that'll entice the user to push the invisible buttons that we'll add soon:

3. In Scene 2, select frame 1 of the **text** layer and drag an instance of **girl** out of the library and position it under the '**you selected pink!**' text.

4. Now select frame 15 and position an instance of **boy** under '**you selected blue!**'

5. Still in **Scene 2**, create a new layer called **buttons** and drag it down so that it's underneath the other two layers. Create a keyframe in this layer at frame 15.

6. Select frame 1 in the **buttons** layer and then click on your **button** symbol in the library and drag it onto the stage behind the **girl** symbol.

7. Scale the button so that it completely surrounds **girl**. You should have something like this:

   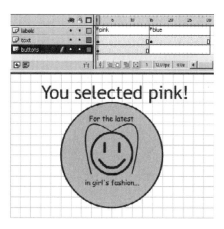

Now we want to go to take the user to a new web page when they click on the button behind **girl**.

The ActionScript we attach to this button will tell Flash "when the user clicks and releases the mouse over this button, go to the web page we specify". We do this using the **Get URL** action.

8. With the new button selected, open the **Object Actions** window if it isn't already open. Double-click on the sixth basic action in the list - **Get URL**:

Notice that the event handler automatically assumes we want it to detect an on (release) mouse event. This is the default setting, and if you know you're going to use it you don't need to double-click On Mouse Event, but can go straight to your second piece of ActionScript. The event handler will detect the mouse being released over the button just as it did in the previous exercise.

9. In the **URL** field at the bottom of the window type '**http://www.friendsofed.com**' - or a URL of your choice - it can even point to a file on your own machine if you wish.

You'll notice that we have added the whole URL here, including the http:// bit, making the address an *absolute* one. It's always a good idea to do this in Flash, otherwise the command may have strange effects on certain servers.

Our button will now take the user to a web page (not exactly full of suitable clothes, but you see the principle...). However, the button is spoiling our lovely drawing. An invisible button would make our movie look much more pleasing.

10. With the button still selected go to the **Effect** panel (**Window > Panels > Effects** if not already open) and select **Alpha** from the drop down menu. Set the button's alpha value to **0%**:

This is a very powerful but simple technique. By making our button transparent, we can put it on top of or below any other bitmap or symbol, making the user think that the symbol or bitmap is the button. And to do all this, we've still only used the same old master button symbol we created.

Now to create the invisible button and URL specification for the blue option.

11. In Scene 2, insert a keyframe at frame 15 of the **buttons** layer and drag in the button symbol.

12. Scale the button, and then add the ActionScript to it - this time make the URL **'http://www.wrox.com'** (or your own choice), and then use the alpha effect to make the button instance invisible.

13. Test your movie.

    It will now take the user to one of two new destinations.

We've learnt a lot in this chapter so far...

We have learnt that buttons in Flash are a prime means of adding interactivity and sound to a web site. We have seen that buttons do not have to actually look like real life buttons, and can be anything from invisible ghosts to entire movies in their own right. They can be any shape or size we choose, and we can use the same button over and over again and make each one look different.

We have learnt how to give Flash instructions to jump to new parts of our movie when it detects the user pushing a button. Not only have we learnt how to attach ActionScript to buttons that tell Flash what to do, we have learnt how to add ActionScript to the timeline as well, so that we can make Flash go through its timeline in a non linear way if we choose to do so.

Let's finish off with the case study.

Case Study

This final tutorial is another continuation of the project we've been working on in the preceding chapters.

So far in our case study web site, we have a lot of pieces of functioning but free-floating, isolated content. It's time to put that right by using ActionScript to add some controlling actions. As we already know, ActionScript is the string that ties our site together.

The first thing to look at is the main timeline. We want the timeline to stop when it reaches the last frame. That doesn't mean that the web site will freeze up, it just means that the timeline itself will wait, displaying the background and the buttons until a button is pressed telling Flash to go do something else.

ActionScript-enabling the Timeline

It's always a good idea to put timeline-triggered actions in their own layer – this keeps them separate and makes them easier to find and amend, and gives us a *control layer* or 'scripting layer'.

1. Open up your case study movie and add a new layer called **actions** to the main timeline:

2. We want the timeline to stop at the last frame, so select that frame (it should be frame 60) and add a blank keyframe there.

3. Bring up the **Frame Actions** panel and click on **Basic Actions** in the left panel if it isn't already open:

4. From the list of **Basic Action**s, double-click on **Stop**.

And that's it! A **stop ()**; command will appear in the right pane of **Frame Actions**, and the familiar small 'a' will show up in the frame:

You could have done exactly the same thing by using the little + button on the top left corner of the **Frame Actions** window. You just need to click on it and select **Basic Action > Stop**:

You'll notice that there are a lot of keyboard shortcuts listed here. It might be a good idea to learn the one for **Stop** right about now... you're going to be using it a lot very soon!

We also want to add a button allowing the viewer to *email* us.

You've already seen how buttons can be used to go to a new web location using the **Get URL** action. Well, allowing the user to send you an email is achieved in a very similar way: this time, though, rather than a URL, the address includes an ActionScript instruction called **mailto:**, followed by an email address. The '**mailto**' part tells your browser that the address is not a web address, but an email address. You don't add actions to buttons until they're on the stage, so before we add the action, let's put the button somewhere on the stage.

We want to insert this button into another section of the **information** movieclip.

5. Open up the **information** movie clip symbol for editing.

6. In the **info** layer of **information**, add a keyframe at frame 50, and pull the **Email us** button out of the library and onto the stage. Place the button underneath the registration point in the same way that you did for the Clients and Services information - we want the email information to occupy the same position when it's displayed:

Now add a **Contact** title and address as shown in the screenshot:

The **CONTACT** title and the postal address below the **Email us** button are both text boxes, remember, and the underline can be pasted from one of the other titles on the same layer. As before, make sure the title lines up so that the titles don't jiggle around when the user swaps between them using different buttons:

You might want to change the text inside the **Email us** button to reflect your own address.

Notice that, because we won't be adding more to the other layers, we don't have to add blank keyframes to 'empty them' as we did in the last chapter. This time, because the other layers stop at frame 45, nothing else will appear on the stage simply because there are no other layers around by frame 46 to display anything.

Now to add some actions to the button so it works as an emailer.

7. To attach the button action, select the **Email us** button and bring up the **Object Actions** window.

    We want to add an **on (release)** action and a **getURL** action to the **Email us** button. Because we're attaching something to a button, Flash always assumes an on (release) mouse event as the first action even if we don't. So, all we really have to do is add the getURL.

8. Select **Basic Actions > GetURL** from the left hand panel or via the + button:

    Your ActionScript so far will look like this:

    ```
    on (release) {
    getURL ("");
    }
    ```

    All we have to do now is tell the getURL action what our actual email address is.

9.   With the **getURL ("")** action selected, click on the **URL** field at the bottom of
the window and enter **mailto: yourEmail**, entering your own address in the
yourEmail part. Leave the other two fields (**Window** and **Variables**) as they
are, but make sure that the **Expression** box next to the **URL** field is
unchecked:

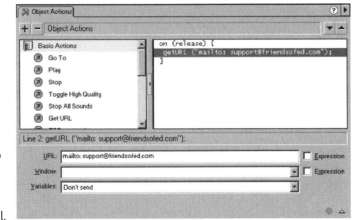

The button is
now set up to
open up your
default mail
program and
send us a mail.

Now let's have a further think about the information movie clip and the
actions we need to add to it.

*   Controlling the information movie clip

The information movie clip contains several different sections:

*   An **About our Company** section (frames 1 to 19):

- A **Services** section (frames 20 to 26):

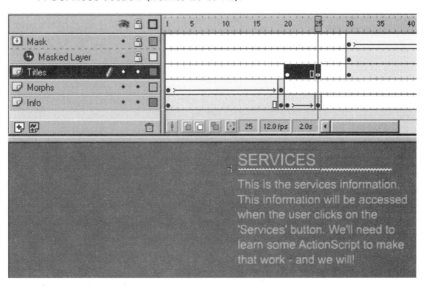

- A **Client** list section (frames 30 to 45):

- The **Contact Information** and **email** button we just added at frame 50:

At the moment Flash will just play the movie clip from frame 1 to frame 45, with no regard for where each distinct section starts or ends, whereas we want each segment to be displayed when the user clicks on the relevant button. Later on in the book, we'll be starting the information movie at frames 1, 20 or 30, depending on which section we want to display. We need a way to stop the movie again once the isolated section has played out. How?

You guessed it: more ActionScript Stop commands.

10. Add stop commands at the end of each section of the info layer as follows:

- At the end of the **About** section (frame 19)

- At the end of the **Services** section (frame 25)

- In a new keyframe at the end of the **Client** list section (frame 45)

- At the end of the **Contact** section (frame 50)

When you've done this, the layer will look like this:

We haven't really needed to add a new layer solely to house the actions, because all the actions are on a single layer in any case. Also, note that you really don't want to put stop actions in the empty keyframes, because then you would stop at a blank screen (and spend hours wondering where everything had gone when you ran the movie!).

We're almost there now with this project. It all comes together in the next chapter.

Summary

In this chapter, we introduced the important concept of interactivity, and we started to see how Flash implements this using ActionScript. This was an important chapter because the simple applications of ActionScripting that we've seen here will be a foundation that you can build on, both in the next chapter specifically and in the rest of the book more generally.

We saw that:

◆ Interactivity is about bringing the Flash movie to life, and giving the user an interesting and satisfying experience

◆ At the heart of interactivity are the principles of events and event handlers. Things happen - events, like a user clicking on a button, and we create actions or behavior that will respond and cope with these events

◆ A powerful way of adding interaction in Flash is by using buttons. Buttons can have behavior - such as animation, sound, and movie clips - embedded in their default states, and they can be made even more intelligent by attaching ActionScript to the mouse events that buttons can detect

◆ ActionScript is the string that ties together all the components of a Flash movie or web site

◆ ActionScript is the internal programming language that Flash uses to create actions in the Actions window, either in Normal or Expert mode

◆ ActionScript can be attached to frames in the timeline, or to objects - typically buttons - on the stage

◆ We can use ActionScript to jump to specific areas inside our movies, and we can even jump to specified web pages and sites

◆ In the case study, we used ActionScript Stop commands to control the playback of the information movie clip, and saw how to make our Email us button respond to a user's click

In the next chapter, we'll explore ActionScript in a more depth and see more ways that it can work for us.

10 Intelligent Actions

What we'll cover in this chapter:

- *Further ActionScripting*

  - *Increasing interaction*

  - *Using ActionScript to direct instructions to specific objects on the stage and tell them what to do*

- *Variables and conditional statements*

  - *Storing values for later use within scripts*

  - *Allowing Flash to make choices about what to do*

In the previous chapter you used ActionScripts to make a multi-scene, multi-section interactive Flash movie that allowed the user to navigate their way through the alternative routes.

That was just the beginning. ActionScripting can be used to do much, much more: frames and buttons that have ActionScripts attached to them suddenly become supercharged and much more talented than their ordinary cousins. This is at the heart of why Flash is a much richer and more flexible environment for web page production than HTML, and the reason why Flash can be used to produce sites that are more interactive and more dynamic in the way they allow the user to move around. Some Flash sites even appear to think for themselves.

This chapter will show you how to start giving your Flash sites these qualities.

You may find this chapter a little daunting at first, particularly because ActionScripting may appear frightening to those of you who are coming into Flash from a Photoshop/graphic design background. You don't need to worry though: Flash actually helps you so much that it practically writes the ActionScript for you! As a beginner, you only have to do two things:

1. Have a clear idea of what you want your ActionScript to do

2. Press some buttons and check boxes to make Flash build up the ActionScript code

Trust us, there is no need to use math or obscure logic unless that's what you want to do.

The Power of ActionScript

We learnt in the previous chapter that ActionScripts are *event driven*. This means that the actions we've told Flash to perform are only carried out when an event we've specified takes place - when the mouse cursor does something specific, or when a frame containing an ActionScript is encountered on the timeline. This makes ActionScripts easy to write. For example, once you've created a working button, all you have to do is attach an ActionScript to it telling Flash what the button should do. There's no long obscure program to write, you just decide what you want Flash to do, generate the appropriate bit of ActionScript, and then move on.

A designer wrote recently: "whenever I think of Flash scripts, I have this irrational mental image of a little superhero with a letter 'A' on his chest. Made up of normal Flash Frames, he has come to us from the planet Interactivity to free us from the clutches of his arch enemy, a secret organization known only by the initials HTML. Ridding the world of boring, static web pages wherever they may exist, with powers that give one command the abilities of 100 lines of JavaScript...Is it a bird? Is it a plane? No. It's *ActionScript*!"

Normal frames

ActionScript is fundamentally much more dynamic than, say a button rollover or an animated movie. With ActionScript, you can control just about every attribute of just about everything on the stage. Surreal as it sounds, ActionScript enables individual elements of your movie to talk to each other. A button symbol can say to a movie symbol, "When instance X of me is pressed, you start playing from frame Y". Buttons no longer just control navigation as in plain old HTML, they *also control other objects*, such as movies and graphics. This is done using the **Tell Target** action.

Defining Symbols as 'Tellers' and 'Targets'

As we've said, and as the name of implies, the tellTarget action is used to make one object (the teller) in our animation tell another object (the target) what to do. Before we can demonstrate this action we need to create a couple of symbols - one to do the telling, and one to be told.

Lets create a little face to talk to. Something we can tell to be happy, or to be sad.

> *Make sure you save the 'smiler' movie we work on throughout this chapter: we'll be enhancing its capabilities with ActionScript as we progress through this book.*

1. In a fresh Flash movie, create a new movie clip symbol called **smiler**.

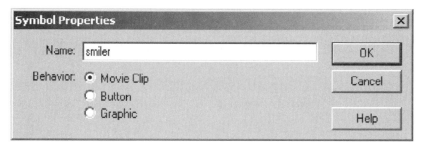

2. Inside **smiler**, create two new layers. From the bottom up, rename your three layers **face**, **eyes** and **smile**. These layers are to hold the separate parts that will make up our face.

3. Place a yellow circle with a black stroke of thickness 8 in the **face** layer, in the centre of the stage as shown. Center the circle at 0,0 using the **Info** panel if you're a bit out. If you have **Show Grid** and **Snap to Grid** on, you'll have no problem doing it by sight:

4. Next, in layer **eyes**, add, well... two eyes. Use two lines with the same stroke width as your circle:

5. Select the smile layer and add a horizontal line approximately where the mouth should be:

We know what you're thinking: he should be smiling.

6. Make all the layers 15 frames long and add a keyframe to the **smile** layer at frame 15:

What we'll do next is animate the mouth so that it goes from a smile to a frown, passing through all the intermediate mood expressions in between. To do this we'll set up a shape tween from frame 1(smiling) to frame 15 (frowning). For the next part to work, you must **not** have the mouth selected (if you find you have, simply click on a blank part of the stage).

7. Select the Arrow tool and go to frame 1. Put the pointer on the mid-point of the mouth until the cursor develops the curve attachment and drag the center of the mouth down to make your face smile:

8. In the **smile** layer, select frame 1. Using the **Frame** panel, add a label **happy** to this frame and change the tweening from **none** to **shape**:

A light green shape tween will now extend from frame 1 to frame 15.

You'll notice that we have nothing else on the **smile** layer. This is a requirement in *all* tween animation, as you'll remember from earlier in this book: you'll confuse Flash if you have more than one item in the layer, and your tween won't work. Also, note that the smile object is just a drawn shape and *not* a symbol, if it was a symbol this would also prevent the shape tween from working.

9. Now select frame 15 of **smile**. Your face here is in its expressionless, or neutral, position. By using the pointer in the same way as before, make the face *frown*.

10. Use the **Frame** panel to add a label called **sad** to the keyframe at frame 15. (You won't see this label on the timeline because there's not enough space to show it, but you *will* see a little flag in the frame to show that it's been labeled):

11. You can see the motion **smiler** will perform by selecting it in the library window and clicking on the **Play** button, or by using the onion skin tool to see all the frames at once:

Play button

We also want to label the 'neutral' face expression. The exact position of this will depend on how you drew your mouth, but it should be somewhere near the middle of the movie.

12. Click and drag the playhead up and down the timeline until it is on the frame where the 'smile' is the straight horizontal line you drew originally.

13. Insert a keyframe at this frame (don't try to select the individual frame, just make sure you've selected layer smile and that the playhead is on the correct frame. Using the **Frame** panel to label it **neutral**:

Each of these labels corresponds to a different expression: we want to be able to target the expression we want to see. To do this, we need a button to press...

14. Create a new graphic symbol and call it **rectangle**. This symbol will form the basis of our button:

15. Inside the graphic symbol, draw a yellow rectangle:

We're going to be putting text over the top of our button eventually, so make sure the body of your rectangle is an appropriate size for typing onto.

16. Now create a button symbol called **rectangle button**.

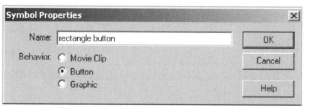

17. Inside the button symbol, drag an instance of the **rectangle** symbol onto the screen and use the **Info** panel to set its position to **X:0.0**; **Y: 0.0** and make sure it's in the center of the screen:

As we've mentioned before, it's important that the graphics in a button's states all line up. For that reason, it's a good idea to always set a button's X and Y positions to zero as a rule. Then, if a button ever starts to look wobbly when it's used in your final movie, you'll know all you have to do to correct the problem is set its position in all states to X:0.0; Y:0.0.

18. Add keyframes to the Over state and the Hit state.

    We suggested earlier in the book that it was a good idea to make the 'hittable' shape in the Hit state a distinctive color. Here, however, because we know that the square is solid, we don't need to change the shape in the Hit state from yellow to a distinctive black by adjusting the brightness, but you may wish to do so for practice.

    We'll let the user know they're over the button's 'press' area by making the button become a lighter shade in the Over state.

19. Select the button in the Over state. Now choose the **Brightness** option from the **Effect** panel drop down menu and set it to 40% using the slider:

20. Go back to the main stage in Scene 1 and add two new layers. Rename your three layers, from the bottom up, **face**, **buttons** and **text**:

21. Select the **face** layer and drag an instance of **smiler** onto the stage from the library. Then, in the **buttons** layer, add two instances of the **rectangle** button symbol. Your stage should look like this one:

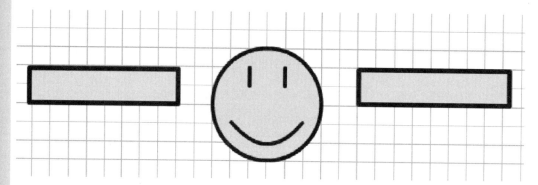

Now to give the user some hints about which buttons they might want to press.

22. In the text layer, use the Text tool and the **Character** panel to add the words **'better'** and **'worse'** on top of the buttons as shown, and along the top of the stage type **'How do you feel?'**:

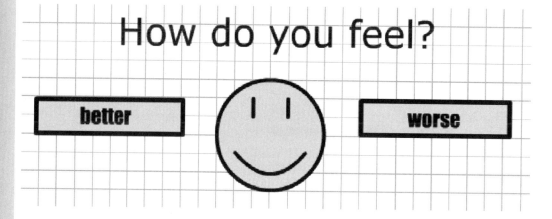

You can test the movie now if you wish. When you go over the buttons, they should become lighter, and the face will continuously animate from happy to sad, but nothing will happen when you press either button.

The next step is to use the buttons to control what mood **smiler** is in, but before we begin adding the **Tell Target** ActionScript that'll tell smiler how it feels, let's look at how **tellTarget** works in theory.

How Tell Target Works

Understanding how **tellTarget** works will allow you to use ActionScript to build really complex-looking sites with a simple technique.

As we said at the start of this chapter, the **tellTarget** action enables the elements of our animation to 'talk to one another' so that how one element behaves can be made dependent on what another element is doing. But this doesn't work on just any object in your animation - **tellTarget** is a function that only works on individual, *named* *instances* of a symbol. Let's make sure we're clear on what an instance is and why we use them.

The original 'master' symbol that sits in the library is the *template* that all the instances of it we put on the stage will adhere to. The version in the Library is the 'parent' and the 'child' instance is permanently linked to it. An instance will **always** look and behave like its parent: when the parent changes, **all** it's instances also change. This characteristic is what differentiates an *instance* from a *copy*: if you drew a square on the stage, copied it, and pasted the copy next to the original, and then went back to the original and changed it, the copy would not be affected in any way as a *copy* has no link to its parent.

You can see this link between parents and instances for yourself by altering the **rectangle** symbol you created in the last exercise.

Parents and Instances

1. In the library window, select the **rectangle** symbol and go to **Options > Edit**.

2. Select the whole of the yellow rectangle with the Arrow tool and use the **'Scale'** option to stretch it at the top and the bottom:

3. Click on **Scene 1** at the top of the timeline to go back to the main stage and notice that **all** the instances of **rectangle** have mimicked the change made to their parent:

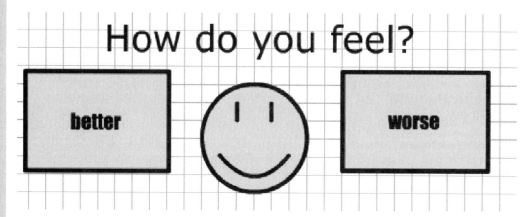

The instances of **rectangle** we put in each state of **rectangle button** have changed, and consequently the instances of **rectangle button** on the stage have changed as well. The changes we made to the parent symbol have rippled through to all of the instances spawned from it.

This is a big advantage for editing and changing your web site. Because of this link between parent and instance, when we change a symbol in the library Flash can follow the link to each instance and apply the same change. When we change a symbol, we alter its **attributes**. Attributes are the features of our symbol and include things such as size, position, and color. For a *movie clip*, attributes also include values like its 'current frame'. We'll be looking in more depth at this aspect of Flash in the two *Intermediate ActionScript* chapters later in the book.

So, Flash is able to change the attributes of **smiler** because it knows what a 'smiler' type of object is - thanks to the template in the library. However, in a truly interactive and flexible movie, we want Flash to be able to change the attributes of single, *individual* instances on the stage, all while leaving the parent symbol untouched. In order for Flash to do this, each instance must be *unique* and identifiable. In propeller-head computing languages, making a specific incarnation of a symbol identifiable is called **instantiation** - which basically means giving each instance a *name*.

Changing Attributes with Tell Target

Let's instantiate - name - the instance of **smiler** we have on our stage.

1. Select **smiler** and open the **Instance** panel using **Window > Panels > Instance**.

2. The panel tells you that this is an instance of a symbol called **smiler** and that it's a movie clip. In the **Name** field, give this instance the name **face**:

Because we've now given this specific instance of **smiler** a name, Flash now knows enough about it to let us control it directly. It knows that this particular instance is called **face**, and can now differentiate it from any other instance of **smiler** we might place on the stage in the future. What's more, we can now direct commands to this instance in a way that parallels our use of labels in the previous chapter.

The **face** instance is now going to be the 'target' of our **tellTarget** ActionScript. At the moment, **smiler** plays continuously during our movie, but we want it to stay on the neutral expression until one of the buttons is pressed - one button will make it happy, and one will make it sad.

To do this we're going to control the **smiler** instance's **'current frame'** attribute.

3. On the movie's main timeline, create a new layer called **control**. Select the first frame on this new layer and use the **Frame** panel to add a label to it called **initialize**:

4. Double-click this frame to open the **Frame Actions** window or, with the frame selected, go to **Window > Actions**. If your **Basic Actions** book is closed, click on it to bring up the list of basic actions you can use.

5. Double-click on the tellTarget command (It's the tenth one down), and this code...

```
tellTarget ("") {
}
```

...will appear in the right pane of the **Frame Actions** window.

At the bottom of the window, an entry field marked **Target** has appeared. Flash is asking you 'which instance do you want me to control with this **tellTarget** statement?'

You can type the name of the instance directly into the box, but if you get it *wrong* Flash won't tell you so, and your ActionScript won't work. There is a better way...

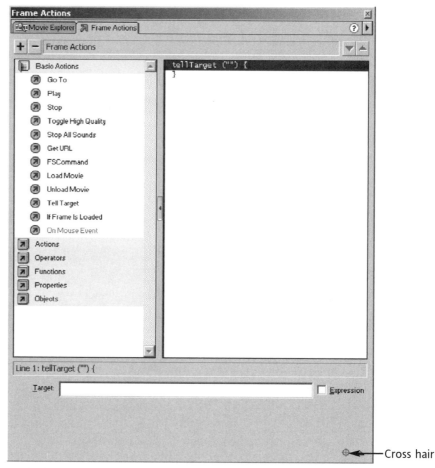

At the bottom right of the window is a little crosshair (as in target...).

6. Click in the **Target** field to ensure you have the cursor there. You're now able to click on the crosshair, which will open this window:

This shows all potential targets in the movie that you can control (i.e. all of the instances that have been instantiated, or named).

7. Click on **face** to select it, and leave the rest of the window unchanged. Now click on *OK*:

The tellTarget ActionScript will have been updated from...

```
tellTarget ("") {
}
```

...to...

```
tellTarget ("face") {
}
```

We've now pointed Flash at the correct target - next, we now to tell Flash what we want it to *do* with that target.

What we want Flash to do is make the **smiler** movie start on its neutral, expressionless face. Remember, we're attaching this ActionScript to the first frame of our main timeline, so what we really want to say to Flash is: "when you encounter the frame labeled **initialize** in the timeline (the first frame), tell the instance **face** to jump to the neutral label on its internal timeline and stay there":

Main timeline:

'smiler' instance timeline:

Let's tell Flash exactly where to go...

8. Double-click on the **Go To** action in the Frame Actions window to add the statement to your script.

9. At the bottom of the window, leave <**current scene**> in the **Scene** field, but select **Frame Label** from the **Type** field.

10. Click on the Frame field's drop-down menu arrow.
Notice that only the frame label **initialize** appears in the **Frame** drop down menu. We're telling **face** to go to the **neutral** frame label, so we'll have to enter it manually.

11. Click on the **Frame** field to select it and type **neutral**.

12. We also want **smiler** to stay on its neutral expression when Flash jumps to the label, so **uncheck** the **Go to and Play** box at the bottom of the window:

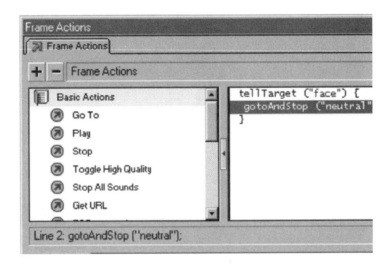

The last piece of ActionScript we need to attach to this frame is a **Stop** action. You should be careful not to add this in a way that makes Flash think its part of the **TellTarget** action. This instruction is *not* aimed at the target (**face**). Rather, it's telling Flash to stop the animation at *this* frame.

13. Click on the last line of script in the right pane of the window. It will contain only a curly brace:

}

14. Now double-click on the **Stop** action in the Frame Actions window to generate the **Stop** command. You should now have the same ActionScript in the right pane as that shown here:

This particular movie would run in exactly the same way with or without this command. However, if you were to add a second scene the movie would run straight into it before the user had had a chance to interact with **smiler**.

Now we need to add ActionScript to the *buttons*. Before we do, let's see the different way Flash 'reads' an instance and a non-instance:

15. Select the text that's over the left hand button and open the **Instance** panel if it's not already on screen:

Notice that everything is grayed out. Flash doesn't know *anything* about this object.

16. Now click on the button itself, and you'll see something like this:

The arrow icon at the far bottom right of this window can be used to open or close the **Object Actions** window.

17. Click on the arrow icon now with the left hand button still selected.

We want to create ActionScript that basically says to Flash, "When this button is pressed, make face smile". More accurately, it will instruct Flash that when it detects the user clicking and releasing their mouse over this button, it must make **face** jump to the **happy** label on the **smiler** movie's timeline.

We've used this ActionScript before, so you should be able to confidently create these commands.

18. Double-click on the **tellTarget** command in the **Object Actions** window. Notice that, as we saw in the previous chapter, Flash assumes that you want the button to detect an **on (release)** mouse event before it fires off the **tellTarget** command, and inserts that ActionScript accordingly:

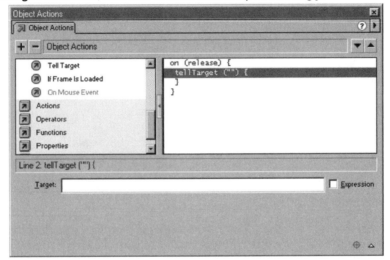

19. Click on the crosshair icon (making sure your cursor is in the **Target** field) and then click on **face** in the **Insert Target Path** window that appears. Click **OK**.

20. Now double-click on the **Go To** action in the left pane. Choose **<current scene>** and **Frame Label** from the **Scene** and **Type** drop down menus.

21. Type **happy** into the **Frame** field and uncheck the **Go to and Play** box.

Your **Object Actions** window should look like this one:

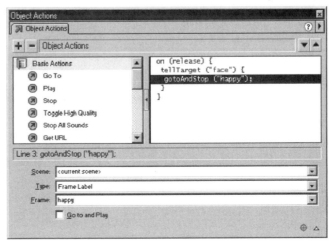

22. Repeat these steps for the button on the right, but this time type **sad** in the **Frame** field as this button will make **face** frown.

23. Test your movie.

Smiler will now start off on its **neutral** face position because of the ActionScript we attached to the timeline. When we press the **better** button, **face** smiles, and when we press the **worse** button, **face** frowns.

The ActionScript attached to each button is controlling the attributes of another object (the instance of our **smiler** movie symbol). This very simple way of linking elements together is extremely powerful and can be extended much further to link more and more objects to each other.

We now know how to use **tellTarget** actions to control instances and enable bits of our animation to boss each other around. But we can also give Flash the power to make decisions for itself by using two more of ActionScript's special powers: **variables** and **conditional structures**.

Teaching your Movie to Think for Itself

The ability to use ActionScript to help Flash make structured decisions means that very advanced Flash interfaces can be built. This feature allows Flash to move beyond being merely a graphical interface for web pages and to enter the domain of fully-fledged web applications and games. By adding ActionScript to a Flash web page you can do more than just make it interactive. You can give it a brain.

At the moment we only ever see the frames of the **smiler** movie that we labeled: **happy**, **neutral** and **sad**. It would be nice if we could see all the intermediate frames and expressions as well.

When you press the **better** button at the moment, it takes you to the 'best' expression, and the **worse** button takes you to the 'worst' expression. What we want to be able to do when we press the **better** button is to make the movie go one frame nearer the **happy** label, or frame 1, and show us a *slightly* happier expression. Similarly, when we press the **worse** button, we want the movie to go one frame nearer the **sad** label at frame 15, and show us a *slightly* sadder expression. We want to give **smiler** a more nuanced range of expressions rather than the two extremes it presents us with at the moment.

Essentially, what we want to do is go to the **previous** frame if the **better** button is pressed, and to the **next** frame when the **worse** button is pressed.

So, we want the ActionScript we create to say to Flash, in simple terms, "When the **better** button is pressed, make **face** move *back* one frame in the **smiler** movie timeline" and "When the **worse** button is pressed, make **face** move *forward* one frame in the **smiler** movie timeline"

But - and it's a big 'but' - what happens when we reach the first or last frame of the movie?

If the **better** button is pressed when **face** is at frame one, or if the **worse** button is pressed when **face** is at frame 15, the actions we told Flash to carry out will be impossible and our instructions won't make any sense.

We need Flash to be able to decide what action it should take in these circumstances - whether it should move to another frame, or stay where it is. To be able to do this Flash must know what frame it's currently at. We can tell Flash where it's at by making use of **variables**.

Variables

A variable is a named container where you store values or data that you want to use over and over again while a program - or Flash movie - is running. A variable is essentially a bit of computer memory that you give a name to. You store information in this memory location, and when you give Flash the name of the variable, it knows where to go and look for the information you stored.

There are two types of variable in Flash we need to look at here - **literal variables** and **expressions**.

A *literal* variable is a value that you want to treat as a 'literal' value: that is, whenever you send Flash to find that variable, the value that it finds in the memory location will be something like a name, an address, or the color of your eyes. It's a value that you want to read of as a 'fixed' thing, something that you won't want to modify once you've set it.

The color of your eyes, for example, could be stored as a literal variable. If you wanted to tell Flash your eyes were blue, you would define this variable like so:

Eyes = "blue"

The "" around the value denotes that it's a literal variable. It won't change until you change your eye color: although your eyes could have been any color at all, Flash will deduce that now they're blue they'll always be blue - until you tell Flash otherwise. Whenever Flash uses this variable, it will read it as a single, integrated value.

An **expression** is different from a literal variable. An expression doesn't necessarily have a fixed value that's waiting to be read out of a particular memory location: instead, an expression has to be *evaluated* - Flash has to do a little working out before it can decide what the value of the expression is.

For example, the statement 'Number of dollars in my pocket + number of dollars in my paycheck' is an expression: it has two component parts, each of which needs to be evaluated and added together before a final figure can be arrived at. Essentially, an expression is any statement that will ultimately return a value.

You could call the money in your pocket 'Dollars', and tell Flash you had 10 of them by writing:

Dollars = 10

Notice that when we write an expression variable we don't enclose it in "". By writing our variable like this Flash knows it's an expression.

Having given Flash this information, you can now forget how much money you have and get Flash to keep track of your accounts. If you were to now find a dollar on the floor and put that one in your pocket, you could just say to "Flash, I now have one more dollar than I had before." You would write this:

Dollars = Dollars + 1

Flash will now make the value of dollars equal to eleven, so if we find another dollar under the couch we would again say, "Flash, I have one more dollar than I had before."

We can apply this knowledge to our movie and get Flash to keep track of what frame of **smiler** we're on. We'll create a variable, and we'll call it **smilerframe**. We can store the current frame number inside this variable. Once Flash looks at this variable and knows which frame we're starting from, it can add one or subtract one frame from this variable each time a button is pressed. The value of **smilerframe** will change using an expression that essentially says:

smilerframe = smilerframe + 1

or

smilerframe = smilerframe - 1

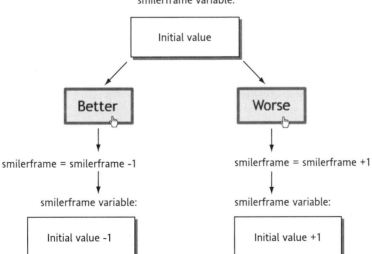

These expressions will create the new value of **smilerframe** and store it in the variable.

Let's put this into practice.

Using Variables

Our first step is to find the frame number that corresponds to the neutral expression of **face**. We can then store this value in the **smilerframe** variable and use it as the starting point for the frame by frame movement from 'happy' to 'sad'.

Earlier, we attached ActionScript to the **initialize** frame which told Flash that, at the start of the movie, **face** should be on the frame labeled **neutral**. This is the frame number that we'll use as the initial value for our **smilerframe** variable.

1. Double-click on the movie symbol icon of **smiler** in the library to go into Edit Symbols mode.

2. Move the playhead to the frame containing the **neutral** label. You'll be able to see exactly what frame this is by looking in the little frame-counter pane at the bottom of the timeline:

Frame Counter

In this example, **neutral** is on frame 9, but in your movie it could be different depending on how you drew the mouth. We can now make our **smilerframe** variable equal to '**9**' (or whatever the value is in your movie).

3. On the main stage, double-click the **initialize** frame on the **control** layer to bring up the **Frame Actions** window.

As we'll be writing a fair bit of ActionScript here, let's give our eyes a little r'n'r by making the font in the Actions window larger.

4. Click on the right facing arrow at the top of the Actions window to bring up the menu. Click on **Font Size** and then on **Large** in the next menu that appears:

5. The particular action we want to use, **set variable**, is not in the **Basic actions** book but in **Actions**, which is the next book down. Click on **Actions** to open it. You will notice that there's lots of actions in here to learn once you get the hang of all this!

6. Select the first line of the ActionScript - **tellTarget**.

7. Find the **set variable** action and double-click on it (it's quite a long way down the list of actions, so you may need to use the scroll bars to find it).

   The following ActionScript statements will appear in the right-hand pane:

Some of the ActionScript that appears is in red, which is Flash's way of telling us that there's currently an error in our ActionScript, and that it won't work properly unless we fix it.

In this case, we've got this red alert because we haven't defined our variable name yet. Flash is telling us this just below the two Actions panes, where it says:

Line 2: <not set yet> = ""; [A variable name is required.]

8. With the new ActionScript line still selected, enter **smilerframe** in the **Variable** field.

9. In the Value field, enter the frame number where the neutral label is located in your movie. The value in this book's example is '9'.

Notice that at first Flash writes the **smilerframe** value as **"9"** - taking it to be a literal variable:

During our movie, as the user clicks on the **better** and **worse** buttons, we're going to want the value of **smilerframe** to change to anything between 1 and 15.This means that we need to tell Flash that we want **smilerframe** to be an expression variable that can be operated on and updated as the user makes their choices.

10. Check the **expression** box to the right of the **Value** field - **not** the one by the **Variable** field.

As the ActionScript is currently written, the **set variable** action is part of the **tellTarget** action, which we don't want it to be. The **set variable** action here is designed to 'initialize' the variable at the beginning of the script so that Flash can use it later: this is a discrete piece of information that we're giving to Flash for future reference so that it knows what the initial value of **smilerframe** is. For this reason, we need it to be the *first* line of ActionScript.

Lines of ActionScript can be moved up and down using the direction arrows at the top right of the window.

11. With the **smilerframe = 9** ; line selected, click on the up arrow to move the line to the top of the pane. Your script should now look like this:

Up and Down Arrows

Expression check box

This script now sets the **smilername** variable to its initial vale at the center of the happy/sad continuum as soon as the movie starts. It also directs the movie to the middle of the **face** instance's timeline, pausing the movie there with a neutral facial expression and waiting for the user's input.

Now we need to change the ActionScript instructions that are attached to each of the buttons. Instead of telling **face** to go all the way to the **happy** or **sad** labels of the **smiler** movie clip as soon as they're clicked, we want them to tell **face** to move forward or back *one frame*.

When we found a dollar, the new value the money in our pocket became Dollars + 1. Similarly, when a button is pressed and the timeline moves one frame forward or one frame back, we want to *update* the value of **smilerframe** as either:

> smilerframe = smilerframe + 1

or

> smilerframe = smilerframe - 1

We'll still be using the **Go To** action to make **face** move up and down the **smiler** movie clip timeline, but we'll now tell it to go to the *previous* frame or the *next* frame. Fortunately, Flash has in-built facilities to help us do this.

However, we still have the problem of what Flash will do when we get to either end of the timeline and it can't physically *go* to the previous or next frame. How do we stop Flash going off the end of the movie?

Well, to solve this, we use a **conditional statement**.

Conditional Statements

A conditional statement allows our Flash movie to make choices, based on the situation it finds itself in. This means we can tell Flash to only follow the instructions we've given it **if** certain conditions apply. Helpfully, '**If**' is the name of the action we'll use to insert a conditional statement in our button ActionScript.

If, in our 'dollars' example, our pockets were only big enough to hold a hundred dollars, we'd add a conditional statement to our instructions to Flash. We'd say, "Every time we find a dollar, only put it in our pocket **if** Dollars (the variable) is less than one hundred." If Dollars was already equal to one hundred, Flash would know to ignore the rest of the instruction.

Let's define the conditions that must apply in our **smiler** movie for Flash to follow our instructions. When the **better** button is pressed we want it to tell **face** to go to the previous frame of **smiler** if - and only if - **smiler** is not *currently* on frame 1. If **smiler** is currently on frame 1, then the **smilerframe** variable will equal 1. If **smiler** is *not* on frame 1, then **smilerframe** will be greater than 1.

Flash will now understand that we're happy to go to the previous frame if we're at a frame greater than 1 (**smilerframe > 1**). If **smilerframe** actually equals 1, then the movie will know not to move when the **better** button is pressed:

Frame 1:
smilerframe = 1

Frame 2:
smilerframe > 2

Frame 3:
smilerframe > 3

Frame 4:
smilerframe > 4

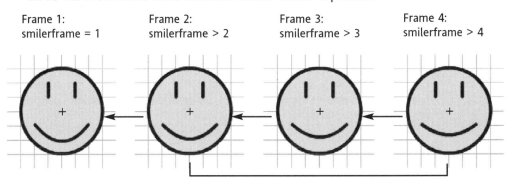

go to previous frame if smilerframe>1

Let's add this instruction and conditional statement to the **better** button.

Updating the Buttons with Sexier ActionScript

1. Select the **better** button and open the **Object Actions** window.

    We're going to significantly change the ActionScript for this button, so it'll be easier to start from scratch.

2. Delete every line in the button's current script by selecting the top line of script in the right-hand pane and clicking on the 'minus' button at the top-left of the window.

3. Double-click **On Mouse Event** in the **Basic Actions** book and leave it as an **On Release** event.

    Before we tell **face** to go to the previous frame of **smiler** when it's clicked, we need to add our conditional statement. Remember, we only want our instructions carried out **if smilerframe > 1**.

4. Open the **Actions** book and double-click on the if action to add it to your script.

5. In the **Condition** field that appears at the bottom of the window, type **smilerframe > 1**. Be careful to get the spelling of **smilerframe** exactly right, otherwise Flash will think you're talking about something else:

We now have to tell Flash that if **smilerframe** actually is greater than 1, it should decrease that value by 1 in preparation for the next time the button is pressed: we have to update the value of **smilerframe** to reflect the fact that the playhead has moved along one frame. By keeping track of the value of

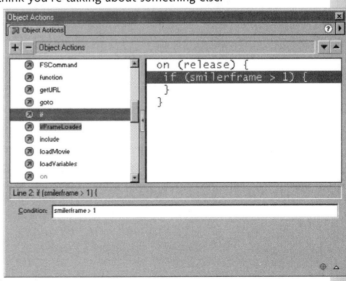

smilerframe in the same way as it would with our dollars, Flash will always know where on the **smiler** timeline **face** actually is.

6. With the **if (smilerframe > 1)** statement still selected on the right-hand pane, double-click on the **set variable** action in the left-hand pane to add it to the script.

7. Now enter **smilerframe** in the **Variable** field and **smilerframe -1** in the **Value** field.

8. Check the **Expression** box next to the **Value** field, as **smilerframe -1** is an expression, in the same way that Dollars + 1 is:

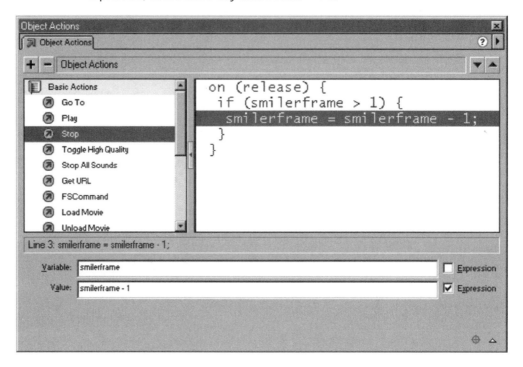

The three components of this expression - the current value of **smilerframe**, the subtraction symbol, and the value 1 - are resolved by Flash to determine the *new* value for the **smilerframe** variable.

Next, we need to tell Flash what to do next - actually move the playhead along the timeline in **face**.

9. With the **smilerframe = smilerframe - 1**; line selected, scroll down the list and double-click **tellTarget**.

10. Now click on the **Target** field, and then use the crosshair tool to select **face** as your target, as we did earlier in the chapter.

11. With the line **tellTarget ("face")** { still selected, double-click on the **Go To** action. We're going to add a special version of the **Go To** action called **prevframe** or Go To Previous Frame.

12. Leave **<current scene>** in the **Scene** field but from the **Type** drop-down menu, select **Previous Frame**. Notice that this grays out the options underneath it:

```
on (release) {
    if (smilerframe > 1) {
        smilerframe = smilerframe - 1;
        tellTarget ("face") {
            prevFrame ();
        }
    }
}
```

The **better** button is now ready to use.

13. Test the movie. You'll see that **face** will get happier each time the **better** button is pressed, whereas it will go straight to its sad expression when the **worse** button is pressed.

   OK, now to make the worse button fully functional. We need to repeat the same sequence of steps as we did for the better button, but with some significant changes to our conditional statement and to the instructions we shoot at face. Follow through the next set of instructions carefully.

14. Select the **worse** button and open the **Object Actions** window.

15. Delete all of the button's current script: select the top line of script and click on the 'minus' button.

16. Double-click **On Mouse Event** in the **Basic Actions** book and leave it as an **On Release** event.

17. Open the **Actions** book and double-click on the **if** action.

18. In the **Condition** field at the bottom of the window, type **smilerframe < 15**. Take care to get the spelling of **smilerframe** spot on.

   Now to tell Flash that if **smilerframe** *is* less than 15, we should increase that value by 1.

19. With the **if (smilerframe < 15)** statement still selected, add a **set variable** action.

20. Enter **smilerframe** in the **Variable** field and **smilerframe + 1** in the **Value** field.

21. Check the **Expression** box next to the **Value** field.

22. With the **smilerframe = smilerframe + 1**; line selected, scroll down the list and double-click **tellTarget**.

23. Click on the **Target** field and select **face** as your target.

24. With the **tellTarget** line still selected, double-click on the **Go To** action.

25. Leave **<current scene>** in the **Scene** field but select **Next Frame**. from the **Type** drop-down menu.

When you've finished, the right pane of the **Object Action**s window should contain the same ActionScript as the one here:

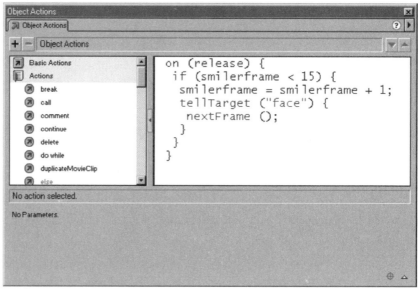

And now the **worse** button is ready to roll!

26. Test the movie again. Now *both* of the buttons will make the mouth move incrementally. You'll see **face** change its expression smoothly from happy, to neutral, to sad and back again as the buttons are pressed.

27. Save the movie. We'll work on it some more later.

There has been a lot to take in in this chapter, but in it you've learnt fundamental concepts for creating top quality Flash sites.

Understanding what **instances** are and how the **tellTarget** action can be used to control them will enable you to give your sites a far greater degree of interaction for the user to enjoy and marvel at. He or she will be able to do things like start or stop movies, affect the appearance and behavior of movie elements, all in addition to merely navigating the site. You can actually do a whole lot more with tell Target, and the basic skills you've gained here will provide a solid footing for learning the more fancy stuff later in your Flash career. Indeed, we have two more advanced chapters on ActionScript later in the book, so we hope that this has whetted your appetite.

You've also been introduced to the use of variables and conditional statements. These are the tools that give Flash the ability to think for itself. When used together, they give Flash some fairly powerful decision making abilities.

Case Study

We're finally in a position where we can start to make the case study web site's components talk to each other. Here, we'll add the actions required to make the buttons start talking to the **Information** movie clip using **tellTarget**. These ActionScript components will mean that when the user clicks on a button, the related content inside the information movie clip will be played back on the screen.

Wiring Up the Buttons

First, we want to make sure that we've given the instance of the **Information** movie symbol a name.

1. Open up your case study movie and add a new layer to it, right at the top. Name the layer **info display**:

2. With the **info display** layer selected, drag an instance of the information movie clip symbol out of the timeline and onto the stage. Place it roughly at the top-right of the stage:

3. At frame 1 in the **display info** layer's timeline, select the instance and use the **Instance** panel to name it **information**:

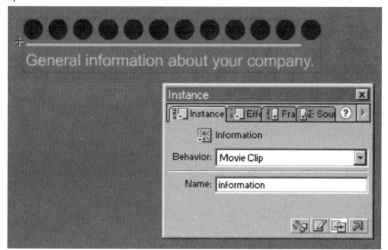

The **information** movie has different sections that we discussed in the previous chapter. As a refresher, here are the sections again:

- An **About our company**, or 'Home' section (frames 1 to 19)

- A **Services** section (frames 20 to 26)

- A **Client** list section (frames 30 to 45)

- The **Contact information** and **email** button (frames 46 to 50)

We want to use **tellTarget** to tell the movie what to do when the buttons are pressed so that:

- When the '**About**' button is pressed, **Information** plays from frame 1 through frame 19 (the Stop action will then prevent the next section from being played too)

- When the '**Services**' button is pressed, **information** plays from frame 20 through frame 26

- When the '**Clients**' button is pressed, **information** plays from frame 30 through frame 45

- And finally, when the '**Contact**' button is pressed, information plays frame 50

You'll recall that we put **Stop** actions at the end of each section to stop Flash from playing on into the next section once the current section has finished.

All the button actions are identical, apart from the targeted frames in **information** that they want to be pointed at so that clicking on them plays the correct part of the movie clip. We'll use **tellTarget** to point the buttons at the correct frames inside the **information** movie clip.

Let's do the first button. In the main timeline, we want to select the **Home** button and attach the appropriate **tellTarget** instruction to it. There are an awful lot of layers here and we want to make sure we work on the correct one.

4. Lock all the layers on the main stage by selecting the topmost padlock symbol on the timeline, and then unlock just the **Button - Home** layer by clicking on its padlock symbol.

The first question is, which *version* of the button do we want to attach the action to? The button has two keyframes, one at frame 30, and one at frame 60. Frame 60 is the one we want to attach the action to, because this is when the button finally stops moving.

5. With the timeline at frame 60, select the button on the stage:

6. Bring up the **Object Actions** window (**Window > Actions**). Flash knows this object is a button, so it will add an **on (release)** action for us when we add our **tellTarget** action. Double-click on **tellTarget**:

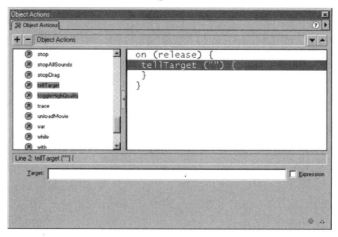

Now we have to tell Flash what our target is. We'll do something a little different here by adding the full path manually.

7. With the **tellTarget** action highlighted in the script pane, enter **_root.information** as the target:

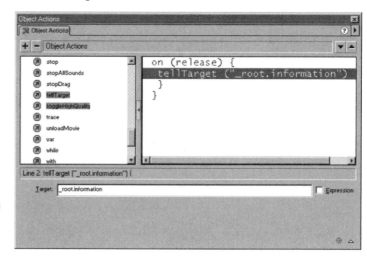

Make sure that the entered text is correct, because Flash will not correct it for you!

What does piece of script mean? Well, **_root** is the default identity that Flash gives to the main timeline, and **_root.information** is the *path* of the instance of the **information** movie clip we put on the stage and gave a label to using the **Instance** panel. If there was *another* movie embedded inside the **information** movie clip, its path would be **_root.information.info1**. We can refer to clips within clips using this 'dot notation'. This will all be explored further in our two chapters on intermediate ActionScript later in the book. However, as a little taster of how powerful this notation is, you might want to go away and have a think about what would happen if you issued a **tellTarget** from a movie with **_root** as the target...

Now that we have defined the target, we want to add the **Go To** action that'll tell Flash which frame of the information movie clip to start playing from, revealing the information associated with that button.

8. With the **tellTarget** line highlighted in the right-hand pane, double-click the **Go To** action and leave the options set as the default.

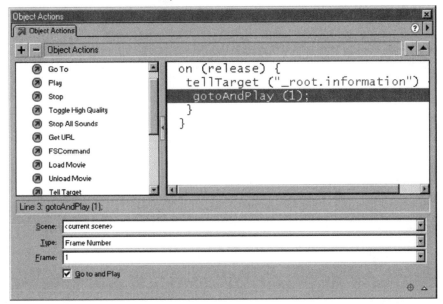

This script will now play frames 1 through 19 of the information movie clip when the **Home** button is pressed.

9. Test the movie by pressing *F12*. When the movie plays in the browser, click on the **Home** button, and the information movie clip will play the section of the movie clip you want to see.

You need to now add similar ActionScript to each button: only the **Go To** ActionScript line needs to be different for each button:

- the Services button's Go To ActionScript will read gotoAndPlay(20)

- the Client button's Go To ActionScript will read gotoAndPlay(30)

- and the Contact button's Go To ActionScript will read gotoAndPlay(50)

Instead of building the scripts for each button line by line, you can follow this sneaky shortcut procedure:

10. Select the Home button in frame 60 and bring up the Actions window.

11. Click on the last line of the script, and then **Shift-Click** on the *top* of the script. This will select all of the script:

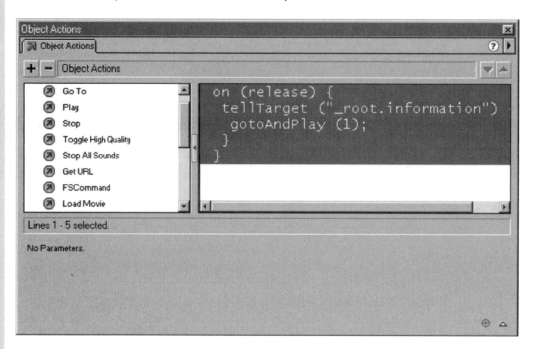

12. Right -click on the selected script to copy it to the clipboard.

13. Unlock the **Button - Clients** layer and click on the **Clients** button in the last frame of the layer.

14. Bring up the Actions window, right-click on the empty right-hand frame, and paste the copied script into the window.

15. Select the **gotoAndPlay** line, and then enter the correct frame number into the **Frame** box - for the **Clients** button, it's frame 30:

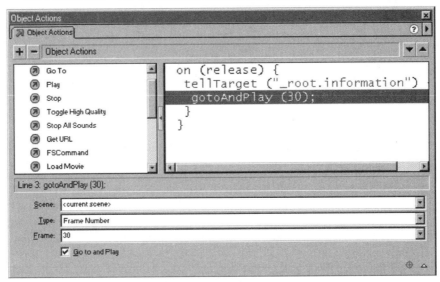

16. Repeat these copy, paste, and amendment steps for the remaining two buttons, changing the **gotoAndPlay** lines in each one according to the bulleted list above (20 for **Services**, and 50 for **Contact**). Remember that you want to add the ActionScript to the *last* keyframe of each button's layer - where the button finishes up once it's motion tweened onto the stage.

The website navigation will now be functioning. Clicking on any of the buttons will cause the **information** movie to start playing the appropriate animation.

17. Press *F12* to preview the movie and try out the buttons.

18. Save your movie away.

You can refine the playing of the animation by adding labels at the start of each section in the information movie - at frames 1, 20, 30, and 50. For example, add a label at frame 1 call it **about**, then select the ActionScript line **gotoAndPlay (1)** in the Home button, and enter **Frame Label** in the **Type** field, and **about** in the **Frame** field. Then ActionScript will now read **gotoAndPlay("about")**. This will have the same effect as the numeric targeting of the frames. The advantage of using labels is that if you add more frames, the labels will get moved along by the right amount and the buttons will still make **information** play from the right place, but we will leave that to you to play with for yourself.

We will add some sound in the next chapter, but the website is now substantially finished. You could even start thinking about customizing it for your own purposes...

Summary

This chapter has built further on the ActionScripting foundation we established in the previous chapter. We've taken an important step towards being able to create well-integrated, intelligent, responsive movies using ActionScript.

We saw that:

- In our **smiler** movie, **labels** provide reference points for us to jump to using ActionScript

- We can name specific instances of movie clip symbols on the stage using the **Instance** panel. Naming an instance - instantiating it - means that we can use that name in scripts and manipulate that instance using ActionScript commands

- We can use the **tellTarget** action to 'point' at a particular instance on the stage and pass it instructions about how it should behave

- The **Go To** action is used to jump to an individual frame number or label within a movie clip's timeline

- We can add intelligence and decision-making to our movies using variables and conditional statements

  - Variables are memory locations where we can store values and information for reuse later

  - We use the **Set Variable** action to initialize a variable by entering its **name** and **value** in the Actions window

  - **Conditional statements** let Flash decide what action to take, depending upon the conditions it finds

  - We used the if conditional statement to move the playhead backwards or forwards based on the value of the **smilerframe** variable

If you want to do serious, industrial strength work with Flash, you need to learn ActionScript. We'll be returning to explore ActionScript in much more detail later in the book.

In the next chapter - **sound**

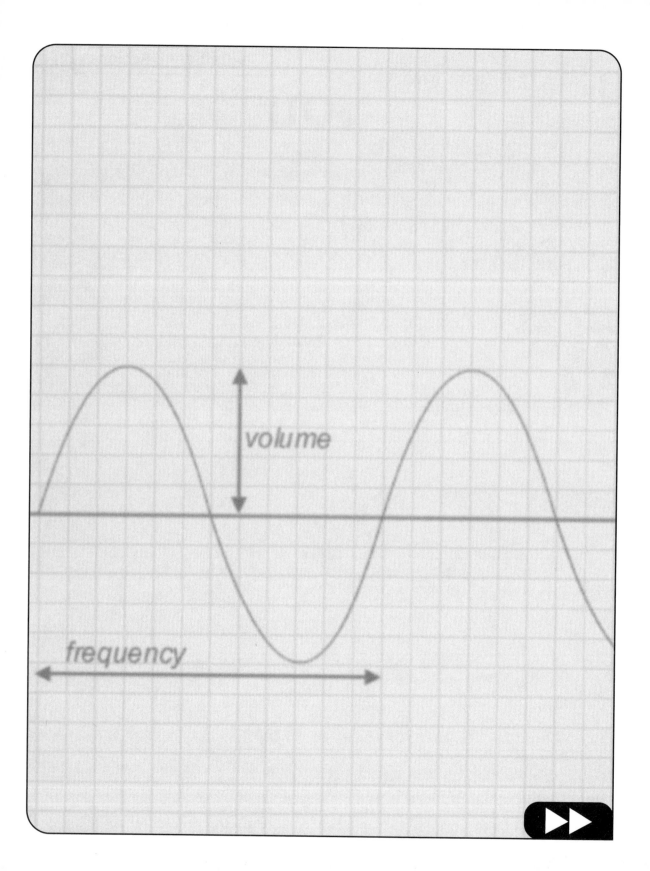

11 Sound

What we'll cover in this chapter:

◆ **Creating sound** - *creating or acquiring sounds and music to use in your movies*

◆ **Importing and exporting sound** - *looks at the types of sound that Flash can handle, and the best ways to get sound into and out of Flash*

◆ **Using sound in Flash** - *manipulating sound inside of Flash once you've got it there*

◆ **Flash sound issues** - *tips on the particular 'issues' (i.e. pitfalls and strange effects) related to sound implementation in Flash*

▶

This chapter is about using sound in your Flash movies. We've already attached a simple sound to a button in a previous chapter, but here we'll be opening up the world of Flash sound and climbing right inside.

The combination of sound and Flash, has not really taken off on the web until quite recently. As well as explaining some of the ins and outs of sound, we'll be explaining all of Flash's little 'issues' with sound, so that you'll be able to understand the pitfalls and how to get round them. We recommend that you download the set of sounds from our web site to get the most out of the examples in this chapter.

The key to getting good soundtracks onto the Web without compromising loading times is *optimization*, so we'll go through all the things you'll need to consider when you finally come to exporting your movie.

In this chapter, you'll be constructing a soundtrack that'll play alongside your web site's visual content. In this example, we're keeping the soundtrack and the visual content separate to keep download time to a minimum. In this way, the web site will load first, allowing people to begin exploring, while the soundtrack loads in the background and starts playing when it's ready. There's another advantage to keeping the sound and visual components apart: if you want to change or replace your soundtrack at a later date, it's much easier to implement this on a separate soundtrack than trying to extract sound files from within your movie and inserting new ones.

Plug in those speakers and let's rumble.

Sound on the Web

Sound on the web was always problematic, and then a little thing called MP3 came along and blew everything else out of the water. Before the advent of MP3 there were really only two options for the web-designer: **MIDI** and **sampled sound files**.

MIDI (Music Instrument Digital Interface) is a format that's understood by all digital music instruments, all music cards, and most soundcards.

For most sound formats, the sound file contains a *digital representation* of the actual sounds, with the corollary that a higher quality representation of the sound implies a larger file. The advantage of MIDI is that it doesn't hold representations of the sounds themselves, just the instructions for how to *play them* on a specific instrument. This means that MIDI files are very small and compact compared to other formats. It's a bit like raster and vector graphics: a MIDI file is similar to a vector in that it's an *instruction* to do something, and not a direct representation of the thing (the sound) itself. MIDI can also be embedded in simple HTML.

A MIDI sound card contains a bank of instruments which the MIDI file instructs to play at certain times, at different volumes, pitches and so on. This can be a problem in that only the instruments embedded in the card can be played. New instruments can sometimes be added to the card, but this means a loss of standardization, as you can't guarantee that everyone will have the correct instrument, resulting in another instrument being substituted for it.

The problems with MIDI are that it's not a universal standard, and that the final sound output depends on the quality of your MIDI-compatible synthesizer or music card. More importantly, MIDI is a music language only: it can't be used to create vocal sounds or non-musical effects - such as a door slamming.

The other pre-MP3 option was to have sampled data via the various sound formats of the time, things like WAVs, SNDs and AIFFs. These were big and bulky, and tended to be a major headache during download. Waiting an extra thirty seconds for a voice to say 'Hi there!' at a website homepage did not really cut the mustard! Additionally, not all sound formats were understood by both PC and Mac platforms, causing further bugs and uncertainties.

Then along came MP3. This was a sound format that compressed sounds intelligently via several different filters to give a much smaller file size for a given quality than any other sound compression system (with the exception of MIDI, which as explained above, is really an electronic music language for instruments). MP3 is now the standard for music files on the web, in the same way that Flash is *the* standard for high-impact, highly interactive web sites. It therefore comes as no surprise that Flash supports MP3.

Flash and MP3

A major advantage of using Flash and MP3 together is that the music, once embedded into Flash, can be listened to on the web but can't be copied in the same way that normal MP3 data can be downloaded (illegally) across the web. This factor is expected to make the Flash and MP3 combination really take off in the near future, so now is the time to get those Flash music skills honed.

Although MP3 simplifies the sound export options available from Flash considerably, there's still the problem of getting the sound *into* Flash in the first place. In this chapter we'll briefly experiment with different ways of doing this.

So, without further ado, let's start using sound. Creating and manipulating sound is probably something novel to many new Flash users, so we have five separate tutorials in this chapter. The Sound Sampling appendix at the end of this book describes the fundamentals of digital sound. You might like to look at that too if you're totally new to digital sound.

Let's begin - logically enough - with how to create or source the sounds you want to use.

Creating Sound

The first problem with getting sound into Flash is acquiring your sound files. There are generally only two options:

- Get them from a sound library CD or from a website offering public domain sounds

- Create the sound samples yourself

There are a lot of sites out there that rip off their sounds from obscure dance or hip-hop records. The implications of this may not be too serious when you're starting out, but when you create sites commercially, being found out can be both costly and embarrassing. The easy and safe option is to get your sounds and loops from a royalty-free web site. For those who go for this option, there's a list of useful sources in the Sound Sampling appendix, so just nip to the web, download a couple of sounds, and fast-forward to the next section.

Now we'll briefly illustrate a typical route for *creating* sounds for Flash.

There are two main types of sound you'll want to capture: incidental sounds, and music. Incidental sounds are things like doors slamming or cows mooing, which can easily be recorded with just a microphone, a handy cow, and the free sound recording software that comes with your computer (Sound Recorder on the PC or the Sound control panel on a Mac). You could record music in the same way, but the results would be huge files with poor quality. The best way to get high quality music onto a computer is to create it yourself.

One of the techniques that you'll learn later in this chapter is how to create a full sound score, optimized for the web. One of the best ways to utilize sound on the internet is by creating a **sound loop**. This means that you start and stop with exactly the same noise, meaning that you can repeat the sound endlessly and smoothly without any obvious breaks in it. The advantage of this is that you only need to download one small file that can carry on playing for a long time. Because music loops are one of the hardest sounds to create well, we'll work through the thought process that goes into them, then finally onto the actual creation itself.

To create music professionally, you'd use a sequencing program along with a battery of expensive synthesizers and instruments, but you can obtain simple (and relatively cheap) entry-level sequencers from the web (see the Sound Sampling appendix for a few to try). Instead of using expensive 'physical' instruments, you can actually use the sequencer to control your soundcard's *built-in* instruments via MIDI. The real advantage of this method is that all current soundcards support playback of sampled sound (as well as sound capture via a microphone). If you have a half-decent soundcard, you probably have a full synthesizer and sampler sitting in a slot in your computer even as we speak. The sound quality of internal soundcards won't be a problem because you'll be compressing the sounds extensively for web transport, and in the end there won't be much difference between them. Once you've created your musical masterpiece, it's necessary to *export* it from your sequencer as audio.

We created this chapter's accompanying sound files by importing the sequencer/synthesizer output into Sound Forge - a popular sound editing program, with a cheaper cut-down version available - at 44 KHz and 16 bit, which is the equivalent of CD quality. Using Sound Forge, you can also *normalize* the sounds. Normalization takes the loudest sound in the sample and increases/decreases the overall volume based on this level. Normalization finds the loudest sound in your sample and sets this to be highest point in the possible *range* of sounds in your movie. This ensures that there's a much greater range available for the quieter sounds in your file, thus avoiding excessively loud quantization noise (hissing) during the sampling process (see Appendix A for an explanation of quantization). If you don't have any really quiet sounds in your file, then this isn't really necessary.

After this Sound Forge based processing, the sounds were passed through a package called Acid (from the same makers as Sound Forge) to create a seamless loop, then saved on to the computer. The most common formats for saving are .WAV files (PC) or .AIFF files (Mac). We'll be using WAVs as the default file format for our sounds throughout this chapter, but if you're using a Mac just substitute this for AIFFs - all of the processes will remain the same.

The files are now ready for importing into Flash.

To allow you to use the individual sounds, we've included them amongst the files at the code section of our web site. We've kept the sound files at CD quality throughout the sound capture process, for two reasons:

- The maximum (best) sound quality that Flash can export is limited by the sound quality you import at. The better your input, the more flexibility you have with the output. There's always the chance that you may want to use better quality sounds as Internet transmission speeds creep up and more people have faster connections. By keeping the files at CD quality, you're never in danger of having to re-record samples.

- You may want to create screensavers or other non-web applications, and these will be able to use CD quality sound because bandwidth won't be an issue. In this case, you wouldn't have to re-record the sounds, as they would already be at the highest quality.

Of course, you may not have CD quality *output* available, particularly if you're using non-optical connections and/or a soundcard as your synthesizer. In that and any other case, keep your sounds at the highest quality your set-up can manage - you may just save yourself from major hassle later on.

Importing and Exporting Sound with Flash

In the last section we gave a brief overview of how to get audio into your computer so that it's ready for importing into Flash. We'll now look at how to actually get it into Flash, and how to optimize it for *export* onto the Internet.

To import a sound, all you have to do is use the **File > Import** menu.

Flash can import a number of sound formats, WAV, AIFF and MP3 being probably the three most popular. If you've created your own sounds, it's strongly recommended that you keep them as full quality WAV files, because MP3 is what's called a **lossy** format. This means that to get the highest amount of compression, the computer intelligently discards sounds that it thinks you won't hear. The problem with this is that there's a drop in quality, and once the sound information is discarded, it's lost forever. Although you may not be able to hear the differences, you'll see them in programs like Sound Forge and Acid, and you may start to have trouble synchronizing the lower quality sounds as precisely: this is because the waveforms have started to 'blur', making accurately locating the sound's start and stop positions much more difficult.

Let's get our fingers busy and work with some real sounds.

> *If you haven't already visited our site and downloaded the sound files that accompany this chapter, do so now. Go to www.friendsofED.com, follow the links to the Code page, and find the relevant sounds download file. We've included both CD quality and Flash-optimized (and therefore smaller) versions of the files.*

Bringing Sound into the Mix

1. Open up a new movie.

2. Save it away as Soundtrack.fla, and save it in the same folder as the case study movie we've been building throughout the book. We'll be using this movie throughout this chapter, and on into later chapters, so keep updating and saving it.

3. Use the **File > Import** command to open up the Import dialog box, and select **All Sound Formats** from the drop-down menu as shown on the following page:

4. From here, navigate to where you've saved your downloaded sound files and **Open** them all, adding them to your library (you can do multiple selections in the PC dialog box using *Shift-* or *Ctrl-click*.

5. Once the sounds are imported, they'll appear in your library, as illustrated here.

   The preview window will show a waveform representation of the selected sound. If you see two separate waveforms it means that the sound was imported in stereo. If you click on the Play button in the preview window, Flash will play one loop of your *original* sound. It's important to remember this, as Flash will play the sound as it was when you imported it, ignoring any compression you may have added inside of Flash since the original import.

6. Bring up the **Sound Properties** window for the **Percussion1** sound either by double-clicking on it in the library, or by selecting it and pressing the **Properties** button at the bottom of the library window:

This window displays the basic information for the selected sound file, and also shows how the sound will be exported in the final movie. The form Flash will export the sound in is dependent on the compression selection that we set in the **Export Settings** drop-down box.

7. Click on the **Test** button, and your sound will play in its original state. If you leave this set to **Default**, Flash will take the settings from your **Publish Settings** window (this window will be covered fully in the Optimization chapter later in the book). At the moment the default compression settings are **MP3** at 16 bit, but you won't *hear* this difference until your movie is published.

8. Now change the Compression setting to MP3:

This will open up another list of options:

The important part to look at here is the text at the bottom of the window. This text tells you how big your file is, and how much it has been compressed. For example, the original file was 1236.4 KB. Using MP3 compression, we've got the size down to 14.0 KB, an amazing 1.1% of the original file size.

9. By clicking on **Test** now, you'll hear the compressed sound. Notice that it doesn't sound quite the same as your original sound.

   You can juggle the file size against the quality by playing with the MP3 settings until you reach a happy medium. The **Bit Rate** is another way of expressing the sampling rate of the sound: it's found by multiplying the *sampling* rate (in Hz) by the *number of bits* per sample.

10. When you've tweaked your sound to what you consider to be the best balance, click **OK** to choose the settings. If you decide later that your sounds are taking up too much room, you can always go back and change the settings to give a smaller size.

11. Now tweak the rest of the sounds to give the best results that work for you. We'll use these optimized sounds later.

12. Save the movie.

> *Sounds can form a major part of the download for the final movie. If you're using sounds, then it's recommended that you do not simply accept the default sound settings or set the export options globally. Play around with the settings for each sound individually, and choose the most appropriate setting for each one by considering the sound quality you hear and offsetting this against the relative importance of the sound. Be fairly brutal in this, because sound files may make your final website un-viewable if they are allowed to stay large and uncompressed.*

In particular, you might consider:

- Making button 'click' sounds as small as the compression allows - The sounds will be a lot deeper and a bit muffled, but hey, what's the difference between one momentary click sound and another?

- Making less prominent sounds lower quality - If you have a big thumping bass line and percussion up front, do you really need all those background effects to be high quality?

- The human ear is very poor at sensing the direction of deep sounds, so stereo is not really necessary for them, MP3 takes this into account during its compression, but other methods may not.

We'll end this section with a discussion of the different sound compression methods (called **codecs** which stands for **CO**mpression - **DEC**ompression). In practice, the only way to be really sure you've used the best settings is to keep on tweaking and testing until you're happy with the audible result.

ADPCM is mainly there for compatibility with Flash 3. It can sometimes give good results for short sounds such as button-clicks, but for longer sounds or musical samples it's best to stick with MP3. As always, the only way to be certain is to try them all and pick the one that's best for you.

MP3 is the compression codec of choice for the Internet in general. You'll find that it tends to give the best sound for the smallest file size. It works by splitting the sound up into frequency bands and then applying numerous filters and tricks, based on which sounds the human ear would actually hear. This weeds out redundant information before recompiling the sound.

If you have a definite maximum file size that you can use, then just work your way down the **Bit Rate** menu until the desired file size is reached. You can also select a *quality* to encode the file at. It's recommended that you leave this set to **Fast**, as on slower machines a higher quality may result in your sounds playing out of sync with the rest of your movie. MP3 also allows you to select stereo when going above 16 Kbps, but because of the way MP3 compression works, this won't always make a huge difference. Often on a stereo track, most of the sounds in one channel are mirrored in the other: part of the MP3 compression cycle is to compare the two channels and delete all of the mirrored information from one of them and then just mark the differences in the other channel. When the track is played back, one channel plays in stereo until it comes across a marked difference and it plays that difference in the other channel. By this method, the size of the track is almost halved while still remaining true to the original. MP3 then performs a number of other more complicated routines to get the track size down even further.

Raw has no compression routine, and, as its name suggests, it exports raw digitized sound. You can actually reduce the file size by specifying a lower quality, but your final file size will generally be much higher than using any of the other methods. You would only use this method if you were running the final movie from a hard-drive in applications such as Flash screensavers.

In all the options listed above it's important to note that putting the sound quality higher than the original imported sound won't produce better quality sound, although it will increase the final file size - just with lots of redundant bits that do nothing useful.

Using Sound in Flash

We've already looked at how to attach sound to buttons in our Actions and Interactions chapter. Attaching sound to the timeline is almost identical in nature, but there are additional sound features Flash offers that we've not yet touched on. We'll repair that state of affairs right now.

Attaching Sounds to the Timeline

This is as easy as it sounds: you create a keyframe, and attach a sound to it. There are, however, several options that can be selected to make full use of the sound, and extra optimization facilities offered by Flash. Although the number of pull down menus may seem a little daunting, it all fits together in a fluid movement when you're actually adding sound. The best way to illustrate this is to try it.

Attaching Sounds to the Timeline

1. Carrying on from the last exercise, change the name of the **soundtrack** movie's default layer to **Percussion1**. Next, insert a keyframe in frame 5. You should now have this basic set-up:

2. Now open up the Sound panel (**Window > Panels > Sound**). From here we can attach our sound, and add effects and different timings to it in the process:

3. If the keyframe in frame 5 is not already highlighted, click on it now. Open up the **Sound** drop-down menu from the **Sound** panel - all of the sounds in your library will appear in a list:

   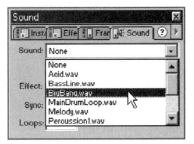

4. To attach a sound to your keyframe you just select it from this list, scroll down the list and click on **Percussion1**. Once you've selected your sound, a little waveform appears in the keyframe:

At the moment it will just look like a straight line because you can only see a small fragment of it.

5. To rectify this, add additional frames using the 'click, drag, press **F5**' method so that you can see the end of the waveform just poking into frame 89:

6. Now test your movie. You should hear a short pause, and then the sound will begin playing at frame 5.

7. Next, click on your sound in the timeline and return to the **Sound** panel. The next thing to look at is the **Effect** option:

This option allows you to add audio effects via a **volume envelope**. The envelope allows you to see and control the volume in different parts of the sound.

8. For an example of this, select **Fade Left to Right** from the **Effect** drop-down menu, then click on **Edit** to be taken to the **Edit Envelope** window:

Once the **Edit Envelope** window appears, use the **Zoom** buttons on the bottom right until you can see the full waveform.

Stereo sounds are split into two **channels**, one for the left speaker, and one for the right. This window contains two panes, showing the waveforms for the left audio channel at the top, and those for the right channel at the bottom. You'll always see two channels, even if the sound you're editing is mono - the one channel will just be repeated twice. The scale between the two panes represents time, and can be measured in seconds or in frames. You can toggle between the scales with the two buttons on the bottom right. You can test your sound at any time by using the **Play** button.

Superimposed on top of the waveforms are a couple of lines with little white squares on either end. These lines depict the volume envelope, and they can be used to control the volume of your sound. The top of the pane represents 100% volume, and the bottom is silence. Because you've selected **Fade Left to Right**, the top pane (the left channel) will have a diagonal line running from the top at the beginning of the sound to the bottom at the end, and the bottom pane will show the opposite. This will mean the sound in the left speaker will start at full volume and drop to nothing, and the sound in the right speaker will start at nothing and rise to full volume, giving the effect of the sound panning from one side to the other.

9. Press the **Play** button now to hear the effect.

10. The squares on the lines are control points, much like on bezier curves, and they can be dragged to change the shape of the envelope - try it now.

11. Drag the control points higher and lower, and use the **Play** button to preview your changes. You can add more control points, up to a maximum of 8, by clicking anywhere on either the top or bottom pane. When you add a point in one pane, Flash adds an identical point in the other. You can easily make some pretty strange sound effects by playing with these settings:

12. To get an idea of some basic effects, run through the **Effect** drop-down list at the top of the window, and notice how the envelope changes to reflect your selection.

    Always play your sounds after you make an alteration to ensure you're achieving the effect you want. As with most things, the best way to appreciate how it works is to play about with it and learn by listening to the effects you make. Notice that you can still zoom in and out using the magnifying glass icons while you're editing the envelope - this allows for precise volume control.

13. We're going to set the **Effect** to **None**, as we want the sound to start straight away, but feel free to leave your experimental effects on if you wish.

14. Click **OK** to close the window with your chosen effects applied to your sound.

    As you may already have begun to realise, the volume envelope can be very powerful when creating sound effects. For example, the sound of an approaching car can easily be simulated by importing a basic engine noise, and using the envelope controls to make it slowly increase in volume. The same engine noise could also be used to simulate the car moving from left to right across the screen by using the **Fade Left to Right** effect. By clever use of the envelope controls, you could even incorporate both of these effects into the same sound. Many more complicated effects are possible with these controls, but they are beyond the scope of this book. For now, just knowing these basics will stand you in good stead.

15. Open the **Sync** drop-down menu in the Sound panel. This will give you a list of four options - **Event**, **Start**, **Stop**, and **Stream**:

    The most important of these options are Event and Stream. Although the selection of these Sync types will have little effect on your movie while you're testing it within Flash, they have a profound effect on how Flash loads the sounds during Internet playback.

16. Leave this selection set to **Event**.

17. Save the movie.

Sounds in Flash take precedence over animations and follow their own separate 'lifetime'. For example, imagine you have an animation that's 10 seconds long, and a sound that also lasts for 10 seconds. You could tell Flash to *start* them both at the same time and expect them both to *finish* at the same time. In reality though, if someone runs your movie on a slow computer, your sounds can easily get out of sync, especially if you're streaming sounds (sending the file down bit by bit as it plays). If you ran the 10 second animation/sound example on a slow computer, it might get half way through the sound and animation without a problem, but then have to pause the animation as it waited to load the next part of the sound as it arrived down the wire. If it was the other way and the animation was the problem, Flash would try to skip frames to allow the sound to play smoothly.

- The Event option tells Flash to treat the sound in the same way as it treats movie symbols. It will only load one version of the sound into its library when the movie is first played, and will re-use the sound if it has to play it more than once. Event sounds are not played until the whole sound has been loaded, and they are not locked to the timeline. If you have an event sound lasting 10 seconds, but the user's computer is too slow to maintain the frame rate, the frame you would have expected the sound to end on may not be the one that the sound actually does end on. The problem with this is that your movie may take longer to begin playing, because Flash is loading all of the sounds before it starts.

- Stream tells Flash to start loading the sound directly from the Internet as a constant sound stream. Flash starts playing the sound as soon as it has approximately 5 seconds of the sound loaded. If you repeat the same sound several times, Flash will re-load the sound each time, as it's not kept in the computer's memory. Where you have several sounds all streaming at the same time and stopping at the same time, Flash will mix them all together when it creates the SWF file for Internet playback, and will stream back only one channel. Additionally, Flash will lock the sound to the timeline. This means that if the sound gets ahead or behind of the main timeline, Flash will stop or skip frames to make sure the sound stops at the right instant. This can cause choppy animations as Flash tries to keehe frame rate up with the sound.

Having said all that, the choice of whether to use **Event** or **Stream** is usually easily made. If the sound is relatively short and will be played more than once or looped, select **Event**, and if your sound is a long, non-repeating introductory tune that has to start playing immediately, then select **Stream**. It's usually more economical to purpose-build tailored sounds from scratch for your movies, and which can be easily looped if they need to be. In this case, you'll rarely have to use the **Stream** option, and will therefore save your sounds from having to be reloaded when you want to reuse them.

- The **Start** option is almost identical to **Event**, except that it won't allow more than one version of the same sound to play at the same time. Without this, if you have a long sound attached to a button it will normally replay every time the button is pressed: rather than stopping the first sound if the button is pressed again, Flash will just start playing the new sound over the top of the original one. As you can imagine, this can make a mess of your carefully constructed sounds!

- The **Stop** option does just what it says it does. There's an action to stop all sounds at once, but if you just want to stop one sound, or a limited group of sounds, you would make the soundtrack jump to a frame with this command attached to it. This comes in useful when you have a soundtrack playing in the background and button click noises over the top. If you had an option to turn the soundtrack off, but you still wanted to have your other noises, you would use a button linked to this option to stop the soundtrack playing.

These options will become a lot clearer when we discuss streaming and publishing your movies in later chapters.

- The final option on the **Sound** panel is **Loops**. Flash will play the sound from end to end as many times as you specify here. If you leave this set to **0**, the sound won't loop, i.e. it will play once and then stop. There are numerous tricks you can perform with this option: for instance, if you set **Loops** to a huge number like 9999, and then put a **Stop** action in the keyframe containing the start of the sound, you could create a sound that will effectively play forever. When you have a looping sound, the volume envelope will extend across all of the loops, allowing you to apply fades and effects across the whole sound, not just each individual loop. This is useful for repetitive sounds like car engines and helicopter whirrs.

Now let's examine some of quirks of sound in Flash.

Flash Sound Issues

There are a fair number of unexpected things that can happen when you're using sound in Flash. These 'features' have put off many otherwise competent Flash web designers from dabbling much further than adding sound to the odd button click in Flash. It's important that you're aware of these from the beginning so that you won't have too much trouble with them later.

- Flash sometimes doesn't seem to like it if you play sound in the first frame of your movie. The Flash player sometimes seems to get its synchronization wrong if all the sounds start on the first frame of your movie or the first frame of any scene. For this reason, it's a good idea to start all sounds at about frame 5.

- From time to time, **Event** synced sounds may not last as long as they should, or may not sound as if they start on the same frame, even though they are set to do so on the timeline. There's a little trick that you can use to correct this: as well as starting your sounds at frame 5, try adding a new layer with a one-frame sound in frame 4 and setting it to **Stream**. We'll call this a 'kicker' layer, because it seems to kick the Flash player into action, and make it behave like it should. It doesn't matter which sound you use, but remember to set its volume envelope to nothing, so you won't hear anything when it plays. You'll need to do this for every new scene you have that contains any **Event** sounds that are supposed to start at the same instant. Alternatively, you can create a very short sound sample specifically for use as the kicker in all your projects.

- **Event** sounds are only synchronized to the timeline when they're started. If, for some reason, the computer fails to keep up with the frame rate, your carefully triggered sounds can start to play too late, leaving gaps and - worse - becoming unsynchronized. There are three ways around this:

  - Change scene often, and have a kicker at the beginning of each to bring Flash back in line. Although this fixes the problem after it has occurred, it doesn't stop the problem occurring in the first place.

  - When you come to publish your movie (more on this in the Publishing chapter), set your movie playback to **Auto High**. If you've set your movie to **High** quality, Flash will try to maintain the picture quality of your animations at a maximum, and won't be too bothered about maintaining a constant frame rate. This may result in your sounds been triggered too late, because the timeline itself is 'getting behind'. You can lower the quality to **Auto High** from the **HTML** tab of the **File > Publish Settings** menu. This tells Flash to maintain a high quality until it's in danger of becoming too slow, at which point Flash will drop the picture quality to keep up. Flash can therefore compensate intelligently.

  - Drop the frame rate.

- Whether you're producing a professional or home web site, it's still best to test it out on a minimum spec computer. Although this used to be a major issue, it's becoming less so as the average computer becomes faster. The other option is to forget the issue completely unless someone reports a problem, which is less likely as time goes on, but still can stop that person from ever returning to your site.

Now that you know about how to acquire or create sound loops, and how to avoid some of the pitfalls associated with sound, it's time to do something a bit more useful than attaching the odd click to a button or a few low-quality sound effects to the timeline.

Integrating Sound

In this part of the chapter we'll create a full soundtrack. There are few web sites that actually have such a thing, possibly because of all the problems that've been encountered with Flash's **Event** sound type, so you're now beginning to walk a trail less trodden, one that many before you have been afraid to follow. You may be a beginner, but that's no excuse for being afraid. Enjoy.

Creating a Movie Soundtrack

A feature of Flash that we've not talked about yet is the **Load Movie** action. This action allows Flash to run *more than once at the same time*. One of these movies could be your web site's visual content, and the other one could be the soundtrack.

In this chapter we'll create a soundtrack movie, and we'll show you how to add it to a web site movie when we talk about publishing in our Publishing chapter. Our soundtrack will not be like a traditional Flash movie, because it'll have a blank stage - the timeline in the soundtrack movie will control sound only. Don't be put off by this, as it will all begin to blend together in the Publishing chapter. For now, let's paste together the loops we imported earlier and make a polished soundtrack.

1. In your **Soundtrack** movie, you should already have a full, optimized library, and one layer containing a percussion sound:

   These sounds have been specially selected to allow the creation of a number of different compositions, or in the more modern parlance, they allow different re-mixes of the same tune. So you can bring certain elements to the fore or delete others to give completely different styles - for example, using strings and melodies for an ambient sound, or focusing on percussion for a more insistent dub sound.

As you saw earlier, the sounds were created for looping and re-use, so we'll be using **Event** syncing throughout. Taking into account the problems that can occur with **Event** sounds, the first thing we must do is to add a 'kicker'.

2. Create a new layer and name it **Kicker**.

3. Insert a keyframe in frame 4 of the Kicker layer, then attach the **BassLine** sound (although you could have used any sound) to the keyframe:

4. In the **Sound** panel, set the **Sync** drop-down menu to **Stream**.

5. Insert a **blank** keyframe in frame 5 of the kicker. As we've set the sound to **Stream**, we want to make sure that the sound only plays for one frame before stopping. This will do that for us.

6. Click back onto frame 4, and then click on the **Edit** button to open the **Edit Envelope** window for the **BassLine** sound. Drag the control points to the bottom set the volume to zero, then close the window:

There's no need to change the **Loop** option in the **Sound** panel because we only want our sound to play once.

7. Because this composition will be long, and it's imperative to know where in the timeline you are at all times (you'll have to be constantly counting beats and frames to sync everything up just right), we'll also add a long comments layer to hold labels. Add a new layer above your **Kicker** layer, and name it **Comments**.

8. The layer will automatically be made to the length of your longest layer - in this case, the percussion layer. If it needs to be any longer at any stage, you can always lengthen it later. You could also make this layer a guide layer if you wanted, so that it doesn't get exported into the final movie, but since it actually contains nothing in it but labels, it won't make much real difference.

9. Insert a keyframe in frame 4 of the **Comments** layer, above your 'kicker' sound. Use the Frame panel to put a label in this keyframe which reads **Kicker & Percussion1**. This will let you quickly see what's happening, and when, in your soundtrack:

10. Make sure that your percussion sound is set to be an **Event** sound that doesn't loop. Unless otherwise stated, this will be the setting for all of the other sounds, too. Don't forget!

Just as a safety check, let's make sure that this sample looks as we're expecting it to. In Sonic Foundry's Acid program, the samples were 7 seconds long each. The movie is playing at 12 frames per second, which for seven seconds equates to 84 frames. The sample starts at frame 5 and ends at 89, which seems about right.

The percussion sound is two bars long, and so for that matter, are all of the other samples. We're writing a dance track, so the pattern we must follow is to do four bars before inserting a change. This is the standard pattern for all dance and most pop music, so it's one to remember. This means that we need another two bars before we can have a new pattern, so we must repeat this pattern once more.

11. Insert a keyframe in frame 89 of the **Percussion1** layer, and attach another **Percussion1** sound to it by dragging another instance of the sound out of the library.

12. Now play your sound through to make sure there are no glitches in it. Insert frames as you did before, until you can see the whole sound wave on the timeline - this will allow you to easily sync other sounds to the end of it. If your sounds do sound a little out of sync, try moving their starting keyframe forwards or backwards until you find where they sound best:

    You may be wondering why we didn't just repeat the first sample for two loops using the **Sound** panel. You *could* have done that, but remember that **Event** sounds are only synchronized to the timeline *when they're started*. The longer the event sound lasts before you attach a new version to the timeline, the more chance there is of your sound getting slightly out of sync with the timeline.

    Next, you'll be adding a new loop, **Percussion2**, which is a slightly fuller rhythm with more bass.

13. Firstly, add a new layer called **Percussion2** to put the sound in, and move this layer to the bottom of the list. This means that your layer order follows the order of the samples in the soundtrack. If you need to see all of your layers at once, click on the bottom of the timeline and drag it down until they are all in view:

14. Now add a keyframe in this layer at the frame immediately after the first percussion loop finishes, and attach the **Percussion2** sound to it:

15. Add a keyframe to your **Comments** layer above where you started the new sound and label it **Percussion2**:

This label is there to remind you that you're now in the second set of four bars, and that you're using the second percussion sample. Documentation of music files is pretty much a necessity. You may recognize all the individual waveforms now, but in six months time when you want to spruce up your website, and decide on a celebratory re-mix, it may take you some time to find where each new sound comes in on the composition.

16. In accordance with the four bar rule, repeat the **Percussion2** sound in the same way as you did for **Percussion1**.

17. Next we'll be adding two sounds that will start at the same time in the third set of four bars. Prepare the timeline by adding two new layers to the bottom, call them **Percussion3** and **BigBang**:

Insert your new sounds in their respective layers immediately after the end of the second **Percussion2** sound:

18. Update your **Comments** layer to include the new sounds:

19. Preview your movie to hear your soundtrack. Now that you've more than one sound playing at the same time, you start to have one being overshadowed by the other. This can be corrected by messing about with the relative volume of each track to make for a more pleasing composition.

20. We want to bring the **BigBang** sound to the fore, so open up the **Edit Envelope** window for the **Percussion3** sound, and lower its volume by dragging the control points down a bit. Now return to your movie and play it again. If the volume needs to be adjusted again, go back and drag the points a little lower. Repeat this until you're happy with the results.

You can also easily bring the volume back up to 100% after the **BigBang** effect has played. By doing this, you can then insert another **Percussion3** track afterwards at full volume without having a noticeable jump in the sound.

21. Look on your timeline, and note which frame the **BigBang** sound finishes in:

22. Now go back into the **Edit Envelope** window for **Percussion3** and change the timer to frames.

23. You can now move along the sound until you come to the frame where you noted the **BigBang** sound as finishing, and put another control point in:

24. Then move about 10 frames forward, to give a gradual volume increase, and put in another control point at 100% in both panes:

25. Now play back your soundtrack. It should play smoothly all the way through, and you probably won't even notice the change in volume at the end.

   So, to sum up, the process for adding new sounds is:

   - Create a new layer and name it after the sound

   - Insert a keyframe in the new layer where you want the sound to start

   - Attach the sound to the keyframe using the Sound panel

   - Add a label to your Comments layer so you can track what's happening

   - Add enough frames to the layer until you can see the end of the waveform

   - Play the soundtrack and decide if you want to make any volume or syncing changes

   - Make any changes you need to, and play the sound again to make sure you're happy with it

   - Either add another copy of the sound afterwards, or start a new sound on its own layer

26. Now use the other sounds we've provided you with - or ones you've created yourself - and put them together to create your own complete soundtrack. Don't worry if it ends up quite long, that's what the soundtrack is for

- to provide a backdrop while the visitor is on your site.

At the end of the soundtrack, we're going to put in a loop so that a section of it will carry on playing forever.

27. Add a label in your **Comments** layer at the end of your last sound and call it **End Loop**.

28. Now insert one set of the sounds that you want to carry on looping. Here is our final selection:

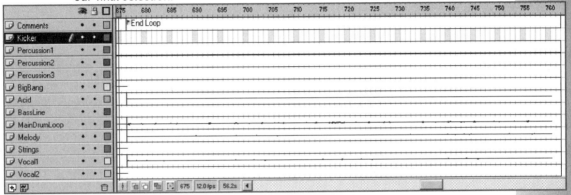

29. Using the Sound panel, set all of the sounds in your final loop to play 999 times, which should be longer than even the most avid fan of your music will remain:

Because the sounds start at the same time, they're synchronized to each other and won't fall out of time with one another. They may fall out of time with the *timeline*, but that doesn't really matter anymore, as no new sounds will be started that need to be synchronized to any particular event.

30. The final thing to do is to put a **Stop** action in the **End Loop** keyframe in the **Comments** layer. If you wanted to have a number of separate soundtracks, say for different sections of your movie, then you could keep them all as different scenes in your one main soundtrack movie, and call them when you needed them. By putting a **Stop** action in here, you're making sure that Flash won't start playing these when it gets to the end of your first soundtrack.

31. That's it, your musical masterpiece is finished. Now just crank up the volume, press play, kick back your heels and enjoy, until you get sick of it and turn it off.

32. Save your movie.

And that's more or less all there is to the basics of putting music in Flash. Simply add or subtract sounds every 4 bars and you're away. The only thing we haven't talked about sound-wise is how to allow the user to turn the sound *off*. Because the control for this will have to be in your website movie and not the soundtrack, we'll leave that for later.

Well designed sounds that can be seamlessly looped are gold dust to the Flash designer, because they make the production of optimized soundtracks to go with your website just a matter of dragging and dropping sounds onto the timeline. Also, an understanding of how and how not to lay down sound in Flash will prevent you falling into the traps that befall many Flash beginners. The use of sound in Flash for soundtracks and incidental effects will hopefully help lift your web site designs above their mute contemporaries.

We'll revisit the soundtrack movie in the Publishing chapter, where we'll show you how to finally add it to your web site via the **LoadMovie** commands.

Case Study

As the final amendment to our web site, we'll add some sound to its buttons. We'll walk through attaching sound to one of the buttons' Over states. You'll need to repeat this for the other buttons.

1. Open up your case study movie.

First, of course, we need to import a button sound.

2. Use the **File > Import** menu and import a suitable button sound from whatever sounds you have available on your machine.

The next thing to do after you've imported a sound is to optimize it.

3. Double-click on the newly imported sound and by using you ears and the various settings available, find the best compromise between sound-quality and size.

Now it's just a matter of attaching it to the appropriate button state.

4. Double click on the **Home** button symbol in the library to enter Edit Symbols mode.

5. Make sure that you add a keyframe to the **Main Button** layer's Down state (you'll need to do this for the other buttons too as you work through them).

It's a good idea to add a new layer for sounds, to keep them separate from the other parts of the button.

6. Add a new layer to the button and call it **sound**.

7. In the **sound** layer, add a keyframe to the button's Over state.

8. Use the **Sound** panel to attach the sound to the Over state. The sound was designed to be used as a button click so there's no need to play with any of the effects.

9. Make sure that the **Sync** is set to **Event** and you're done.

10. Now when you preview your movie, the sound will play when you run the mouse over the button.

11. Next, add a new keyframe to the sound layer's Down state, and attach a different sound to it. This sound will play when the button is pressed.

12. Preview the movie again and press the button to check out the two different sounds

13. Next, in the same way, add sounds to each of the other buttons. The sequence is:

- Open the relevant button symbol for editing from the library

- Add a keyframe to the **Main Button** layer's Down state

- Insert a new **sound** layer into the button and add keyframes to its Over and Down states

- Use the Sound panel to attach sounds to the two state keyframes in the **sound** layer

At the end of this process, each of your buttons will now look something like this:

You now have the beginnings of a burgeoning multimedia web site.

Now the real fun starts. Those of you who are confident enough to go away and write a soundtrack for your website, don't forget to have a look at the sound appendix in this book before you start. Once you start writing soundtracks, you'll realize that it can be one of the most fun parts of the Flash design process, and can really lift the presentation up to new heights. Good luck!

Summary

Sound, if used well, can add an extra dimension to your Flash movies and web sites. We already knew that we could attach sounds to buttons, and in this chapter we've also looked at how to incorporate multiple sound elements onto the Flash timeline.

We saw that:

◆ You can import generic or purpose-built sounds into your Flash movie

◆ You can process and optimize a sound file's **properties** once you've imported the sound into the Flash library

◆ You attach sounds to keyframes in the main timeline (or inside a movie clip's timeline) using the **Sound** panel

◆ The **Sound** panel also gives you access to an extensive range of panning, volume, syncing and looping effects

◆ You can create a complete, independent soundtrack movie that will play alongside your visual movie - we'll see how to integrate these two components in the Publishing chapter

◆ We finished the construction work on the Case Study movie's content

Next, we're going to look at **optimizing** your movies so that your audience get the best experience they can.

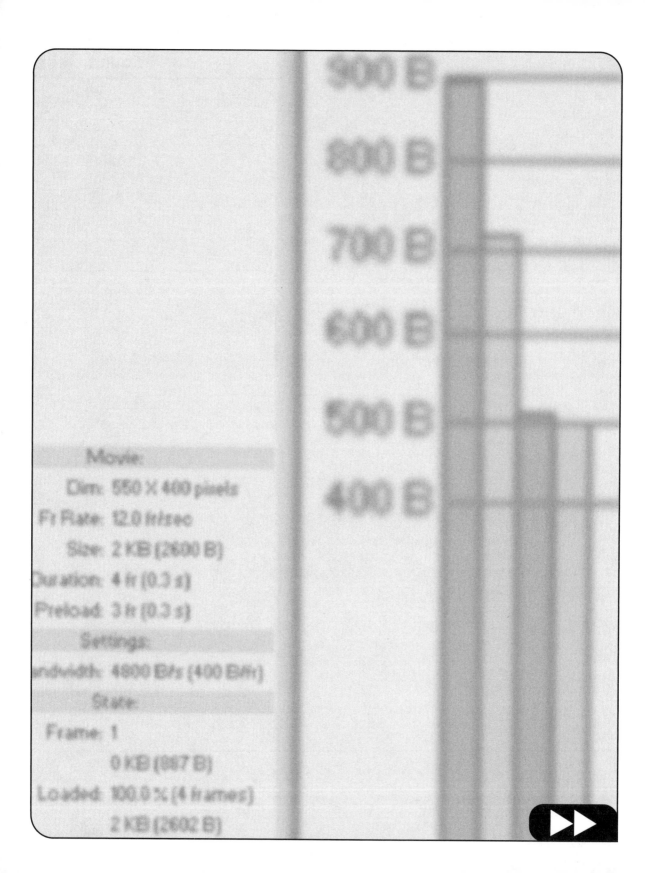

12 Optimizing

What we'll cover in this chapter:

- *The nature of the Internet, and how this affects your Flash movie*

- *Thinking about your target audience*

- *How Flash can transmit content across the Internet effectively using* **streaming**

- *Flash's tools for optimizing your movies and seeing how they'll download and display on the Internet*

- *How to design optimized Flash movies*

Picture the scene: you finish your Flash web site and it looks great. Excitedly, you put it up on the server that's hosting your site, replacing that boring old HTML site you've had for years. You're sure to get more visitors as word spreads about the multimedia extravaganza your site has become.

Two days later, you check the number of visitors, anticipating a massive surge. But wait...surely not! The number of visitors has actually gone *down*.

There's a very good reason for this, and one that the first time Flash designer needs to take careful note of. The site may look great when it's running from your hard drive, but once it's up on the Internet, the rules are very different. All those multimedia bells and whistles have made for a bigger, fatter site with a longer download time. The average web surfer has a very short attention span, and while they're waiting for your site to appear, the rest of the Internet is trying to entice them away from your sluggish download and onto *their* web pages.

Once you've learnt all the new and exiting features that Flash has to offer, the next lesson is **always** the hard reality of download time. It's something that you must always bear in mind when designing Flash sites that'll be accessed over the net.

Flash and the Internet

Now that we've broken your dream a little, we'll use the rest of this chapter to do what the US Army does: build you back up, and give you some insights into the practicalities and disciplines you're going to need to turn your Flash dreams into usable reality.

Before we start to look at how our Flash files behave on the Internet, let's recap on what the Internet and World Wide Web actually are, and revisit some other terms you'll have heard but, maybe, never really understood.

The Internet

The Internet's existence was instigated by the US Department of Defense, who needed a fault-tolerant system that provided basic communications services between computers: file transfer, email, remote logon and remote control of computers - all of which had to work, irrespective of different computer types or operating systems. The solution was designed to be able to take the hits a communications system would get in battlefield use. To achieve this, the system had to be able to carry on even if parts of it were knocked out, and it had to be accessible by a number of different computers (from hand held laptops to big dirty mainframes, and everything in between).

The technology that achieves this, and which makes the Internet work the way it does, is a **transmission protocol**, something that goes by the catchy title of **TCP/IP**. This transmission protocol is the universal 'vehicle' that everyone uses on their networks to move data between remote computers. As the slash in TCP/IP suggests, this vehicle comes in two parts.

IP (Internet Protocol) is the tractor that shunts data around across the network, based on a destination address called the *IP number*. The IP number is a unique numeric code used to identify any computer on the Internet. It's a four-byte value expressed by converting each byte into a decimal number from 0 to 255, and then separating each byte with a period, so an example IP could be: 245.239.99.34, or 22.254.0.128. The Internet Protocol is a technology that takes the thing that you want to send - a file, an email, whatever - and encodes it as a series of little data packets that can be sent down the wires that connect up the different IP numbers.

The data that's passed between different IP numbers is directed across the Internet by special communications computers called **routers**. Routers are like switching stations that direct data to its target destination. Each router passes the data that it receives on to the next closest *working* router to the target address. The routers are arranged to be intelligent enough to pick the fastest available route for the data to take. As the network is in a constant state of flux, your data might be directed via an infinite number of possible routes - but the router will do its best to pick the best route for you.

TCP (Transmission Control Protocol) is the technology that *verifies* the data actually got to its destination. IP doesn't care if the packets of data are sent out of order, or even not sent at all. It's up to its big brother TCP to make sure that all the data eventually gets to where it's sender intended.

In terms of *hardware*, the Internet looks like a lot of nodes (or computers) all connected together. Although it may seem rather anarchic and organic, there is actually a broad structure:

Nodes tend to be grouped together in clusters, and these have a large, high bandwidth transmission point called a **hub** at their center. Such hubs are sometimes connected together by very large bandwidth links called **backbones**, which connect large population areas or continents.

The World Wide Web

The Internet then, is a network of physical networks across which you can send, receive and view text files, using the transport methods of TCP/IP. The World Wide Web (WWW, more casually known as 'the web') is a more recent development that came about because there was a need to access multimedia files containing music, pictures and video across the network of machines.

The web consists of two parts: **Browsers** - software that allows the computers that are part of the Internet to read and view multimedia files, and **Servers** - computers that can host and disseminate these documents.

It's the universally agreed components of the web, coupled with the expandability and versatility of the underlying TCP/IP and communications hardware, that have made the Internet such a success. One of the key web components are **Uniform Resource Locators**, or URLs. We use these in the same way we use file names, but a URL designates a file that can exist on any computer within a network, such as the Internet. Another component is HTML (**Hypertext Mark Up Language**), which is a system-independent way of telling a browser how to render information.

So, when a client asks you what the Internet is, you can tell them. But one of the key things we need to know about before we put our work out on the net is **bandwidth**.

Bandwidth

Whenever people talk about the future of the Internet, one of the things that's invariably discussed is bandwidth. Bandwidth essentially denotes how much data will travel along a given path in a given time, or how much information a modem can download and how quickly.

Bandwidth is measured in bits or bytes per second - a bit being the smallest individual morsel of computerized data. The higher the bandwidth, the faster things get to and from your computer. Different types of content demand different amounts of bandwidth to let them be used effectively - for example, it takes more bandwidth to download an animation in one second than it does to download a static text page in the same time. Because the size of the 'pipe' you send the data down to a user's computer is fixed by the capacity of their modem, you need to think about the size of your movie, and how long it's going to take to get down the pipe and onto their screen. Photographs, sound files and video clips all add to the bandwidth required to quickly download a file.

Data sent over the Internet will usually get to its destination, but neither the sender nor the receiver knows *when* this will occur, or the *route* that will be taken. Over time, the average transmission rate becomes fairly constant, but because of the nature of TCP/IP and the way that it parcels data into little packets as they're transmitted, it's unwise to assume a given transmission rate over a short period. Again, there are implications here for the way you design your movies - as you'll see when we discuss *streaming* later.

A full Internet connection is only as fast as the *slowest* node, meaning that slow sections will tend to drag down the average transmission time across the whole network - the difference between a 33.6K modem and a 56K modem in download times was not that great until the transmission lines across the internet began to be upgraded. Although this 'lowest common denominator' factor is not so much of a problem now, it can still rear its ugly head during peak times, when it's the Internet itself that's the slowest component in the whole system. Here's an example:

A large number of people are trying to access the same server or web page. The closer a router is to the target server, the number of available alternative routes drops, whereas the amount of data being shuttled goes *up*, creating a bottleneck of queuing information. So what do the poor routers do? They give up and throw your data away! You, and everyone else, try again, and the re-tries generate even more traffic, grinding the whole thing to a standstill.

These problems show up sometimes as numerous re-tries and connection losses when trying to connect to popular pages, or a sudden drop in bandwidth for no apparent reason (but most likely due to the loss of a route, causing traffic to be suddenly shoveled on your local routers!).

So, the important thing to remember is this: the time it will take your potential viewer to download your Flash site file depends on what's in your file and (within the constraints of the Internet we've just discussed) how quickly their computer can read it. This means that when you make a Flash site you not only have to consider *what* you put in your Flash movie file, but *who* you want to be able to see it. Who is your audience, and what assumptions do you make about their computer equipment?

The End User - Your Audience

If you're coding your site on a super fast G4 Mac, what happens if the user has a slow PC? There have been all sorts of little discussions about this on the Flash newsgroups for some years, spilling over into accusations of elitism and/or Flash snobbery on the one hand, and the 'take no chances' corporate Flash designers on the other.

Here are some general rules to keep in mind before putting your site on the web:

- No user will wait more than fifteen seconds for your site to download if nothing *interesting* is happening at the same time (now read that again) unless you're a cool enough Flash designer to warrant the wait

- A cutting-edge, designer Flash web site should be viewable using a standard two-year-old computer's hardware configuration

- A commercial Flash site should be viewable on a standard three-year-old computer

- The speed of connection you can assume is largely dependant on two things:

  - Whether your target is a business or design audience (assume whatever was 'cutting-edge' 18 months ago), or a domestic user (assume the worst!)

  - The relative affluence of your target audience

Now you've absorbed all this techno-jargon, you'll be aware just how easy it is to lose your movie file in the digital jungle that is the Internet. To ensure your file survives that jungle environment, it's essential to understand the concept of streaming, and to consider how to use it when designing Flash movies for the Internet.

Streaming

As we've said, the bits of your Flash file that will make your site stand out from the crowd - your movies, sound effects, and so on - are the bits that will take a long time to download. If you have them all at frame 1 of the timeline, your user's modem will be unable to download your movie straight away and the user will have to sit and look at nothing until the download is complete. They'll most likely get bored and take their business elsewhere.

When **streaming** is used, however, your Flash presentation starts playing before all of it has loaded into the user's browser. By starting the Flash page as soon as there is enough information to show *something* rather than waiting until the whole thing has loaded up first, the user has to wait much less time to see part of the web site. This means that you can hold the user's attention while the cast of your all singing, all dancing, interactive masterpiece of a site is downloaded by the their computer.

> *Well thought-out Flash sites often have a specific scene at the beginning that loads up immediately, allowing the viewer to watch it as the rest of the movie is downloaded. This type of scene is called a preloader, and we'll look at preloaders more thoroughly later in the chapter.*

Streaming, as we saw when using sound in our movies earlier on, is therefore 'a very good thing'. Although it doesn't actually make things load faster down the user's pipe, it intelligently organizes what's needed in the movie, and when, so that everything is loaded up in the best order. Used efficiently, streaming can ensure that everything in your movie is downloaded before it's needed on the stage, meaning that the movie will play smoothly without any pauses to wait for an image or a movie clip to appear.

When a user requests a Flash web page across the Internet, Flash has to send the user two things:

*   The Flash movie's timeline; including attached ActionScripts and 'non-instanced' components (i.e. things that aren't stored as symbols) such as text and drawn shapes that haven't been converted into symbols

- The Flash library; including the sounds, symbols and bitmaps used in the movie

When Flash sends this data across the net, it will send the movie timeline in *frame order*. If the movie is split into separate scenes, it will send the scenes in the order they appear in the **Scene** panel. Flash will also arrange the transmission of library symbols so that they're sent in the sequence in which they appear in the timeline.

You can think of our web-bound movie as having two markers traveling along its timeline. The first one is the '*streamer*' which tracks how much of the movie has been downloaded and is ready to play. The second is the '*player*' - which points to the current frame being played:

Streamer: "how much have I downoaded?"

Player: "what frame am I on?"

For streaming to work, the *streamer* always has to be in front of the *player*. If the *player* catches the *streamer* the movie will pause, as it means that the next frame of animation has not yet been loaded. To avoid the player constantly playing tag with the streamer, causing a pause every time it catches up, it's a good idea to give the streamer a head start. We call this head start a **streaming buffer**. A streaming buffer operates by starting off the streaming process before the playback is started, giving Flash the chance to download some of the movie onto the user's computer in advance of the playback starting.

To illustrate this, imagine a movie that has a movie clip symbol called **A** in frame 10 and 30, a graphic symbol **B** at frame 20, and a drawing on frame 40 that isn't a symbol, like this:

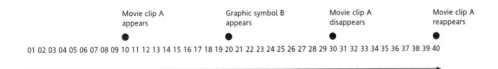

Flash would follow this sequence during streaming:

- Start off the **streamer**, sending the timeline data, beginning with frame 1. As it sends each frame, Flash will also send all timeline ActionScripts. If the *streamer* reaches frame 10 before the *player*, movie clip A will start to load. If, during this process, the player catches up to the *streamer*, the movie will pause as it waits for the movie clip to load.

- Once the movie clip has loaded, the *streamer* will race on towards frame 20, leaving the *player* plodding along the timeline, playing back the content that's been downloaded so far. Hopefully, the graphic symbol **B** will have loaded by the time the *player* reaches frame 20.

- At frame 30, the *streamer* sees symbol **A**, which it's already used once before. It doesn't have to load it up again because the information is already in the library. It just adds the instance name (and any other instance-specific information on the timeline) to the symbol template in the library and recreates the instance without having to download it again.

- At frame 40, the streaming marker sees a drawing on the stage that has not been converted to a symbol. The information for this drawing is not in the library - instead, it's attached to the frame in which it was drawn. The *streamer* will load the information as part of the frame data, but because the data is not in the library, the drawing cannot be re-used in the same way as happened in frame 30, and it will have to be loaded again if it is encountered in another keyframe.

The idea of *streamers* and *players* may be a little hard to visualize, but Flash has something that actually lets you see these two markers in action, allowing you to work out how Internet download times will affect your Flash presentation's delivery to the user's browser - and that's what we're going to look at next - the **bandwidth profiler**.

The Bandwidth Profiler

The bandwidth profiler lets you preview how your movie will behave as it downloads in the real world.

The first thing to be aware of is that Flash's bandwidth profiler assumes *constant* transfer rates. Having read the introduction to what the Internet actually is, you'll realize that this is a close approximation at the best of times, and a downright fiction at peak traffic times. However, you can use the profiler to get a good idea of which stages of your movie are going to be problematic for a user to download, even if you can't get *exact* precision for all times.

Using the Bandwidth Profiler

1. Create a new movie and make it 20 frames long by clicking on the timeline, dragging to frame 20, and then pressing *F5*:

2. In frame 1, add the text 'This is a test to see how I can optimize this movie using the bandwidth profiler' in the center of the stage in 24 point Times New Roman:

> This is a test to see how I can optimize
> this movie using the bandwidth profiler

3. Make the text into a graphic symbol with *F8* or **Insert > Convert to Symbol**. Call the symbol **text1**.

4. Still at frame 1, and under the text you've already placed on the stage, add a new text box containing this text - '**Flash will be made to load two pieces of text in different fonts, and we will use the bandwidth profiler to optimize the movie**' in Arial, 16 point.

5. Make the text a graphic symbol as before, and call it **text2**. Your stage will look something like this:

> This is a test to see how I can optimize
> this movie using the bandwidth profiler
>
> Flash will be made to load two pieces of text in
> different fonts, and we will use the bandwidth
> profiler to optimize the movie

6. Test your movie by pressing *Ctrl-Enter*.

7. While the movie's playing, go to **View > Bandwidth Profiler**, or press *Ctrl-B*. A graph will appear:

At the far left of the graph there's lots of useful looking information under the headings **Movie**, **Settings** and **State**. To the right is a little bar graph that tells you how much data is downloaded during each frame. Under **Settings**, you'll see something like **Bandwidth: 4800B/s (400 B/fr)**. This tells you the amount of information, in bytes, that can be read per second and per frame. The red line at the 400B point on the graph also shows this. This is the **Bandwidth Limit** and it represents the maximum throughput a particular modem can handle.

Your Bandwidth and Bandwidth Limit figures may read differently from those shown in the screenshot: there are three different values it can have, as you'll see now.

8. Look in the **Debug** drop down menu. You'll see something like this:

You'll see the numbers **14.4**, **28.8**, **56K** listed on this menu, with one of them ticked. Do those numbers sound familiar? They're modem speeds, and these options represent the download rates that the bandwidth profiler can simulate.

9. Our bandwidth profiler is currently simulating download using a 56K modem, set yours to the same.

If you look under the Movie heading in the left of the profiler window, you can see **Size 4KB** and **Preload: 12fr (1.0s)**. This is telling us that the movie is a 4kB download in total. Because everything appears in frame 1 of our movie, Flash has to preload everything *before* frame 1 can be played. This preload time, the time the user will wait to see the movie, is 1 second.

Try changing to a 28.8 modem, and if you really want to see how we used to live, try out the 14.4 modem as well. As you can see from the **Size** and **Preload** figures at these different settings, some people are going to have to wait longer than others to see this movie. Now you have a feel for how different modems have different download times, let's see what we can do about it.

If you look towards the top of the profiler, you can see a little marker that whizzes back and forth while the movie is running. This is the *player* we described earlier. What a help it would be to see the *streamer* as well. We can...

10. Select **View > Show Streaming**. Did you catch that? Let's see it again in slo-mo.

11. Select the 14.4 modem setting from the **Debug** menu and select **View > Show Streaming** again.

    Nothing happens for a second or so, except some frantic activity going on under the State heading at the bottom left of the profiler. Then you'll suddenly see a green band along the top of the profiler. The data in the frames covered by the green band is what has already been loaded.

    The leading edge of this band is the *streamer* and the distance the green band is ahead of the *player* is our streaming buffer.

    In this movie we have no streaming buffer at all. The *player* catches the *streamer* at frame 1 as it waits for our symbols to load. We need to go back and redesign our movie to allow streaming to take place so we can spare our user that 1 second of waiting. As I'm sure you'll appreciate, this wait can be a lot longer for more complex movies - but the method needed to avoid it is the same as we're about to use.

12. Go back to the main stage from the test movie screen.

13. Delete all the text from frame 1 and add two new blank keyframes at frames *5* and *15*:

14. With the keyframe at frame 5 selected, drag an instance of the **text1** graphic symbol onto the center of the stage. At frame 15, do the same with **text2**.

15. Test the movie - making sure the bandwidth profiler is still running (***Ctrl-B***) - and use the **Debug** window to set the modem to 14.4.

16. To see the streamer again, go to **View > Show Streaming**.
    You will see something like the graph to start with. The green bar, or *streamer*, will race ahead to frame 4 almost straight away - even on the 14.4 modem - because these are blank frames.

431

These blank frames are our streaming buffer - the time we have to start streaming before the player starts trying to play back the movie in the user's browser. The *player* will move along at its usual 'frame every twelfth of a second' pace until it catches the *streamer* at frame 4, where the streamer has been delayed by the first peak in the data graph.

Frame 4 is the *end* of the streaming buffer. The *player* will now have to wait while the extra data that's needed for frame 5 (the text1 symbol) is loaded before it can play that frame.

When you test the movie with **Show Streaming** turned *off*, the extended pause at frame 4 is not shown. By using **Show Streaming**, we're simulating what the movie would actually look like during transfer and playback across the Internet.

However, we can see that there will be a pause before frame 5 just by using the graph. The first download spike on the graph is telling you that the modem can't preload all the data needed before the frame is due to be played:

This is perhaps not surprising for a 14.4 modem, as the bandwidth limit allows only 100 bytes per frame to be downloaded.

The spike on the graph also tells us how much we've exceeded the bandwidth limit by, enabling us to judge how long the pause in playback will be.

> *Notice that the profile scale is not linear. This scale, from the 1KB line upwards is an exponential function of 2. Don't worry if you never paid attention in math when you did exponential functions, all it means here is that every value on the scale is double the value below it. Flash will create an appropriate scale for whatever amounts of data it needs to display.*

We can see that the data contained in frame 5 is over 2KB more than can be downloaded in one frame. The modem we're currently simulating takes a second to download 1200Bytes, so the movie will pause for almost two seconds. To give the modem enough time to download the data for frame 5 we'd need to add over 20 blank frames to the start of our movie - keeping the viewer waiting for playback to start and giving them a very dull first impression of our site.

Even then, our movie will pause once more at the second spike on the graph where **text2** is being loaded, and fixing this will require yet further lengthening of our already protracted movie.

So, on a 14.4 modem it's still very difficult to avoid pauses due to the very low bandwidth limit. In this case you may have to accept that even streaming can't solve the problem. You can easily switch to something more current by selecting the 56K modem from the **Debug** menu.

As you can see the use of a 56K modem makes the second spike disappear, but you're still stuck with the first one at frame 5 when the data required for **text1** again takes us over our bandwidth limit.

17. Go back to the movie and add three blank frames before the first keyframe:

18. If you test the movie now, you'll get a bandwidth profile like this:

Notice that the bars *never* go above the bandwidth limit. This means that when downloaded by a 56K modem, the movie will run smoothly with no pauses. The *streamer* will always be ahead of the *player* because all the data needed for each frame is loaded before it needs to be played - we have given our movie a sufficient streaming buffer.

In short, the movie will look and behave the same whether it is viewed from your hard drive or over the Internet with a 56K modem.

The movie we just created was fairly simplistic, but the theory we applied is the same when you start creating much bigger sites. Here's a bandwidth profile for a real commercial site:

There's an initial preload at frame 1, but after that, the site is always inside the bandwidth requirements of a 56K modem. Why did its designer choose a 56K modem? Well, this particular site was for a nightclub. Its designer considered two of the guidelines we spoke of earlier: who the target audience for the site was, in this case 18 to 26 year olds; and the relative affluence of this audience. Thinking about these factors allowed the designer to reason that the people coming to view the site would have at *least* a 56K modem at the time the site was going out. He or she reasoned rightly, because the hit rate for the nightclub trebled when this Flash site was used!

> *If you see a peak on the bandwidth profiler for one of your movies and want to know which frame is causing it, click on the peak and the movie will go directly to the offending movie frame. Remember though, the bar graph is arranged in the order that streaming will take place, and the bar you click on will rarely represent the frame the numbering along the top of the graph (which is the current frame being played) suggests it should. You can see which frame you have clicked on by looking under State to the bottom left of the screen.*

As you can see, the bandwidth profiler is a vital tool. With it, you can tailor your movie to meet the bandwidth constraints of your target user. With the **Show Streaming** option activated, you can actually see how bandwidth will affect your movie in real time, and alter things accordingly.

There are some sites that don't use streaming at all. Instead, they load the whole movie in one go. For example, Flash animations that lip-synch to sound don't use streaming, as even a slight slowing down of playback would greatly affect the movie. However, the designers judge their viewers will be prepared to wait for this spectacle.

A lot of 'unstreamed' sites are Flash showcase sites where Flash designers show off to other Flash designers or potential clients. As fledgling Flash users you're unlikely to be aiming your sites at these people and consequently your audience is unlikely to have the same level of technical equipment to view sites as these people do.

For most web audiences, long waits for web sites are a real turnoff. Although the Internet is getting faster all the time, low bandwidths will be with us at least for the shelf life of Flash 5, so we must learn to overcome them. The bandwidth profiler is a powerful weapon to have in your armory in this respect.

Optimizing and Fine-tuning Flash Movies

There are a number of things you can do to make your movies more compact and lean for Internet download. In the rest of this chapter we'll summarize all the Flash methods that allow you to achieve responsive sites. Firstly, we'll look at what to consider when planning our site.

Structure

Perhaps the most important aspect to get right for a responsive site is a well-defined structure and download flow. You need to sit down and think about which scenes the user will see, and in what order, before you jump into Flash and start creating the movie. For example, an MP3 site would probably consist of the following scenes:

- Preloader

- Intro

- Main

- About

- Downloads

- Links

When visiting the site, the viewer would most likely:

- See the *preloader*, and be taken to the *intro*

- From there, end up in the *main* scene

- Because he or she has come here looking for MP3 files, go straight to *downloads*

- Once they've set off a music file download, the viewer will probably browse the *about* scene to find out more about the music

- Finally, the viewer will most likely exit from *about* or via your *links* section

This analysis of the way that your site will be used dictates that you want *preloader*, *intro* and *main* to be your first three streamed scenes, because these are the scenes that the viewer is likely to look at first. Remember, Flash will stream the scenes in the order that they appear in the **Scene** panel. You can choose which scene to follow these with, but by second-guessing what your audience will do, and streaming the scenes in the appropriate order, you'll make your site more responsive for most visitors. In this case, our preference would be to make *downloads* the next scene, followed by *about*, and finally *links*. If you put your scenes in a random order you have no way of ensuring that the scenes will be loaded and ready to use when they are accessed by the user.

In a slightly more subtle vein, the average user in this example will spend little time in the *main* section, seeing this as just a route to the *downloads* section. You can design that into the site by making the main scene easy for the user's modem to download, thus buying time for the *downloads* section to be loaded more quickly as well. Structuring your Flash site in this strategic way is the hallmark of a good web designer. It will come with practice, and all designers will always be somewhere on that particular learning curve, struggling with the same problem as you'll face as a beginner!

Use the Right Components in Your Movie

Choosing the correct basic components to build up your site with is another area where forethought is required.

It's wise to use symbols wherever possible, the reason being that symbols possess two very desirable properties that make them bandwidth friendly. These are:

- The attributes of a symbol (size, color etc) can be changed for an individual instance via the **Effects** option on the **Instance** panel.

- Flash downloads each symbol only *once*, and bases all instances of the symbol on the single downloaded library version.

This means that instead of building a blue button and a red button separately, you can have a single gray button that Flash will only have to download once but will use to produce two tinted instances. If you don't make an object a symbol, Flash will not store it in the library once it has downloaded it, and will have to download it again the next time a separate copy of it appears in the movie.

There's one component that's an exception to this rule: a 'starting-credits' movie that you want the user to see first. If this is the case, and you make your starting credits a movie clip symbol, Flash will not begin playing it until it has completely loaded. If, however, you created it as the first scene of your movie, Flash would begin to play the movie as soon as the first frame had streamed in.

The way you use *fonts* in your final movie will also affect the download time. If your movie contains text written in a sans serif font such as Helvetica, a serif font such as Times, and a Typewriter style font such as Courier, all three font files will need to be downloaded before the movie can be viewed. If, however, you use the generic _sans, _serif or _typewriter styles to write your text in your original file, the text in the downloaded version will be written using fonts on the user's hard drive that match these styles. No font files will have to be downloaded as part of the Flash file, and the download time will be reduced.

In general, every time you use a new font face, Flash will have to download the font shapes you've used. If you're designing a site that contains a lot of text, make sure that you use the same font throughout. Because some fonts look very similar on the screen, you may not notice you're using two different fonts and are inadvertently adding to the download time of your movie. Be wary, also, of using complex font faces:

Before you use such fonts, look to see how big the font files are. They may really look cool, but some really complex font faces can take up to 32K just for ten or so characters leading to unnecessary download delays...try before you buy!

Optimizing Components

It's important to do everything possible to keep the file size of your Flash movie as low as you can. We're going to have a quick look at the tools Flash provides for lowering the amount of data taken up by the *individual components* of a movie.

Reducing the Memory used by Vector Shapes

1. Create a new movie and add three blank keyframes to the timeline so that there are four in total.

2. Use the Pencil tool, in the **Ink** mode, to draw an abstract shape at frame 1. Make your shape excessively curvy, like ours:

   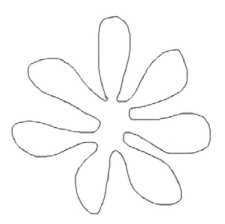

3. Select your shape and copy it. Next, select frame 2 and use the **Edit > Paste in Place** command to copy your shape onto the stage in this frame. Do the same at frames 3 and 4.

4. Select the shape in frame 2 and go to **Modify > Smooth**.

5. Select the shape in frame 3 and go to **Modify > Straighten**.

6. Lastly, select the shape in frame 4 and go to **Modify > Optimize** and drag the slider to maximum.

The **Smooth** option will make our shape more rounded, in the way that shapes drawn with the 'smoothed' Pencil tool appear, and **Straighten**, as you've no doubt surmised, will make our shape more angular in the way shapes drawn with the 'straightened' pencil tool appear. These commands can be repeated over and over again to make the shape more and more rounded, or more and more angular.

The **Optimize** option will reduce the number of curves that make up the shape. Like the previous two commands, it can be applied multiple times - but only until Flash reaches a point where no more curves can be removed.

7. Test your movie, and make sure the **Bandwidth Profiler** is turned on (**View > Bandwidth Profiler**).

The graph will be the same shape whichever modem setting you use. It shows us that the modified versions of our shape will download more quickly than the original drawing. As designers, we must decide how much we're prepared to alter the appearance of our movie components in our quest for a lower download time.

One designing eye also needs to be kept on the size of any sound clips or bitmap images we use, as the bigger they are the longer they'll take to download. We learnt how to optimize bitmaps and sound files earlier in the book. We need to balance how much they add to the movie's appeal against how long the user has to wait to see them.

Optimizing Tricks and Tips

To end this chapter, here are a few simple tricks that'll get you started on the route to efficient and responsive sites.

As we've said earlier in the chapter, the key to good design is structuring your site so the components load in the order they're needed. Make sure you load up all the functional and informative components first, such as the buttons that enable the site to be navigated, and let the eye candy that you have put in to show off appear later, as not everyone will be prepared to wait for it.

Here's the main page of the author's current personal home-site:

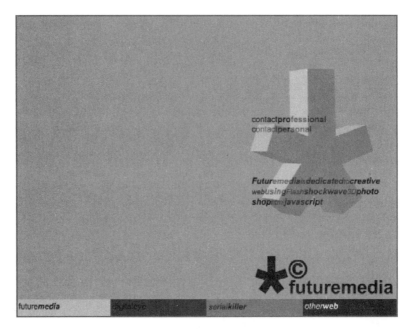

As you can see, it consists of a simple menu-bar at the bottom, with a 3D rotating symbol (created using the Flash-compatible Swift 3D rendering program) to the right. If this was your site, you wouldn't want the user to have to wait for the 3D symbol to appear before they could press a button and go to the screen of their choice, where they would be more willing to wait to see what's on it.

The way you'd arrange for that to happen is shown here:.

- At frame 1: the buttons that make up the menu-bar load up - they're in the **buttons** layer.

- At frame 2: the 3D rotating logo appears - it's in the **logo** layer - and a Stop action in the **control** layer - notice the little a - pauses the movie to allow the user to choose which button to press.

The menu bar is four different colored instances of the same button. This means only one component needs to be downloaded for it to appear, so it will show up immediately even for low bandwidth users. If the user waits for the further 20K that's needed for frame 2 to be loaded up, they'll see the logo animation. During this time, the user can select any of the menu options. Users with a high bandwidth connection, such as a T1, will see the whole page immediately, but everyone will be able to move on into the rest of the website as soon as they like.

One question that sometimes pops up is: how do you make Flash load up symbols *before* they're needed? You would need to do this if, for example, you wanted a responsive site and were prepared for Flash to pause at the beginning while essential symbols were loaded up. It's done using a **preloader**. A preloader is a scene created purely to occupy the user's attention while the symbols your site requires for later use are downloaded. Remember, once they're in the library, Flash doesn't need to reload them every time they appear.

In order to load the symbols without the user seeing them, you tell Flash they're appearing in the frame that's playing, but you place them in the work area *outside* the visible stage. However, you'd want the viewer to be looking at something so that they didn't get bored and lose patience with your downloading site.

So, what a good preloader needs is a simple animation to play as the download takes place, and some informative text to let the user know they won't have to wait too long:

Here's this preloader's timeline:

While the animation in the **logo** layer entertains the user, a different symbol from the later scenes is loaded up in the **loader** layer as each frame plays. In Frame 1, for example, all the site's essential buttons are loaded, and in frame 2 some of the vector graphic symbols that will be needed soon are loaded. Flash is made to download components that it'll now keep in the library - allowing the rest of the site to be wait-free. (The 3D animation that you saw on the previous screenshots are *not* loaded as part of the preload because they're not essential to the site - they're already beginning to look outdated in the fast expanding fashion that is Flash). To keep the viewer informed about what's going on, each frame of the **loader text** layer will contain a sentence that tells them what's going on. In frame 1 it would say something like, "Loading Interface" and so on...

If you can't think of ten interesting things that could be in the process of being loaded up, you could use a 'loading bar' (like the progress bars used in so many applications). This is simply a tweened rectangle that stretches across the screen during the ten frames of loading. Alternatively, you could give the viewer a 'percentage loaded' figure: you would arrange all the objects you needed to download amongst the ten frames of the preloader so that each contained 10% of the total download (the bandwidth profiler could be used to fine-tune this). Then the text in each frame of loader text just needs to indicate the percentage of the download completed. These two methods, however, can be seen as overkill; if you have to give 'percentage loaded' figures, your download is probably too long!

In the author's site, once the download is complete, there's a **Go To** action in frame 11 that takes the user into the main scene of the site, where the ready-downloaded symbols can now be put to full use. The whole thing takes less than ten seconds, during which time the viewer has been kept pretty well entertained.

Last Minute Checks

Armed with the information from this chapter, we're now able to ensure our Flash site will be suitable for exposure on the World Wide Web. Once you've completed your movie, view it with **Show Streaming** on and ask yourself the following questions:

- Does the movie run smoothly when using the modem my target audience is most likely to have?

- Does it ever pause at inappropriate times because of streaming?

- Is the user made aware that they'll have to wait (and for how long) whenever a preload is required?

- If my site is running slow because of high bandwidth, what can I get rid of - is the tune that plays every time a button is pressed really necessary?

Summary

We've now seen the technicalities of how we make sure our Flash movie gets where we want it to go in the form we intended, and in a way that's satisfactory for the user.

We saw that:

- ◆ The **bandwidth profiler** lets us see:

    - ◆ How our movie will play on the Internet

    - ◆ Where the pauses in playback will occur

- ◆ **Streaming** is used to smoothly download the components of our movie before they are needed on the stage

- ◆ A **preloader** can buy us time to download our entire movie in one go

In the next chapter, we're going to look at the issues involved in preparing our movie for publishing on the web.

Load Order: [Bottom up ▼]

Options: ☐ Generate size report
☐ Omit Trace actions
☐ Protect from import
☐ Debugging Permitted

Password [   ]

JPEG Quality [▭▭▭▭▭▭▭▭] [80]
. . . .
0   100

Audio Stream: MP3, 16 kbps, Mono

Audio Event: MP3, 16 kbps, Mono

☐ Override sound settings

Version: [Flash 5 ▼]

▶▶

13 Publishing

What we'll cover in this chapter:

- ◆ The different formats available to you for publishing, and when to use them

- ◆ How to create the necessary files to get your movie ready for the Internet

- ◆ The principles of putting your files on the Internet

- ◆ Tying together your case study movie and its soundtrack

OK, so you've spent days - weeks, maybe - creating the perfect movie, and you're bursting to show it to the world, but so far only your dog and a few bewildered family members have been able to see it. Relax - the waiting's over: this chapter is here to help you and your movie make the transition from the cozy world of the local hard drive to the hustle and bustle of the Internet. It's time to go public.

The essential process is this: when you're happy with your movie, you use Flash's **File > Publish** menu to create a viewable file that you can share with the world. This file can then be put on your web site.

When you're preparing your movie for display on the web, there are a number of different output formats you can choose from when you finally publish the movie.

Web Formats

One of the things that's made Flash so successful on the web is its small file size, and this is where publishing comes in. Up until now you've only been working with FLAs, the authoring files where you work on your movie as its creation is in progress. When you publish your movie, Flash compresses the FLA and removes all of the redundant information leaving just the instructions for a sleek, streamlined, multimedia presentation. The default output file from the Flash publishing process is a SWF ('swiff'), but there are several other formats available to you. The more common ones you'll come across, and their usual file extensions, are:

- Flash - .swf

- HTML - .htm

- Animated Gifs - .gif

- QuickTime - .mov

There's a rich choice to choose from, and you can make things as simple or as complicated as you want. Flash's publishing process means that you point and click to select the output options you want, and Flash does the rest for you, producing files that can be migrated straight onto your web site and put into the public domain.

Let's look at each of the common output formats in turn.

Flash

The full name for the standard Flash file format is **Shockwave for Flash**, hence SWF. The Flash player plug-in is the piece of software that plays these SWF files on the user's browser. The Flash player is now a standard across the Internet, and you can more or less assume that anyone who wants to watch Flash movies already has the Flash plug-in. In the transition from Flash 4 to Flash 5, there's a slight hitch: new movies built in Flash 5 are not compatible with the old Flash 4 player, so people will have to download the new plug-in to be able to see your movies. There *is* an option to export your movie in Flash 4 format when you publish it, but by doing this you won't be able to use any of the new features in Flash 5. For most of the things we've covered so far in the book, this won't be a problem, but when you start to use more advanced ActionScript techniques you'll have to export your movie as Flash 5. It's a trade off: if you want to reach the widest audience, you'll be advised to always put a Flash 4 compatible movie onto the Internet at the moment, at least until Flash 5 has been around for a few more months, but if you want to show-off some of the new functionality you've learned, you'll have to use Flash 5.

The Shockwave for Flash format is part of a larger standard called Shockwave. This standard is used in Macromedia's Director software, and it means you can incorporate your Flash movie seamlessly into Director. Director is a general multimedia-authoring tool, and is designed to produce multimedia presentations for applications such as CD-ROMs and screensavers, as well as web applications. The main difference between Flash and Director is that Director has been designed for general multimedia, and not just small, size-optimized web graphics. Director can do many things that Flash is not designed to do, such as play video and provide greater synchronization between multimedia streams.

If you ever reach the point where you want to create more heavy-duty multimedia presentations, Director is a good place to start.

HTML

HTML stands for HyperText Markup Language. HTML is not a language in the same way that ActionScript is - it's a **formatting** language whereas ActionScript is a **scripting** language. Basically this means that HTML consists of special instructions telling the browser how to format the text and graphics on a web page. It's these instructions or *tags* that are the heart of HTML, and they are also its major weakness. HTML was only designed to present simple text data and static images. At its inception this was enough, but as the Internet has taken off, HTML has looked more and more old-fashioned and heavy. On the plus side, HTML is an integral, universal feature of the World Wide Web. Its ease of use and total compatibility make it a good choice if you want simple information to be readable by absolutely everyone. One of its main features, the ability to have links from one page to any other, was a defining feature that led to the current popularity of the Web as a tool for quickly acquiring information. And of course, you don't need a plug-in for HTML to work.

The real problems with HTML start when you want to do multimedia. Because HTML wasn't designed for this, you have to use JavaScript, the scripting language that ActionScript is based on, over the top of it, and by doing this you start to lose compatibility. There are new versions of HTML, and other supporting languages, for multimedia and wireless devices in the works, but for the time being at least, there will be much less support for them on the Web than there is for the Flash plug-in.

As a Flash designer, you have to know a bit about HTML because it's what carries your movie on the web: to make your movie accessible over the web, your movie file will be hosted inside an HTML file. Luckily, it's easy to publish your movie embedded right in an HTML file, which you can then simply integrate into your web site. As we'll see later in this chapter, all you have to do is tell Flash a few simple things about how you want the final movie to behave in the browser window, and it will generate the appropriate HTML file. You still may need to do other things with this Flash-generated HTML, however, because parts of your HTML document can perform tasks that Flash does not do, like making descriptions and keywords for the web page available to search engines.

Furthermore, most Flash web pages don't just consist of a Flash movie on its own: they're usually made up of many separate elements, things like hit counters and advertising banners, and your Flash movie must integrate seamlessly with these. In this book, we'll be discussing Flash's HTML publishing controls, but not the HTML site design and creation side of things: that's a whole subject of its own. We've included a couple of good HTML resource sites in the HTML and Flash appendix, and there are many books dedicated to HTML if you want a more thorough understanding.

Animated GIFs

Animated GIFs were an early attempt at animated content on the web. We've already touched on them briefly when we imported them into Flash in an earlier chapter, but you can also *export* your Flash movie as a GIF. Why would you want to do this? For the simple reason that you don't need a special plug-in to view them. You can guarantee that everyone who can view images on the web (and that really is just about everyone) will be able to view your movie. This is the reason why all banner ads are created as animated GIFs - they're universally viewable, and thus assault the maximum number of eyeballs. You can harness this accessibility in your own sites by having both a Flash, and an animated GIF/HTML version of your site on the Internet, and allowing people to visit either depending on their preferences. It's possible to export some, or all, of your Flash movie as animated GIFs, via the export options, which we'll touch on later.

QuickTime

QuickTime is Apple's Internet multimedia technology. The advantage of using it rather than Flash is that, like Director, it supports other things - such as full video - that Flash does not. You can embed a Flash SWF file in QuickTime as a multimedia channel, but at the time of writing, Flash 5.0 is not supported. Take care when using QuickTime delivery on a PC platform, because you need QuickTime 4 or better for Flash compatibility, and this version does not yet have wide coverage. You can also export your Flash presentation as a QuickTime MOV file via the publish options.

So, how do you actually publish the movie?

Putting on the Show

Once you've produced your movie, you have to create the necessary files for people to view it outside of the Flash authoring environment. The way this happens is controlled by the settings in the **File > Publish Settings** window:

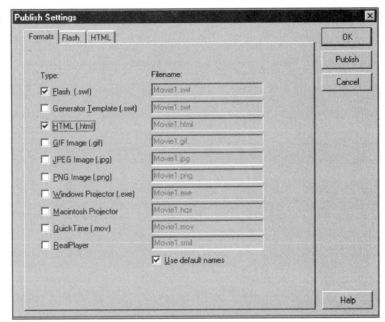

Each of these different formats is for playing your movie in a different environment, such as the Internet, a QuickTime movie, a standalone file that can be run on a computer without the Flash player installed, or even as a static picture. It's important to realise that the file you've been creating so far won't be the file that's finally used in any of the above applications. The 'work in progress' FLA file will be converted to one or more new files that can be read by the target software.

The general method is as follows;

- Select how you want to publish your movie via the **Publish Settings** window

- Preview the movie

- Once you're happy with your Publish Settings, publish the movie

- Transfer the published movie onto your web site.

Let's walk through the publishing process.

Creating and Publishing a Basic Movie

To start off with, we'll concentrate on the simplest and easily the most popular option: publishing a Flash movie in a form that'll be viewed by anyone who's got a browser with the Flash plug-in attached. Firstly, we'll create a simple movie to publish.

1. Start a new movie and write '**This is a test movie**' in a big, bold font on the stage:

> # This is a test movie

2. Use the Alignment tool to make sure your text is in the exact centre of the stage.

3. Insert a keyframe in frame 20 of your movie.

4. Using the **Frame** panel, add a motion tween between the two keyframes and set it to rotate clockwise one time:

5. Test your movie (**Ctrl-Enter**). It's a simple movie, but it'll be effective for our purposes here.

6. Create a new folder on your desktop, and save your movie in it as movie.fla.

   If you look in your folder, there will be one file in it - the FLA that you just saved. When you publish your movie, Flash will automatically put all of its output files in the same folder as the one your FLA is saved in, so if you're building a big project it's a good idea to keep everything in a dedicated folder.

7. Go back to Flash, and select **File > Publish Preview**. A sub-menu will appear with the publishing options on it:

   If your copy of Flash is in the same condition it was when you installed it, you'll see three options available: **Default**, **Flash** and **HTML**. When you publish your movie, Flash will create output files in all of the formats that are in bold letters on the **Publish Preview** menu - in this case, SWF and HTML. By previewing a file, Flash will still publish all of the highlighted file types, but it will open the one you've selected in its associated viewer.

8. Select the **Flash** option: this will take you to the familiar 'test movie' screen.

   When you're on this screen, Flash is showing you what the movie will look like on its own. It has complied your source FLA file and produced a SWF file, which is what you're seeing being played.

9. Go back to the **Publish Preview** menu and select the **HTML** option. You'll see the same movie, except this time it's being played in your default browser. When you select this option, Flash will create an HTML file and embed the SWF into it.

Go take a look at the folder you stored movie.fla in. You'll see that there are now three files in it:

Name	Size	Type	Modified
Movie.fla	9KB	Flash Movie	14/10/00 18:49
Movie.html	1KB	Microsoft HTML Document 5.0	14/10/00 18:54
Movie.swf	2KB	Flash Player Movie	14/10/00 18:54

The SWF is the movie file that's playable in the Flash player, and the HTML file is just a text HTML document containing the formatting tags needed to display the page in a browser, plus a link to the SWF (on the eleventh line down in this text):

SWF file link →

```
<HTML>
<HEAD>
<TITLE>movie</TITLE>
</HEAD>
<BODY bgcolor="#FFFFFF">
<!-- URL's used in the movie-->
<!-- text used in the movie-->
<!--This is a test movie --><OBJECT classid="clsid:D27CDB6E-AE6D-11cf-96B8-444553540000"
 codebase="http://download.macromedia.com/pub/shockwave/cabs/flash/swflash.cab#version=5,0,0,0"
 WIDTH=550 HEIGHT=400>
<PARAM NAME=movie VALUE="movie.swf"> <PARAM NAME=quality VALUE=high> <PARAM NAME=bgcolor VALUE=#FFFFFF> <EMBED
src="movie.swf" quality=high bgcolor=#FFFFFF  WIDTH=550 HEIGHT=400 TYPE="application/x-shockwave-flash"
PLUGINSPAGE="http://www.macromedia.com/shockwave/download/index.cgi?P1_Prod_Version=ShockwaveFlash"></EMBED>
</OBJECT>
</BODY>
</HTML>
```

When this HTML file is loaded into the browser, it'll give you this result:

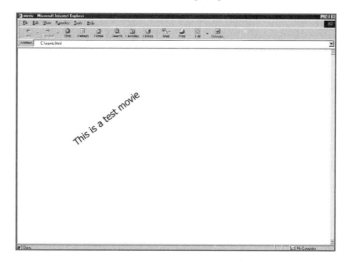

There's a slight problem with the way our movie is being shown in the browser. The size is right - it's at the dimensions set in the **Movie Properties**

dialog box - but it appears in the top-left corner of the screen. We can change all that by giving Flash some different publishing settings to work with.

10. Select **File > Publish Settings**, and bring up the **Publish Settings** window:

The Formats tab of the **Publish Settings** window, shown here, is where you can select the file formats your movie will be published in. You'll see that at the moment there are check marks in the boxes for **Flash** and **HTML** - these correspond to the options that were available to us on the **Publish Preview** menu. At the top of the window there are tabs corresponding to these two selected options. (Don't worry if your **Generator Template** option in the **Type** list is grayed out - this option will only appear if you chose to include the Generator add-ons when you first installed Flash on your computer.)

11. Click in the **GIF Image** check box, and you'll see a new **GIF** tab appear at the top of the window:

Uncheck the box, the tab will disappear. The tabs contain the individual settings for each of the file types that you've got checked in the **Type** list.

12. Click on the **HTML** tab, you'll be taken to the **HTML Publish Settings** window:

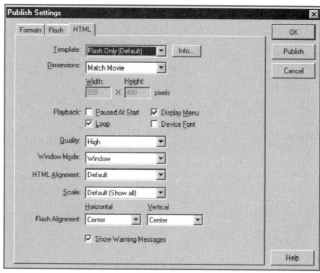

We'll be covering all of the options in detail later in the chapter, but for now, let's sort out getting your movie to play how you want it to.

13. We want the movie to take up the *whole* of the screen when it plays, and this is done through the **Dimensions** menu:

At the moment, this is set to **Match Movie**, so your browser will always keep the movie at the size set in the **Movie Properties** - in this case, the default 550 x 400 pixels. If you resize your browser window, your Flash movie will stay at the same size and will begin to be cut off when the window gets too small:

The other problem with using a pixel measurement is that if someone is using a different screen resolution to you, your movie will come out a different size. If you design your movie to be the perfect size on your

1280 x 960 pixel monitor and your audience are viewing it on their 800 x 600 screen, what they see won't be quite what you intended. You can stop this from happening by changing the **Dimensions** setting to **Percent**. The **Percent** option refers to the size in the browser window, not the pixel size of the movie, so 100% will always fill the entire browser window, no matter what size or resolution it is. Neat.

14. Change the settings to **Percent**, ensure the **Width** and **Height** boxes both read 100, and **File > Publish Preview** (*F12*) your movie again.

These settings are *good* because you know your movie will always stay central and fill the window...

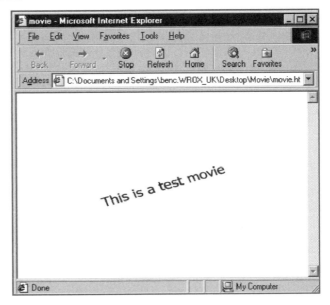

...but bad because the movie no longer maintains the correct proportions, sometimes making your movie incomprehensible:

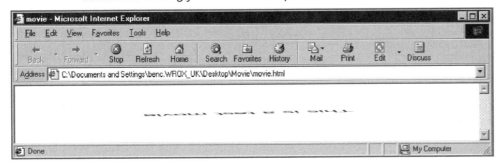

Here, the text is so distorted by the compressed browser window that it's almost unrecognizable.

The choice of which of the **Dimensions** options to use is up to you: if you want your movie to be in an exact area on your web page and to remain in the same proportions, then leave the **match movie** settings on, but if you want it to play at a certain percentage of the screen size on any computer at any resolution, then choose the **Percent** setting.

15. Go back to the **Publish Settings** window and click on the **Formats** tab.

   Notice that each of the file formats has a grayed out box next to it with the name of your movie in. These boxes show what your movie will be called when you publish it. It's vital to be able to see which of your files corresponds to which format, and if the extensions are not visible on your computer then it can be a problem telling them apart at a glance. For example, GIF, JPEG, and PNG will often all have the same icon as they can be associated with the same program. To make this difference more obvious, it's useful to be able to change the names of the files to suit the format you're saving it in.

16. Uncheck the **Use default names** box:

   The grayed out boxes will now become editable. Change the names of your two selected file types to movie_flash.swf and movie_html.html respectively: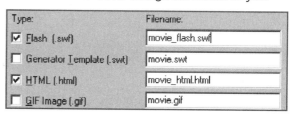

17. Now click on the **Publish** button. If you look in the folder where you originally saved your movie, you'll see a whole host of files there now:

You can see how much quicker and easier it is to locate specific files, and this can be a lifesaver in a large project. Looking in the **Type** column of the screenshot shown here, the **Flash Movie** file is your original FLA, and the **Flash Player Movie** files are the SWFs that'll open in the standalone Flash Player. When you were using the Bandwidth Profiler in the last chapter, the

SWF was the file you were testing. You can see how much smaller the compressed SWFs are compared to the original FLA.

18. Double-click on the movie_flash file shown in your folder, and your movie will start to play in the standalone player (provided you installed the Flash player when you loaded Flash onto your machine, of course!):

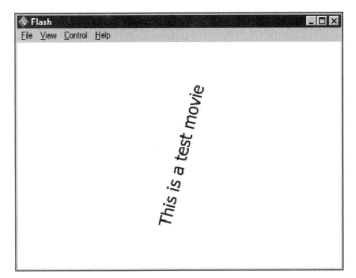

19. Close the player and double-click on the movie_html file, and your movie will now start playing in your web browser.

> *These two files - the SWF and the HTML file - are all that you need to put your movie on the Internet.*

If you wanted, you could delete your FLA file now, and still be able to display your work on the web. This isn't recommended though, as if you ever wanted to go back and edit your movie, you'd need to have the FLA. You should try to keep all of your project files in one folder so you can easily find them again if you need to. It's also always a good idea to archive your FLAs onto CD or some other backup media.

Now that you've gone through the process once, we'll take a more detailed look at the different publishing options, looking at how and why you'd use them.

The Many Faces of Flash

Flash is a powerful creature, but it's a modest creature as well. It recognizes that while it can do a lot of things, it can't do *everything*. For this reason, there are many different publishing options, allowing you to do much more with your Flash movie than just creating a SWF.

1. Open the **Publish Settings** window, and check *all* the **Type** boxes. Depending on whether you have Generator installed or not, your tabs may spill over onto a second line. Sometimes the first row of tabs will disappear when this happens: to get them back, just click on one of the visible tabs.

2. For ease of reference later, go through and change the name of each file to include its format as you did before. The **Projector** files are standalone executable files that don't have any options, so we won't be looking at them here. These files are used if you're creating movies for viewing off-line, such as screen-savers, or if you want to e-mail your movie to a friend, and they don't have the Flash player. The projector files contain a miniaturised Flash player inside them so people can view your movie even if they don't have a Flash player installed.

3. When you've finished, you'll have a screen like this:

The two most important and influential tabs are **Flash** and **HTML**, so we'll focus on these two.

Flash File Publishing Options

The **Flash** Tab is where you specify exactly how the SWF file will be created.

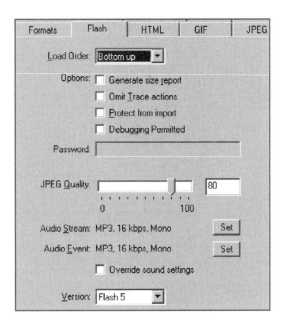

It contains the following options:

Load Order	This specifies the order in Flash which will load the layers for the first frame of your movie. It can either load from the bottom layer up, or from the top layer down. This option only really has an effect when your movie is being viewed over a slow connection, when the failure to load layers that are critical to the display first - such as the layer containing the navigation buttons - could result in a degraded user experience.
Options	**Generate size report** - creates a text file that tells you all about the final SWF file. The file can be useful when you're optimizing your movie, as it gives you a frame by frame breakdown of the movie's size, and useful information about any symbols, sounds, pictures, and text that you have in there. The exact content of this file is a bit beyond the scope of this book, but it's fairly straightforward when you view the file.
	Omit Trace actions - makes Flash ignore any Trace actions you might have included in your movie. Trace actions are commands

Options cont.	that allow you to track the value of a variable in your movie and display it in an Output window while the movie is running. This is very helpful for you when you're debugging your movie, but you don't want it popping up when someone else plays your file. **Protect from import** - this stops anyone from taking your SWF file and importing it back into Flash, and then copying all of your hard work. **Debugging Permitted** allows you to use the debugger window on the final presentation, which can be selected from the Flash player pop-up menu. This is useful for you when you're trying to track any bugs in your final movie, but again, it's not something that you normally want other people to be able to use. It's also possible to password protect this option by putting a word into the **Password** box, this permits only those who know the password to use the debugging options.
Quality	There are **Quality** settings for imported artwork and sounds. These are global settings, and they will only affect the movie components that you did not optimize separately. As you discovered in earlier chapters, it's always best to optimize all aspects of your movie separately, as this allows for the best compression to quality ratio. There's an option to Override sound settings, but you should never need to do this.
Version	Lastly, there's a drop-down menu to specify which version of the Flash player you want to use. You're recommended to select Flash 4 until the Flash 5 player has time to become widespread across the Internet. The only time you should definitely use Flash 5 is when you need to include some of Flash 5's extra functionality, such as the advanced ActionScript commands. You can tell these commands because they are highlighted in yellow in the **Actions** window. Another thing to remember is that the RealPlayer option will only work with Flash 4 files.

HTML File Publishing Options

The **HTML** tab specifies how you want to configure the HTML file that'll be published. For those of you who want to fine-tune the default Flash-generated HTML by hand, the HTML and Flash appendix explains the key issues, and expands on the use of Dreamweaver with Flash.

Template	This specifies the type of HTML file you want the SWF to be embedded into: each different template will include specific types of HTML tags which allow you to extend the HTML file's functionality. The **Info** button:
	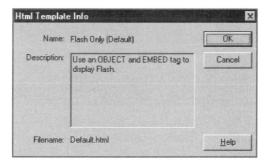
	will give you a brief description of the selected template, and which file it is. The HTML template files are actually kept in the /HTML directory of your Flash 5 folder, so if you're an HTML whiz and want

	to change them, back up the originals and have a play. For the beginner though, the **Flash Only** option will be fine.
Dimensions	As you've already seen, this allows you to change how your movie is displayed on the screen. You can use your movie dimensions, specify another movie size, or scale your movie to a percentage of the user's browser dimensions.
Playback	**Pause At Start** means the user has to tell the movie to play before it will do anything. **Display Menu** will change whether or not a menu appears when the user right-clicks on your movie: This menu allows the user to control the playback of the movie, and to zoom in and see all that lovely vector detail. **Loop** will play your movie continuously if selected, or only once if it's not. This option is overridden by any **Stop** actions that you have, and can also be overridden by the user. **Device Font** is only useful for Windows users: it replace any static text in your movie with a system font, which can cut down on file size.
Quality	This option allows you to set the rendering quality that your movie will play at: the lower the quality setting the faster it will run on a slower computer. As we said in the Optimization chapter, you're recommended to set this to **Auto High** to allow Flash to drop the quality to maintain frame rate and synchronization if it needs to. It's not worth worrying about setting this to a low quality, as if the user's having problems with the quality, they can change it themselves at their end.

Window Mode	These options affect how some advanced Dynamic HTML commands can interact with your movie in certain browsers. Most of the time, you'll want to leave this set to **Window**.
HTML Alignment	This allows you to specify the position of your movie window inside the browser window. **Default** will center the movie, and the other options will align it along the desired edge.
Scale	If you've changed the size of your movie with the **Dimensions** option earlier, you can use this option to define how your movie is scaled to fit into the browser window.
Flash Alignment	These two options allow you to set the vertical and horizontal alignment of your masterpiece inside the movie window, and how it will be cropped if it needs to be.
Show Warning Messages	When this box is checked, any errors that are discovered when the HTML file is played - things like images that aren't where they say they are - are displayed as messages on your screen.

Until you become more familiar with the intricacies of HTML coding, you won't need to alter many - if any - of these options. The **Dimensions** are the most important things to be aware of at this stage, and you can experiment with the rest when you become more experienced.

The remaining publishing formats are fairly self-explanatory. We'll give you a brief run down of them and highlight the most important options.

Generator Template

Generator is another Macromedia program that can be combined with Flash to expand its functionality. With Generator, you can add dynamic content to your movie by using a template to feed text and images from a database or other data store into your Flash front-end. Generator integrates these features with Flash, and allows you to create data-driven Flash sites (as do many other dynamic content technologies such as Swift Generator, Flash Turbine and others - these technologies are beyond this book's scope, but friends of ED are publishing a book dedicated to them).

The options allow you to override certain settings in your movie, like frame rate and background color. There are also more detailed Generator specific options that'll affect how it works together with Flash.

GIF, JPEG and PNG

These bitmap export options are of particular interest to the Flash designer, as they allow the easy creation of both a Flash *and* an HTML version of your web site. All of these formats will publish the first frame of your movie as a static image. The exception to this are GIFs, which can also be animated. You can specify an individual frame for Flash to publish by putting **#Static** as a label on that frame:

GIF seems to be the best option for publishing a static image, as its compression routines are well suited to Flash's solid colors. If you use a lot of gradients in your movie though, these can come out horribly dithered, and it's worth checking the **Remove Gradients** box and replacing the gradients with solid colors to achieve a better quality image.

GIF files also have the option to be animated. When you publish your movie as an animated GIF, Flash will save each frame of your movie as a GIF frame that'll then be played through in a flipbook manner to give the appearance of animation. This is best for HTML versions of sites, or for doing small animations such as advertising banners that you want to be viewable on all computers.

If the image you're exporting contains a lot of gradients or imported artwork, the best option for publishing it is a JPEG file. The lower you move the **Quality** slider, the smaller the file size and the worse the picture - and vice versa. It's worth playing with this option in conjunction with the **Publish Preview** option to find the best balance for your image. There's also an option to set the image as a **Progressive** JPEG. This is a method for loading images on slower computers: the computer will load an interlaced version of the file, say every 5th line, then progressively fill in the image, one set of lines at a time.

PNG is the only image format supported by Flash that includes an alpha channel for transparency. Remember that a transparent GIF can only be fully transparent, or fully opaque, but a PNG image can contain degrees of transparency. To use this option, you must have the **Bit Depth** set to **24-bit with Alpha**.

QuickTime Movies

Publishing your movies in QuickTime format allows you to incorporate full video with your Flash content. The Flash movie will be published on its own 'track' inside the QuickTime file, and this can then be edited from inside QuickTime Pro, a program from Apple for the creation and editing of QuickTime files. The options here control how the Flash track will interact with other tracks inside the movie, and which type of QuickTime controller to use to play the movie. It's a good idea to check the **Flatten** box, as this tells Flash to build all of the external files (for example graphics or movies) into the final QuickTime file, allowing it to be played standalone on any computer. If this box is *not* checked, the final file will be smaller, but it will depend on links to the external files. If these files are moved or renamed, the movie won't display correctly.

RealPlayer

The RealPlayer format is a streaming format that's popular across the Internet. When you publish a RealPlayer file, you need to take into consideration which version of the RealServer you're publishing to. Version 8 includes support for Flash 4, but versions below that only support Flash 2. Flash 5 support has not yet been built into the RealPlayer software, so many ActionScript commands won't work. RealPlayer also only supports streaming sounds in Raw uncompressed form, so to publish your audio files you'll have to make sure you change their settings to reflect this, and set the **Audio Event** option on the **Flash** tab to
Disable:

Audio _S_tream: Raw, 22kHz, Stereo		Set
Audio _E_vent: Disable,		Set

When you publish to RealPlayer, Flash creates three files:

- A 'tuned' SWF file - this is distinguishable from the normal SWF file by having a 't' appended to the filename, for example your movie.swf would become moviet.swf. This file contains the animations in your movie

- A RealMedia file with the extension RM. This file contains all of the sounds from your movie compressed into the RealPlayer streaming format

- A SMIL file that ties together the animation and the audio and makes sure they are synchronized

For descriptions of the advanced features, consult the documentation that came with your copies of QuickTime and RealPlayer.

Now you've got your files together, the final hurdle is getting them up to the server and onto the Internet.

Uploading your Files to the Host Web Site

To finally make your movies available to the viewer, you need to upload them onto your hosting server so that people can access them over the Internet. This task is always fraught with danger the first time you ever do it, but, like riding a bike, after you get it right once it'll just seem to come naturally. The options available to you when you upload your files will depend on the Internet Service Provider (ISP) you're using, and it would be impractical to provide you with practical instructions on how to do it all in detail. We'll cover some of the basic principles here, but always check with your ISP to make sure you know all of its distinctive ins and outs.

The key stages in the process are:

- Choose your ISP and establish how much space they'll give you for your web site, and what features they'll support

- Find out the specific upload locations and procedures for your ISP

- Transfer your movie files up to the host site based on these procedures

The first problem you come across when you're getting your web page up and running is knowing exactly which files you need to upload. The only files that you need to are your SWF and your HTML files: remember that the FLA file is just the authoring file, and it isn't required once you've published your movie. Also, you don't need to upload any of the fonts, images or other external files, as Flash will embed these into your final SWF movie.

The second problem you'll come across is knowing what to *call* your HTML file. If the file is going to be a page inside your web site then you can call it whatever you like as long as you include a link to that filename from another web page. If, however, your movie is going to be the *first* page of your web site, you'll need to rename it according to the protocols of your ISP. Typically, the first HTML page of a site is called index.html, but you'll need to check this with your ISP. (When you type a web address into your browser, you'll normally just type the URL, for example www.friendsofed.com, and the browser automatically searches for the web page called www.friendsofed.com/index.html. It's just a convention designed to save people from having to type /index.html at the end of every web address. If you did not rename your file, the user would have to know to type www.friendsofed.com/movie_html.html into their browser to get to your movie.)

The final hurdle is actually getting the files up onto the server. To perform file transfers to the server you use a special protocol called **ftp**, which stands for **file transfer protocol**. You can either use a shareware program to do this (see the Resources appendix for some examples), or one of the many site creation programs, such as Microsoft FrontPage or Macromedia Dreamweaver, which contain built-in features to help you do it.

From here, you pass beyond the bounds of Flash, and out into the brave new world of the Internet.

Case Study

Remember that soundtrack that you created back in the Sound chapter? Well, it's finally time to add it to your movie by using one of Flash's clever little ActionScript tricks - **LoadMovie**.

LoadMovie is an ActionScript command that allows you to load SWF files *on top of each other*. The files go into slots called **levels**. Level 0 is the default level, and is where the first SWF is loaded, which in this case it will be your case study movie with all its buttons and tweens. There will then be a **LoadMovie** command in your movie telling Flash to load the soundtrack into level 1. The two levels will then play alongside each other.

LoadMovie is a good way of splitting a large initial download into lots of smaller downloads that can occur on demand. For example, you could have the navigation menu strip for a large site load up at level 0, and have further SWFs loaded in on demand onto other levels, making sure that none of them overlap the menu area:

Each navigation button would have a **LoadMovie** action attached to it, specifying which sub-movie to load in when the button was pressed. Each separate movie would encapsulate a particular aspect of the site, and be loaded on demand.

If you want to replace a particular level, you can simply load another movie at that level (including level 0).

Levels work rather like layers: anything that's in the higher level sits *above* the lower level. All the movies take on the size of the movie sitting at level 0, and their background color is shown as transparent. This means that you'll still be able to see the lower levels through the upper ones.

> *One thing to be aware of with levels is that the buttons of lower levels continue to work, even though they might be obstructed by something on the higher levels.*

OK that's the theory, let's put it into practice. You should by now have your movie and soundtrack FLAs safely optimized and tucked away in the same folder somewhere on your hard drive. To use the LoadMovie command, you need to have a SWF file to link to it.

Loading the Soundtrack

1. Open your soundtrack.fla authoring file from the Sound chapter.

2. Make sure your **Publish Settings** are set up to publish in the Flash format, and use the **File > Publish** command to create an SWF file in the same folder as your movie.

3. Now you need to modify your main case study movie to load the newly created SWF. Open your final case study FLA, and double-click on the first frame of the **actions** layer to bring up the **Frame Actions** window.

4. Double-click on the **LoadMovie** action (it's in **Basic Actions**) to add it to the frame:

Because there's nothing on the stage in your soundtrack movie, you don't need to worry about anything in the level below it being obscured.

5. Type soundtrack.swf into the **URL** field, and set the **Location** to **Level 1**:

And that's it. When the case study movie loads, this simple action will pull in the soundtrack movie and play it concurrently with the visual part of the case study web site.

Line 1: loadMovieNum ("soundtrack.swf", 1);
URL: soundtrack.swf
Location: Level ▼ 1
Variables: Don't send

> *Your soundtrack movie needs to be in the same folder as the case study movie for Flash to find it.*

6. All that's left to do now is publish your movie as an HTML file and test it out. The soundtrack should play as your case study movie goes through its paces.

When you upload your final movie to the Internet, don't forget that you need to put up the soundtrack.swf as well, because this is an external file linked to the movie.

Summary

In this chapter, we've given a brief survey of the issues related to getting your finished movies ready for viewing up on the web.

We saw that:

◆ Flash has **publishing options** that will build all the output files you need to get your movie online

◆ The commonest publishing option for Flash is to embed a **SWF** file inside an **HTML** page

◆ Flash will create the HTML file that hosts your movie, and you can tweak the HTML if you wish

◆ You can adjust the way your movie displays in the user's browser - and other attributes, too - by manipulating the values in the **Publish Settings** window

- ◆ Once you've created the viewable files, you need to consult with your ISP about getting your files up on your web site

- ◆ In the case study, we saw how to use the **LoadMovie** action to load our soundtrack SWF alongside the main movie

- ◆ **LoadMovie** can be used to load different SWF files 'on demand' - such as when a user clicks on a particular button. Each loaded movie can reside in its own specified **level**

In the next two chapters, we're going to delve deep into the heart of ActionScript and give you a taste of the future.

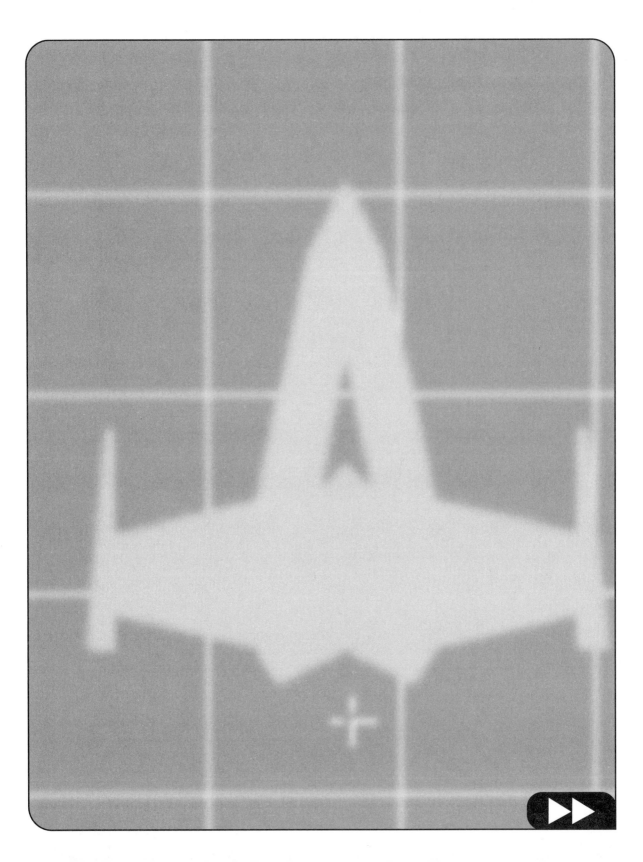

14

Intermediate ActionScript 1

What we'll cover in this chapter:

- The first steps of intermediate ActionScripting:

  - Planning larger scale ActionScripts

  - Basic input and output

- Taking ActionScript further:

  - Flash 5 dot notation: the logic of a Flash movie's internal structure and why dot notation is a major advance

  - Getting movies to talk to each other using dot notation in ActionScript

  - Animating objects dynamically with ActionScript and user input

▶

So far in this book you've gained enough Flash know-how to earn the grade 'beginner' - you're not a novice any more, that's for sure. However, the rest of the book is going to take you beyond this and allow you to earn your wings as an 'intermediate' Flash user. The impressive effects on cutting-edge Flash sites will no longer baffle you - after the next two chapters you'll have an insight into the methods that top Flash designers use to create those cool-looking sites.

This is the starting point of your road towards mastering Flash and this chapter, along with the next, is going to teach you the three main programming techniques you need to get going on your journey. They are:

- Intelligently breaking down a problem and forming a structured plan to resolve it

- Treating a movie clip symbol as an **object** and understanding its relationship to the main timeline *and* to other movie clips

- Object-oriented programming

We'll cover the first two points here, and introduce the basics of the third so you can hit the ground running when we get to Chapter 15.

From now on the book has a much steeper learning curve than in the previous chapters, and assumes you know how to attach basic actions (which we learnt in chapters 9 and 10) without being shown all the steps explicitly. However, we want as many readers as possible to get their wings, so, if you feel that you haven't mastered one of these skills once you've read the relevant section, go back and practice a little until you get the hang of it. The things we'll discuss in this chapter are the things that will make the difference between a plain vanilla Flash site and one that's packed with interesting and engaging features.

Planning a Complex ActionScript: Practical Overview

This chapter's author has worked in several 'software heavy' environments before going into multimedia and web design. These were at the sharper end of the equation: from industrial display systems up to safety-critical computer-control systems at nuclear plants. Working with this intense level of coding teaches two things about effective programming which are equally applicable to complex ActionScripting - which is really programming by another name:

- You must start by looking at the *problem* and *not* the solution, and then refine the problem until you have a collection of simpler problems to solve

- You must treat these individual problems as small, self-contained tasks, and be able to code and test each small solution as you go along to make sure it's working properly. Once the discrete components are tested and working, you can integrate them and test again

We're going to put these ideas into practice by modifying the Smiler movie that we created in Chapter 10.

Some people are very sensitive about their age, so when anyone asks you , "How old do you think I am?", you need to reply with care. If you guess close, you'll please them. But if you're a long way out, in either direction, you're likely to offend, and may need to retreat quickly.

We're going to make our Smiler equally sensitive about its age. Fishing for a complement, it'll invite you to guess its age. If your guess is way wrong, it'll put on a big frown, but as your guesses get closer to its actual age, the happier Smiler will get. When you guess dead right, you'll see Smiler's biggest possible smile.

This is going to involve quite a big change to the existing Smiler code. Following the advice above, the first question we need to ask is, "What exactly is the problem we're trying to address with our complex ActionScript?".

Defining a Problem

Is 'guessing Smiler's age' the ActionScripting problem? No. That's the *user's* problem: we're creating the code for Flash to *deal* with the user's guess. Let's think about exactly what we want Flash to do by walking through the user's typical interaction with Smiler - this will help us identify the contours of the problem and the sub-problems that it's composed of:

1. We want to define a number that the user doesn't know - Smiler's age - and we want to constantly check this number against the user's guess

2. We want to detect when the user is wrong and, if so, by how much, and then convert the size of the user's error into an expression on Smiler's face

3. The more wrong the guess is, the more Smiler will move towards its biggest frown, at the 'sad' frame

4. As the user's guesses get nearer to Smiler's age, the happier it'll get - moving towards the 'happy' frame When the user guesses the exact value of Smiler's age, Smiler will put on its biggest smile and the game is finished

How do we now check that we've defined the problem correctly? Well, we think it through in our heads and ensure there's nothing else we want our program to do. If necessary, we talk to our client to ensure that we've analyzed the problem correctly.

At this stage, it's important to think only in terms of what you're going to want Flash to do - now isn't the time to think about exactly how you're going to make Flash do it. We need to keep our minds untainted by solutions until we've got a clear idea of the problem and its component sub-problems.

You'll find that most problems can be stated in a similar form to that we've just used, even if they're very complex. A programmer would call the list of things that the ActionScript needs to do a list of **requirements**. This list doesn't state the solution, it just states *what needs to be done*. Because these are the only requirements we have for the interaction of Smiler and the user, we can be reasonably confident that our list is a general statement of the *whole* problem. A programmer would call these the **high level requirements**, and would then break each requirement down into a list of smaller, more detailed requirements for the program. This list is called a **requirements specification**.

The many billion dollar 'super-computer' programs that refuse to work don't usually fail because they've been coded incorrectly. They fail - almost without exception - because the *wrong problem* is defined at the planning stage, meaning that the programming solution that's built based on that definition doesn't fulfill the requirements of the *actual* problem that you set out to address! This can mean that the programmers are not all working towards the same clearly defined goal: although all the sections of the program work in isolation, when they're put together, the different chunks can't be integrated properly and nothing works. This emphasizes the importance of planning, and it's why we're not going to jump straight into creating the ActionScript for the new, improved Smiler. Instead, we're going to take things stage by stage, and guarantee that we come up with an effective solution.

Breaking Down the Smiler Problem

We now need to break down, or *decompose*, our high level requirements into more detailed basic requirements. We keep breaking things down in repeated iterations until we have the simplest list possible - things that can't be broken down any further.

A first iteration has sub-points of each original point (1.1, 1.2; 2.1, 2.2...) and a second iteration has sub-points of each of these (1.1.1, 1.1.2, 1.1.3...).

Let's work out Smiler's detailed requirements specification, based on the high level requirement we've already agreed above:

1. Define a number representing Smiler's 'age'

2. Acquire a number - let's call it *guess* from the user, and check it against *age*

3. Compare the difference between *age* and *guess*, apply this value to the Smiler movie to make it go to a particular frame to indicate how close the guess is

4. If the difference is zero, make Smiler to go to the 'happy' label on the timeline - Smiler's biggest smile - and stop. If the difference is not zero, repeat from point 2.

We can now break this down further in our first iteration by asking ourselves more questions about the nature of the problem. For example:

- How big a number can *age* be? Can it be 450? Can it be 6.124569081?

- Can *guess* be the *word* 'five' or does it have to be *number* '5'?

- How many frames should Smiler have?

This is what our first iteration might look like:

- 1.1 Get Flash to define a variable - *age* - which is between 1 and 99

- 2.1 Elicit a text entry from the user that's numeric

- 2.2 Assign this text entry to a variable, *guess*

- 2.3 If *guess* is not between 1 and 99, then repeat from 2.1

- 3.1 Create a new variable, *difference*, which is equal to *age* minus *guess*

- 3.2 If *difference* is a negative number, convert it to a positive number of equal magnitude

- 3.3 In the Smiler movie clip, go to a frame number that's equal to *difference* to represent how far out the user's guess is

- 4.1 If *difference* is zero, stop. Otherwise repeat from 2.1

Through refining our problem we've almost written ourselves a set of instructions to solve it with.

If we put 1.1 to 4.1 in order, we actually end up with a list of what we need to do to reach a solution to the overall Smiler ActionScripting problem. This powerful technique goes by the name of **top-down design**: We've defined the high level problem - the 'top' - and then worked 'down' into the problem by splitting up the requirements into their simplest forms. By the end of the process we have a problem that's so well defined it has become the answer itself - and the path to the final specification is traceable all the way back to the top level problem we're trying to solve.

The Smiler example is a fairly simple problem, and we probably could have worked out the answer in our heads without listing our requirements. However, when you're working on a bigger coding project you won't have that luxury. The top-down method of planning and problem definition will save a lot of time and brainpower when solving more complex problems, and will help to ensure you're solving the right problem in the right way.

By giving your problem a defined structure, you are forcing your ActionScript to follow a similar, structured form. You will write ActionScript that doesn't look like it was hacked together, but something that's well thought out, considered and which addresses each requirement in turn.

For the beginner, thinking of the task in terms of the *problem* rather then the actual ActionScript has yet another, rather more subtle advantage: if you think only in terms of the code solution, you'll only ever use the Flash skills you've already got to grips with. However, if you define the problem properly before thinking about the code, you may well hit upon the requirement for tasks you can't yet do, like creating a 'loop' where a set of instructions are repeated until a certain condition is met. You'll be forced to try new methods to achieve this - instead of repeating the knowledge you already have and allowing your Flash programs to become stale. By looking at what skills you need to solve a problem, rather than what problems you can solve with the skills you already have, you'll constantly improve your skills and upgrade your Flash technique.

We now know what we need to change in the old Smiler to create a new, age-sensitive version. However, before we can solve the problem defined by our requirement specification, there're one or two pieces of Flash know-how we need to acquire. For instance, point 2 asks us to get the user to guess Smiler's age: so we need to know how to allow the user to *input* text and how to get Flash to <u>use</u> that input.

Basic Input and Output

So far in this book, we've seen that ActionScript allows us to create *variables* that we can store values in, and that Flash uses these variables in the background without the user being aware of them.

Sometimes, as in the Smiler movie, we want to have these variables visible on the screen so that we, and the user, can see what they are. In Flash, the getting and displaying of variables - whose values can change, remember - is done with **input text** boxes and **dynamic text** boxes. The text boxes we've used up to now have contained **static text**, which, as its name suggests, doesn't do anything but sit in its box (even if the box itself is animated). Before we explain the two new types of text, there's something about the text boxes themselves that you may or may not already have noticed and needs to be explained .

If you just *click* once on the stage with the Text tool, you'll create a text box that will extend indefinitely as you type into it, only moving to a new line when you press the **Enter** key. This text box, with 'undefined' width, will have a *circle* in the top right corner:

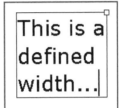

If, however, you *click and drag* on the stage with the Text tool and make your text box a wide rectangle, this box will have a width defined by the size of the box you dragged

out. The text you type into it will wrap onto the line below as the text reaches the edge of the box. This text box, with a *defined* width, will have a *square* in the top right corner:

Note also that an undefined text box will become a defined text box if you alter the width of it at any time.

OK - now to use text boxes for input and update them dynamically.

Input Text and Dynamic Text

Let's try an experiment.

1. Create a new movie and use the Text tool to drag out a text box on the stage. Make it about two inches wide.

2. Click on the **Text Options** tab on the **Character** panel and use the drop-down menu to change the text from **Static Text** to **Input Text**:

    Notice that the square at the top right of the text box has moved to the bottom right of the box, and that there are also the new fields visible on the panel.

    This text box is now enabled as an input box in the finished movie. The additional fields on the **Text Options** tab allow us to control the behavior of that input box.

Let's use these fields to tell Flash we want to store the user's input in a variable.

3. In the **Variable** field enter **usertext**, change the **Max Chars** (maximum characters) field to **10** and check the **Border/Bg** check box. Your panel will now look like this:

By entering '**usertext**' in the **Variable** field, we're telling Flash that when the user enters text into this box in the finished movie, we want Flash to store that text inside a variable called '**usertext**':

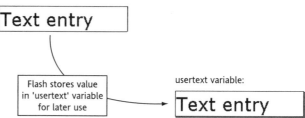

Text box in finished movie:

Text entry

Flash stores value in 'usertext' variable for later use

usertext variable:

Text entry

Checking the **Border/Bg** option means that the outline of the text box will appear in the movie - this can be very important for the user, as they don't want to have to search too hard for the text input area.

4. Now test the movie.

5. Click on the box and try entering some text. You'll find you can enter up to 10 characters, the maximum we specified.

OK, we've created a text input area for the user on the screen, and the text typed into here will be assigned to the **usertext** variable. When we assign a value to a variable, we're just 'populating' that variable with a value we want to refer to later using the variable name.

We can now also create an *output* text area that'll keep us informed about the current value of the variable.

6. Paste a copy of the text box you just created underneath the original.

7. Working with the new text box, change the text type to **Dynamic Text** using the drop-down menu.

8. Now *uncheck* on the **Border/Bg** option, and *uncheck* the **Selectable** check box.

9. In the **Variable** field, enter the **usertext** variable name. This is the same variable we're inputting in the top window - we're telling Flash to display this variable in the new dynamic text box on the screen:

Notice that when not selected the dynamic text box has a dotted line around it, whereas the input text box has a solid line:

10. Now test the movie.

You can enter text in the upper window, but you can't select the lower window. Whatever you enter in the upper window also appears in the lower window.

What's happening here? Well, both text areas are showing the same variable, **usertext**. The top window has been set up to allow user input of **usertext**, and the lower window has been set up to allow display of it. Rather than tell the user what he or she already knows, as we're doing here, we can instead make Flash do something useful to the data we input before it displays it, or outputs it, for our viewing.

11. Select the lower text box again and change it to so that it's an **Input Text** type box. Check the **Border/Bg** box and enter 10 in **Max Char**. In the **Variable** field, type **usertext2**:

We're going to get Flash add the input to usertext and **usertext2** together and display the result in a third text area. We need to define this third text area next.

12. Draw a third text box and make it a dynamic text box.

13. Make sure the **Selectable** field is unchecked but the **Border/Bg** box remains checked.

14. In the Variable field type **textadd**. Because **textadd** is the addition of the previous two variables, it may be up to 20 characters long. Make sure you create a large enough text box to fit all those characters in.

15. Place the two input boxes on the left of the stage, one above the other, and the new, dynamic text box on the right of the stage:

Now we need to let the user add the two text entries together.

16. Create a new button symbol.

17. Using a standard (static text) text box, type a large '+' sign in the button symbol's Up state and add keyframes to the other states:

18. In the Down state, change the '+' in the text box to an '=' sign, and in the Hit state add a filled square that completely covers the '+'. This will give the user a larger button to press than just the '+' sign.

19. Back on the main stage, place an instance of the button symbol in the center of the stage next to the two input boxes:

That's the front-end part of the movie set up. Now we need to create a little ActionScript that will add together the contents of the two input boxes and display the result in the dynamic text box on the right. This ActionScript will work with the two input variables and assign the result of the calculation to the **textadd** variable.

To achieve this, we'll create an ActionScript that'll use a **setVariable** action to calculate **usertext + usertext2**, assign the result to the **textadd** variable, and then display the result. We want the user to enter **usertext** and **usertext2** before we do the addition, so we'll attach the addition ActionScript to the '+' button that we just added to the movie. This way, Flash will perform the calculation when two numbers have been entered and the button is pressed.

However, there's a problem. If we just ask Flash to add **usertext2** to **usertext**, it will simply join them together. For example, if the user typed '**35**' and '**45**', Flash would assign the result to **textadd** as '**3545**'. Flash would treat the inputs as *string values* - ordinary text - whereas we want them to be treated as *numbers*. To do this, we use the function **number()** to tell Flash to treat the value of whatever we put in the brackets (which will be our variable names) as a number.

Let's build that ActionScript.

20. With the button instance selected on the stage, bring up the **Object Actions** window and double-click on the **Set Variable** action (it's in the **Actions** book, remember).

21. Type **textadd** in the **Variable** field and click on the **Value** field. Now select the **Number** function from the **Functions** book. Your scripting window will now look like this:

You'll see that the word **expression** is highlighted in the **Value** field. Flash is waiting for the name of the variable that we want it to treat as a number.

22. Overtype **expression** with the variable name **usertext**, and then type a '+' after the bracket in the **Value** window:

23. Click just after the '+', type a space, and then click on the **Number** function again.

24. Overtype the second **expression** with **usertext2**:

25. Finally, check the **Expression** field. Your **Object Actions** window will now contain the following ActionScript:

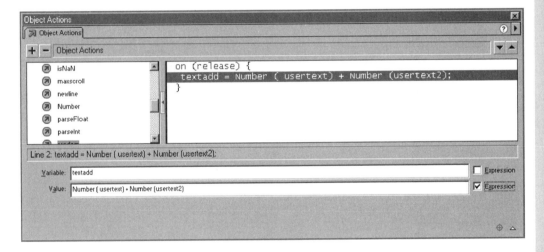

26. Now test the movie.

27. Type two numbers into the input boxes and press the big '+' button:

28. It works! And you can even add decimals.

29. Try typing letters into one, or both of the fields and pressing the '+' button. The **textadd** dynamic text field shows **NaN**, or 'Not a Number':

There's an informal rule in programming that states 'If you're taking input from the user, assume that the user is a monkey'. We're not talking about the monkey with a keyboard whose random typing produced, by chance, *Hamlet*. We're talking about the monkey next to it that *didn't*. Your input boxes have to cater for all the *wrong* inputs as well as the *right* one. So your code has to be able to cope if the user types '**89g6!trc**' instead of '**896**'. Let's see how to add an 'intelligence filter' to an input box.

30. Select one of the text boxes and look at the **Text Options** panel:

There are some icons at the bottom and an unlabelled text entry field at the bottom right: this field and the icons let you specify what can be typed into or displayed in this input or dynamic text box. Flash assumes you want to allow input of everything unless you select one or more of the icons.

31. We only want *numbers* to be entered in the input boxes, so select each box in turn and click the icon marked **123**.

32. We also want the decimal point and the minus sign in case someone wants to enter a negative decimal like **-234.567453**. Enter a '.' (period) and a '-' (minus sign) in the bottom text field for each of the input boxes to specify that we want to be able to input these characters as well as numbers:

33. Test your movie again. Now you can monkey about all you want. Flash will only allow you to type in up to 10 characters, and they must be integers from 0 to 9 or '.' or '-'.

Flash possesses a math library, containing functions such as sin, cos, tan etc, that would allow us to develop this simple movie into a working calculator program.

Remember the Smiler specification we were planning before? We've just learnt an important building block that allows us to code it up in Flash: now we've got the hang of input and output, getting the user to guess Smiler's age later in the chapter will be no problem at all.

First though, we need to learn about a sophisticated way that Flash can allow different parts of a movie to communicate with each other, and how we can exploit this ability in ActionScript. If you thought that **tellTarget** was cool, you're about to be blown away. Stand by to be wowed by Flash's **dot notation**.

Dot Notation

It may not sound very exciting, but Flash 5's new dot notation will create incredible new possibilities for you and your Flash movies.

Remember the structured planning we went through at the beginning of this chapter? We broke the Smiler problem down into manageable chunks or sub-problems. If we now structure our movie correctly, we can address each of our requirements *in a separate movie clip*. We can then use dot notation to make these movie clips converse with each other and control the movie as a whole. This method allows us to perform **dynamic animation**, which means that we can animate things based on values that the user supplies.

Dynamic animation is animation that is controlled 'on the fly' by ActionScript. The big advantage of doing this is that, unlike timeline-based tweening animation, you can change the animation in response to other things that happen, such as the user moving the mouse. You can't really do this with tweening because the animation is linear and *fixed*.

We learned some useful lessons about ActionScripting when we used **tellTarget**, but now we're going to thank faithful **tellTarget** for its service, and move on to a method that's more sophisticated and versatile, and yet simpler and neater once mastered. Advanced dot notation allows for a much richer ActionScripting environment, something you will thank yourself for taking the time to get to grips with.

What is Dot Notation?

Dot notation in Flash and ActionScript is a way of expressing a **path** through a movie: it gives us a way of targeting a particular object and telling it what to do, irrespective of its position in the movie's structure. So, if we want to direct a particular piece of

ActionScript at a specific movie clip, or if we want to tell an instance of a 'square' symbol to change it's Alpha value, we can do that by specifying that object's location using dot notation.

Here's an analogy: on your computer you have a hard drive with various folders and sub-folders - often nested many deep. To get to a particular folder you use Windows Explorer, or click on the drive's icon on the Mac to open up the folders you want to look at.

On our computer, the path for the folder of this text file (the one that's been edited, printed and shipped to your bookstore, is based on its position in the folder hierarchy:

So, the actual path for this file is:

C:\Home Edit\Chapter 14\Ch 14 Second Edit AC.doc

This path tells us how to get to this text file starting from the harddrive, **C:/**, which is the lowest level, or **root level**. (You will note the tree-like nature of the way these networks are linked.) What we're saying here is that to get to the file I have to go into a folder called *Home Edit*, where I'll find another folder called *Chapter 14*, and if I open *that* folder, the file I want will be there. This path through the folder hierarchy gives me the entire journey, starting from the lowest level - the hard drive. If I specify the path in this way, starting from the hard drive level, it's referred to as the total or *absolute* path.

If I was *already* at C:/Home Edit, then I could express the route to the document *relative* to where I'm starting from - I don't have to go back via the hard drive level. The path from C:/Home Edit would be expressed as:

Chapter 14/

This is saying "Starting from where you are, open the folder *Chapter 14*, and you'll find the file you want."

Flash uses a similar structure, except that instead of seeing levels of hard drives and folders, it refers to .swf files and movie clips or, to be more accurate, it refers to their *timelines* and *sub-timelines*.

Consider a SWF file that has:

- A main timeline (or root timeline, called _root in Flash) that has one scene - Scene 1

- A movie clip called FoED on frame 27 of Scene 1

- A movie clip called FoundationFlash on FoED's timeline at frame 20

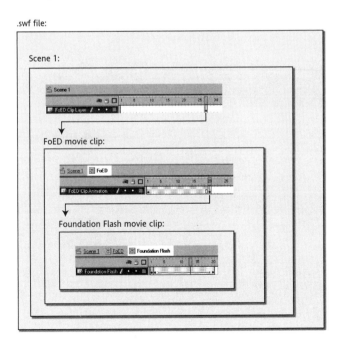

To access an object or frame on FoundationFlash's timeline I could use the following absolute path in my ActionScript:

_root.FoED.FoundationFlash

> *Because the path shown above is an absolute path, starting at the _root and working its way through the nested timelines, I can safely issue it from anywhere and know that Flash will be able to find its way, down the path, to the FoundationFlash movie clip's timeline.*

Note that each of the levels in this hierarchy is separated by a dot - hence the term **dot notation**. We can use this notation to specify the path that we want Flash to follow - and we can use it to point to any object, anywhere in the movie.

What if I wanted to access something in FoundationFlash's timeline from within the FoED movie clip? I *could* use the full, absolute path defined above, but I could also use a simpler method: because I'm *almost* where I want to be; I can just give a shorter *relative* path in ActionScript as follows:

FoundationFlash

This path will start from where I am, and look for the next level of the path *inside* of the FoED movie clip:

FoED movie clip:

'Foundation Flash'
ActionScript

Foundation Flash movie clip:

And there's a special ActionScript command if I want to go back a level (ie from FoundationFlash back up to the FoED clip):

_parent

FoED movie clip:

'_parent'
ActionScript

Foundation Flash movie clip:

You can also string these commands together to go back more than one level:

_parent._parent

_root movie:

FoED movie clip:

'_parent._parent' ActionScript

Foundation Flash movie clip:

Going back to our hard drive, you'll notice that we actually have more than just a C:/ drive. We also have **A**, **D**, **E**, **H** and **X** drives:

We can navigate to those drives by specifying their paths - such as **X:/**.

Similarly, we can include *external* movies in the paths we use in ActionScript. Remember how we previously loaded a soundtrack *.swf* over the top of our case study movie SWF file? To access a separate SWF using dot notation, you just replace _root with a reference to the external SWF's level: _Level0 for the SWF at level 0, _Level1 for the movie at level 1, all the way to level 16000 which is the maximum number of levels you can have. (16000 is the maximum number of symbols you can have in the library. In fact, 16000 is the limit for most everything in Flash.)

So, in terms of the original analogy of our hard drives:

- SWF files - movies - are the equivalent of our separate hard drives

- a movie's main timeline is the equivalent of the root path of each hard drive

- individual movie clips are the equivalent of folders and sub-folders

On our hard drives, we use paths to access *files*. What will Flash allow us to access? It allows me to access *variables*.

To specify a variable at the end of a path, you just precede it by a ':' (colon). So the full path for a variable called '**userinput**' in the FoundationFlash movie clip would be:

    _root.FoED.FoundationFlash:userinput

or

    _level0:FoED.FoundationFlash:userinput

In your Flash movies, you'll find the root level displayed as level 0.

Before we put this new notation into practice, let' think about the dynamic animation we promised you at the start of the chapter.

Dynamic Animation

For dynamic animation to work, we have to be able to target a movie clip and alter some aspects of its appearance or behavior. To do that, we work with a movie's *properties*. We can view these properties by looking at the movie in Debug mode.

Viewing a Movie Clip's Properties

1. Open one of your movies - preferably one with a movie clip attached to the main timeline.

2. Now choose the **Control > Debug Movie** menu option to bring up the Debugger window with the movie in test mode.

3. Click on the **Properties** tab of the **Debugger** window.

> *Note that Flash sometimes doesn't work properly in debug mode unless you have run the movie in test mode at least once. If the Debugger window appears completely blank, simply go back and do a* **Control > Test Movie***, and then try the Debug menu option again. Alternatively, choose the* **Control > Debug Movie** *option.*

When you get the **Debugger** window up, you'll see something like this:

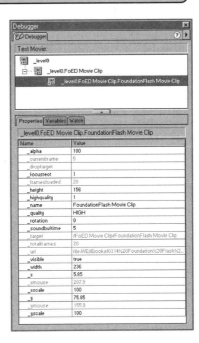

The top pane here shows us the hierarchy of movie clips in the movie. It also gives us the path for each nested movie clip, starting at the root with the main timeline, all the way down to the FoundationFlash movie clip inside the FoED clip. Note the dots separating each nested clip:

Movie clips have other aspects apart from just the variables that we define and set. The names and values shown in the bottom pane of the **Debugger** window when you click on the different movie clips are the properties of the movie clip. All movie clips will have this same set of **properties**, but the values for the properties in an individual movie clip will differ.

Essentially, properties are just like variables except that they relate to a particular aspect of the movie clip such as its size, rotation, whether all its frames have streamed in yet, or its position on the stage. There's one difference between variables and properties that you may already have guessed: if we change a property of our movie clip at any stage, we'll alter its appearance on the screen - it'll be animated. We're going to do this now with dot notation.

Dynamic Animation with Dot Notation

You can now use this knowledge of levels, variables and properties to execute a simple example of a new kind of animation and control. We'll create a dynamic animation that responds to user keyboard inputs.

1. Open a new movie, change the background color to black and set the size to 550 pixels x 400 pixels.

2. Create a new movie clip symbol called **ship**, create a new layer called **space**, and draw yourself a spaceship that looks like it just emerged from a 1980s video game. Don't make the spacecraft too complicated: partly because we're aiming for a retro feel here, and partly because Flash will be moving our ship around the screen, and this will be easier and smoother with a less complex shape. Make sure that the center line of the spaceship is also the center of the movieclip (denoted by a little cross):

3. In the root timeline (remember, that's the timeline on the main stage) create three layers, **actions**, **input** and **ship**.

4. In the new **ship** layer, drag an instance of the your **ship** movie clip onto the stage. Position it at the bottom of the stage and scale it so that it looks like player 1's spacecraft from a Space Invaders arcade game. Using the **Instance** panel, give the **ship** movie clip an instance name - **ship**:

We want to be able to move this spacecraft left and right as it dodges the alien hordes in its epic battle to save the planet - whatever. To do this we need to know two things about this spaceship:

- Its position

- How fast it will move

To get this information all we need to know is the ship movie clip's **_x property**, which is its position on the x-axis of the screen - how far from the right of the screen the space ship is. The ship is at the extreme *left* when **_x=0**, and the extreme *right* when **_x=550**. Once we have this value, we can then assign it to a variable called **ship_pos**, which we'll use to keep track of where the ship is.

5. In the root timeline's **actions** layer, at frame 1, open up the **Actions** window and double-click on the **setVariable** action in the **Actions** book. Type **ship_pos** in the **Variable** field.

6. Select the **Value** field and then click on the 'target' crosshairs at the bottom of the window. Select **ship** as the target path:

Notice the two radio buttons at the bottom right - **Relative** and **Absolute**: these allow us to choose how we want the path to be displayed in our ActionScript. We're going to leave ours at **Absolute** so that we see the **_root** reference in the ActionScript.

7. Back in the **Value** field, type a '.' after **ship** - this is to tell Flash that we want to explore the properties that are associated with the **ship** movie clip:

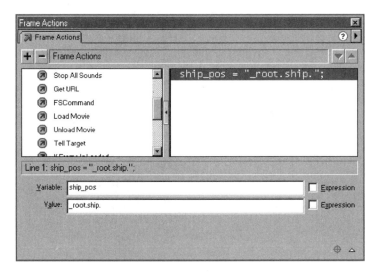

8. Now open the **Properties** book in the left-hand pane:

This reveals the properties of the **ship** movie clip that we can manipulate.

9. Scroll down the properties list and double-click on **_x**. (Use the tool tip that appears as you roll over each property to ensure you select the correct one.)

The property name will appear in the **Value** field, appended to the path for the movie clip:

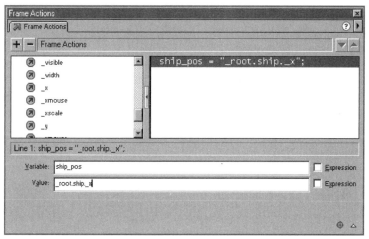

10. Now, check the **Expression** box is checked next to the **Value** field.

Your ActionScript should now read:

ship_pos = _root.ship._x;

This ActionScript will populate the **ship_pos** variable with the value of the ship movie clip's x position.

We need to assign two more variables: **speed**, to set how fast our spacecraft will move (in pixels per keypress) and **shipdead**, which will be either 'true' or 'false' depending on whether our ship is dead or not.

11. Still in the first frame of the actions layer, use the **setVariable** action twice more to assign these two variables: set the value of **shipdead** to **false**, and the value of **speed** to **5,** leaving this frame's finished ActionScript looking like this:

For the **shipdead** variable, you can simply type in **false**, or select it from the **Functions** book in the left pane. Notice that if you click away from it, it will turn blue to show that it's one of Flash's set instructions.

> *Remember to make all the values of these variables expressions. We're going to be assigning more variables throughout the chapter so you need to note carefully whether the values in the ActionScripts we show you are in quotes ("") or not.*

12. Use the **Frame** panel to label this frame as **initialized**, to signify that this is the initialization of the variables.

Now we'll add the *input* part. We've looked at keyboard input into text boxes, but that's not really what we want to do here. Instead, we want our animation to react to a particular key being pressed - the left arrow key. When this is pressed, we want to move the **ship** movie clip instance 5 pixels to the left.

This works in a similar way to a button press, and we need to create a button to enable us to do it. This button will never actually appear on the user's screen, but it will act as a 'funnel' that captures their keyboard input and feeds it into Flash.

13. Create a new button symbol called **input**, and insert a keyframe on its Up state. In a static text box in the Up state, type '**input**'.

14. We don't want this button to ever be selected, so insert a blank keyframe (*F7*) in its Hit state. To ensure that it's never seen (as well as never being selected), go back to the root timeline and place an instance of the button in the work area, outside the stage in frame 1 of the input layer:

15. Select the button and bring up the **Object Actions** window. Double-click the basic action **On Mouse Event**.

Earlier in the book we discussed the alternatives to having an **on (release)** event. One we didn't mention was the on (**KeyPress**) event. We use this event to tell Flash to carry out an instruction when a *particular* key is pressed.

16. Uncheck the **Release** box and check the **Key Press** box at the bottom of the **Object Actions** window:

17. Click in the box to the right of **Key Press** and press the *left arrow* key on your keyboard. The phrase **<Left>** will appear in the box:

The hidden button will now respond to the press of the *left* arrow key.

Next, we have to tell Flash what to do when the left arrow key is pressed. We want it to move five pixels to the left of its current position, or to **_x - speed**. Flash already knows that **speed = 5** from the initialization frame.

18. With the **on (keyPress "<Left>") {** line selected in the Actions window, insert a **set variable** action.

19. Now type **_root.ship._x** into the **Variable** field: we want to change the value of the movie clip instance's **_x position**, remember.

20. Next, use the crosshair icon to add the **ship** path to the **Value** field, add a dot and then _x. Add an '**=**' sign after this, and then use a combination of the crosshairs, the **Properties** book, and your typing fingers to add **_root.ship._x - speed** after the = sign.

Notice that you have great flexibility in how you build up the ActionScript: the more comfortable you become, the more you'll find yourself keying things in by hand rather than selecting actions, properties and targets using the books and path windows.

The **Object Actions** window should now look like this:

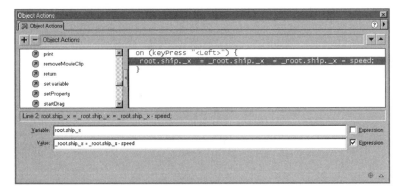

Note that the **Expression** box is checked.

This piece of ActionScript will now decrement the x position of **ship** every time the user presses the left arrow key.

Now we're going to make the ship move five pixels to the right when the *right arrow* is pressed. This means we want the ship movie clip's **_x** property to increase by five, so we'll write **_x + speed**.

21. Starting with an **On Mouse Event** action added with the last line of script selected, repeat and adapt the previous steps to create this next piece of ActionScript for the rightward movement of the ship:

    ```
    on (keyPress "<Right>") {
        _root.ship._x = _root.ship._x = _root.ship._x + speed;
    }
    ```

So now your script is like this:

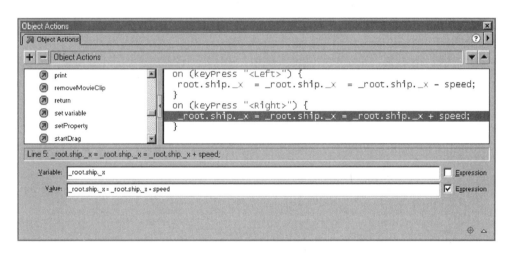

22. Test your movie. You can use the left and right arrow keys to move the spaceship left and right. How cool is *that*?

    This is currently a pretty basic movement, but we're using the main principles of dot notation to alter the properties of the **ship** movie clip and are therefore able to move it at will - its movement is not fixed as it would be in a simple motion tween. This kind of dynamic animation is often called **sprite movement**.

    We haven't finished yet. Next, we're going to simulate the effect of our spaceship being killed by the marauding hordes of alien invaders: we're not going to create the aliens themselves, but your knowledge will soon be sufficient for you to do that yourself. When our ship is destroyed, we want to change the value of the **shipdead** variable we initialized in the movie's first frame: we want to change its value from 'false' to 'true'.

23. In the root timeline, select the button and open the **Object Actions** window.

24. Add an on (**Key Press**) event that responds to the *spacebar* being pressed, and a **setVariable** command that reacts to the **Key Press** event by setting the **shipdead** variable to **true** (you can select true from the **Functions** book in the left pane). Your ActionScript for the button should now look like this:

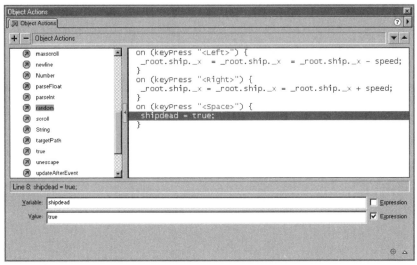

OK, we've set the movie up for all the user input. Now we need to make the **ship** display change in response to the *space bar* being pressed.

25. Add a new layer called **actions** *inside* the **ship** movie clip, and add keyframes at frames 1, 2, 5 and 9.

26. Label frame 5 **dead**:

In frames 1 and 2, we want to set up a 'loop' that constantly checks whether the root timeline has decided that the ship is dead - i.e., whether the space bar has been pressed, and whether the value of **shipdead** is true or false.

27. In frame 1 of the new **actions** layer, insert an **if** action and type
    _root:shipdead into the **Condition** field.

    This action will go back to the root timeline and determine if **shipdead =
    true** (i.e. if the space bar been pressed).

28. Next, add a **goto** action after the **if** statement, select **Frame Label** in the
    Type field and **dead** in the **Frame** field. Leave the **Go to and Play** box
    checked:

    This ActionScript will now jump to frame 5 if the ship has been destroyed by
    the user pressing the space bar. If the ship is still alive, the playhead will go on
    to frame 2. Here, we'll want it to go back to the start of the loop again.

29. At frame 2, we want to go back to frame 1 – the beginning of the loop – so
    add a **goto** action and select **Frame Number** and **1** from the bottom two
    entry boxes. This frame's ActionScript will read:

gotoAndPlay (1);

The movie clip will now loop between frames 1 and 2 until it detects that the space bar has been pressed and that the ship is dead.

30. Still inside the **ship** movie clip, extend the **ship** layer to frame 7, and at frame 9 in the **actions** layer use the **Go To** command to add a **gotoAndPlay("dead")** action:

31. This means that once the root timeline tells us **shipdead = true**, we go into a 'dead loop' where our movie clip plays from frame 5 to frame 9 over and over again. Our ship will disappear at frame 7 and then reappear when the sequence loops, giving the impression of a destroyed ship.

32. Now test the movie again. You'll see that when you press the space bar, the space ship will flash. (You can add the obligatory 'blooop blooop... blooop blooop... ping!' noise later if you feel the need.)

    (Note that if you try and publish the movie as it stands, the keys won't work until the user has clicked on the screen with the mouse.)

    What happens when we press the *space bar* is that the root timeline sets the **shipdead** variable to **true**. The **ship** movie clip is constantly looking at this variable's status via the two-frame loop inside the **ship** movie clip, and as soon as it sees that it's true, it skips from the 'I am alive' loop to the 'I am dead' loop.

This is a significantly different set-up from what we've done before. In particular:

- All animations in this FLA are created totally from ActionScripting. No part of the animation process is tied to the timeline via tween keyframes, and as a result the animation is entirely controlled by the user, and will be different every time.

- Rather than being a way of separating out animations into different parts, in the way each of our buttons did in the case study web site, movie clips are being used in a much more complex way. They are no longer just sitting on the root timeline and being told what to do. They are now actively controlling themselves based on variables derived from user input, and beginning to act in a much more pro-active way.

As well as controlling the spaceship's position on the x-axis, you could just as easily control any other *property* of the movie clip. For example, using the *rotation* property you could get the ship to rotate clockwise and counterclockwise in response to the arrow keys. You could also create a draggable slider and use its position to vary the Alpha property of a movie clip instance. The variations are really beyond the scope of this book, but you can start to get a feel for the possibilities by looking through the options in the **Properties** book.

We spoke earlier of the alien hordes we'd need to create to complete this game. Each alien would need to have variables such as '**invader_pos**', '**invaderdead**' and '**fire_photon_torpedo**'. Controlling the properties of all of our invaders individually is much simpler than you may imagine, as the next brief example will illustrate.

Many Movie Clips, Many Variables

So far, all of the variables that we've used inside of our simple movies have been associated with the whole movie: that is. They were defined in ActionScript in the main timeline, and when their values changed, every movie clip that used those variables saw the changed value. These variables have what's known as '*global* scope' - they look the same to everything in the movie, and any changes in value are applied globally across the whole movie.

This is fine if we have a simple movie and a few variables - it's not to difficult to track and maintain these variable values in ActionScript. Imagine, though, if you had twenty aliens on your screen, each inside its own movie clip instance, each one of them needing to have its x and y positions tracked and amended as the movie played. In this situation, it's considerably more difficult to track and update these aliens' associated variables if these variables are all kept on the main timeline.

Fortunately, we can create variables that are specific to particular movie clips, and whose value changes only affect the movie clip that the variable is associated with. This means that each alien movie clip can have its own **alien_pos** variable, independent of the other nineteen (or thirty-nine, or six hundred) aliens.

Let's look at how this works in a brief exercise.

Movie Clip-specific Variables

1. Open a new movie.

2. In the root timeline (that's on the main stage, remember - we're going to be speaking in this new jargon from now on) add three layers, **actions**, **text** and **clips**:

3. In frame 1 of the **actions** layer, use the **Frame Actions** window to add a **setVariable** action and set **a=3**; (type '**a**' in the **Variable** field and '**3**' in the **Value** field - making '**3**' an expression).

4. In the **text** layer, add a dynamic text box using the Text tool and the **Text Options** panel. Make it 'non selectable' by leaving the **Selectable** box unchecked, and give it a border by checking the **Border/Bg** box.

    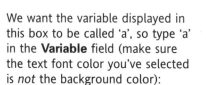

    We want the variable displayed in this box to be called 'a', so type 'a' in the **Variable** field (make sure the text font color you've selected is *not* the background color):

    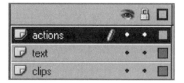

    When you run this single frame movie, you'll just see a text box with '**3**' in it. Not the most exciting movie we've made in this book. Bear with us, though, as the point this example illustrates will open your eyes to a wealth of exciting possible movies.

5. Now create a new movie clip called **Mclip**. Add new **actions** and **text** layers to it as you did for the root timeline. Create a similar non-selectable dynamic text box in frame 1 of the **text** layer, but this time set it to display the variable '**b**':

6. To help us remember that this text box shows a variable that's *inside* **Mclip** we're going to label it. Draw a static text box next to the dynamic one and type '**This is inside Mclip**' into it (You could also use the **Character** tab to select a different text color from the text that appears inside **Mclip**):

7. In frame 1 of the **Mclip** movie clip's actions layer, use the **Frame Actions** window to add a **setVariable** action with an (expression) value of **b=10**:

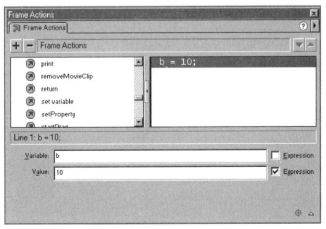

8. Place an instance of the finished **Mclip** on the clips layer in the root timeline, and give it the instance name **Mclip** using the **Instance** panel.

9. Test the movie:

This is inside Mclip

So now you have a variable in root called '**a**', which is equal to **3,** and a variable in the movie **Mclip** called '**b**', which is **10**. Here's the current variable/text box relationship:

Now we're going to see how it's possible to have a variable name that has more than one value...

10. Inside of **Mclip**, change the ActionScript in frame 1 from **b=10**; to **a=10**.

11. Select the dynamic text box in **Mclip** and change the **Variable** field on the **Text Options** panel from '**b**' to '**a**'.

You've now set two variables, both called '**a**' to two different values in two different places. The **a=10** ActionScript inside of **Mclip** is initializing a *new* variable called **a**, *inside* **Mclip**. This **Mclip**-specific variable is a *different variable* from the variable **a** that's being initialized on the main timeline. You can think of them as:

•   _root:a

•   _root.Mclip:a

Each variable is associated with the timeline that it was initialized on.

12. Test the movie to see how Flash implements this:

> 3
>
> 10

Both text fields will show the same values as they did before. Although both text areas are displaying an '**a**' variable, one is showing 10 and the other is showing 3, because the two different variables have different *scope*. The '**a**' variable spawned from the main timeline applies to the main timeline, and the '**a**' variable spawned inside **Mclip** applies to the movie clip only.

Try running the movie again, but this time select **Control > Debug Movie** instead of **Control > Test Movie** and take a look in the **Debugger** window:

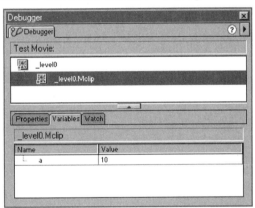

Again, remember that the **Debugger** can be a little temperamental, so persevere...

Once again, Flash is showing us the path to each of our movie components: the path for the main stage/timeline is **_level0**, and the path to the movie clip is **_level0.Mclip** - showing us **Mclip** is inside **_level0**.

As the icons suggest, the main or root timeline is *really* just another movie clip: **_level** is represented by the same kind of icon as **Mclip**. This is something worth remembering as you advance further into Flash, because all of the things that you learn to do with movie clips can also be applied to the root movie itself.

If you click on the **Variables** tab in the **Debugger** window with one of the paths selected, Flash will display the values we've assigned to our variables.

With **_level0.Mclip** selected we'll see that the value of **a** is **10**, and if we then select **_level0** we'll see that here it has the value **3**. (Here, you'll also see a variable that represents the version of Flash Player that is running. We can ignore this as it doesn't affect our programming.)

Although we have two variables called '**a**', one is called **_root:a** and the other is called **_root.mclip:a**. Each variable is defined on a separate timeline, and exists in only one place. The version of '**a**' inside **Mclip** only applies to that movie clip. It is **local** to **Mclip**.

Local variables are exceptionally useful because they allow us to re-use a movie clip. For example, imagine we built a movie clip that controlled a single space invader using the internal, movie clip-specific variables we mentioned earlier - '**invader_pos**', '**invaderdead**' and '**fire_photon_torpedo**'. If we then put another ten alien movie clips onto the stage, we would have ten space invaders with ten sets of discrete, internal, *local* variables, *all* being individually controlled.

> *The use of global/local variables and dot notation is important as it's an extremely powerful technique. We will talk about it in more detail when the third area of Flash mastery is looked at - object-oriented programming (OOP). OOP is one of the things that separates supreme Flash Masters from mortal Flash designers. It's difficult to learn, so we've set aside the whole of the next chapter to cover it.*

The techniques we've introduced here are the raw materials of the really advanced and slick looking Flash web site interfaces you may have seen, and you have now taken the second step on your road towards mastering Flash.

Armed as we are with our new found knowledge of input text fields, dot notation and 'sprite' animation, we're now ready to implement the changes we planned for our Smiler movie.

Making Smiler Age-sensitive

If you don't have your fully-functional version of Smiler saved from Chapter 10, you can download a ready-made Smiler among the downloadable files for this book on our web site.

Guess Smiler's Age

Let's remind ourselves what our requirements specification was:

- **1.1** Define a variable, *age*, with values between 1 and 99

- **2.1** Input a numeric text entry from the user

- **2.2** Assign this text entry to a variable called *guess*

- **2.3** If *guess* is not between 1 and 99, then repeat from 2.1

- **3.1** Create a new variable, *difference*, which is equal to *age-guess*

- **3.2** If *difference* is negative, make it positive

- **3.3** Go to a frame number that's equal to *difference* in the Smiler animated movie clip

- **4.1** If *difference* is zero, then stop, otherwise repeat from 2.1

- **5.1** Define a variable, age, which is between 1 and 99

    Let's walk through this step by step

The first thing we need to do is get Flash to come up with an age for Smiler that it can compare the user's guess against. It would be a good idea to make this a *random* value, so that it's different for every run of the game. We can do this easily with Flash's **Random()** function, which returns a random value between 0 and whatever number you put in the brackets. There's a slight twist here: if you enter...

```
age = random(10);
```

...the **age** variable will come back as 0, 1, 2, 3, 4, 5, 6, 7, 8 or 9, but not 10. The result of this function is *zero-based*, meaning that it starts at 0. If we want to generate a number between 1 and 99, and we use **Random(99)**, this will give us a number between 0 and 98 - the function will always give you a number one digit lower than the one you entered in the brackets.

To generate a number between 1 and 99, we have to enter:

```
age = random(99) + 1;
```

This piece of ActionScript will tell Flash to add 1 to the random number generated by the **Random** function.

We want to generate the random number right at the start of our game, during *initialization*, so that the age variable is populated, ready and waiting for the user's guess.

1. In frame 1 of the **control** layer in the existing smiler movie (as it was at the end of Chapter 10) we already have this ActionScript:

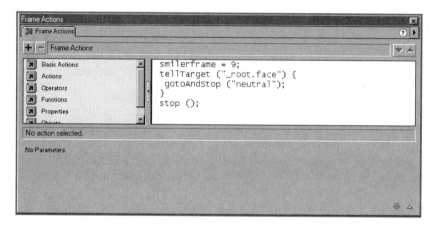

We want to assign a new variable, age, so the first thing we need is a new **set variable** action.

2. Delete the **smilerframe = 9;** action using the '-' button, and add a new **set variable** action (from the **Actions** book in the left-hand pane).

3. In the **Variable** field, enter **age**, and move this line of script to the top of the window:

4. Click in the **Value** field, and then select **random** from the **Functions** book:

Now to complete the **random()** part of the action.

5. In the **Value** field, delete number and type in **99** in its place. Type **+1** after the bracket, and once you've checked the **Expression** box your window should look like this:

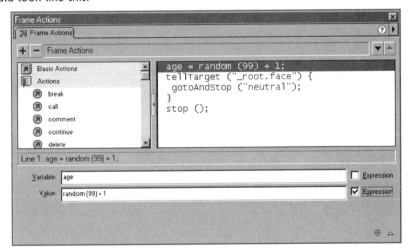

Because we want to start using our new ability to write in dot notation form, we'll also clean up the **tellTarget()** part of this script before we create the more efficient Flash 5 version.

6. Delete the **tellTarget()** action by selecting its first line and pressing the window's '-' key. Delete the **stop()** action too.

The next command you need to enter is not in any of the books in the left-hand side: you'll have to enter it using the **Actions** window's **Expert Mode**. Yes, expert - and at the start of the chapter you were a beginner.

In expert mode, Flash assumes you know exactly how to hand-code the ActionScript you're creating, and it'll consequently offer you less help than it's done previously. The various fields and tick-boxes that you previously prompted your input will not appear, and you'll have to enter everything yourself. The good thing about being in expert mode is that (a) you're able to enter commands in a much more streamlined form and (b) you'll pick up much more advanced techniques, learning by heart the ActionScript syntax.

7. Click on the right arrow-head button on the top right of the **Frame Actions** window:

8. **Normal Mode** should currently be ticked. Select **Expert Mode** to change into top gear.

Notice that the area at the bottom of the window is reduced in size, and that there are no hints or text to tell you what to do:

Also note that if you click on a line of script now, it isn't highlighted. Flash is trusting you to do things right!

9. With your cursor in the next free line, click on the target icon at the bottom of the window.

10. Select the **face** instance as the target path. Type in a '.' after it and then select the **gotoAndStop** command from the **Actions** book. Delete **frame** from within the brackets and type "**neutral**" (including the quotation marks):

If you've entered your ActionScript correctly, you should see no red areas on the line you've just typed. The **gotoAndStop** action should appear on the screen in blue (to show that it's a command), as will the **_root part**, and the rest of the script should be in black.

This command is saying 'using the **face** instance, go to the label called **neutral** and stop'. Flash knows that we're talking about a label because it's in quotation marks. You could also have used this command:

    _level0.face.gotoAndStop("neutral");

which gives the full path to the **face** instance.

Before we can run this script, we want to be sure that it has no errors in it. In *expert mode*, Flash does no error checking. If the movie doesn't work when you run it, Flash won't hint why that is. If you were in *normal mode*, however, Flash would be constantly checking your commands for correct syntax.

We can overcome this by slipping back into normal mode before testing our movie. This is a trick that affords you the best of both worlds. By entering your script in expert mode you can work much more quickly once you're familiar with the ActionScript commands and syntax, and without having to fill in check boxes and entry fields. However, when you switch back to normal mode you get Flash to double-check your code for you - and save yourself a lot of head scratching if the movie doesn't work. If you *do* have any errors when you change back into normal mode, Flash won't let you back in until you've corrected them. It will show you them in the Output window.

For example, if you'd left out a quotation mark around **neutral** in the third line of ActionScript and you tried to switch to normal mode, Flash would have thrown up this dialog box...

Flash 5

This script contains errors. It is not possible to convert from Expert Mode to Normal Mode until you fix these errors.

OK

...and displayed this error message in the **Output** window:

```
Output                                                                Options
Scene=Scene 1, Layer=control, Frame=1: Line 2: String literal was not properly terminated
    _root.face.gotoAndStop ("neutral);

Scene=Scene 1, Layer=control, Frame=1: Line 3: ')' or ',' expected
```

Flash tells us:

- Which line is in error

- What is wrong, in general terms, with the line

We'd recommend all new Flash users having a go in Flash expert mode in this way for a few lines of code at a time. As time goes on, you will find yourself using normal mode less and less. It's well worth learning: Macromedia did not call it expert mode for nothing - it lets you get really close to the ActionScript, and you'll also find your text input becomes a lot quicker.

OK, back to **Smiler**.

11. Go back into normal mode, and your window should look like this:

Testing the movie will not make Smiler do anything at the moment, but our level of coding has just gone up a few notches.

Let's work on the rest of our specification.

2.1 Input a text entry from the user that is a numeric

2.2 Assign it to variable, guess.

2.3 If guess is not between 1 and 99, then repeat from 2.1

12. Add frames to all the root timeline layers up to frame 20 (using click, drag, *F5*) and add a keyframe at frame 10 in the **control** layer.

13. Label this frame **loop** and add a **setVariable** action. Enter **guess** in the **Variable** field and leave the **Value** field blank and the **Expression** box unchecked. Next, add a **stop** command and your ActionScript should look like this:

```
guess = "";
stop ();
```

Your timeline will look like this:

14. At frame 1 of the buttons layer, delete the **better** button and its text, and move the **worse** button down so it's in the lower right part of the stage. Change the text inside it from **worse** to **Enter**.

15. Create an *input text* box next to the **Enter** button. Give it a border by checking **Border/Bg** and associate it with the **guess** variable by typing **guess** into the **Variable** field. Make the maximum characters the user can enter **2**, and select the 'numbers' icon at the bottom of the panel. By doing this we are limiting the possible input to numbers up to 99:

We'll set guess to **0** initially, and change it to the value the user enters once they press the **Enter** button.

16. Click on the **Enter** button (being careful not to select the text over it), and bring up its **Object Actions** window. The current ActionScript is not required, so you can delete it all with the '-' button. Now insert an **if** action - Flash will add an **on (release)** action automatically.

17. In the **Condition** field select **isNaN** from the Functions book where we found **random** and change **number** to **guess** manually:

18. From the **Actions** book, insert an **else** command, and then a **Play** command from **Basic Actions**. The window should contain the same ActionScript as ours:

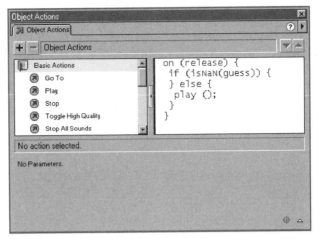

The **isNaN(guess)**; part looks to see whether the user's input, **guess**, is 'not a number'. Since we want to carry on only if it *is* a number, we have put the **play()** action in an **else** branch, which is the same as saying 'play *only* if guess *is* a number'.

Consider this example:

If an apple can only be red or green, what *else* can it be if it's *not* red?

guess can only be 'a number' or 'not a number' in the same way as the apple can only be red or green.

Because our input text field will only accept numbers, we know that if the movie starts to play after the mouse has been clicked and released, a number between 1 and 99 was definitely keyed in. This prevents the movie starting when the mouse is pressed but no guess has been entered.

> *Be careful never to put '=' in **if** statements. You should always use the '=='
> which means 'check to see if the left side is equal to the right side. Putting
> '=' will actually change the left hand side of your equation to be equal to
> the right-hand side, when all you want Flash to do is check it! This is quite
> a common mistake for new Flash 5 programmers, so don't get caught
> out.*

You can now test the movie. It will wait for an input until you enter a value that is between 0 and 99. Try to see if you can enter anything else.

Now for the next requirements:

> **3.1 Create a new variable, difference, which is equal to age-guess.**
>
> **3.2 If difference is negative, make it positive.**
>
> **3.3 Go to a frame number that is equal to difference in movie Smiler.**

We want the **Smiler** movie to have 98 frames, because that's the maximum amount we can be wrong by when we guess its age.

19. Inside the **Smiler** movie, add frames (*F5*) to the *left* of the **neutral** keyframe to shift it up to frame 49, and then extend the layer to frame 98 as shown here by adding frames to the *right* of **neutral**. Finally, extend the **eyes** and **face** layers up to frame 98:

We now need create the variable that represents the *difference* between the guess and the actual age, and create the ActionScript that'll make the **face** instance go to the frame number that matches that difference.

20. In the root timeline, add a new keyframe at frame 15 of the **control** layer and enter the following actions in the **Frame Actions** window:

```
difference = age - guess;
if (difference < 0) {
    difference = - difference;
}
face.gotoAndStop(difference);
```

We've done the first three actions a few times now, so this will just test your memory. We've only created an action like the one in the last line *once* before, so here's a reminder: go into expert mode as we did earlier, use the target crosshairs to select **face** as the target path, type a period, then select **gotoAndStop** from **Actions** and type **difference** in the brackets. Take a breath.

This script tells Flash how to calculate the **difference** variable (line 1). If the calculation produces a negative number (less than zero), we convert it to make the value positive (lines 2 and 3). Then, whatever number difference is, we want Flash to go to that number frame on the **smiler** timeline inside the **face** instance and stop (line 5).

And the next requirement, please...

4.1 - If difference is zero, then stop, otherwise repeat from 2.1

21. Under the actions you've just added to frame 15, and back in normal mode, insert an **if** action and type **difference <>0** in the **Condition** field. Then insert a **Go To** action and tell Flash to go to the frame labeled **loop** and play the movie:

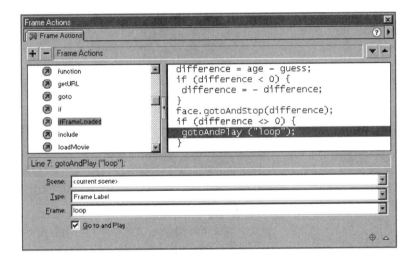

This is telling Flash that if the difference is greater than or less than 0 (which would mean that the user's guess was incorrect) then it must go back to the frame labeled **loop** where it will await another guess.

Finally, we need to alter the text at the top, which is still asking us 'How do you feel?'

22. In frame 1 of the **text** layer, change the text at the top to '**Guess my age!**' and, in frame 20 of the **control** layer, add a keyframe and put a **stop()** action in it.

23. In frame 20 of the **text** layer, add a keyframe and change the text in this new keyframe to read 'You got it!'

24. Test the movie.

And that's it. We've followed our top-down requirements specification, solved our problem and finished our game.

You might want to give Smiler a bit more personality. For example, you could have a dynamic text box that displays a statement showing how Smiler feels about your last guess. If difference is greater than 30 it could say:

'Miles away!'

Or if the difference is less than 30 it could say:

'Getting warmer'

And when the user guesses within 10 of the age it could say:

'Red hot!'

All that can be done by adding **if** and **else** actions that relate to the variable you've assigned to the text box. There are many other things that you can add to this program to make Smiler more intelligent, just using the commands and techniques you've now learnt.

You've now reached the top of the intermediate learning slope. We haven't told you everything you need to know, but you now know all the basic principles and have had enough practice to allow you to quickly learn other structures that will increase your ability.

Summary

In this chapter, we've been exploring the ActionScripting features which make Flash a powerhouse for sophisticated, powerful web applications. Once you've learnt these principles and applied them, using the full array of actions and options, you can build the kind of web sites you've dreamed of making. We hope you started to see that with ActionScript, the possibilities in Flash are infinite.

Specifically, we saw that:

- The **top-down design** approach is a great way to approach complex programming and ActionScripting tasks:

  - Define the general problem to be solved

  - Break the problem down iteratively into its smallest components

- ◆ Reassemble these components in a logical list of **requirements**

- ◆ Build solutions to each requirement. Test, integrate, test again!

◆ Rudimentary **user input** can be captured using a simple **input text box**

◆ Input text can be assigned to a variable and redisplayed in a **dynamic text box**

◆ User input and variables can be manipulated with ActionScript: for instance, we used a big '+' sign on a button to add together two numbers and display the result

◆ **Dot notation** gives us a secure and flexible way of targeting named movie clip instances inside our movies

◆ Dot notation gives us access to the **hierarchy** of movie clip timelines implicit in every Flash movie

◆ Movie clips have **properties** which we can target and modify in ActionScript, allowing us to alter a movie clip's appearance, behavior and animation characteristics

◆ We can modify movie clip properties and behavior based on user input and other movie events

◆ Variables can be **scoped** and targeted using movie clip timelines and dot notation

We're now ready to move on to and tackle the remaining area of Flash knowledge you need to round off your Flash initiation - **object-oriented programming**. All the hard work and theory will seem worth it as we use these principles to build something we *nearly* built twice in this chapter: a proper game.

15 Intermediate ActionScript 2

What we'll cover in this chapter:

- ◆ *Fundamental Concepts of **Object-Oriented Design***

- ◆ *How Flash can use objects*

- ◆ *Building a simple Flash game*

The real power of Flash 5 over Flash 4 is hidden in its code. Flash 5 is full of huge additions that really expand its usefulness. For the first time, Flash allows proper coding techniques to be applied to ActionScript, the only problem being that you have to be already fairly advanced up the ladder to appreciate it. Luckily for you, you're high enough to appreciate the differences - it's just the full application that's yet to come.

In this chapter, we'll try to show you what all the fuss is about. It's now easier than ever to create animations and effects that are controlled directly from Flash using the dynamic animation techniques discussed in the last chapter, but it's also the ease of specifying paths, and the subtle changes that have occurred to the movie clip symbol that gives Flash 5 its extra power, as you'll soon see.

Part of the reason for Flash 5's quantum leap in functionality is that it allows us to implement the principles of **object-oriented design**. Object-oriented design and programming is too vast a topic to cover definitively in a single chapter like this. For a richer coverage of the theory and practice of object-oriented analysis, design, and programming, you should consult a book dedicated to the subject. What we'll do here is give you a taste of the *principles* of the object-oriented approach, and see how they can be applied in the Flash context, and how they might make you think differently about your Flash movies.

Object-Oriented Design

Object-oriented programming and design has become a standard approach in the computing industry. The reason for this is that it allows you to build computer systems that are robust enough to do their job, while at the same time being flexible enough to be easily maintained and altered as the nature of the problem that they were set out to solve changes. How is that? Well, the essential truth of the object-oriented approach is that it models the problems it's setting out to solve in as abstract a way as possible: that is, it's always trying to distill a problem down to an essence that's unencumbered with surface detail. By *abstracting* the problem you have create a series of solutions that can easily be reorganized to deal with a different problem.

As an example of this, consider the task of making a cup of your favorite instant coffee.

Making Coffee

First, let's think about how you'd analyze this in terms the top-down approach that we considered in the previous chapter.

In the top-down design you take the problem and break it down into sub-problems. As you keep breaking it down, you're making the individual functional items smaller and more compact until you can start to see the solution in the sub-problems, because the sub-problems become more and more manageable and easier to understand. Take this problem definition;

To make a cup of coffee, with milk and one sugar

First iteration:

1. Create some hot water
2. Have a cup ready with coffee in it and some sugar
3. When the water has boiled, pour the water into the cup
4. Stir mixture for twenty seconds and add milk

Second iteration:

1.1 Fill kettle full of water
1.2 Connect kettle to power and switch on

2.1 Get one teaspoon of sugar from sugar bowl and transfer to cup
2.2 Get one teaspoon of coffee from jar and transfer to cup

3.1 Wait until kettle has boiled
3.2 Pour water from kettle into cup
3.3 etc.....

Here, you're breaking things down until the problem is so basic that its components can be coded. The result of building a system based on this kind of analysis would be a combination of steps that carried out each stage of the task. A computer system developed in this way will usually consist of a series of carefully targeted, tightly constrained code elements - procedures - which each perform a small piece of the overall task. This approach is fine, until you want the system to do something different - say, make a cup of lemon tea, or an iced coffee. To reprogram the system to do this, you'd need to re-engineer multiple elements in the system to allow them to perform a different task. The top-down method of decomposing the problem tends to 'hard wire' the solution to the problem and make it a less adaptable when your needs change.

An Object-Oriented Cup of Coffee

In object-oriented design, you try and look *beyond* the specific problem and analyze the nature of the *things* that make up that problem. That sounds a bit woolly - what does that mean? Well, if we were looking at the 'making a cup of coffee' process in an object-oriented way, we'd ignore the brand of coffee, and how hot the water needed to be, and how long you were supposed to stir the beverage. Instead, we'd think about the *general* processes involved, and try and conceptualize them.

The process of object-oriented design is a little like being in an episode of one of those drama series where fantastically wealthy, stylish and attractive thirty-somethings agonize over their inner torment, questioning the meaning and content of every aspect of their existence. OK, it's not *that* bad, but you *do* have to philosophize on 'What is making coffee all about?'.

The generalized, philosophical answers to this question would be things like: "Well, there's liquid and powder involved, switching things on and seeing when they're done, moving things from one container to another, and finishing."

You're abstracting the problem down into building blocks, but into building blocks that are more 'loosely tied' to the actual components involved in the physical act of making a cup of coffee. You're not thinking about specific functionally any more, but are thinking about general principles like 'moving things from one container to another', 'liquid flowing', 'turning things on' and 'detecting when things have finished'.

Once you can express the process in these generalized terms, you can start creating *generic* routines that embody these general principles in code. You might create, for example, a routine that catered for the process called 'prepare the liquid'. This routine would embody the general function of preparing liquid, but it wouldn't be tied to preparing a particular *type* of liquid. Instead, this routine would be able to carry out the basic process using values that we supplied to it when we started that process. For instance, we might tell it the kind of liquid to use and give it a temperature to heat (or chill) the liquid to:

"Prepare the liquid" routine:

What drink do we want to make? → Liquid type value → Process for preparing the liquid

How hot we want it to be → Temperature information value → Process for preparing the liquid

The generic routines are flexible, and, because we've distilled them down to the very essence of their functionality, they can be applied to a number of different tasks - making tea, making an iced drink, making a milkshake and so on. The 'prepare the liquid' routine is the same, but the details of an individual implementation of this process - making *this* cup of coffee or *this* iced tea - can be specified in each particular instance.

The 'prepare the liquid' routine is one part of the solution for the overall 'making a beverage' problem, and it would act in choreographed collaboration with the other generalized routines to achieve the overall aim.

The generalized routines are 'templates' for carrying out each aspect of the task, created to serve us, and waiting to do so. When we come to perform a beverage-making task, we'll initialize *instances* of each of these templates, feeding them the *specific* information that they need to perform this *specific* task properly:

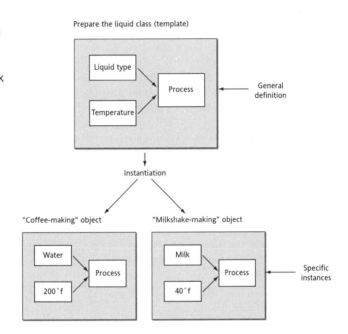

In object-oriented design terms, the templates are a **class**. The class describes the essentials of a process or an item, specifying the characteristics of the process that make it uniquely different from any other kind of process. The definition of the 'prepare the liquid' class might include: the capacity to specify a type of liquid; a variable that describes the amount of liquid, and a variable that controls the prepared liquid's temperature. The functionality for carrying out the task, and for coordinating activity with other routines, is encapsulated by the class.

To make an **object** to carry out the task, we instantiate - bring into existence - an object based on the class definition. So, if our class is called **Prepare Liquid**, we'll issue an instantiation that says:

Object Get Coffee Water Ready = Prepare Liquid (water, 1 cup, 200 degrees fahrenheit)

The part on the left of the equals sign is just saying 'Create me an object called '**Get Coffee Water Ready**'.

The part on the right of the equals sign specifies the *class* you want this object to be based on - **Prepare Liquid** - and the values that you want to set for this particular object/process - the liquid type, the quantity, and the temperature. You have to feed these values in because the class defines them as being part of this general process. A class will also define the way that this class can interact with other classes, and it'll define interfaces for communicating with other classes.

Once the object is instantiated, it will run through the task it's been built to perform, using the definitions embodied in the class, plus the specific attributes that we've assigned to this object.

A class is like a 'black box' that embodies a general process that solves part of a larger problem, and an object is an instance of that class that you create to perform a specific function - making *this* cup of coffee.

So what's the point of this? Why would you want to go through all this extra thinking, and dip your toes into the world of object-oriented design (which is all we've done here?). The answer is that object-oriented solutions are more robust and flexible, and they're easier to maintain and upgrade. Because you've designed the solution in terms of generalized and self-sufficient components, you can reuse these components in other tasks that have a similar element in them - maybe a 'preparing a bath' task could reuse our 'prepare the liquid' component. Furthermore, as each class communicates with other entities using interfaces, you can completely change the instructions inside a class and not affect the overall solution - provided that you keep the same interfaces: each class - and the objects that are derived from it - can be reworked in isolation. Here, in essence are the benefits of the object oriented approach:

- Reusability

- Encapsulation - functionality embedded in a self-contained object

- Maintainability

- Extensibility

- Flexibility

The object-oriented approach helps you build solutions that can change as the world that they're modeling changes, and the strength of **OO** design lies in its ability to generalize: generalized solutions based on these design principles are not 'locked in' to the problem you initially set out to solve, because elements can be used elsewhere and change when different problems arrive.

What's this got to do with Flash?

That's a good question.

Flash 5 and Objects

The simple answer is:

- Reusability

- Encapsulation - functionality embedded in a self-contained object

- Maintainability

- Extensibility

- Flexibility

Flash 5's code has been restructured to allow you to implement the object-oriented approach more easily, and that's one of its major internal differences from Flash 4. In fact, Flash 5 actually gives you the facilities to define classes and instantiate objects from them - unfortunately, the ActionScript you need to do this in a rigorous way is a little beyond our scope here. Instead, we're going to look at a particular basic object that you're already really familiar with: Flash lets you implement the object-oriented design principles we've discussed using **movie clips**.

A movie clip instance on the stage is essentially a specific named object based on the movie clip *class* embedded in a symbol in the library:

A movie clip object has standard, basic properties like 'size' and 'number of frames', and once you've built up the individual instance by adding a few actions and frames of content to it, it can start to do things.

An object has a standard general structure. At its simplest level, it calculates a certain, small but well-defined chunk of a solution (or movie), and it has well-defined interfaces that allow it to communicate with the other objects that deal with the other parts of the problem (movie). Remember that to follow the object-oriented route you have to:

- Identify the basic elements of your problem in terms of what you can see happening (or what you *want* to happen in your movie)

- Identify what these basic elements actually are (conceptualize) and see whether you can generalize them into basic groups (classes)

- Create movie clips in the library that map to these basic groups and perform the functions associated with the group

- Instantiate (drag out of the library) individual movie clips (objects) on the stage and if necessary, give them instance names so that you can target them with ActionScript

The important point here is that the movie clips must be *self-contained*. They must be able to solve their part of the problem, by themselves, and they must be able to do this independently of whatever else is going on in parallel in the movie.

Objects work best in situations where there are multiple instances of a few very similar processes to be performed. We can illustrate this with a graphical effect in a Flash movie. A lot of computer graphic effects use a few basic rules that are applied many times over to give the illusion of complex behavior. Here, we'll see how a very simple movie clip object with a single simple behavior can be replicated many times on the screen to create a much more complex looking effect.

A Simple Mouse Trail

The great thing about object-oriented design is that it allows you to *play* - you don't even need to have a high-level problem or task to solve. You can just say, "This effect looks interesting, let's break it down into its objects and see what we can build from them." Like child's play, you can use this as a creative thought process, and not necessarily as a logical, analytical problem solving process. The reason for this is very simple: in Flash your objects are not long-winded and obscure data elements - they're visual movie clips with animation and sound, which can be much more fun.

A mouse trail is a little group of characters or text that follows the mouse pointer. An effective mouse trail will usually contain some very complex math, using things like inertia and trigonometry to calculate the cursor position and the relative position of the trail. By stopping and thinking about it, though, you'll realize that instead of using heavy math and shifting movie clips around behind the cursor, you could just use lots of static movie clips that *react* when the cursor moves over them. Basically, you're turning the problem on its head.

There are two stages to building our mouse trail: (1) building the basic movie clip object that we'll use multiple copies of later; (2) integrating the multiple copies into the movie.

Creating the Basic Movie Clip

The first thing to realize is that all of those fancy mouse trails have one thing in common: the character furthest away from the cursor is *least* affected by what the mouse is doing now, and the closest is *most* affected.

In essence, we've abstracted the problem down to a generalization of the type of animation that's required to create the desired effect: the animation on any particular character should get weaker based on: (1) increasing distance from the mouse; (2) how long ago the mouse was near it - longer ago means weaker animation effect.

The only thing we've encountered so far that's affected by the mouse is a button symbol, so maybe if you had loads of buttons all over the screen, you could make Flash do all the hard work for you. That's all you need to know. It seems pretty vague, but that's okay, it allows you more room to experiment...

1. Start a new movie, and in **Modify > Movie**, change the background color to black. Make sure also that **View > Grid > Show Grid** and **Snap to Grid** are both selected.

2. Create a new graphic symbol and call it **sy.circle**: make it a blue circle with a diameter of about **90** pixels, and center it at **0,0** by using the **Info** panel:

3. Now create a movie clip and call it **mc.circle**. Change the name of the current layer to **circle**.

4. Leave frame 1 of this movie clip empty, but add a keyframe in frame 2. Drag a copy of **sy.circle** into this keyframe, and center it on the stage at **0,0**.

5. Next, using the **Effect** panel, select **Alpha** from the drop-down menu and give the circle a value of **70%**:

6. Add another keyframe at frame 20. In this frame, use the **Effect** panel again, but this time, select the **Advanced** drop-down menu option. The **Alpha** will already be set to **70%** from before, but give the circle a red hue by moving the second **Red** slider (the one that's a *number* rather than a percentage) all the way up to **255**:

7. Back in the **Info** panel, set the width and height to **1**. Finally, create a motion tween from frame 2 to frame 20.

8. If you drag this movie clip onto the stage and test your movie you'll see a blue circle that starts off big and blue and then gets smaller and redder until it finally disappears.

   You've now created your simple 'diminishing' effect. The next thing that you need to do is change the clip so that it'll only play when the mouse goes over it, when it will run through once and stop until the mouse goes over it again. The more recently the mouse was near it, the bigger the circle. This carries on for 20 frames, by which time the circle is so small it disappears. You also have to somehow persuade your object to acquire the mouse input that will control its appearance and behavior. You *could* get it to look at how close the mouse is to it, but there is a simpler option to try first.

9. Duplicate **sy.circle** by selecting it in the library window and clicking on **Options > Duplicate** from the top of the library. Now make the new symbol into a button via the **Symbol Properties** dialog box and call the button **bu.circle**.

10. The button should be transparent, and the same size as the movie clip. In **bu.circle** insert a keyframe in the Hit state, and delete the circle from the Up state. You now have a circular button that has no Up, Over, or Down state, but *does* have a Hit state, which makes it invisible but selectable:

11. We want to add this button, plus some simple actions, into **mc.circle**, so go into **mc.circle** and add two new layers called **actions** and **button**:

12. In the **button** layer, add the **bu.circle** symbol and center it at **0,0**. Then remove all of the other frames from this layer, so that the button only exists on frame 1.

13. Finally, attach some ActionScript to the button. Use the **On Mouse Event** action and check the **Roll Over** box, and uncheck the **Release** box too. Finally, add a **Play** action. This should leave you with the following code:

```
on (rollOver) {
    play ();
}
```

14. Next, add two even simpler actions to the actions layer. At frame 1 attach a **Stop** action, then insert a keyframe in frame 20 and add a **Go to** action. Uncheck the **Go to and Play** box to make it **Go to and Stop**, and leave it pointing to frame 1.

And that's it. You've created a movie clip that does the following:

- Waits at a blank first frame until it's rolled over

- When it's rolled over by the mouse, it plays

- When it has played once, it goes back to the blank first frame

15. Test your movie. You'll see a blank screen until your mouse happens to move over the button. As soon as this happens, a circle will appear, getting smaller as time goes by, until it disappears completely. That was the basic object we started out trying to create: an effect that diminishes based on either 'time since it was started' or 'distance the mouse is away from it'.

Notice that up until now we haven't even thought how we're going to use this object. We just wanted to create an object that waited until the mouse was near, and then displayed a diminishing animation. We've forgotten the initial problem completely, and concentrated on creating this object.

Building the Movie

The next step is to test the object to see if this simple animation repeated many times could be used to produce the complex behavior we're looking for.

1. To start with, build up a single row of your movie clips by using the grid to create a regular overlapping pattern:

2. Keep placing new clips on until you have a complete row across the stage:

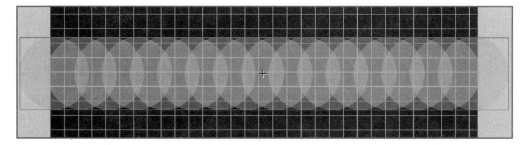

3. Then, when you have a full row, select them all and then press **F8** to convert the whole row into a new movie clip symbol, and call it **mc.circle.row**.

4. Finally, keep adding rows above and below your starting row until you've filled the screen with a neat grid:

And now comes the moment of truth. Remember, we set ourselves the task of creating a trail that would start from wherever the mouse was and gradually fade as the mouse moved away, or as time passed. Did we do it? There's only one way to find out - test that movie:

It seems to have worked perfectly. Cool. You could tweak it to have smaller circles and closer gaps if you wanted, and have your animations last half as long to tie them closer to the cursor. In fact, why use circles at all? You can change the animation to be whatever you want - sparkling stars, jumping sheep - the possibilities are endless. The next step is to play and create!

Notice that in making this movie, all you've done is thought about an effect, decided what its most basic behavior was, and created an object with that behavior. Then you've made a more complex looking overall effect by making lots of copies of the simple effect. Although this movie isn't truly object-oriented, the thinking behind it *is*. One of the fundamental advantages of objects is that they're self-contained, and therefore reusable. What's more, because they are generalized solutions, they can be rearranged to fit new problems.

We'll now show you how objects and the theories behind them can be reapplied to different tasks: we're going to create a fully playable, albeit basic, Flash game.

Putting it all Together

We're going to be looking at a simple memory game sometimes called 'pairs'. The first thing we'll do is define the basic rules:

- The player is presented with an even number of face-down tiles with symbols on their face-down side. For each tile there is at least one other identical tile

- The player has to match each tile with another matching tile by turning a pair of tiles over per turn. If the tiles are an identical pair, the tiles are left face-up. If the tiles don't match, the tiles are returned back to their face-down state

- The game has finished when all tiles are face-up

This game can be implemented using either a top-down or an object-oriented approach. If you want, you can try it using the top-down approach, but you're guaranteed to end up with a bunch of if-then-else statements as long as your arm, and more variables than you would believe!

Instead, let's look at it from an object-oriented point of view.

Your first thoughts should be about what the fundamental objects of the game are. In this case it's quite obvious - the only things being manipulated in this game are the *tiles*. So if we can create a generalized tile object with an appropriate range of behaviors, then we've cracked the whole game. What do we want the tile to be able to do?

At a guess, we'd want it to be able to do the following:

- Be face down when it's unselected

- Turn face up when it's selected, and tell the user and Flash what symbol it has on it

- Be able to ask Flash when the current turn has finished, and if it's not one of a pair, to turn back to its initial state, or stay face up if it *is* one of a pair

Notice that there are a few things we *haven't* defined as necessary to know. Things like:

- How many tiles there are

- How many different tile symbols there will be

- How many tiles are already face up

- How many tiles are already face down

We don't need to know these things because the object we're looking at creating will represent only one tile. All these bits of information don't apply to *one* tile, they apply to *many* tiles working alongside each other. So, using our object-oriented design method, we'll first create the object, and then when that's working fine we'll go on to the next step up and build the object into the game - it's the game structure that provides the *context* for the tile's behavior, whereas the behavior is all built into the tile itself.

But wait a minute...

Part of this definition sounds strangely familiar. The mouse trail we just created stays still when it's not selected, and then does something when it *has* been selected. This is a subset of the same sort of behavior we want for our tile. The only difference is that the mouse trail circles were all identical, but the tiles we want to create will be different. Can we re-use part of the previous exercise? It might be a good starting point.

Creating the Tile

1. Start a new movie. In **Modify > Movie** set the movie background to purple, and the dimensions to **800x800**.

    In the last tutorial we created a circle to start off with, and created a button that was the same size and shape to 'trigger' the movie into action, and we'll do the same thing here.

2. Create a new graphic symbol and call it **sy.tile**.

3. Next, create a tile shape by drawing a rectangle with rounded edges, the same as you did for your playing cards earlier in the book - you could even use them, but remember to take the character off the front, as we want them to be blank for now. Center your tile on the stage:

4. Use the **Option** menu from the library to duplicate the symbol as a button, the same way as you did in the last example. Call this symbol **bu.transparent** - the reason for this name will become clear in a moment.

5. Add a keyframe in the button's Hit state and clear its Up state to create a button that's invisible, but still hittable.

6. The next thing we need are some pictures to go on the tiles. We've provided a set of pictures of fruit on our web site that you can download and use, otherwise feel free to come up with whatever you want. For this example we'll be using four different pictures: a tomato, an orange, a lemon, and a pear:

   Import them, and convert your four individual images to graphic symbols, and give them appropriate names: we've called ours **sy.fruit.tomato**, **sy.fruit.orange**, **sy.fruit.lemon**, and **sy.fruit.pear**.

7. Now you need to put all of these together to make your tile. First of all, create a new movie clip symbol and call it **mc.tile**.

   We know that we'll need to have a button and an animation in this object, so we'll put them in now.

8. Rename the first layer tile, then create a new layer and name it **button**.

   In the tile layer, we'll create an animation of the tile turning over, and to create this effect we'll use the same kind of illusion we implemented for the 'flipping face' tween in Chapter 7.

9. In frame 1 of the tile layer, drag in a copy of **sy.tile** from the library and center it at **0,0**. Now add keyframes at frames 5 and 10.

10. The next thing is to create an animation of the tile flipping over. To do this, we'll make the tile get progressively shorter as it moves between frames 1 to 5, and then grow again until it's back up to its normal size in frame 10. This will give the illusion that the tile is flipping over. Click on frame 5 and use the **Info** panel to set the height (**H**) value to 1:

11. Now add two separate motion tweens between frames 1 and 5, and frames 5 and 10:

At the moment your flipping tile won't really seem very convincing as both sides look the same, but when the picture is on one side the illusion will be complete.

12. Create a new layer and call it **fruit**. What we want to do is make the fruit start to appear from frame 5 onwards, and grow in size until it's full size in frame 10.

13. Insert a keyframe in frame 10 of your **fruit** layer and drag a copy of one of your graphic symbols onto the stage - we're using the tomato symbol. Center your symbol and resize it until it fits nicely onto your tile:

14. Add a new keyframe at frame 5, then copy the fruit from frame 10 and paste it in place into frame 5. Now, here's the trick: we want the tomato to be as thin as the tile at frame 5, so using the **Info** panel, change the tomato's **H:** value to 1, the same value as the tile. At frame 5 you should now have a 'squashed' tile and a 'squashed' tomato over the top of it.

15. Finally, create a motion tween from frame 5 to 10. Your animation should now give a convincing impression of a tile flipping over:

The tile should start of blank then shrink to nothing, before growing back to full size again with the tomato image on it.

16. Once the tile has flipped over face up, the next thing we'll want it to do is flip it back over to its initial face down position. This motion would simply look like the animation we've created so far in frames 1 to 10, but in reverse. Create a new keyframe in frame 15 of your **fruit** and **tile** layers.

17. Select frames 1 through 10 on the tile layer and use the **Edit > Copy Frames** command to copy them to the clipboard.

18. Now click in Frame 15 of the layer and use the **Edit > Paste Frames** command to paste the frames into the timeline:

You don't need to reverse these frames, as you'll see it looks fine if you play the movie clip.

19. If you were to do the same thing with the tomato animation though, it would be the wrong way round. Click in frame 5 on the **fruit** layer and again, use the **Edit > Copy Frames** command to copy it to the clipboard.

20. Now click in frame 19 on the same layer and paste the frame there. Finally, set up a motion tween between frames 15 and 19:

Now when you play back your movie clip, it should run through with no trouble.

So you now have a tile that starts face-down, flips face-up, then flips back to face-down again. The next thing you need are the actions...

Making the Tile Work

The tile should only flip when it's selected, so you need to incorporate a button into the movie clip to trigger this behavior.

The button will go into frame 1 of the **button** layer. This layer should only have a single frame in it: once the tile has started flipping we don't want the user to be able to select it again as this could create problems later on in the game.

1. Drag your **bu.transparent** symbol from your library and onto the stage, and center it on your existing tile. If you find it easier, you may want to hide and lock the other two layers by clicking on the eye and lock icons on the timeline.

   The first thing we want the button to do when we click on it is to start playing the movie clip. We can do this with some simple ActionScript.

2. Open up the **Object Actions** window for your button and insert an **On Mouse Event** action, change the **Event** from **Release** to **Press**, then put a **Play** action in. You should be left with this code:

   ```
   on (press) {
       play ();
   }
   ```

3. We'll be adding a lot of actions to the tile object, so to keep things neat create a new layer at the top of the stack and name it **actions**.

4. The first actions we need to put in are the easiest, we want the tile to pause in the first frame until the button is clicked, so put a **Stop** action into frame 1.

5. We also want to be able to refer to the frame by name, so put a label in it and call it **facedown**.

6. The other simple thing we want the tile to do is to return to the first frame when it finishes running through the animation. We can do this by putting a keyframe with a **Go To** action into frame 24. Change the frame to point to the **Frame Label** called **facedown** and make it **Go to and Stop**. This should leave you with the following code:

   ```
   gotoAndStop ("facedown");
   ```

7. Go back to the main stage and drag a copy of your movie clip out from the library. It doesn't matter where you place it, as it's only there so we can test the movie.

8. Now play your movie. The tile should stay blank until you click on it, then it will cycle through its animation and return to the face-down state. You should only be able to click on it in its fully face-down state.

The next thing you need to do is to have the tile stop when it's fully face-up.

9.   Unfortunately, you'll need a little more than a **Stop** action in this frame - we also want the tile to tell the user, and Flash, what symbol it has on it. The user bit's easy, as they can see the picture on top of the tile, but telling Flash is a little more complicated. The questions that you should be asking are:

  • Who or what do we tell?

  • How do we tell it, and what does it need to know?

One of the fundamental things to realize when you're creating object-oriented programs is that you have to know which parts of the program fit inside of one object, and which parts fit into another object or into external code. This is a difficult concept to grasp at first, but if you think '*What's the game doing? What can a tile do, and should it be able to do that?*' it quickly becomes obvious that the pieces of a game - the tiles - should not be the *controllers* of the action. So what *should* be controlling the game? The rules should, or a referee who knows the rules.

The referee for this game will be the main timeline, and it's that which will be in control. The tiles are just saying things like 'Okay, I am a tile object, and I have just flipped over', and nothing more. This is because we need to be able to add as many tile objects to the final game as we like. This is the beauty of object-oriented design: the tiles are just objects that we can plug in to the program any number of times without having to recode them. They are *self-contained*.

As you know from the last chapter, the main timeline is called **_root**. While using the root would be fine for our movie, it would stop it from being truly object oriented. Remember what we said earlier about objects being reusable? Well, to keep this reusability as open as possible, we don't want to always tie things to the main timeline. The way we can get round this is to instead give control of the movie clip to the next level up: by doing this, we'll be able to move the code around within the levels of a movie and still have it work. The name for the next level up in Flash is the **parent**. By telling the movie clip to talk to the parent level, we're keeping it as a separate portable object - wherever you place a tile in a movie hierarchy, this notation will ensure that it always talks to the next level up, irrespective of the name of that level's timeline.

That answers the first question, but now we know we should be talking to the parent, what do we want to tell it? The parent needs to know what's on the tile, and in this case it's a *tomato*.

10. In your movie clip, insert a keyframe into frame 9 of the **actions** layer and attach a set variable action to it. In the **Variable** field put **_parent.fruit**, and put **tomato** into the **Value** field. Leave both of the **Expression** boxes unchecked:

Why is this action on frame 9, and not in its logical place on frame 10? Well, we know that there will be a lot more actions to come that deal with the number of tiles turned over, and whether they're a pair or not, so to keep things as tidy as possible we're keeping this piece of code separate from that piece.

The next thing to do is test to see whether Flash can now tell which fruit is on the tile.

11. Go back to the main movie timeline and draw a text field below the tile. Make the text field dynamic and non-selectable, and check the **Border/BG** box to make Flash draw a box around your text. Finally, assign it to the variable **fruit**:

12. Now test the movie.

This time just as the tile has flipped over, and you'll see the tile communicating with the **_parent**, telling it what the variable **fruit** now is:

tomato

You could also have used the **Debugger** window to tell you the same information.

You've now got one tile working pretty well, but the game won't be much fun with only one tile! The next thing to do is test it with *multiple* tiles, and see what sort of problems arise.

Using Multiple Tiles

You now need to start thinking how you want each tile to work when there is more than one tile on the stage.

1. Add another three tiles to your main stage to make a row of four in all. You can tidy up the row by using the **Align** panel:

2. Now test the movie. There are a few things to notice here:

- Your text field won't change after you've selected the first tile because *all* of the tiles are tomatoes

- It's possible to flip more than two tiles at the same time

- The first tile doesn't wait until the second tile has been flipped before it flips itself back round, so you'd have to be pretty quick to match a pair

The first problem should sort itself out once we start using different fruit, so we don't need to worry about that.

For the second problem, we need to count the number of tiles that are now face-up: if it's two or more, we shouldn't allow any other tiles to flip. To do this, we'll need a variable to count the number of tiles that have been flipped.

To fix the third problem, we need the first tile to wait until one other tile is face-up before it flips itself back over.

3. Go back to the movie clip and open up the actions for frame 9. We've already told the parent that the fruit on this symbol is a tomato, so this is also a good place to tell it that a button has just been pressed.

4. Add a **set variable** action to the frame, type **_parent.buttonpress** into the **Variable** field, and in the **Value** field write **++ _parent.buttonpress** and make it an **Expression**:

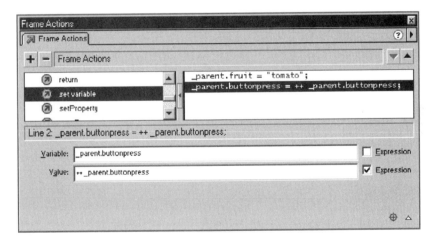

You haven't yet encountered the **++** command. What it means is 'add one to this', so in our example it will add one to **_parent.buttonpress** every time the movie clip is played. It's a handy code shortcut that you'll come to use time and time again in your ActionScript. Once you start to use the **Actions** window in expert mode, you'll come across an even shorter form of writing this, but for now we'll stay with the relatively simple normal mode.

Now that you know how many times a button has been pressed, you can set about telling Flash to stop more than two tiles being flipped at the same time.

5. Click on the button symbol in the **button** layer and view its actions in the **Object Actions** window. You already have a couple of actions in the button,

but now you need another one. Attach an **If** action to the button and type **_parent.buttonpress < 2** in the **Condition** field. Finally, use the up and down arrows to make sure that your ActionScript looks like this:

```
on (press) {
  if (_parent.buttonpress < 2) {
    play ();
  }
}
```

This checks our variable called **buttonpress** in the parent timeline. It says, 'If we've already pressed *any* two other buttons, don't respond to any more button presses'. The beauty of tying **buttonpress** to the parent and not to each tile is that all of the tile objects will look at the same variable. They don't need to know *which* other buttons have been pressed, they will respond as soon as any two buttons are pressed.

6. Test the movie to confirm this.

   The third problem is a bit more involved. What we want to do is:

   • Make the parent count how many times *any* button has been pressed

   • Keep the first tile flipped until a second is face up

   • Make some decisions on whether the tiles match or not

   Hang on, the first part of that sounds a bit familiar: **buttonpress** already does that - it tells the main timeline how many buttons have been pressed so far, and when this number is equal to two we know that the player has picked a pair, and that the current turn is over whether they match or not.

   The next part of our task is to make the tile stay face up until our referee tells it that the current turn is over. We'll create a new variable called **hadgo** to help us with that.

7. Create a new layer in the main timeline and name it **actions**. Name the other layer **tiles**.

   The first frame of the **actions** layer will set up the variables that apply to the whole game, and the second will hold those that deal with each turn.

8. Insert a keyframe into frame 2 of the **actions** layer. There are three things that we want to happen at the beginning of every go: (1) we want the **fruit** variable to be reset; (2) we want the **buttonpress** variable to be put back to 0; (3) we want our new variable **hadgo** to be implemented.

9. To do this we need three **set variable** actions:

   ```
   fruit = "";
   buttonpress = 0;
   hadgo = false;
   ```

   - For **fruit**, leave the **Value** field and the **Expression** box blank

   - For **buttonpress**, put **0** into the **Value** field and make it an expression

   - For **hadgo**, put **false** into the **Value** field and make it an expression

   That's all of our initializations done. Now it's time to set up our turn loop using **hadgo**.

10. Open the **actions** layer of your movie clip and create keyframes at frames 10 and 11.

11. Put a label in frame 10 and call it **buttonloop**.

12. Now we'll add some actions to frame 11. First, add an **If** action with the **Condition: _parent.hadgo == false**. (Don't forget the double equals sign!)

13. Now add a **Goto** action pointing back to your **buttonloop** label.

    This should leave you with the following code:

    ```
    if (_parent.hadgo == false) {
        gotoAndPlay ("buttonloop");
    }
    ```

    This bit of code looks to see if the player has had their turn, and stays face up until the turn has finished by constantly looping back to the previous frame labeled **buttonloop**. At the moment, this will be an infinite loop as **hadgo** is *always* false. Don't worry, this'll all be working after we get a bit more code in.

14. Go back to the **actions** layer on the main timeline and insert keyframes in frames 4 and 5. In these frames we want to wait until two tiles have been turned over, and we know that this will be when **buttonpress** is equal to 2. So, we want a similar loop to the one that we've just used, but with **buttonpress** as the condition rather than **hadgo**. We also need to set up a new label for the loop.

15. Click in frame 4 and label it **pressloop**.

16. Now we need to add our code in frame 5. The **If** action is straightforward:

```
if (buttonpress == 2) {
}
```

But this time, if the condition is true, and therefore the user has flipped two tiles over, we want to set **hadgo** to *true*.

17. Insert a **set variable** action inside the **If** statement to this effect:

```
hadgo = true;
```

Remember to make this an expression.

18. The last thing to do is to finish the loop by putting a **Go to** action at the end to send it back our **pressloop** label. Your code for this frame should look like this:

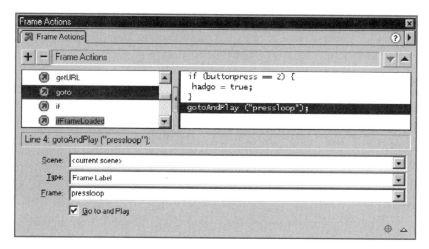

19. Use **F5**, to insert a frame at frame 5 of the **tiles** layer. We need to do this to make sure the tiles are visible throughout the movie. Now you can test your game...

There are now two separate loops running at the same time, one waiting for **buttonpress** to equal 2, and one waiting for **hadgo** to be true. Flash will stay within frames 4 and 5 on the main timeline until two tiles have been turned face-up. When this happens it will set **hadgo** to true. As soon as **hadgo** is true, the loop in frame 11 of the two face-up tiles will open and the animation will run through to the end and flip the tiles back over. We haven't yet put an action in to set **hadgo** back to false, so at the moment it will only run through once.

Notice that there is no need to control the tiles that have not been touched in this turn. What this means is that you could add as many tiles as you wanted now, and Flash wouldn't care because it's only looking for two face-up tiles and isn't counting the face-down ones. The reason you've been able to design in this way is because you've used an object-oriented approach - the problem was abstracted down to its minimum variables and conditions. Things that you might have thought the referee and the tiles would have needed to know turn out to be irrelevant. How do you know they are irrelevant? Well you don't really, you just know that it seems to work without them, and if it isn't broken, why fix it? It may seem a bit simpleminded to not even consider any other things, but simplicity is the key to object-oriented design, and being simpleminded takes a lot of practice.

We've almost completed the game now, the only things left to do are to run through what happens at the end of each turn, and then tell it to start the next one.

Sorting Out the Main Timeline

So, the things we want to happen at the end of each turn are:

- When a matching pair has been uncovered we need to tell the tiles to stay face up

- When a matching pair has been uncovered we need to note that there is one less pair to find

- When all the pairs have been found Flash must be able to detect this, and finish the game

  Notice again that we're not actually interested in things that you might think we should be, like the number of tiles and the number of different symbols there are on the tiles. They are not part of the problem even though they are part of the game. The important thing in this game is to find pairs, and it's this that determines our definition of the referee.

  We'll start with a 4 x 4 playing board, which will include 8 pairs. This will be constant for every game, so this value will go in frame 1 of the **actions** layer on the main timeline. This layer is blank at the moment, but remember that we decided this frame would contain the variables that would be initialized only once for each game.

1. On the main timeline, click in frame 1 of the **actions** layer, and add a **set variable** action. This variable will tell Flash how many pairs there are, so it will know that when it's flipped over this many pairs, the game is over. Set the variable to **pairs**, give it a value of **8**, and make it an expression:

    pairs = 8;

2. In frame 2, we've already initialized **fruit**, **buttonpress**, and **hadgo**. Now we also want to initialize variables that allow us to decide if there was a match or not. We need to know which fruit was on the first tile and which fruit was on the second tile, and we can then work out if they match. So, we need to add another three set variable actions to this frame.

    One to say what's on the first tile:

    fruit1 = "";

    One to say what's on the second tile:

    fruit2 = "";

    And a final one to say if they match:

    match = false;

    The ActionScript for this frame will now look like this:

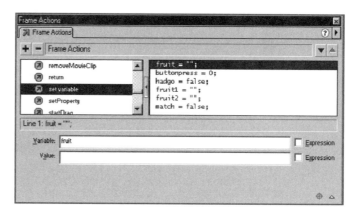

    We now need to alter our loop in frame 5 to include these new values. There are three possible conditions our referee will have to look at in this loop:

    •   No tiles have been flipped

- One tile has been flipped - Flash will need to know what the revealed fruit was and put it in **fruit1**

- Two tiles have been flipped - Flash will need to know what the second revealed fruit was and put it in **fruit2**

If two tiles have been pressed then the turn has finished, so we need to do a couple more things. We need to see if **fruit1** and **fruit2** are the same, and if they are we need to set **match** to true. Then when **match** is true, we need to reduce the number of pairs by 1 so Flash will know when the game is over.

3. Open the actions for frame 5. At the moment we just have a **buttonpress** loop running here, but we need to modify this quite heavily. So that we can see clearly what we're doing in this frame, delete all of the actions that are in it.

4. Add an **If** action to the blank frame 5, with the condition **buttonpress == 0**.

5. Attach a **Goto** action telling Flash to loop back and play the frame labeled **pressloop**. This is just a basic **If** statement to keep on looping until a button is pressed.

6. Put in an **Else If** action and set the condition to **buttonpress == 1**.

7. Now add a **set variable** action setting the variable **fruit1** to the value **fruit**, and make it an expression.

8. Attach another **Goto pressloop** command. This loop has stored what was on the first tile and looped back to allow the user to select a second tile.

9. Put in another **Else If** action, and give it the condition **buttonpress == 2**.

10. Now set the variable **fruit2** to the value of **fruit** (for the second tile) and make it an expression.

11. That's now the end of the user's go because two tiles has been flipped over, so set **hadgo** to **true**, and make it an expression the same as you had it before. Your ActionScript should now look like this:

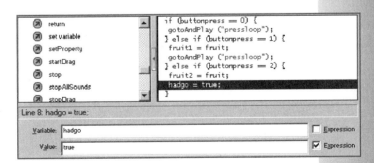

Now you need to put in the final code that'll test to see if the tiles match. The first thing you need to be able to do is to compare the **fruit1** and **fruit2**. This can be done using the same **==** that we've been using because we're comparing variables. If we had been comparing strings, Flash would have just compared the number of characters in each string.

12. Add another **If** action with the condition **fruit1 == fruit2**.

13. Finally, we need to put in what we want to happen if the tiles *do* match. Attach another couple of **set variable** actions. The first should decrease **pairs** by 1, so **pairs = -- pairs** (remember that **++** means add 1 to, so it follows that -- means take one away from). The second needs to tell Flash that we've found a match, so **match = true**. Both of these values should be expressions.

14. Your completed code for this frame should read:

```
if (buttonpress == 0) {
    gotoAndPlay ("pressloop");
} else if (buttonpress == 1) {
    fruit1 = fruit;
    gotoAndPlay ("pressloop");
} else if (buttonpress == 2) {
    fruit2 = fruit;
    hadgo = true;
    if (fruit1 == fruit2) {
        pairs = -- pairs;
        match = true;
    }
}
```

15. Test your movie.

You'll be able to flip over a tile, and then Flash will wait for you to flip over another tile before carrying on. When you've flipped over two tiles, Flash will start back at the beginning of the game. At the moment, when two tiles have been flipped over, Flash is going all the way back to frame 1 and starting again. This is a problem: we only wanted frame 1 to be played once at the very beginning of every game, whereas after two tiles are turned over we only want Flash to go back as far as frame 2.

16. Click on frame 2 in the **actions** layer of the main movie, and label it **mainloop**.

The next thing we need to do is set up a loop to make Flash go back to **mainloop** at the end of each turn. We want to give the player the chance to have another go unless they have already found all of the pairs. So we only want to take another turn if **pairs** has not yet been reduced to zero.

After frame 5, the tiles will be flipping back to their face-down state, so we'll allow a bit of time for this before we start adding more actions to the main timeline.

17. Add a keyframe in frame 11. Additionally, put a normal frame in frame 11 of the **tiles** layer to keep them displayed on the screen throughout the game:

18. Add an **If** statement to frame 11 on the **actions** layer with the condition **pairs > 0**. Then put a **Goto** action in to send it back to **mainloop**, giving you the code:

```
if (pairs > 0) {
    gotoAndPlay ("mainloop");
}
```

There's one more thing to do before you test your movie: when the user's found all of the pairs, we want them to get a reward. For simplicity, we're just going to have a screen saying 'Well Done', but we'll put it on another layer to give you room to go to town with it.

19. Add a new layer to the main timeline and name it **finished**, then put a keyframe in frame 26. Add a keyframe to frame 26 of the **actions** layer as well, but only put a normal frame in frame 25 of the **tiles** layer. This is because we don't want the tiles to be visible on the victory screen. Of course, if you want the user to be able to carry on admiring their handiwork, you can keep the tiles in all the way to frame 26.

20. Put a **Stop** action in frame 26 in the **actions** layer.

21. Now draw your victory screen in frame 26 of the **finished** layer. We've just put "**Congratulations, You've Completed the Game!!!**" in big green letters across the stage. Handsome.

And that's the main timeline done. You can now test your game, as the whole thing should be working perfectly. Because we've currently only got one fruit on the stage, you'll have to select eight pairs of the same thing, but you can see how spectacular it will be when we have the full range of flora in there.

Adding the Final Touches

The only thing left to do is tell our tiles to stay face-up when they are a pair, we'll also put in a little animation to make them look different when they're matched.

Back in the movie clip, the crucial frame is frame 11. This frame is the brains behind the whole object because it decides what the tile is going to do next once it has flipped face up. At the moment, it's just looking for the root to tell it whether the current turn has finished via **hadgo**. Once **hadgo** is true, either one or the other of two conditions will exist:

- This tile is one of a matching pair, and _parent.match is true

- This tile is not one of a matching pair, and _parent.match is false

1. At the end of the current **If** statement on frame 11 (the line with the **Goto** action on), add an **else if** action with the condition **_parent.match == true**.

   You *could* just put a **Stop** action in next to keep the frame face up if it's part of a pair, but we're going to go one step further and put in a little animation. There's no need to check whether **_parent.match** is false because if it isn't true, then it can clearly only be false. In our code, if it's false the timeline just carries on to the 'flip back over' animation, which is what we want to happen for a turn that ends in no match anyway.

2. Add a **Goto** action pointing to a label, and type **done** into the Frame **field**. You should have this code:

   ```
   if (_parent.hadgo == false) {
       gotoAndPlay ("buttonloop");
   } else if (_parent.match == true) {
       gotoAndPlay ("done");
   }
   ```

   At the moment there is no frame called **done**, so we'll have to make one.

3. Put a keyframe into frame 35 of the actions layer and label it **done**. Then put another keyframe into frame 43 and put a **Stop** action in it:

4. Put a blank keyframe into frame 20 of the **fruit** layer, then put a normal keyframe in frame 35, and a plain frame in 43. Finally, copy the tomato from frame 15 and paste it in place in frame 35.

5. On the tile layer, put a keyframe in frames 35 and 43. Your timeline should now be complete:

6. Use the **Effects Panel** to set the **Brightness** of the tile in frame 43 to **100%**, then put a motion tween between frames 35 and 43 to make it glow when a pair is found.

   You can test this glow effect now by playing the movie and turning over two tiles. Unfortunately, now that we've put in this last piece of code, the game is no longer 'completable'. We've told it that there are eight pairs to be found, but we've only got two pairs on the stage. It's time to add the rest of our fruit and get the game working.

7. We need a new tile object for each of our four fruits, the one that we've been using so far has got a tomato on it, so rename it **mc.tile.tomato**.

8. Duplicate this object three times in the library, and name the copies **mc.tile.lemon**, **mc.tile.orange** and **mc.tile.pear** respectively.

   We'll change the lemon movie clip now, then you can go back and do the same to the orange and the pear clips. There are two things that we need to do to make our transformation complete: change all of the pictures of tomatoes into lemons, and change the ActionScript that tells the timeline which fruit it is.

9. Start by locking all of the layers except for **fruit**. We know that all of the keyframes on this layer currently contain a tomato, and we need to change them even when they're squashed so much that you can't see them.

10. Click on the first keyframe in frame 5, and use the **Swap Symbol** button on the **Instance Panel** to change the tomato for **sy.fruit.lemon**.

11. Now run through the rest of the keyframes, and perform the same operation on each.

Once you've done this to all 5 keyframes, your tomato will look like a lemon, but it will still *think* it's a tomato. So we need to retrain it - luckily this isn't as hard as it sounds.

12. Open up the actions for frame 9 in the **actions** layer. At the moment the variable reads:

   _parent.fruit = "tomato";

So this needs to be changed to read:

   _parent.fruit = "lemon";

And that's it. Now you just need to go back through the two fruit conversion stages for your pear and orange movie clips, and you're ready to make the game board.

13. Go back to the tiles layer of your main timeline and delete everything that's currently on the stage. Now randomly place four of each movie clip into the stage in a 4 x 4 grid. Use the **Align** panel to tidy up the tiles and get them into neat rows:

And that's it. You're now ready to show off your first complete Flash game. Congratulations.

Possible Improvements and Modifications to your Game

You're probably staring in disbelief at this title: it's taken you long enough to get the game working, and there's *no way* you're going to change it now. At the back of your mind though, there's a niggling little voice saying, "It would be nice if there were a few more fruits so I only needed *one* pair of each, and maybe if there were a few more tiles, and while I'm at it that victory screen could really do with improving..." This section has been dictated by that voice.

- You can add as many as you want, creating a 16x16 or even a 32x32 grid if your eyes are up to seeing tiles that small. All you have to do is to change the initial value of **pairs** (in frame 1 of the main timeline's **actions** layer) to how may pairs there are to find

- You could make a timer, or a turn counter to score each game

- You could make a scoring system where the player scores 5 points for each correct tile, but lose 2 for each wrong tile

- For those feeling really confident, you could figure out how to make the game deal a random set of tiles every time a new game is started

This game is more advanced than the simple mouse trail it's derived from. You can use it as the basis of other, even more advanced games. You could, for example, take the basic **mc.tile** and, realizing that it allows you to model a generalized 'playing card' object, go ahead and make some rather cool card games.

But what has this to do with web site design? Well, web sites and games are two branches of a tree called *interactivity*. There is an offshoot from the web site branch that's very close to the game branch, and that offshoot is called *advanced web site design*. Both make use of lots of clever bits of ActionScript to create their animations, interfaces and effects. By learning simple games, you're priming yourself for the design and coding of *complex* sites.

The next chapter will start to look at web site design and point you on your way. You've reached base camp one on the ActionScript Everest, and, armed with what you've learned so far, combined with that little niggling voice that keeps on asking questions and telling you to try new things, the only way is up. Never lose sight of the main goal, and have fun - it'll be worth it.

Summary

In this chapter, we've dipped our toe into the vast ocean that is object oriented design and programming. We've looked at the basic principles of the **OO** approach, and seen how we can map this onto the movie clip objects we use in Flash.

We saw that:

- Object oriented design and programming delivers solutions that are:

    - Reusable

    - Extensible

    - Flexible

- The key to OO design and programming is the ability to abstract yourself away from the surface detail of a problem until you can define its absolutely essential components

- A class defines the characteristics of one of those components - what it is, what it can do, what its characteristics are, and how it communicates with other components. The class is a template

- An object is an individual instance built using the class template

- In Flash, you can think of a named movie clip instance on the stage as an object. This object is derived from the original library movie clip symbol. All instances of the symbol on the stage will share the same essential properties, but we can customize them so that their behavior and properties 'individualize' them

    - Simple movie clip objects can be combined to produce complex effects

In the next chapter, we're going to look at the considerations you need to take into account when you're **designing** your Flash site.

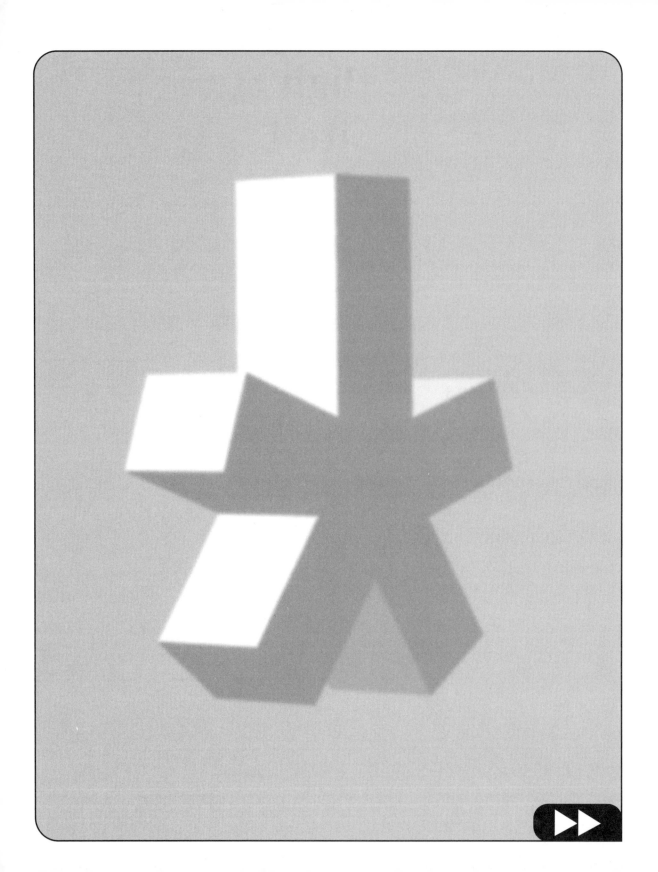

16

High Level
Site Design

What we'll cover in this chapter:

- *The principles of good design*

- *Introduction to site formation*

- *A look at dynamic site design*

- *The authors' recommended web sites*

At this point in the book you can afford to congratulate yourself on your new status as an intermediate Flash programmer/designer. It's been a hard road, but it was worth it. Before you rush off into the crowded world of web design though, there are a couple more things to think about. So far, this book has been about the actual technical implementation of your ideas inside Flash, but this chapter will run through some tips on what to do when you first have that spark of inspiration, and how to make sure it will work on the web. It's here to give you a rough guide to some of the 'do's and 'don'ts' of designing for the web, both by reminding you of some of the considerations we've discussed earlier in the book, and by drawing new ones to your attention. At the end of the chapter there's a list of sites recommended by two of the authors, Pat and Amanda, to fire your imagination into action and get those designs flowing. Before that though, Sham, the third member of our team, is going to discuss some of the principles he follows when creating his designs, and talk you through a few of the sites he's created himself.

The Principles of Good Design

When I was in my early twenties, I worked in a design team that was creating VDU display screens for use in a nuclear power plant. The screens were going to be used by the operators as their primary point of reference to see what was going on in the plant. In an emergency, the reactor engineers had to be able to access the information they needed as quickly as possible, and it had to be shown in a form they could understand immediately. If the engineers had to move to another location to find more detailed information, the path they needed to follow had to be clearly laid out. It was important that the screens never showed too much information - just the relevant information that the engineer had asked to see.

The rules I followed to resolve this project are just as important to the work I do today because now, as then, my projects have the same basic requirements: **usability and clarity**. Of course, web sites have to be engaging, interesting and entertaining as well, but that's really down to the choice of *content* you display. To be engaged, interested and entertained, the user has to be able to *find* the content first. There are sites out there that intentionally break the rules, and are entertaining because of it. But the people who are able to get away with this are always *aware* of the rules they're breaking.

These principles, important as they are for the usability of your site, will not bring you success on their own: *originality* is another defining feature of good web design. Sites that don't catch the eye and draw in the mind with good ideas and solid graphic design will get fewer visitors.

Flash is a cost *and* bandwidth effective design tool with bucket loads of features that enable you to capture your visitors with compelling visuals and sound. One of the reasons that Flash has taken over the net is its high number of creative options compared to HTML - all of them viewable with a small and simple plug-in. However, over-indulgence will make viewers leave your site if they've already 'seen it all before' or are fed up with the two-minute download time. There's a fine line between multimedia and 'junkmedia', and the designer must always be aware of which side they're on. In your design career, you're going to have to learn to balance creativity with practicality - in this chapter I'm going to talk about both.

File Structure and File Sizes

Whenever you do anything on the web, you have to be aware - even if it's only at the back of your mind - of what the web *is* and what it will do to your presentation as your files are downloaded or streamed across the web. We talked about these issues in the Optimization and Publishing chapters, but we'll re-iterate some of the main points again here:

- Be aware of download times and optimize as much as possible to lower them

- Differentiate between what's *central* to the message you're trying to get across, and what's just eye (or ear) candy. If download times are an issue, you should know which parts of your movie can be the first to end up on the cutting room floor

- Consider a multiple **loadMovie** download strategy (as shown in the Publishing chapter) to avoid a large initial download

- Take special care with bitmaps and sound. Optimize them all individually and don't rely on the global export settings to do the job for you

- Choose your symbols carefully and use a 'one symbol often' approach in preference to 'lots of symbols used once each'

- Remember that ActionScript-based 'sprite' animation is particularly bandwidth friendly: it requires far fewer frames than the corresponding tween-based animations

The chapters on Optimizing and Publishing told us all about structuring our movies correctly, but I'm going to reiterate the main points again because your increased understanding of ActionScript will help you to understand the basis of more advanced solutions.

Preloaders

One of the things we looked at earlier was the **preloader**. I work with three levels of preloader so I'll give you a brief description of their varying degrees of complexity:

Basic: Timeline-based Loader

The most basic preloader has been introduced in the Optimization chapter, and I would recommend anyone who doesn't want to get their hands dirty with ActionScript, or has a relatively simple and small .swf, to go for this option.

Intermediate: ActionScript-based Loader

You can build a very efficient ActionScript preloader by looking at the **_framesloaded** and **_totalframes** properties of your movie. These are two properties of the main timeline that you can view just like any other variable - for example, using the **Properties** tab in the
Debugger window:

When these two values are equal, you know that the whole of your .swf has been loaded. Essentially, what you would do here is create a simple animation to keep the user interested while the main site loads up, and use ActionScript to tell it to stop playing and go to the main site once the movie properties **_totalframes** and **_framesloaded** and equal to each other.

Intermediate/Advanced: Bandwidth Manager Object

The most sophisticated preloader I have is a 'loading manager' object that I coded recently. It constantly looks at what's currently being loaded, and if nothing is, it looks to see if there are any other .swf levels to load via **loadMovie** and sets them off loading in the background. All the additional loaded .swfs have a blank frame 1 with a **Stop** action in it: they just sit there, hidden (because the first frame is empty), until the lowest level sets them off with a **Play** action. You can tell that 'nothing is being loaded' if

_totalframes and **_framesloaded** are equal for the last level of .swf that you set off loading.

If you decide to embark on this project, remember **never to unload an already loaded .swf level** - instead, you can just send it back to its first (blank) frame, where it will remain invisible to watching eyes. A problem arises here if the user requests a .swf other than the one that the manager is currently loading, but explaining that is beyond the scope of this chapter. When your knowledge is sufficient to solve this problem you'll be ready to code the loading manager, and you'll have an extremely efficient method of loading your web sites - which, as we've said, is one of the main practical concerns of any web designer.

Intros

What you show during your preload is another major concern. A good intro (the animation that hides your pre-load) will draw the viewer into the main web site, whereas a poor one will resemble a cheesy rock band's guitar solo - it'll go on for *far* too long.

As a general rule, always have something interesting going on whilst the main site is loading. As we've said, the average Internet surfer will not stay long if you've a 'please wait, loading...' screen up, and it's in this context that an intro really becomes useful. In my view, your intro must:

- Show the user what'll be missed if they click away

- Give an indication of the quality of the web site proper

- Give the viewer the option to skip past it if they want to

Different types of website require different intros. If you were creating a website advertising you as a web site designer, you'd want to show off your technical ability and give the potential client a showcase of your advanced understanding of complex animation and your graphic design ability. This would not be the case if you were designing an information service for a bank. In this case, the viewer wants to see the information they came to look at, and they want it *fast and clear*. They need to be attracted to the site by a cool and slick Flash design, but once they decide to open an account the route to the 'sign me up' web page must just be a click away and free of over-indulgent Flash animation and tricks. Making your design *appropriate* to your client and audience is another vital consideration.

Tailoring Your Designs

Summarizing the large number of constraints and features that make up a good web site in a single paragraph is an impossible task (watch this space for future friends of ED books...). However, there are a number of checklist items that you should at least be aware of when you come to sit down and build your main site:

Timescales

We all want to build the coolest Flash sites possible, but if you are doing this for a living, you need to think about how soon the site is required. A good site, delivered on time will always get you a satisfied customer, whereas a brilliant cutting edge site delivered three weeks late *won't*. Remember, it's very difficult to change a site once it's up (people tend to become accustomed to the navigation and style) so be careful - unless, of course the change is the *client's* idea and they're paying by the hour...;-).

Site Style

The style you choose for the site is defined in part by the content and the impression that the client wants to get across to the viewer. When defining a style, be careful to choose one because it's actually suited to the message, not because it's easy to create in Flash. A lot of the time, the client already has a brief or advertising campaign that the site will be part of, so you should be flexible enough to take on their ideas and jump between styles.

Content

Unless you're creating a site based on a very specific brief, where the client has provided all the site graphics and type, you'll have to find a way to hold the audience's attention long enough to put the site's message across. The coolest visual Flash interface will be ignored if it's not properly integrated with something *interesting*.

Navigation

The content of your site will greatly influence the navigation you create for it. In some (especially commercial) sites there's a 'route that you'd prefer the visitor to take' - meaning the one that'll most likely result in a sale or a 'click-through' to your sponsor. Your navigation must make this route clear. Other sites are based around a central 'hub', with numerous links going out to sub-topics. In these sites, it's important that the user can quickly access *any* area of the site, and, as a general rule, they should be able to do it *within two clicks*.

In all of these things, there's no substitute for practical experience. To this end, I've included walk-throughs of some site designs I've been involved in, to illustrate different methods of visualizing and creating a web site.

Case Study 1: Online Showcase

A few years ago (which equates to several decades in Flash years), I found a really old looking poetry book that contained a lot of verse dating back to Victorian England. Reading it, I was particularly taken by how different their thinking was to that of the twentieth century: whereas we live in an age where everything is out in the open (especially on the web), they had a much more closed and hidden society.

I decided to update this book and put a fully interactive version onto the web, using all the new technology available to me. I had to create a web site that had the same sort of feel as the book, because I wanted to use the language of the book to present this bygone world and give a sense of the cultural and behavioral beliefs implicit in the book. But I wanted to present it via Flash animations.

Before I went into the Flash implementation I had to have a very clear idea of what I wanted to create, because I could see this being a very large project. I'd have to do two things:

- Create a set of storyboards and sketches that gave me a graphical direction and template

- Create the text, making sure that it matched the graphical style

Storyboarding

I had to define the look of the final web site before I could continue and I knew that to work, the whole site would have to be true to the original concept. I decided that the original book would have to play a part in the final look.

However, I had a problem: to navigate within a book you turn pages, sometimes lots of pages. This sounded like something that wouldn't work on the web. To go to a particular page is easy when you're holding the book because you have an idea of the paper's *thickness*, so you know if you want to go a point a third of the way into the book, you just open the book at a third of its thickness. You can't do that with a 2D representation on a monitor. Here's the sketch that solved the problem:

tabs

By looking at the way address books use 'tabs' to allow you to quickly find a particular section of names - the Newmans and the Newton-Johns under 'N' for example - I was able to create a 2D representation of a book that was still easy to navigate.

On a whim, I used a cheap flatbed scanner to scan in an image of a small notebook I've carried with me in my coat pocket for close on a year. Then I got some newspaper that had faded to yellow in the sun and scanned that in too, to get the effect of old book pages. In Photoshop I cobbled it all together so that it looked like this:

I now had an idea of what my open book would look like. The idea was that the animated poems would appear in the page area as Flash SWF files. I still needed to create my navigation tabs though...

As well as the chapter tabs, I needed something to allow the user to move between the individual pages of each chapter. I needed last page and next page buttons. I also needed a help button somewhere, so I sketched that in as well:

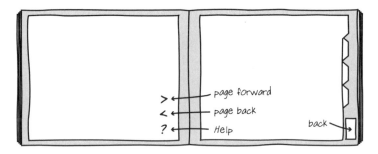

These sketches were created using a Wacom pen tablet. It's as quick a way of doing initial sketches as drawing on paper, and it helps workflow because you can import the electronic image directly into Flash (or whatever program you're using), rather than having to scan them in and then fiddle with image resolution, color depth and so on.

With my basic site structure worked out, I needed to make sure I could create a convincing set of tabs for navigation before I started devoting time to Flash programming. I went back into Photoshop to mock it all up:

By putting each tab in a separate layer and simulating the effect of each tabbed page being turned over, I was able to check that my digital creation still looked like a book. This was obviously essential for the effect I was trying to create. I also used Adobe ImageReady, a web page preparation tool, and some JavaScript to create a simple HTML version of the book to see if the navigation was workable - and thankfully it was:

As you can see, removing tabs gives the impression that we have moved further into the book. Luckily, the fact that our virtual book still has the same number of pages left no matter how far into the book you are doesn't seem to kill the illusion.

By mocking up my ideas in Photoshop first, I proved to myself that the concept of a virtual book was a viable one without wasting my time trying to get it working in Flash straight away. As an added advantage, I now also had some bitmap images I could trace into Flash.

Content

The book was to be called *Passages*, and was to be about the one journey we all make - the one through life. Victorian society was full of double standards, with a very rich upper class segment and a chronically poor underclass (so, things haven't changed *that* much, then...). Using this as a starting point, I wanted the book to liken existence to the life of a young child who is forced to break into a rich man's mansion, to see what's there on offer, and take whatever they can.

Here are two initial storyboards done in Photoshop:

The first one is an introduction to the whole book, and the second is called *crush*. Both of these compositions are multi-layer Photoshop files. By moving the individual layers around in real time, I gave myself a good idea of how the text should appear and how the individual elements should move. These shots represent the last frame in each animation. There are approximately 40 animations for the whole *Passages* sequence, following our young thief through an entire lifetime on their trip through the mansion. By now I had lots of images, sketches and text, and I was ready to mold it into a site. Time to start looking at Flash.

Integration

The first thing was that the book had to look real. It had to have pages that turned. Contemporary native Photoshop files can't be imported into Flash (which is a good thing considering they tend to be about 10Mb each), but you can split the layers up and export them as separate GIFs or JPEGs which will compress the information you're importing. The separated Photoshop images were first converted to vectors and re-built as fully animated movie clips. Here's the final Flash symbol of the front of the *Passages* book, which is fairly faithful to the book that started all this off:

The pages were also made to turn with a simple tween animation, which you can see in this 'under construction' shot:

Here's the finished, open book in Flash. The whole book and associated animations comes in at a little over 20K:

I now built a simple intro to play as the book animations and graphics loaded in (the separate poems would come in as **OnLoad** movie levels, using the loading manager I mentioned earlier).

I wanted to introduce definite symbols to represent the themes of *Passages*: The Victorian ideas of *life* and *mortality*. For *life*, I chose a butterfly, and for mortality I scanned in an image from *Grey's Anatomy*. There were two advantages of this second choice: it was written in the Victorian period, and its engravings are **royalty free** - providing you don't copy the whole book. Neat.

New designers need to pay careful attention to issues of copyright and royalties to avoid getting themselves into unwanted, and perhaps costly, trouble.

The butterfly appears in the introduction, and flits through the book as you turn certain pages. The image of a human spine is shown as a recurring theme throughout the book, representing the Victorian fascination with mortality.

figure 1a
the wonder of existence

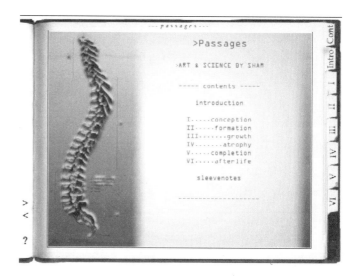

Summary

This walk-through will have shown you how Flash can be used in a creative way to make web sites that are unlike anything else on the Internet. At its lowest level, *Passages* is nothing more than an online showcase of related Flash movies. However, by creating an overall *style* and *ambience* the site will hopefully become much more than its individual components, and the user will forget that they're viewing a Flash web site and become drawn into its imaginary world - in the very way I was when I first found that old book.

The best thing about something like *Passages* is that it has no heavy ActionScripting: it's all about basic artistic skills and ideas. Those of you who are coming into Flash from a Photoshop or graphic design background could create something like this now because you already have the basic Flash skills required to pull it off.

Mocking up the site and prototyping it in Photoshop and ImageReady was one of the most important parts of this site's creation. Flash doesn't have the tools to take in bitmaps and other scanned data in the same way Photoshop does, and for this reason a lot of professional designers use Photoshop for the initial design and storyboarding. Even when used in the simple ways shown here, Photoshop and Flash form the basis of a very powerful set of *visualization* tools for the designer - whatever he or she is designing.

This web site has been up on the web in preliminary forms, but in the end I took it down: the individual SWFS were taking me too long to design, and the gaps between updates became longer as other work became more pressing. The Photoshop mock-ups actually made it to print in *Computer Arts*, a British magazine dedicated to digital art. (I didn't have the heart to mention that they weren't actually finished!) The site will go up again when all forty SWFs are built.

Case Study 2: My Flash Home Site Interface

Designing your own home site is where you get to *play*. Some designers use it to show off and compete with other designers, but I think that's just asking for trouble. Whenever another designer uses a new technique you'll have to go one better. That's kind of 'technological arms race' is not my idea of fun - I prefer to be creative.

The last example was all about design, and how to get those vague ideas in your head down onto a digital canvas, how to tie the ideas down, create a plan and then take the elements and animate them in Flash.

This second example looks at the sites you make without ever really setting out to: what happens is that you have a folder full of half ideas and part-finished FLA files that you don't know what to do with - and then something in your head links them all together and an idea hits you out of nowhere.

Random Idea #1

As I was driving down a busy highway a few months ago, I noticed some large billboards by the side of the road. It put the idea in my head that sometimes size really 'makes' a picture - wouldn't it be nice to have a browser that was as big as a billboard?

So that's what I tried to do. But if you had a really *big* site, how would you see it all? The browser is way too small. Then I remembered reading a book called *Fahrenheit 451* by Ray Bradbury, which had cars that were so fast that the only way people could read the adverts as they drove past was to have huge billboards with stretched images on them. This way, the enormous billboard would zip past but all the images would be stretched out so that they looked normal to you. So I decided to try and do the same with my site design by stretching it out horizontally to give me a really long billboard-type site.

I've seen no one else do this, so at the time of writing it's new for Flash sites. I created a new movie and modified it to make it 2880pixels x 600pixels and then set the publish width to 300% by 95%, just to see what would happen. It looks nice as a design concept, because if you had a logo (I've used mine again because the site isn't up yet) the user would have to scroll from left to right to get to the actual web site at the end, where they'd get an eye full of oversized logo. Because this is a novel format (or will be until you all try it yourselves), the average web user will remember the first site they saw that used it. As we said at the outset of this chapter, originality is an important component of your sites.

Random Idea #2

Another thought was buzzing around my head at around the same time as I was forming Idea #1: my VCR was broken, and whenever you played anything on it, you got a horrible picture that was totally un-viewable, the kind of snowy, fuzzed picture you get when you play a video that's a copy of a copy of a copy. In a funny way, though, I liked the mangled image on the VCR. It worked really well whenever I'd accidentally recorded the test transmission pattern on the screen, making all the colors fade in and out of each other and showing ghost images or random noise within the picture. I imagined, somewhat dramatically, technology breaking out of our control and refusing to be mastered.

With this on my mind I happened to walk past a shop that had a lot of TVs all on at the same time in a 4 x 4 matrix, with no two screens ever showing exactly the same picture: one was brighter than the others, one was redder, and one had a lower saturation.

I imagined the same effect on my browser window - separate 'TVs' all doing their own thing, and I decided to create the effect.

I used an array of little movies that sit over the top of the SWF that I'm trying to see, sort of like this matrix. If you read the chapter on masking you'll no doubt have a good understanding of how this is done:

All I needed now was my broken VCR effect in each segment.

I built a set of little objects that randomly applied noise effects (distorted them) to the underlying image or SWF Remarkably, the whole thing works! It looks a little bit like the video walls you still see in some bars or clubs that show one picture on a matrix of TVs - each TV showing a separate square of the image.

I now needed something to tie my two media related ideas, billboards and broadcast, together.

Integration

I don't know what made me put the television matrix on the end of my billboard, but I did, and it worked. I was just playing around, putting this matrix idea over other SWFs and looking to see how it mangled everything up. I was just having fun. Even when the underlying SWF is motionless, there's plenty of movement going on.

I needed a menu bar to really tie it all together, and I was still in love with the test transmissions I spoke of earlier, so I created a row of rectangles that approximated the test-card color chart. It's shown in grayscale here, but it is in fact the color progression you see on a color TV - white, yellow, cyan, green, magenta, red and blue:

This menu bar is made up of little button objects that the user can press to navigate the site. The buttons 'wobble'. By this, I mean that when you press one, it performs an oscillation that sees it extend and contract as if it were made of Jello. These 'wobblers' are wrapped within a parent object called 'menu'. When one 'wobbler' gets bigger the others get smaller - and vice versa - to preserve the overall length of the menu bar:

It all wobbles with a delay, so it looks a bit like a big elastic band, producing a bouncing effect that's fascinating and disorienting at the same time...

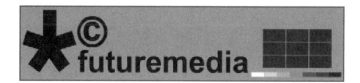

So here's my idea for my new Flash 5 home site. You have to scroll in from left to right, going over the big oversized billboard logo. Once you get to the far right end of the movie and the mouse passes over the TV screens they spring to life and play their little test-cards and video noise until you ask to see something. If you ask to jump to another web site, you don't see it in a new window...it appears in the TV screens! Every now and again one of the screens gets a little brighter or loses synch or something, and the longer you leave the mouse still, the more pronounced the effect becomes.

Sometimes the screens flick to new stuff you never asked to see: little MTV-type animations or Japanese Manga cartoons - or the grainy type of video footage that was taken from the cameras in missile nosecones during *Desert Storm*. I want to add things in those screens that are possibly *better* than the things you've come to see, so you'll say to yourself "never mind looking at the websites...missile command has just shown up in the top left corner! Quick...figure out the keys before it disappears!"

Summary

I hope that, from seeing this example, you all feel enthused to create your own innovative sites. And I also hope you realize that most of the knowledge you need to achieve something like this was given to you in the ActionScript chapters. The 'wobbler' menu uses quite a lot of ActionScript: I simplified my description above, as the objects are in fact nested about five deep - but you could simply use a 'solid' menu instead.

The use of Flash as a tool for just trying out ideas, like any design program, is not to be ignored. Sometimes, you find an effect that you like in a Flash tutorial site, but which has been 'done to death' by repeated use. When you've collected enough ideas like these you can take the best aspects of each and create something unique to use on your own site.

Most designers have a little box of collected effects, but, unfortunately, some never change what they keep in it. The best designers are always on the lookout for new coding ideas. When they offer a client the chance to be the first to use a particular effect, they can ensure they'll have a better chance of getting the job.

Case Study 3: A Dynamic Site

I was asked to create a new front end for an existing HTML site called **freshfroot**. This would be an online visual inspiration resource for web designers, and, unlike other online libraries, it was free.

The site was to be aimed at cutting edge web designers, and a HTML site was not really appropriate. It had to be Flash.

Although there were the normal Flash design issues to think about here, there was the added complication that the information presented by the site had to change every hour on the hour. It was going to be a *dynamic* site.

To change a Flash site dynamically means changing text fields and graphics to reflect the latest, current information. This isn't the same dynamic we spoke of earlier in the book where we made animations that reacted to the user; this is a site that that contains different information every time you look at it. A Flash site is not dynamic in this sense, because no matter how different a Flash site appears each time you run it, it's always running exactly the same SWF file.

A dynamic site in Flash works by creating a SWT file, rather than a SWF file. This file is a template and is designed to interact with an external piece of software. The external software looks at the template and updates parts of it with current information before it is sent to the viewer:

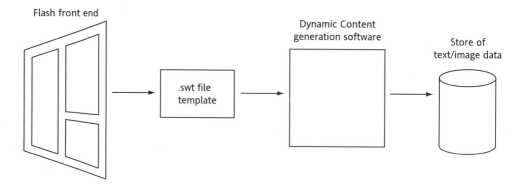

In this way, the Flash presentation can either be updated regularly or customized for each user - the dynamic content that gets fed into the front end can be based on user choices and preferences.

There are a number of software packages that interface with Flash to provide dynamic content, amongst which are:

- Swift Generator

- Macromedia Generator

- Flash Turbine

There are bound to be more coming onto the market as this aspect of Flash becomes more prevalent.

To generate dynamic content, the dynamic content generation software sits between the web server and your browser. Whenever you go to the URL of a dynamic Flash site, the SWT template is accessed by the content generator, which adds the dynamic data to create a full SWF file. This is then sent to your browser.

Although Macromedia Generator has come down in price significantly since the release of Flash 5, Swift Generator still has the advantage of being free (you can get more information about Swift Generator at www.swift-tools.com). We therefore decided to go with Swift Generator, unless we ran into problems that would require us moving up to Macromedia Generator.

In essence, both of these programs look in the SWT file for *placeholders* (which, as you'd imagine, are containers that hold information) and fill them with the latest content it's found on the web server. For text, the placeholders are denoted by anything surrounded by {} brackets. The text message 'Hello {name}' in the SWT file would be accessed by the generator software and replaced by a database variable corresponding to whatever 'name' is for the current dynamic page. So, if Sam had previously added her name to this particular web site's database (probably by filling in a form), the site may come back with 'Hello Sam'.

The detailed workings of the dynamic content generation software is, unfortunately, beyond the scope of this book, but shouldn't prevent us looking at the actual site creation.

This screenshot shows an example of the freshfroot template:

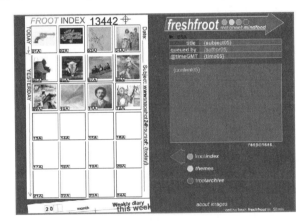

The idea for this site was that there would be a series of 'snapshots' of the web taken over every 24 hour period. The thumbnails in the index shown above change as new content is entered, and the descriptive text that comes up as each picture is selected must also change.

Although this sounds pretty long winded, as a designer you do not have to know much about what the back end (the database linked to your site) is up to and what it will do to your SWT and SWF files. All you have to do is assign all the text to the correct variable within the database, enclosing it with {} in your design. This is much easier when you work closely with the back end programmer and you agree the data structures and naming conventions. When *picture 03* is selected, the text that's assigned to the variables *subject03*, *author03*, *time03*, and *content03* will be displayed in the appropriate fields.

If you're ever involved in active Flash sites, I think it is in your interests to pick up as much as you can from the back end programmers. Dynamic Flash sites look to be the next big thing, and it would be a good idea for you, as a designer, to be as proficient in working with them as possible.

Suggested Sites

Now that you have a better appreciation of how they can be created, perhaps the best place to start looking at Flash sites is the web itself. As promised at the top of the chapter, here are some suggestions from Amanda and Pat:

www.dennisinter.com

The home of Dennis Interactive, creators of the Blender interactive magazine. The site includes some impressive but simple text effects and tweens.

http://www.giger.com/

The official site of H.R Giger, the Swiss artist famous for the initial designs for the original Alien movie, as well as many other Darkwave art pieces. The site includes a link to a 'homage-site' produced with Flash. By keeping the bitmaps small, they're effectively mixed with the vector content to produce a site that includes sharp bitmap images as well as maintaining a healthy frame rate.

http://yigal-azrouel.com/

This site has a modern look, great design, and fantastic navigation as well. It really gets the designer's feeling across to the user. The site is fun, interesting to play with and, importantly, does not get boring. Winner of many prizes at the New York FlashForward 2000 conference.

http://www.mtv2.co.uk/

This site shows excellent use of 3D. It might not be complicated, but it makes great use of objects with a low file size. The site has appropriate sound use that doesn't get annoying - and it's always fun to play with 3D blocks in cyberspace.

http://www.foulds2000.freeserve.co.uk/

This site contains many examples of Flash toys and effects, and is one for you all to use your ActionScript know-how to deconstruct.

http://www.derbauer.de/

This site is just amazing. These people really know how to put their images to use. The programmers and designers have together created a well designed site. Even though the file size is large, the site is easy to navigate and is extremely interactive.

http://www.praystation.com/

Any site where more than 45 minutes passes by unnoticed while you're playing with all the interactive Flash toys has got to be a good one. Even though the toys on this site are simple shapes, lines and effects, the results are extremely engaging.

http://www.studioadhoc.de/rabbitkiller/

Crass but fun. Wait for the hen to lay the eggs and then let the rabbits have it!

http://www.banja.com

Great animations and a great game. Islands, treasures, pirates - the whole thing. Excellent interactivity and well thought out design with fast loading for such a large game.

Flash is ideally suited to web sites that include animated content, and here are a few favorites:

www.heavy.com

http://www.bulbo.com/

http://www.atomfilms.com

Summary

The summary for this chapter is short and sweet:

- ◆ Learn
- ◆ Work
- ◆ Explore
- ◆ Plan
- ◆ Play

Great Flash design comes from continually honing your design and Flash skills, from innovation, and from trying things out as you go. Remember that time spent monkeying around with little movie clips and effects can pay dividends later.

In our final chapter, we're going to look at some other Flash areas that are ripe for exploration as you build your Flash future.

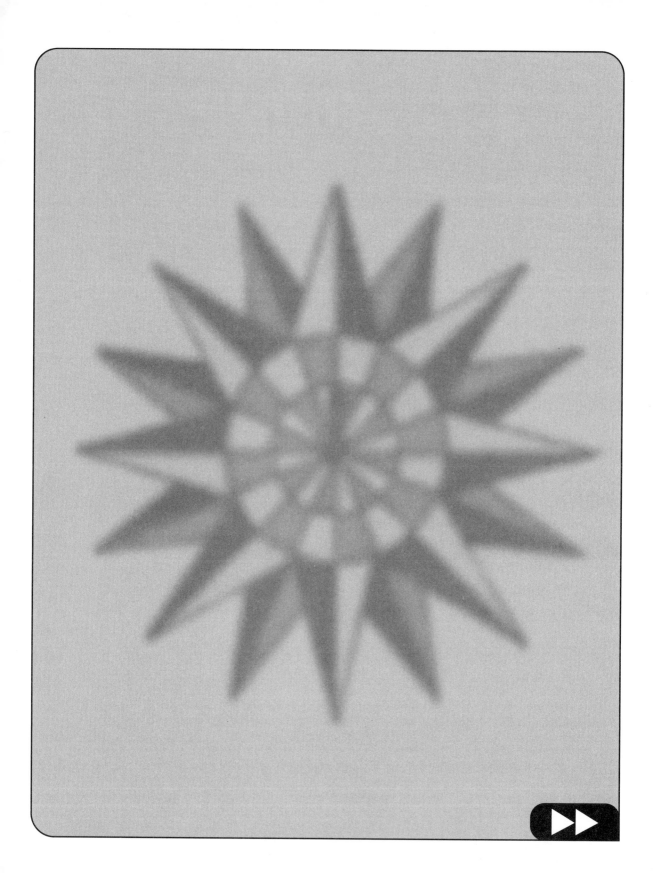

17 Futurescape

Where next?

Flash has come a long way from being just a superb animation package. With its new features, Flash 5 is now capable of producing fully functional web applications that are rich in graphics, sound and interactivity. And its this interactivity - building applications for e-commerce, entertainment, community sites replete with chat rooms and all the rest of it - that we think will be big in the Flash future. Flash can now talk to web servers in a highly sophisticated way, meaning that dynamic content is within the reach of everyone using a little ActionScript, and Flash is increasingly becoming integrated with other web-standard technologies such as XML. Flash has grown up strong, confident and powerful, and now is a great time to be getting into it.

You've now learnt the basic skills required for Flash competence. In the space of a few hundred pages you've gone from a ground level beginner making a mushroom grow to an intermediate programmer coding an interactive game.

Mastering these new skills completely will keep you content and occupied for many months to come as you explore the full range of your powers. But before too long you're going to want to do more. You'll be hungry for new knowledge and new skills, and will want to wring every possible design opportunity from Flash, and from the Internet as a whole.

Using and Improving your Flash Skills

There are numerous Flash tutorial sites out on the web, and most have beginner's sections. Most new Flash effects and interfaces seem to end up deconstructed and presented as a 'how to' tutorial within a very short time, so if there's a particular design effect you want to know more about, check out the web first. Be sure to try the Macromedia newsgroups as well, particularly the **alt.macromedia**... newsgroups. These tend to be a good way of picking up the knowledge of some of the older hands. Our advice, though, is to check out the FAQs of these groups before asking questions of your own as most beginner questions will have been covered.
Here are some places we recommend you take a look at:

http://www.virtual-fx.net/
http://www.were-here.com/
http://www.flashaddict.com
http://www.ibisfernandez.com
http://www.flashmove.com/
http://www.flashplanet.com
http://www.screamdesign.com
http://www.flashlite.net/
http://www.enetserve.com/tutorials
http://www.flashkit.com/
http://www.flashzone.com/tutorials/

Flash web design presents the user with a large number of different fields to look at. You only have to look at a few sites out there created by the Flash Masters to realise that the variation in Flash sites is larger than that exhibited by any other web technology currently on view. From cartoon sites to futuristic looking 3D, Flash has a large amount of the best of the web covered. To give you an idea of some of the areas you may want to find out more about we're going to briefly introduce them to you now.

Flash Games and Toys

Getting noticed as a designer is hard work, so you need to find a way to get your skills recognized. One way to attract attention is by designing quality games for people to play. Games and toys can be a good way to hold a viewer's attention. You could add them to an existing site that's in need of new blood, or make them into a site in their own right, where people can witness your Flash experimentation. If this is the area you're interested in, then perhaps existing sites that need 'perking up' with some Flash interaction would by willing to incorporate your work - if you give them enough of a nudge

Flashed Cartoons

As a pure animation tool, Flash should not be underestimated. Managing the timeline with the skills you've learnt in this book can produce highly professional looking animations. You can generate drawings within Flash itself, scan in photos or drawings you've generated by hand to give a less 'computerized' appearance to your work, or import work from other applications that give you more flexibility when creating your images (as we saw in the walk-throughs in the previous chapter).

The animation features of Flash are used in preliminary work for TV idents and also for mocking up commercials. The current 'in' look in commercial illustration, and animation, is very much the vector style created by Illustrator and Freehand - and of course, Flash.

Using Flash with other Software

As well as using Flash in isolation, many designers are now beginning to look at using Flash with other software, including Quicktime and Director. Both these options allow you to extend the use of Flash beyond web applications and into stand-alone programs. They also let you overcome one of Flash's biggest current disadvantages: its lack of full video support.

Although Flash has its own drawing tools, there's a lot to be said for using programs such as Freehand, Photoshop and others to enhance the available options of Flash presentations. A number of designers appear to have taken this step, particularly in initial design stages. Be sure to optimize anything you bring into Flash though, because some of these applications are not as web savvy as Flash can be.

Sound in Flash is another area to look at getting into. Although creating sound can become very expensive, there are many entry-level options available by using a good soundcard as the main device, and shareware or freeware tracker and sequencer software.

3D in Flash

As some of the examples in this book have shown - and as do many of our recommended sites - adding a 3D element to your work can achieve impressive results, giving your sites an extra edge over conventional Flash work. The applications available are well worth getting involved with; if a client wants a 3D version of their logo on their site, you want to make sure you're in the running for the job.

As the demands placed on web sites increase and more varied, and perhaps realistic, looks are requested, 3D rendering skills will be highly desirable. Adding this ability to your impressive Flash résumé will do you no harm at all. Flash is well suited to the use of 3D images and whether you're trying to make your name as a designer, or are merely using Flash for your own enjoyment, you'll find that using 3D objects will add to your designing enjoyment. Check out *Swift3D* as a Flash-friendly 3D tool that can output SWF files you can load in your movies.

Advanced ActionScript-based Flash Interface Designs

ActionScript is going to become a major force in web programming, and now that you know the basics - more than just the basics in fact - thanks to this book, you will no doubt be bursting to know what other possibilities are offered by this web-wonder. ActionScripting is a skill in itself and knowledge of it will be a tremendous benefit to your designing. We saw in the later stages of the book what effects can be achieved when you've only seen the tip of the ActionScript iceberg. When you really flesh out your ability the Flash designs you'll be able to produce will astound even you.

Dynamic Content

Dynamic content seems set to play a major role in Internet programs, and Flash is no exception. The Macromedia Generator objects that you need to create a functioning SWT file are supplied with Flash 5, and the 'developer' version of Generator has now come down significantly in price (although the high-volume, large site version is still only for operations with deep pockets). This price reduction suggests that Generator will be used much more in the future, and going on past employment demographics, there will soon be a shortage of Flash Generator people. This trend will also apply across the other methods of feeding dynamic content into the Flash front end: as well as the bespoke middleware packages that sit between the SWT and the back-end content store, you can pass data dynamically between the browser and the web server using ActionScript in conjunction with the surfeit of server-side scripting languages (such as Perl, CGI, PHP, ASP et al.)

As we mentioned in the previous chapter, Swift Generator is available free, so it might be a good idea to familiarize yourself with that software in anticipation of the coming 'dynamic boom'.

XML

Flash 5 now also includes support for the eXtensible Markup Language (XML), which is already a web standard for disseminating data in a form that can be interpreted anywhere, on any device, and rendered according to the abilities of that device and the needs of the user.

Because XML tags can be used to actually tell a browser something *about* the included information rather than just *how to display it*, XML is expected to soon take the place of HTML in a number of areas, including the current web buzzwords *e-commerce*, *intelligent search engines* and *wireless devices*. Flash's ability to deal in XML data in ActionScript, coupled with the rich multimedia features that Flash is famous for, mean that Flash can be a powerful player in a world where XML- and data-driven web applications are becoming evermore popular.

Flash will roll out into a whole new set of contexts: people will want Flash content for new generation WAP phones and for all kinds of wireless and non-PC web devices, such as PDAs.

Starting a Career in Flash

Flash has now become the standard for dynamic animation and sound on the web. It follows, therefore, that it's also a discipline that can be used to form part, or all, of a career in web design. The question many people tend to ask is *how do you get your foot in the door?*

If you are so taken with Flash that you're considering attempting to earn a living as a Flash designer, you'll have to stop a moment and consider the following issues:

HTML

Most employers and agencies expect you to know something about HTML. This is something that's becoming less of a constraint as time passes and the majority of operations adopt site-HTML-creation packages like Dreamweaver. However, a lot of Flash web-design positions still require you to be able to *hand code* HTML. Even if this is not the case, we'd be very surprised to find Flash positions that did *not* require an understanding of Dreamweaver. Some understanding of JavaScript is usually an advantage too, as Flash 5 ActionScript is now very similar to JavaScript - good news for you as it means there's much less to learn to achieve competency.

Graphic Design

Web design is an offshoot of a much wider discipline called graphic design. As a web designer, you'll not be expected to get your pencils and paints out, but a knowledge of computer based graphic design and layout packages is usually a distinct advantage - Adobe PhotoShop is usually stipulated as a competency. It's also worth your while considering a point that the earlier chapters alluded to: with the ever-increasing competition for web surfers, your potential clients are going to take it for granted that you can produce a functional site. They're going to want something that's visually appealing *as well* - so your artistic skills need to be up to the job.

Getting In

Having an impressive home site is one of the best ways to get noticed on the web. There are a number of well-known Flash designers who started out by building themselves a killer home site. Having a cutting edge site does not necessarily mean that you have to be an ActionScript or 3D guru: there're plenty of other site styles that will appeal to users - humor, animation, innovation and a distinctive style spring immediately to mind.

There are of course other, more stealthy ways into Flash design, and these seem to be the routes that most of us tend to end up following:

One of the things we'd recommend is that you look at what is already up on the web in your locale. A good starting point when looking for your very first site job (after your own of course) is charities. They tend to be run and organized by volunteers, and many won't turn away a volunteer Flash expert who asks to re-engineer the existing HTML site to fully Flashed status, with the promise of a much more entertaining site and therefore more visitors. This is the way many designers start out, doing odd web site jobs in their spare time and keeping up the day job, slowly increasing their portfolio and gaining a good reputation.

Although your first few Flash sites may be more in the 'solid-but-dependable' ballpark, it won't be long before you have a few sites that you're actually proud of. That's the time to start looking at full time **freelancing**. This is much easier to do now that the web has really taken off, and there are a number of web sites in America and Europe that will email you with weekly lists of contract positions.

A good tip is to add Flash, Dreamweaver, PhotoShop, and JavaScript to your résumé's list of keywords. Be aware that most freelance contracts specify that you work at the client's office, and working from home is much less of an option. Flash web design seems to be attracting more and more of this type of contract work, particularly around October as Christmas nears and hourly rates really start to rise. If you choose this route, our advice would be to find a few sites that allow online portfolios, and add links to your three best sites. You'll find that a lot of traditional employment agencies now scour such entries, and you sometimes find emails from agencies you have never worked with imploring you to get in touch about a contract!

Applying directly to web design houses is another option. However, unless you've already created a stir on the web with your home site or other work, be prepared for a disappointing starting salary. There's a lot of money to be made from the Internet, but junior web designers seem to be seeing a minimal part of it. A lot of people may choose this option despite lack of initial pay, because it can create a very good portfolio of work very quickly. Working with the right company, the work can be very satisfying and you can move up to more senior positions, or into freelance work, after a couple of years. There's much less uncertainty when starting out on this route than there is with freelancing, where you may not be employed all year round.

Flash Farewell - for now

So, the end of this book is very much the beginning of your Flash career - whatever you choose to do with your new skills. You now have a platform of knowledge that'll allow you to branch out into a variety of areas - all with their own pitfalls and possibilities. Flash is already a major force on the web, and is destined to increase its power and influence. There's an opportunity now to ride in on the crest of Flash's wave and all make your mark in the world of web design. Don't rest on your laurels: practice the skills you have and search out new ones and new ways to apply them.

See you on the beach.

The Truth about Flash

Ho**Home**

Important stuff you should know

A Sound Sampling

The first time you glance at this appendix will probably be to locate the downloadable sound files you need to perform the exercises in chapters 9 and 11. And here they are:

MIDI Sequencers

http://www.cubase.net
http://www.cakewalk.com
http://home.c2i.net/jaase/massiva.htm

Sound Editing and Looping

http://www.sonicfoundry.com

Free Sample Sounds

http://music4flash.com
http://deusx.com
http://www.flashsound.com
http://www.flashkit.com

Fun Sound Effects

http://www.wavcentral.com

The rest of this appendix will give you a more detailed understanding of how sound works, and of the things that you need to bear in mind when you're creating your own sounds for use on the Internet.

Sound

Sound travels through the air in waves. The bigger the wave, the louder the sound. To help you visualize sound waves and how they move, think about the ripples that are created when you throw a pebble into a pond. The ripples move outwards from the point of impact at a constant speed (frequency) that's independent of the size of the pebble, but at a height that is determined by the size of the pebble. The water is displaced and pushed along by the pressure that the pebble's impact creates.

A sound wave works in much the same way: pressure caused by objects vibrating displaces air particles and creates a 'ripple' in the air. This ripple of pressure strikes your eardrum, causing it to vibrate, and this vibration is what we hear as sound. The ripple of air particles forms a sound wave:

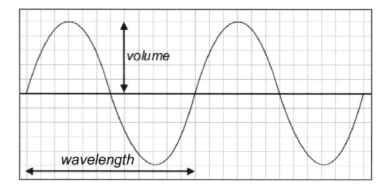

The height of the wave represents its **volume** and is determined by the power of the sound source, or the strength of the initial vibration that created the pressure wave. (Using our pond analogy, the bigger the pebble, the higher the ripples in the water).

The length of one complete wave is called the **wavelength**, and the number of completed waves that pass a fixed point in a fixed unit of time is the **frequency** of the wave, which is measured in Hertz (Hz or KHz).

Digital Sound

Before we can bring any sound into Flash, we have to digitize it. The digitizer will most likely be your soundcard connected to a microphone. The digitizing process involves recording the current height of the sound wave at regular intervals. The length of the interval is called the sampling rate: the higher the rate, the more frequently the samples are taken. This process is sometimes called quantizing or just sampling. Each level is called a sample, and when you put them all together in order they form a digital representation of the sound wave:

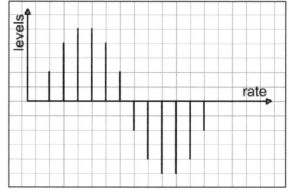

Defining the Sampling Rate

The sampling rate is expressed in either samples per second or, like frequency, in Hertz. The sampling rate defines the highest frequency, or sound range, your sampler will capture. There is a sound sampling law (discovered by Nyquist), which states that if your sample rate is twice the highest frequency that your sound contains, you can actually sample the audio with no loss of quality. For example, the highest frequency we can hear is about 20Khz (for a newborn baby), and about 10 - 16Khz for adults. This means that if a sound is sampled at 40Khz, no one will be able to tell the difference between the real sound and the sampled sound. For this reason, compact discs contain sound sampled at just over 40Khz. In practical terms, you can define your maximum sampling rate (which equates to a perfect digital copy) by the type of sound you are trying to capture. A violin sound contains harmonics that extend beyond the audible range and so would have to be captured with a sampling rate of 40Khz. Normal speech tends not to go much beyond 10Khz so you could sample it with a rate of 20Khz. Finally, a telephone only records sounds up to approximately 2.5 KHz, so you could reproduce vocals at that quality with a sampling rate of just 5Khz.

Many beginners in sampling tend to assume that if, for example, you're sampling a guitar string at 500Hz, then the sample rate should be 1000Hz (1 KHz) to reproduce it correctly, but this is not true. The guitar string has a main frequency (or fundamental frequency) of 500Hz, but has many *harmonics* superimposed upon it. These may extend for quite a distance up the frequency scale, and it is the harmonics that define the difference between a guitar sound at 500Hz, and a trombone playing the same frequency. To get a good musical sample you must therefore use a high sampling rate if you want to get the detailed ambience of the sound that the harmonics will create.

When sampling sound for the Internet, you can get away with quite a lot by making your sounds deep and bassy. Drum and bass beats tend to sample very well at low sampling rates so can be used to overcome the bandwidth limitations you'll inevitably have on the Internet.

Defining the Quantization Levels

As we've seen, the samples at each interval are converted to a level. The number of available levels depends upon the amount of information you're allowing for each sample, and the soundcard will store them as a binary number with a length of 8, 16, 24 or 32 bits.

For 8 bits you can have 256 different levels, which comes from 2^8, and for 16 bits you can have 65536 different levels (2^{16}), and so on. Note that increasing the number of levels from 8 to 16 bits only doubles the size of your sample, but increases the *quality* of your sound 256 times.

Because the samples are encoded into a binary number, which can only be a whole number, the sampling process can only choose between one level and the next. If your sound is actually between two levels, then there will be a difference between the original sound and its sample. This error is called the quantization error, and will be heard as a background buzzing and popping. It's this distortion that makes speech sound tinny and mechanical on a telephone:

The sampling levels here are one square apart in height, so the difference in the levels is the distance between the arrows. As you can see, the sampled signal frequently misses the actual wave, and if you select 8 bit sound as your export bit rate you'll hear it very loudly as it manifests itself as background interference. Remember, the export bit rate you choose will determine the background noise in your final sample. Samples that have high noise content anyway (such as explosions, doors slamming etc) can be sampled at very low bit rates because, although they will sound different from the original, they won't sound any *worse*.

If you're particularly sneaky and allow for quantization noise in your compositions, you can actually mask out the noise in the higher pitched voices by hiding them behind louder and lower pitched drum and bass beats (which, as noted above, tend to sample well). MP3 compression actually uses this to intelligently hide quantization noise completely. When it detects a loud bass sound, it will look to see which higher pitched sounds are being drowned out, and will start to sample them much less frequently, using the extra free bandwidth to sample sounds the listener is more likely to hear.

As a general rule, you can optimize your bandwidth use by assigning high bit export rates to sounds that are more prominent, or loud, in your composition, and get away with lower rates for background sounds. However, take care when sampling quiet passages of sound: they'll result in the largest, and most noticeable, quantization error of all. You can combat this by setting an appropriate **record level**.

Record Levels

The sound levels you sample at have a big effect on the sound quality. Unlike normal sound recording, the quantization error in digital sound is always constant because it's a function of the sampling process itself, rather than a function of the sound. As your sound gets lower in volume, you're using less of the available quantization levels, and the signal to noise level will get worse faster than it would if you were recording using analogue only. The best way to get round this is to always set up your record level so that you're using as many of the quantization levels as possible. This is achieved by making the sound input as loud as possible without distorting the recorded sound:

When you come to play the sound back in Flash, use the sound envelope to set the volume back to its original level within the composition. This way, you're drowning out the constant quantization noise with a louder sound, and may well be able to move down to a lower bit export rate, thus optimising your sound for Internet use.

The Truth about Flash

Important stuff you should know

B | HTML and Flash

For those readers with a knowledge of HTML, or those who might be thinking of looking into it in the near future, here are a couple of examples of more advanced HTML and Flash integration.

Formatting Text with HTML

While working through the later exercises in this book, you may have noticed the **HTML** check box on the **Text Options** panel when an input text or a dynamic text box is created. Flash 5 lets you use limited HTML type formatting within dynamic and input text fields. It's a little quirky and needs some coaxing sometimes, but it's effective. Remember though, it only supports HTML 1.0.

You can add the following formatted text:

- URLs via the <A> tag

- Underline, Bold and Italic via the <U>, <B> and <I> tags

If you're not too hot on HTML hand coding, there are a huge number of sites on the web that include this sort of information, so you'll be spoilt for choice.

As an example to show you how to apply formatting to both text and URLs, we'll use the **Contact** button from the case study.

1. Select the contact button's layer at frame 30. To set up the text field to display the HTML formatted text, drag out a non-selectable dynamic text field onto the main stage of your case study movie and select the **HTML** check box as shown here:

As your formatted text will be more than one line long, you'll need to select Multiline from the second drop down menu.

2. In the **Variable** field assign the variable **formatted_text** to the text field.

   The **contact** button currently has this ActionScript attached to it:

   ```
   on (release) {
     tellTarget ("_root.information") {
       gotoAndPlay (50);
     }
   }
   ```

   We want to change this so that it sets **formatted_text** to the HTML code. If we assign this HTML to a variable called **contact** (which we'll do in a moment), then all we have to do is make appropriate changes to the **contact** button's ActionScript.

3. Change the ActionScript in the contact button's Actions window, using a **set Variable** action, to:

   ```
   on (release) {
     formatted_text = contact;
   }
   ```

4. Make the value an expression.

5. We now have to define the variable **contact**, which we'll do in the keyframe in which our dynamic text box appears. In the Frame Actions window for the keyframe, select a **set Variable** action and enter **contact** in the **Variable** field, and the following HTML code in the **Value** field. Do **not** check the **Expression** check box:

   ```
   <FONT size = "20">Contact</FONT>
   <BR>
   <A HREF="Mailto:yourname@yourdomain.com">
    <FONT color = "#0033FF">yourname@yourdomain.com</FONT>
   </A>
   <BR>
   <FONT size="10">your address</FONT>
   ```

   You have to set text colors manually (even for links) via **color = "#xxxxxx"**, where **xxxxxx** is the Hex color code. You can easily find what the code is by reading it off on the color swatch from the toolbar. The paragraph tag (<P>...</P>) seems a little buggy, and you're advised to ignore it completely and just put in plain text separated by break (<BR>) tags.

It looks a little odd, but it works:

As you have to enter all the code on a single tiny line, it's a good idea to write it all out in a text editor or word processor first, and then block copy it into Flash's **Frame Actions** entry field when you are done, as this method makes it easier to spot any mistakes you may type in.

Your newly formatted text will appear on the screen, the first and last lines will be in the color that you set the text field to, and the URL will be in blue:

The real advantage of using this method is that you can mix URL links with plain text.

To further practise your HTML skills, here are some sites you can look at:

http://www.htmlgoodies.com
http://www.echoecho.com/
http://html.digitalsea.net/

Embedding Your SWF File in an HTML Page

In order to view your .swf file properly on the net, it's a good idea to embed the file into an HTML page. This gives you more control over the layout of the file, and also gives you the ability to use HTML on the Flash page as well. There are many ways that you can embed your .swf file into an HTML page, these are a couple of the easiest.

Embedding with Dreamweaver

If you have Macromedia Dreamweaver, you can embed a Flash file simply by opening the **Window > Objects** panel and using the Common objects.

As you'll see in the screenshot here, this panel contains a Flash icon:

All you need to do is press this icon and a dialog window will appear asking you where your .swf file is. Browse to it and press **OK** and your .swf file is automatically embedded into the HTML page.

Flash button

Of course, the file may not be exactly the way you want it. Dreamweaver will the set the .swf file to its original size and background color by default. If you want to change any of this, you can click on the .swf file in Dreamweaver and it will bring up a dialog window:

You can also open this window by selecting **Window > Properties**.

From this window you can change, amongst other things, the size, file, background color, quality, alignment, vertical and horizontal spacing, and whether the movie will loop or not.

Manually Embedding a Flash Movie

Dreamweaver is by far the quickest and easiest way to integrate your Flash movies into HTML files. However, if you don't have Dreamweaver you can always embed the code into your HTML page manually. Here is the snippet of code that you will need. Replace the width, height, and filename details used here with those from your file:

```
<object classid="clsid:D27CDB6E-AE6D-11cf-96B8-444553540000"
codebase="http://download.macromedia.com/pub/shockwave/cabs/flash/s
wflash.cab#version=4,0,2,0" width="280" height="280">
  <param name=movie value="filename.swf">
  <param name=quality value=high>
  <embed src="filename.swf" quality=high
pluginspage="http://www.macromedia.com/shockwave/download/index.c
gi?P1_Prod_Version=ShockwaveFlash" type="application/x-shockwave-
flash" width="280" height="280">
  </embed>
</object>
```

There is not really that much information to change from the code given above, so embedding this code is quite easy.

If you don't know the width and height of your movie, you'll need to open up the .fla file in Flash and check the movie dimensions under **Modify > Movie**. The width and height are important, as if you do not enter the correct values then your Flash movie will stretch or shrink itself accordingly.

You can also use a percentage instead of pixel width. So instead of **width="280"** you'd use **width="100%"**. Overall, you have a lot of control over how your .swf file is displayed in the HTML page.

Titling and Meta Tags for your Flash page

Titling your Flash page is exactly the same process that you would undertake to title an HTML page. Since your Flash file is "embedded" into the HTML page, then technically you still have all the HTML code to work with. This also applies to Meta tags as well.

Both titles and Meta tags (if you haven't studied HTML), are inserted in between the <head> </head> tags in your HTML. For example if you wanted to title your Flash page "My Flash Portfolio On-Line", then you would type this in between your HTML < head> </head> tags:

> **<title>My Flash Portfolio On-Line</title>**

This also applies to Meta tags. Meta tags are used to help search engines find your page more easily and they also help to push your page up near the top of search engines. A search engine will first look at the title of your page and then it will look at the Meta tags. So you need to make sure that they're very descriptive of what is contained in the Flash movie.

The two most popular Meta tags for search purposes are description and keywords. Between your <head> </head> tags in your HTML you'd place the two Meta tags as listed here:

> **<meta name="description" content="The description of your web page would go here">**
> **<meta name="keywords" content="Flash, web, design, graphics, animation, color, theory, internet">**

All you need to do is change the **content="whatever..."** part. This will ensure that the pages on your web site get searched correctly.

Removing the White Page Border

Many times when you embed your .swf file to take up the full HTML page, there'll be a small margin around the edge between the .swf file and the browser window.

These are the default margins that browsers have, and you have to manually specify their removal. A quick way to do this is with Dreamweaver. This can fix the margins both in Internet Explorer and in Netscape.

To do this in Dreamweaver, open up **Modify > Page Properties** to get the Page Properties dialog window:

You can specify your page margins for Internet Explorer browsers in the **Left Margin** and **Top Margin** fields and for Netscape browsers in the **Margin Width** and **Margin Height** fields.

If you set *all* of these fields to zero it will force the .swf file to butt directly up next to the browser window, meaning that you'll no longer have that annoying gap around the edge of your movie.

Publishing your Flash site with Dreamweaver

Macromedia Dreamweaver has a much wider web designer following than the other program you might use as a beginner. Microsoft's FrontPage seems more popular with businesses building office intranets and the like, probably because of its easy integration with MS Office. As a budding new Flash web professional, you'd be recommended to go for Dreamweaver because of its ease in handling Flash and Director files.

The site management is performed via Dreamweaver's site files window, accessed by pressing **F5**.

To define a new site you need the following information:

- Where the site is on your hard drive

- Where the site will be on the server, and its Internet address

- The file transfer method you will be using

Let's enter this in Dreamweaver. From the site window, select **Site > New site**. The Dreamweaver **Site Definition** window will appear. To the left is a category window. You only need to provide information for the **Local Info** (corresponding to the first point above) and **Web Server Info** (corresponding to the other two points).

Local Info

The **Site name** field is for Dreamweaver's (and your) benefit. On your hard drive, you must create a local folder to put your web site into. For your first attempt, this will probably only consist of a single .swf file and the associated HTML file (which you should normally rename index.htm if it will be the default page). The full path of this folder must be entered in the **Local Root Folder** field, or you can search for it by clicking on the little yellow folder icon to the right. Dreamweaver can assume that this

local location is actually on the server by substituting its path for whatever is in the **HTTP Address** requester. This is the address of your server (which is the same thing as your website URL). Remember to include the 'http://' part of the address, and the 'www' part if your address has one:

Web Server Info

When you first select the Web Server Info category, you'll see a single pull down menu called **Server Access**. This will be set to none.

If you change it to **FTP**, a set of new fields will appear:

You need to enter the FTP address of the server as a minimum, which will be the same as the HTTP Address you have just added to the last window, minus the 'http://'.

If you haven't made your address point to an existing subfolder (unless you know different, chances are you haven't), you don't have to add anything in the **Host Directory** field. You can enter the **Login** and **Password** details if you wish to avoid having to enter them every time you connect.

And that's about all you need. In the **Site Files** window, click the *Connect* button. After you've connected to the server, and assuming all the addresses are okay, a little green light to the left of the button should signify you've now connected. You can now simply drag your files across from the right pane (your local site) over to the left pane (the server). After Dreamweaver has sent the files over to the server via FTP, they should appear in the left hand panel. Now open your browser and enter the address www.mysite.com. And there you are; visitor number 1!

Some servers have a short delay before the uploaded file appears on the web, but most servers now present uploaded material immediately.

A top tip when using Dreamweaver: in **Edit > Preferences > FTP** make sure that the 'dependent files' check boxes are all checked. When you do this, Dreamweaver knows that if you upload the HTML file, it'll need to FTP the .swf (which is a dependent file because it is called for in the HTML) as well.

FTP Clients

In order to publish your finished Flash site you're going to need an FTP program. This can also help you to transfer files across the Internet and to download software and music. Here are some of the places you can get hold of an FTP program.

http://www.cuteftp.com
http://www.coffeecup.com/
http://www.vicomsoft.com

The Truth about Flash

Important stuff you should know

C Glossary

.fla
The Flash authoring file. This is the file that you create initially in Flash and are able to edit while you're building your movie.

.swf
The compressed, streamlined Flash movie that you put up on the web. Once exported, this is no longer in an editable format.

.swt
The template format used to feed dynamic content into a Flash movie.

Actions
Commands that designers and programmers can use to give Flash movies added interactivity and functionality, taking them beyond the level of simple animation and linear playback.

ActionScript
Programming/scripting language in Flash 4 and 5. Used to create more complex and interactive Flash movies.

Alpha
This percentage value refers to the *transparency* of an object. An Alpha of 0 is fully transparent, 100 is opaque.

Anti-alias
Setting in Flash that smoothes edges on lines, text, and bitmaps.

Bandwidth Profiler
The tool used to fine tune a Flash project before final publication. The bandwidth profiler will indicate how much bandwidth or download time a file is using.

▶

Break Apart

Breaks an object down to its most basic level - *lines* and *fills*. Similar in effect to ungrouping an object.

CGI

Common Gateway Interface - A technology for processing information from web page-based forms or similar user entry fields. CGI provides a universal 'processing container' that allows you to run scripts to manipulate and respond to a user's input.

Controller

Found under the **Window > Toolbars** menu, the Controller gives you the ability to play, stop, rewind, and fast-forward through the frames of a Flash Movie. The controller will only play the frames of the given scene.

Device Fonts

Device fonts are not embedded into a Flash movie: instead the Flash player goes hunting on the local computer for the fonts to display. Because Flash is not embedding the font into the movie the file size is much smaller. Flash comes with three device fonts, _sans, _serif and _typewriter. The '_' (underscore) before the font name in a selection box denotes a device font.

Dynamic Text

Text that changes as the variable assigned to the particular text field changes during the movie.

Easing

Effect used during motion tweening to control the apparent acceleration or deceleration of an animated object.

Forms

Forms are screens that collect information from the user. They contain input fields, checkboxes and radio buttons - all aimed at collecting a given set of data. A CGI program commonly processes the data entered into a form.

Frames

The building blocks of your timeline. Objects placed on your stage with a particular frame selected appear in the played back timeline at that particular moment.

Frame Rate

The speed at which a Flash movie plays. The default frame rate is 12 fps (frames per second).

FreeHand

Macromedia's vector-based illustration program. Flash 5 now features tighter integration between the two software packages to allow easier image editing and importing.

Generator

Dynamic content provision package. Macromedia Generator allows a Flash movie to access information held in a separate database and display it as part of the Flash movie. This results in a 'dynamic' site, which is not restricted to running the same data each time it is run. There are other dynamic content providers available, such as Flash Turbine and Swift Generators. A dynamic Flash file is exported as a .swt files rather than a .swf.

Gradients

A graduated blending of two or more colors. Gradients can be *radial*, where the color change is outwards from the center, or linear, where the change stretches from one side to another.

Input Text Field

Field used to enable the user to input text on a Flash front end. Used in forms or interactive applications. Similar to an HTML text box.

Inspectors

Flash 4 feature replaced by Panels in Flash 5. Inspectors were used to view and modify movie components.

Instance

Version of a symbol on the stage. Designers can modify the color, size, and shape of a named instance without affecting the original symbol.

Kerning

Adjusting the space between text characters; moving them apart or closer together.

Launcher

Provides easy access to common panels such as the Movie Explorer, the Actions windows and the library. New to Flash 5, and located in the lower right hand corner of the screen.

Layers

Used to separate objects and symbols to give you more control and organization of your movie. Also used to arrange objects in front of and behind each other.

Library

Stores and organizes the symbols you create and the files you import. You can create folders and move symbols like you would in a regular file browser.

Masking

A *mask* layer selectively hides and reveals whatever is on any *masked* layers below it. The mask layer contains a filled area that acts as a window through to the masked layers. The mask can be static or animated.

Mixer

The Mixer panel contains modifiers for the Paint Bucket and Ink Bottle tools. You can adjust the color and transparency of fills and lines by adjusting the RGB settings and the Alpha value.

Motion Guide

Guides an object's movement by defining the path that the object moves along during motion tweening. Motion guides have their own layer.

Motion Tweening

Animates an object between point A and point B. It can also rotate, scale and change the colors of the objects during the animation.

Movie Clip

A movie that's on the stage, but which runs independently of the main timeline. Has all the features the main timeline does, and is a fully functional 'mini movie' in its own right. A movie clip is a symbol and is stored in your library. It's essentially a 'movie within a movie' when being used.

Movie Explorer

New to Flash 5 - the Movie Explorer is a tool used to view all the components of your Flash movie and their positions within it.

Onion Skins

Displays multiple frames of animation at the same time - showing what's on the stage in each individual frame, either in solid or outline form.

Panels

New to Flash 5 - panels provide easy access to tool modifiers such as the Swatches and the Mixer tabs.

Playhead

Rectangular red marker at the top of the timeline that signifies which frame you are currently working on.

QuickTime

A movie format established by Apple. Flash 5 has the ability to export movies as a QuickTime movie file.

RealPlayer

A streaming media format founded by Real Networks. Flash 5 has the ability to export movies as a RealPlayer file.

RGB Settings

RGB stands for Red, Green, and Blue, and the range for each color value is from 0 to 255. If all three values are 0 the color created is black, and if all three are at their maximum of 255 the color created is white. By changing the RGB values in the Mixer, you can create your desired color.

Scenes

Individual sections of your movie, which play in the order you specify.

Shape Tweening

Sometimes referred to as morphing. This takes an object (which must be ungrouped) and changes (tweens) it into another object over a chosen timeframe.

Snapping

With snapping enabled, Flash will 'stick' an object to the grid at the objects centering point. If you grab an object at the center point the cross will turn into a hollow black circle, called the snapping ring. The snapping ring snaps to the grid at any line but is snapped easiest at an intersection (where vertical and horizontal gridlines meet.)

Soften Edges

Used on fills to make the edges look slightly blurred to give a 'shadow' or a 'blur' effect.

Stacking Order

Objects in Flash, similarly to layers, function in a background/foreground relationship. Flash stacks objects based on the order in which they were created, with the oldest at the bottom.

Stage

The working area of your Flash movie. Whatever you place inside the stage will appear in your final exported movie.

Standalone Projector

Refers to the ability to build a Flash project and compress it into a self-contained executable file, which can then be used on a machine that does not have the whole Flash program. Typically used to put files on CD-ROMs.

Static Text

Text that you put on the stage that stays the same and does not change.

Streaming

Method used to enable the browser plug-in to start displaying the data before the entire file has been downloaded and prevent pauses in the playback of the Flash movie.

Swatches

The panel where the colors, color mixers, and gradients are stored and accessed.

Symbols

Fundamental components of Flash movies. Objects that are converted into symbols get stored in the library. There are three types of symbol: graphic, button and movie clip. Symbols are ways to keep file size low when using the same object more than once, as once downloaded they can be instantly re-used within the movie.

Timeline

The area above the stage that shows all the frames and layers that you've created and their order. It allows you to organize the content and length of your movie.

Transform Menu

This menu contains several modifiers, such as Rotate and Skew, that transform or manipulate an object.

Tweening

Flash term for animation. There are two kinds of tweens in Flash: motion and shape. See separate entries for each.

Vectors vs. Rasters

Flash uses Vector graphics because the size of the images can be changed (they can be scaled) without the quality deteriorating. Everything remains in proportion, irrespective of the resolution at which the viewer is seeing the vector animation. Rasters, on the other hand only look good at the image size they were created at. If they are made larger the individual pixels become visible giving a rough line, and when made smaller the image begins to look fuzzy.

The Truth about Flash

HomHome

Important stuff you should know

Index

X

Z

The Truth about Flash

Important stuff you should know

HomHome

DESIGNER TO DESIGNER™

What's this Book about?

Flash 5 is not just an upgrade to the Flash design tool. It's more like an earthquake in web-design. Apart from the new Bezier drawing tools, the real significance of Version 5 is the development of ActionScript into a full-fledged scripting language and the associated XML support. Professional and aspiring web designers can now turn their wildest creative dreams into interactive web spaces.

This book is about helping you fulfill those dreams as you move from beginner to expert status.

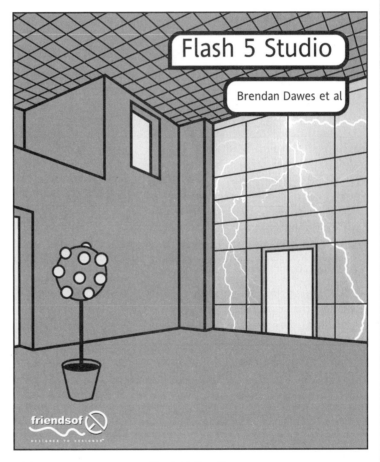

Title:	**Flash 5 Studio**
ISBN:	**1-903450-30-6**
Price:	**US $ 49.99**
	Can $ 74.95
	UK £ 35.99
To be Published:	**January 2001**

What's this Book about?

ActionScript is now an even more important part of the Flash landscape. Flash 5 is the latest version of Macromedia's incredibly successful motion graphics creation package. It contains the exceptional graphical facilities, that makes Flash the de facto standard for interactive, graphically-rich web sites and applications, coupled with a vastly expanded and more powerful range of ActionScript components. The new implementation will make ActionScript an even more vital skill to learn.

To fully exploit this raft of new Flash 5 features, the designer will need to understand the set of programming constructs and principles, that underpins ActionScript.

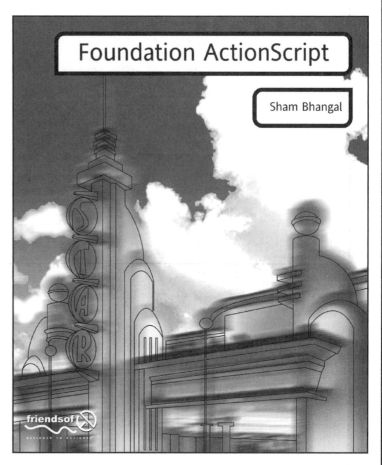

Title:	**Foundation ActionScript**
ISBN:	**1-903450-32-2**
Price:	**US $29.99**
	Can $44.95
	UK £22.99
To be Published:	**December 2000**